Torts

Torts

by Edward J. Kionka

Professor of Law Emeritus
Southern Illinois University at Carbondale

FOURTH EDITION

Mat #40264726

© 1988, 1993 West Publishing Co.
© 2002 by West Group
© 2006 Thomson/West
   610 Opperman Drive
   P.O. Box 64526
   St. Paul, MN 55164–0526
   800–328–9352

ISBN–13: 978–0–314–15414–9
ISBN–10: 0–314–15414–0

 *PRINTED ON 10% POST CONSUMER RECYCLED PAPER*

Preface

This "Black Letter" is designed to help a law student recognize and understand the basic principles and issues of law covered in a law school course. It can be used both as a study aid when preparing for classes and as a review of the subject matter when studying for an examination.

Each "Black Letter" is written by experienced law school teachers who are recognized national authorities on the subject covered.

The law is succinctly stated by the author of this "Black Letter." In addition, the exceptions to the rules are stated in the text. The rules and exceptions have purposely been condensed to facilitate quick review and easy recollection. For an in-depth study of a point of law, citations to major student texts are given. In addition, a **Text Correlation Chart** provides a convenient means of relating material contained in the "Black Letter" to appropriate sections of the casebook the student is using in his or her law school course.

If the subject covered by this text is a code or code-related course, the code section or rule is set forth and discussed wherever applicable.

FORMAT

The format of this "Black Letter" is specially designed for review. (1) **Text.** First, it is recommended that the entire text be studied, and, if deemed necessary, supplemented by the student texts cited. (2) **Capsule Summary.** The Capsule Summary is an abbreviated review of the subject matter which can be used both before and after studying the main body of the text. The headings in the Capsule

Summary follow the main text of the "Black Letter." (3) **Table of Contents.** The Table of Contents is in outline form to help you organize the details of the subject and the Summary of Contents gives you a final overview of the materials. (4) **Practice Examination.** The Practice Examination in Appendix B gives you the opportunity of testing yourself with the type of question asked on an exam, and comparing your answer with a model answer.

In addition, a number of other features are included to help you understand the subject matter and prepare for examinations:

Short Questions and Answers: This feature is designed to help you spot and recognize issues in the examination. We feel that issue recognition is a major ingredient in successfully writing an examination.

Perspective: In this feature, the authors discuss their approach to the topic, the approach used in preparing the materials, and any tips on studying for and writing examinations.

Analysis: This feature, at the beginning of each section, is designed to give a quick summary of a particular section to help you recall the subject matter and to help you determine which areas need the most extensive review.

Examples: This feature is designed to illustrate, through fact situations, the law just stated. This, we believe, should help you analytically approach a question on the examination.

Glossary: This feature is designed to refamiliarize you with the meaning of a particular legal term. We believe that the recognition of words of art used in an examination helps you to better analyze the question. In addition, when writing an examination you should know the precise definition of a word of art you intend to use.

We believe that the materials in this "Black Letter" will facilitate your study of a law school course and assure success in writing examinations not only for the course but for the bar examination. We wish you success.

THE PUBLISHER

Summary of Contents

Table of Contents

PART TWO: INTENTIONAL TORTS

PART THREE: NEGLIGENCE

PART FIVE: SPECIAL LIABILITY RULES FOR PARTICULAR ACTIVITIES

PART SIX: STRICT LIABILITY

PART SEVEN: DAMAGES FOR PHYSICAL HARM

PART EIGHT: SURVIVAL AND WRONGFUL DEATH

PART NINE: NON-PHYSICAL HARM: MISREPRESENTATION, DEFAMATION, AND PRIVACY

APPENDICES

App.

Capsule Summary of Tort Law

■ PART ONE: INTRODUCTION

I. GENERAL CONSIDERATIONS

"Torts" is a general classification encompassing several different civil causes of action providing a private remedy (usually money damages) for an injury to P caused by the tortious conduct of D. Each tort cause of action is separately named and defined, each with its own rules of liability, defenses, and damages. There is no useful general definition of "tort" or "tortious conduct."

Tort law is primarily judge-made law, and no American jurisdiction has yet adopted a tort "code." However, tort law is being increasingly modified by statute.

In tort litigation, judges and juries have distinct functions. Juries decide questions of fact, such as (1) what happened, (2) certain legal consequences of those facts (e.g., was D negligent, was P an invitee), and (3) P's damages. Judges decide issues of law, such as (1) whether D had a duty to P and the nature and extent of that duty, (2) the elements of the cause of action or defense, and (3) whether certain legal rules apply (e.g., can a particular statute be used to set the standard of care). The judge also can decide fact issues if she determines that the evidence overwhelmingly favors one conclusion. The judge also applies rules of civil procedure and evidence.

■ PART TWO: INTENTIONAL TORTS

II. LIABILITY RULES FOR INTENTIONAL TORTS

A. Intent

1. Rule

In tort law, conduct is intentional if the actor (a) desires to cause the consequences of his act, or (b) believes that the consequences are certain to result from it.

2. Proof of Intent

D will be presumed to have intended the natural and probable consequences of his conduct.

3. Intent Distinguished From Motive

Intent is the desire to cause certain immediate consequences; motive is the actor's reason for having that desire. Motive is usually irrelevant on the issue of liability.

4. Intentional Conduct Distinguished From Negligent or Reckless Conduct

If harm is intended, the tort is intentional. If not, and D's conduct merely creates a foreseeable risk of harm, then D's conduct is either negligent or reckless depending upon the magnitude and probability of the risk and D's consciousness of it.

5. Children

Young children may be found capable of intentional torts even though too young to be capable of negligence.

6. Mentally Incompetent Persons

In most jurisdictions, a mentally incompetent or insane person is liable for his intentional torts, even when incapable of forming a purpose or understanding the consequences of his conduct.

7. Transferred Intent

D's intent to commit any one of the original trespass-based torts (assault, battery, false imprisonment, trespass to land or chattels) automatically supplies the intent for any of the other four. It also transfers from X (D's intended victim) to P (D's actual but unintended victim).

8. Scope of Liability (Proximate Cause)

Broader scope of liability rules apply to intentional torts.

B. Battery

1. Rule

Battery is a harmful or offensive contact (direct or indirect) with P's person, caused by D, with the required intent. D must have acted intending to cause a harmful or offensive contact with P (or another), or an apprehension of such a contact.

2. P's Person

P's "person" includes his body and those things in contact with it or closely associated with it.

3. P's Awareness

P need not have been aware of the contact at the time.

4. No Harm Intended

D need only have intended the contact. It does not matter that D intended no harm or offense.

5. Harmful or Offensive Contact

A harmful contact is one which produces bodily harm. An offensive contact is one which offends a reasonable sense of personal dignity, as by being hostile, insulting, loathsome, or unduly personal.

6. Consent

If P consents to the contact, D is privileged to make it and there is no tort.

C. Assault

1. Rule

Assault is an act by D, done with the required intent, which arouses in P a reasonable apprehension of an imminent battery. D must have acted intending to cause a harmful or offensive contact with P (or another), or to cause an imminent apprehension of such a contact.

2. Apprehension

P must have been aware of D's threatening act at the time, before it is terminated. Apprehension is all that is required; P need not be afraid. If D's assault is directed against P, D is subject to liability even though P's apprehension is unreasonable.

An assault may occur even when D's act is directed against a third person, or when it is apparent to P that D intended only an assault, provided P reasonably perceives the threat of a battery to P.

3. Imminent

The contact must be perceived as imminent. There must be an apparent intent and apparent present ability to carry out the threat immediately.

Mere words, unaccompanied by a physical act, are not an assault. But words may give meaning to movement. A conditional threat may be an assault, unless D is privileged to enforce the condition.

D. False Imprisonment

1. Rule

False imprisonment occurs when D, intending to confine P (or another) within boundaries fixed by D, so confines P, and P is conscious of the confinement or is harmed by it.

2. Intent

The requisite intent is merely the intent to confine. A mistake of identity is no excuse, nor is a good faith belief that the confinement is justified.

3. Confinement

Confinement occurs when P is prevented from leaving a given area, even when that area is relatively large. The confinement must be complete, and P must have no reasonable or safe exit or escape known to him. The confinement may be by means of actual or apparent physical barriers, physical force, or credible threats of physical force, or duress sufficient to vitiate P's consent, as where D threatens to harm another or P's valuable property, or restrains such property. However, merely moral or social pressure is not sufficient. Refusal to release from a once-valid confinement is also sufficient.

Confinement by color of legal authority is sometimes called false arrest. If D has or purports to have legal authority to take P into custody, exercises it, P believes that D has or may have such authority, and P submits against his will, there is confinement. P must be aware of the confinement, unless P suffers physical harm from it.

4. Shoplifters

Shopkeepers may have a privilege to detain persons suspected of shoplifting for a reasonable time for the purpose of conducting an investigation.

5. Accessories

To be liable for false imprisonment, D must have been an active and knowing participant in procuring or instigating the confinement, including its wrongful aspect.

E. Intentional or Reckless Infliction of Emotional Distress

1. Rule

When D, by extreme and outrageous conduct, intentionally or recklessly causes severe emotional distress to P, D is subject to liability to P for that emotional distress and for any resulting bodily harm.

2. D's Conduct

D's conduct must be extreme, outrageous, intolerable, and not merely insulting, profane, abusive, annoying, or even threatening. Unless D knows of some special sensitivity of P, mere verbal abuse, namecalling, rudeness, insolence, and threats to do what D has a legal right to do are generally not actionable, absent circumstances of aggravation.

3. P's Response

Only severe emotional distress is actionable. Mere unhappiness, humiliation, or mild despondency for a short time is not sufficient. However, most jurisdictions no longer require that the mental suffering have a physical manifestation or result in bodily harm.

4. Abuse of Power

A common fact situation resulting in liability involves an abuse by D of some relation or status which gives him actual or apparent power to damage P's interests, where D's threats go beyond the ordinary demands or means of persuasion and become flagrant abuses of power in the nature of extortion.

5. Conduct Directed At Third Persons

D's distress-producing conduct directed at a third person (T) is actionable by P if D intentionally or recklessly causes severe emotional distress to P by such conduct, provided *either*: (1) P witnesses D's conduct, T knows of P's presence, and T is a member of P's immediate family; *or* (3) P's severe emotional distress results in bodily harm. In compelling cases, the presence requirement may be relaxed.

6. Proximate Cause

The "eggshell plaintiff" rule does not apply to this tort. D is liable only to the extent that P's emotional response is within the bounds of normal human reactions to D's conduct, unless D knew that P was extraordinarily sensitive.

7. Transferred Intent

The doctrine of transferred intent does not apply insofar as D's intent was to commit some other intentional tort.

8. Public Official and Public Figure Plaintiffs

"Public officials" and "public figures" may not recover for emotional distress resulting from a media publication unless the publication contains a false statement of fact that was made with "actual malice" (under the *NY Times* standard).

9. Mishandling of a Corpse

Next of kin may have a claim for intentional or reckless mishandling of a corpse.

F. Trespass to Land

1. Rule

D trespasses on P's land when he intentionally (a) himself enters the land or causes a thing or third person to do so, (b) remains on the land after his privilege to be there has expired, or (c) fails to remove from the land a thing which he is under a duty to remove. P may sue in trespass only if P is in possession of the land or is entitled to immediate possession.

2. Intent

The intent required is merely to enter upon the land, cause the entry, or remain. D's good faith (but erroneous) belief that he has a right to be there, or his reasonable mistake concerning title, right to possession, consent, or privilege, is no defense.

3. Manner

The trespass may be directly or indirectly caused.

Vertical Boundaries. The boundaries of land extend above and below the surface, and therefore the trespass may be by an intrusion at, above or beneath the surface.

Exception: Aircraft. Aircraft flights over private property present a special problem. Several theories are used to balance the possessor's rights against the needs of aviation.

Causing Trespass by Things. It is no less a trespass if D does not personally enter the land but merely causes some thing to do so.

4. Damages

If the trespass is intentional, the tort is complete without proof of any actual harm. Of course, P may recover for all harm resulting to his property, and persons and things upon it, and a broad range of consequential damage.

5. Reckless or Negligent Intrusions

An intrusion upon P's land may result from D's negligent conduct or abnormally dangerous activity. In such cases liability is determined in the usual fashion by the rules of those other torts. Actual harm must be shown.

G. Chattels

1. Trespass to Chattels

Rule. D commits a trespass to P's chattel when he intentionally interferes with it, either by physical contact or by dispossession. P must be in possession or entitled to future possession of the chattel.

Intent. No wrongful motive is necessary. The intent required is merely to act upon the chattel. Thus, D's good faith, reasonable (but mistaken) belief that he owns the chattel or for some other reason is privileged to deal with it is no defense.

Interference by Physical Contact. One form of trespass is interference by physical contact, which may be direct or indirect, and consists of any impairment of the chattel's condition, quality or value.

Dispossession. A dispossession consists of taking a chattel from P's possession without his consent, or by fraud or duress, or into custody of the law; barring P's access to the chattel; or destroying it while it is in P's possession. Dispossession even for a short time is still a trespass.

Damages. If the trespass consists of physical contact, P must prove actual damages. But any dispossession is a trespass for which at least nominal damages may be awarded.

2. Conversion

Rule. Conversion is an intentional exercise of dominion or control over a chattel which so seriously interferes with P's right to control it that D may justly be required to pay P its full value. It is a trespass to the chattel which is so serious, aggravated, or of such magnitude as to justify forcing D to purchase it.

Test. There is no simple test for determining when the interference is so aggravated as to constitute a conversion. The important factors are: (1) the extent and duration of D's exercise of dominion or control; (2) D's intent to assert a right which is in fact inconsistent with P's right of control; (3) D's good faith; (4) the extent and duration of the resulting interference with P's right of control; (5) the harm done to the chattel; and (6) the inconvenience and expense caused to P.

Intent. While D's beliefs, motives and intentions may be relevant in assessing the seriousness of his interference, the only intent required for the tort is an intent to exercise dominion or control over the chattel. Thus, D's good faith or honest mistake is no defense if the interference is sufficiently great (e.g., destruction).

Ways In Which Conversion May Occur. A conversion may occur when D (1) acquires possession, (2) moves the chattel, (3) makes an unauthorized transfer, delivery, or disposal, (4) withholds possession, (5) destroys or materially alters the chattel, or (6) under certain circumstances, merely uses the chattel.

Types of Chattels. Originally, only tangible chattels could be converted. Today, most courts have extended it to include intangible personal property represented by, or merged into, a document.

Damages. Damages include the full value of the chattel at the time of conversion, plus interest. Under the prevailing view, P is never required to (but may) accept a tender of the chattel's return in mitigation of damages.

3. Trespass and Conversion Distinguished

A conversion is a trespass to a chattel that is so serious that D can be forced to buy it. In such cases, P may choose either action.

III. DEFENSES TO LIABILITY FOR INTENTIONAL TORTS: PRIVILEGES

A. Privilege

1. Introduction

"Privilege" is the general term applied to various defenses in which special circumstances justify conduct which would otherwise be tortious.

2. Other Defenses Distinguished

Privileges differ from other defenses such as contributory negligence and immunities which operate to reduce or bar P's recovery but do not negate the tortious character of D's conduct. Privileges do.

3. Types

Privileges may be divided into two general categories: (a) consent, and (b) privileges created by law irrespective of consent. Today, both types are affirmative defenses.

4. Mistake

In general, D's mistaken belief that he has a privilege is per se no defense to an intentional tort, nor does it negate the required intent. However, D's mistake may be relevant in determining the existence of a privilege.

B. Consent

1. In General

Consent is a defense to almost any tort, but it is applied most frequently to the intentional torts.

2. Existence

There is consent when one is, in fact, willing for conduct to occur. It is a matter of P's subjective state of mind. It is valid whether or not communicated.

3. Apparent Consent

P's words or conduct manifesting consent are sufficient to create a privilege to D to act in light of the apparent consent, even if P's actual (but undisclosed) state of mind was to the contrary.

4. Conduct

Conduct can manifest consent. Even silence and inaction may indicate consent when such conduct would ordinarily be so interpreted.

5. Custom, Prior Relationship

Consent may be inferred from custom and usage, from prior dealings between the parties, or from the existence between them of some relationship.

6. Capacity to Consent

Consent can only be given by one having the capacity to do so, or one authorized to consent for him. Infancy, intoxication, or mental incapacity normally will vitiate effective consent.

7. Implied Consent

When an emergency actually or apparently threatens death or serious bodily harm and there is no time or opportunity to obtain consent, consent will be implied.

8. Scope of Consent

The consent is to D's conduct, and once given, P cannot complain of the consequences of that conduct, however unforeseen. But D's privilege is limited to the conduct consented to or acts substantially similar. The consent may be conditioned or limited as to time, place, duration, area, and extent.

9. Mistake, Ignorance, Misrepresentation

Even though given pursuant to P's material mistake, misunderstanding or ignorance as to the nature or character of D's proposed conduct or the extent of the harm to be expected from it, P's consent is effective as manifested unless D knows of the mistake or induced it by his misrepresentation.

10. Informed Consent

Under the doctrine of informed consent, if D (e.g., a physician) misrepresents or fails to disclose to P the material risks and possible consequences of his conduct (e.g., a medical procedure), P's consent is not an informed one. Under the prevailing view, the failure to disclose mere risks is deemed collateral, and therefore a matter of negligence only. It does not vitiate the consent and therefore there is no battery.

11. Duress

Consent given under duress is not effective. Duress includes threats of immediate harm directed against P, his family or valuable property, but usually not threats of future harm or of economic duress.

12. Consent to Crime

Under the majority view, the consent is not effective if the conduct consented to is a crime, at least in battery cases. The minority and

Restatement view is that consent to criminal conduct is valid unless in violation of a statute making conduct criminal to protect a class of persons irrespective of their consent.

C. Self–Defense and Defense of Others

1. Self–Defense

D has a privilege to use so much force as reasonably appears to be immediately necessary to protect himself against imminent physical harm threatened by the intentional or negligent conduct of another. D may use force likely to inflict death or serious bodily harm only when (a) he reasonably believes that he is in danger of similar harm, and (b) he is not required to retreat or escape.

The privilege exists even when D reasonably but mistakenly believes that self-defense is necessary. The reasonableness of D's belief is judged by the objective standard of the reasonable person of average courage.

2. Defense of Third Persons

Rule. D is privileged to come to the defense of any other person under the same conditions and by the same means as he would be privileged to defend himself.

Effect of Mistake. Under the majority view, D's privilege exists only if and to the extent that the third person in fact had a right of self-defense.

3. Duty to Protect

If D is under a duty to protect another or his land or chattels, he is privileged to use reasonable force or confinement to do so.

D. Defense and Recovery of Property

1. Defense of Property

Rule. A possessor is privileged to use reasonable force to expel another or a chattel from his land, or to prevent another's imminent intrusion upon or interference with his land or chattels, or to prevent his dispossession, even though such conduct would otherwise be a tort.

Request. The possessor must first request that the intruder desist, unless it appears that the request would be useless or cannot be made before substantial harm is done.

Amount of Force. D may then use force or the threat of force, but only such actual force as is minimally required to prevent or terminate the intrusion. Force likely to cause death or great bodily harm is not privileged. The intruder is not privileged to resist.

Watchdogs, Spring Guns. Spring guns, concealed traps, and other mechanical devices, and vicious animals, used to defend D's property, are used at D's risk. D is subject to liability for harm they cause to an intruder which he would not have been privileged to inflict himself if present.

Effect of Mistake. If the intruder in fact has one of these privileges, D has no privilege to defend his property, even though D through ignorance or mistake reasonably believes that the intruder has no privilege, unless the intruder himself was responsible for that mistake. Conversely, the intruder's mistake does not defeat D's privilege unless the mistake was caused by D's fault.

Property of Others. There is a similar privilege to defend the property of others, at least if the third person is a member of D's immediate family or household or is one whose possession D has a duty to protect.

2. Forcible Retaking of Chattels

There is a limited self-help privilege to use force or threats of force to recapture D's chattel, wrongfully and forcibly taken from D's possession, even under claim of right, or obtained by fraud or duress. D must be in fresh pursuit, and first demand its return. Then, only reasonable force may be used.

3. Possession of Land

D, who is entitled to the immediate possession of land, may peacefully enter and retake possession without liability for trespass, and thereafter defend his possession.

E. Necessity

1. Rule

The privilege of necessity may be invoked when D, in the course of defending himself or his property (or others or their property) from some threat of imminent serious harm for which P is not responsible, intentionally does some act reasonably deemed necessary toward that end, which results in injury to P's property and which would otherwise be a trespass or conversion.

2. Public Necessity

If the danger affects an entire community, or so many persons that the public interest is involved, the privilege is complete and D's tort liability is entirely excused.

3. Private Necessity

If the danger threatens only harm to D or his property (or to a third person or his property), D is privileged to commit the act which causes the trespass or conversion, but he is subject to liability for compensatory damages for any resulting actual physical harm.

4. Scope of Privilege

D's reasonable belief that his act is necessary is sufficient; but his conduct must be reasonable considering the extent of the threatened harm in relation to the foreseeable damage to P's property.

F. Authority of Law

1. Rule

One acting under authority of law is privileged, under certain circumstances, to commit acts which would otherwise constitute an assault, battery, confinement, trespass, or conversion. The scope of the privilege varies according to the type of authority being exercised and other factors.

2. Scope: Ministerial vs. Discretionary Acts

If D must exercise significant judgment or discretion in determining whether or how to act, the act is privileged if done in good faith. Ministerial acts are not privileged if done improperly, regardless of D's good faith.

3. Scope: Jurisdiction

Acts done without jurisdiction are not privileged. But acts merely "in excess of" D's jurisdiction are privileged if done in good faith.

4. Types of Acts

The most common types of such acts are arrest and prevention of a crime; execution of civil process, writs, or court orders; and acts required or authorized by legislation.

5. Use of Force

Whether D is privileged to break and enter an enclosure or building, or to use force against P's person, and the amount of such force permitted, depends upon the source and nature of the privilege being exercised.

G. Discipline

Parents. A parent is privileged to apply such reasonable force or to impose such reasonable confinement upon his child as he reasonably believes to be necessary for the child's proper control, training, or education.

Loco Parentis. The privilege extends to persons having responsibility for the custody, control, training, or education of the child, except so far as the parent has restricted their authority to do so.

Reasonableness. The reasonableness of the force or confinement depends upon: (1) whether D is a parent; (2) the age, sex, physical and mental condition of the child; (3) the nature of the offense and D's apparent motive; (4) the influence of the child's example; (5) its necessity and appropriateness to compel obedience to a proper command; and (6) whether disproportionate to the offense, unnecessarily degrading, or likely to cause serious or permanent harm.

Purpose. It must be administered in good faith, for a proper purpose, and without malice.

■ PART THREE: NEGLIGENCE

IV. NEGLIGENCE LIABILITY RULES

A. The Elements of the Negligence Cause of Action

"Negligence" is both (1) the name of a tort *cause of action,* and (2) the term given to *conduct* which falls below the standard which the law requires. The elements of a *negligence* cause of action (prima facie case) are:

(1) A duty by D to act or refrain from acting;

(2) A breach of that duty by D's failure to conform his conduct to the required standard (i.e., "negligence");

(3) A sufficient causal connection between the negligent conduct and P's injury; and

(4) Actual (provable) harm—i.e., harm which the law says is measurable and compensable in money damages.

It is sometimes said that there is a fifth element, "proximate cause"—the harm must be within the scope of liability. Strictly speaking, this is not an element of the negligence cause of action but a liability limitation that cuts off recovery, similar to a duty limitation, even when the four traditional elements are established. In some cases, the court determines the scope of D's liability as a matter of law. But in some cases, the jury determines whether D's negligence was a "proximate cause" of P's harm.

B. Characteristics of Negligent Conduct

1. Definition

"Negligence" is conduct which falls below the standard established by law for the protection of others against unreasonable risks of harm.

2. Objective Test

The test for negligence is objective—not whether D intended to exercise due care, nor whether D did the best he could to be careful, but whether D's conduct was that of a hypothetical "reasonably prudent person" placed in the same or similar circumstances.

3. Care Required

The standard is "reasonable care" (sometimes called "ordinary care" or "due care") under the circumstances. The law does not require D to be perfect, but only to behave as a reasonably prudent person would behave. And D need only protect others against unreasonable risks of harm.

4. Attributes of the Reasonable Person

Knowledge, Experience and Perception. In judging D's conduct, D will be charged with what he actually knew and observed, and also with those things which a reasonable person would have known and perceived. And if D has superior intelligence, memory perception, knowledge, or judgment, he will be held to that standard. But D's deficiency in any of these attributes is ignored; he is still held to the standard of the reasonable (i.e. normal) person.

Knowledge Common to Community. The reasonable person knows those things which at that time are common knowledge in the community—commonly known qualities, habits, and characteristics of human beings, animals, and things.

Activities Requiring Skill. If D chooses to engage in an activity requiring learned skills or certain knowledge, his conduct is measured against the hypothetical person who is reasonably skilled and knowledgeable in that activity.

Physicians. In most jurisdictions, the standard of care of medical doctors (and sometimes other professionals) is conclusively established by the customary practice of reasonably well-qualified practitioners in that field.

Physicians or others who are certified specialists, or who hold themselves out as specialists, are held to the standards of that specialty.

Physical Characteristics. The "reasonable person" standard is subjective to the extent that if D has a physical deficiency or disability, his conduct is measured against that of a reasonably prudent person with his physical characteristics.

Mental Capacity. In judging D's conduct, no allowance is made for deficiencies in D's mental capacity to conform to the "reasonable person" standard of care. The fact that D is mentally deficient, voluntarily intoxicated, or even insane does not matter. His conduct is measured against the reasonably prudent sane, sober and normal person. A few courts apply a subjective standard to insane or mentally disabled persons.

Minors. Minors are an exception. If D is a minor, the test is what is reasonable conduct for a child of D's age, intelligence, and experience under the circumstances. But this exception does not apply to minors engaging in "adult" activities requiring special skills and training, such as driving a car or flying an airplane. Below a certain age (in some states, arbitrarily fixed at seven), a young child is incapable of negligence because he or she lacks the mental maturity and experience to assess and respond to risks.

5. Conduct in Emergencies

The fact that D is confronted with a sudden emergency which requires rapid decision is a factor which may be taken into account in determining the reasonableness of his choice of action. However, D may have been negligent in (a) failing to anticipate the emergency or (b) creating the emergency; as to such negligence, this rule would not apply.

6. Sudden Incapacity

D's conduct during a period of sudden incapacitation or loss of consciousness resulting from physical illness is negligent only if D ought to have foreseen such an incapacity and was negligent in failing to take reasonable precautions to prevent its occurrence

7. Anticipating Conduct of Others

The reasonable person will regulate his conduct in light of what he can anticipate others will do.

8. Failure to Warn or Instruct

It may be negligent to fail to warn or instruct another so that he can take proper precautions for his own safety. Conversely, D's exercise of reasonable care to give others an adequate warning of a danger does not necessarily prevent D's conduct (the subject of the warning) from being negligent. If there is an unreasonable risk of harm inherent in D's conduct, D must reduce that risk so far as reasonably possible; only then will an adequate warning of the remaining risk constitute "reasonable care."

9. Other Types of Negligent Conduct

Any conduct may be negligent under the circumstances. Negligence may consist of an act or a failure to act, lack of competence, or lack of preparation, or a misrepresentation. It may be negligence to prevent protective action by another; to use an incompetent, defective or inappropriate instrumentality; or to permit another to use a thing or engage in an activity under D's control so as to subject another to an unreasonable risk of harm.

10. When Is a Risk "Unreasonable"?

Under the classic formulation, a risk is unreasonable when the foreseeable probability and gravity of the harm outweigh the burden to D of alternative conduct that would have prevented the harm. This is the classic "Hand" test.

Magnitude of Risk. The probability or likelihood that the harm will result, in conjunction with the gravity or seriousness of the potential harm, are placed on one side of the scale. The gravity of the harm includes both the extent of the damage and the relative societal value of the protected interest.

Burden of Alternative Conduct. The burden of reducing or eliminating the risk by alternative conduct is placed on the other side of the scale. Factors relevant in assessing this cost include: (1) the importance or social value of the activity or goal of which D's conduct is a part; (2) the utility of the conduct as a means to that end; (3) the feasibility of alternative, safer conduct; (4) the relative cost of safer conduct; (5) the relative utility of safer conduct; and (6) the relative safety of alternative conduct.

11. Judge and Jury

Whether conduct was or was not negligent is a question of fact for the trier of fact.

C. Sources of Standards of Care

1. Rules of Law

Appellate courts, reviewing fact situations and deciding that there was or was not sufficient evidence of negligence, often state that given conduct is or is not negligent. Such statements may be either (a) guidelines for the review of jury determinations of an issue of fact, or (b) fixed rules of law that given conduct is or is not negligent as a matter of law.

Some such rules of law may be desirable and lend stability to the law, so long as they are not immutable and admit exceptions. But better results are usually achieved if negligence is treated as a question of fact for the jury, and such "rules" are merely regarded as guidelines for the courts in determining that certain conduct in certain recurring situations so clearly is (or is not) negligent that the question may be taken from the jury.

2. Legislation

In General. Legislation (statutes, ordinances, regulations) often pre-scribe standards of conduct for the protection of others from harm. For tort law purposes, two types may be distinguished:

(1) legislation which (a) expressly or (b) by necessary implication creates a civil remedy for damages for violation (e.g., F.E.L.A., F.S.A.A.); and

(2) legislation which does not (limited to criminal penalties).

Courts routinely use legislation of the second type in negligence cases as evidence of, or as establishing, the standard of care which D was required to meet.

Legislative Purpose. Legislation is relevant on the standard of care in a negligence case only if the statute was intended, at least in part, to protect a class of persons which includes P against the particular hazard and kind of harm which resulted.

Licensing Statutes. Violation of a statute requiring a license to engage in a particular trade, profession or activity is generally not admissible to show that D was negligent on a particular occasion.

Effect of Violation

Majority Rule. Most courts hold that violation of a relevant statute is prima facie negligence or negligence per se. This means that if D introduces no evidence to excuse the violation, D's negligence is conclusively established.

Minority View. In some jurisdictions, violation is merely evidence of negligence, which the jury can consider along with all other evidence in determining whether D was negligent. This is the rule in all jurisdictions when a minor violates a relevant statute.

Cause. A violation does not per se establish a sufficient causal relation between the violation and P's injury.

Children. A minor's violation of a statute is only evidence of negligence, not negligence per se.

Defenses. Contributory negligence and assumption of risk defenses (if otherwise available) apply, except in the case of statutes intended to protect a class of persons against their own inability to protect themselves.

Excused Violations

Certain Safety Statutes. A few statutes having a strong safety purpose (e.g., F.S.A.A., child labor laws, some factory and construction safety acts, pure food acts, some motor vehicle equipment and maintenance laws) permit no excused violations.

Other Statutes. As to most other statutes, courts will permit excuses for violations to be shown to rebut the per se or prima facie negligence. These include (a) physical circumstances beyond D's control; (b) innocent ignorance of facts which make the statute applicable; (c) sudden emergencies not of D's making; (d) situations in which it would be more dangerous to comply with the statute than to violate it; (e) violations that are reasonable in light of D's childhood, physical disability, or physical incapacity; and (f) D used reasonable care in attempting to comply with the statute. In jurisdictions where the statute is merely evidence of negligence, any proof tending to excuse or make reasonable the violation would be relevant.

Compliance With Statute. D may ordinarily show compliance with a statute as evidence of his reasonable care, but such compliance is not conclusive since a reasonable person might have taken precautions greater than the statutory minimum.

D. Proof of Negligence

1. Burden of Proof

P must introduce sufficient evidence to support a finding by a preponderance of the evidence on each element of his cause of action—duty, negligence, causation, damages. Whether a duty exists is usually an issue of law for the court; the trier of fact determines the other elements.

2. Presumptions

Each jurisdiction's tort law has its own set of legal presumptions, which are codified rules of circumstantial evidence.

3. Experts and Opinion Evidence

In a large number of tort cases, expert testimony is necessary or desirable to furnish the jury facts beyond its common knowledge. Expert testimony may be required to establish the standard of care in professional negligence cases. Expert witnesses are permitted to testify to opinions when they will be helpful to the jury.

4. Res Ipsa Loquitur

Like presumptions, *res ipsa loquitur* ("the thing speaks for itself") is basically a rule of circumstantial evidence.

Rule. If P can establish a prima facie *res ipsa loquitur* case, he need not prove by direct or other evidence the specific conduct of D which was negligent. If P makes a prima facie showing that (1) his injury was caused by an instrumentality or condition which was under D's exclusive management or control at the relevant time(s), and (2) in the ordinary course of events, P's harm would not have occurred unless D was then and there negligent, then the jury is instructed on *res ipsa loquitur* and may infer that D was negligent.

Control by D. D need not have been in control of the injury-causing instrumentality at the time of P's injury. P need only establish that D's negligence, if any, must have occurred while the instrumentality was in D's control.

Multiple Defendants. The exclusive control requirement ordinarily precludes use of RIL against multiple defendants. However in a few cases, the courts have applied a variation of the doctrine and required each defendant to prove that he was not negligent. If there are multiple defendants but their relationship was such that they were jointly responsible for the instrumentality at the relevant time, or one would be vicariously liable for the conduct of the other, then the doctrine may be applied.

Inference of Negligence. P need not show that D's negligence was the only possible explanation, only that the inference that it was D's negligence outweighs the sum of the other possible causes.

P's Conduct. At one time, P was required to prove that his injury was not due to any "voluntary act" by P, or that P's own conduct was not a significant causative factor, or, most recently, that P was not contributorily negligent. However, with the adoption of comparative negligence, this requirement has been eliminated in most jurisdictions.

Procedural Effect. Once the court determines that P has established a prima facie *res ipsa* case, the issue becomes one for the jury to determine whether or not to draw the inference, taking into consideration D's contrary evidence (if any). Both res ipsa and specific negligence theories may go to the jury, so long as the two are not inconsistent.

Products Liability Cases. There is an analogous circumstantial evidence rule in strict product liability cases. P need not prove the specific defect in the product, so long as the evidence tends to show that the product malfunctioned in such a way that the existence of a defect may be inferred and also tends to exclude possible causes other than a product defect.

5. Custom, Character

Custom and Usage. In determining whether conduct is negligent, the customary conduct of the community, industry, profession, or other relevant group in similar circumstances is relevant but not conclusive. *Exception*: In professional negligence cases involving physicians and certain other professionals, customary conduct usually is conclusive as to the standard of care.

Character. Evidence that D or P was or was not a careful person is not admissible to prove that he acted or failed to act carefully on the occasion in question.

6. Trade Rules and Standards

Rules and standards for the conduct of an activity promulgated by authoritative groups, if relevant and recognized as authoritative, are similar to custom and often admitted as some evidence of the standard of care.

7. D's Own Rules and Standards

D's own rules and standards are admissible but not conclusive as evidence of the appropriate standard of care.

E. Degrees of Negligence

1. Degrees of Care

The duty of those who conduct certain dangerous activities is sometimes stated as greater than "ordinary" or "reasonable" care.

In some jurisdictions, common carriers (operators of airplanes, ships, buses, trains, taxicabs, and even elevators, escalators and amusement devices) are said to owe their passengers "the highest degree of care consistent with the mode of conveyance used and the practical operation of their business." In some jurisdictions, persons responsible for certain **dangerous instrumentalities** (e.g., high-voltage electricity, explosives) must exercise a "high degree of care," commensurate with the danger.

The trend is to reject such special duty rules, holding that "under the circumstances" achieves the same result without modifying the standard duty.

2. Degrees of Negligence

Occasionally, efforts have been made to subdivide the negligence concept into finer gradations—"slight," "ordinary," and "gross" negligence. These distinctions have proved unworkable and are rarely used.

F. Reckless Conduct ("Wilful and Wanton Misconduct")

1. Definition

Conduct is in "reckless disregard of the safety of another" (also called "wilful and wanton misconduct") when D knows or has reason to know that (1) it creates an unreasonable risk of harm and (2) the risk is relatively high, either in degree or in the probability that harm will occur.

2. Distinguished From Negligent Conduct

Negligent conduct merely creates an unreasonable risk; no awareness of that risk is required. For conduct to be reckless, D must be conscious (or a reasonable person in D's situation would have been conscious) that it creates a relatively high risk of harm to another.

3. Distinguished From Intentional Torts

Conduct is intentional when D either intends to bring about the consequences or knows that they are substantially certain to occur. Reckless conduct lacks that certainty of result.

4. When Required

Certain statutes and common law rules exempt D from liability for ordinary negligence, thereby requiring proof of reckless conduct for liability.

5. Effect

Defenses. In some jurisdictions, ordinary contributory negligence is not a defense or damage-reducing factor if D's conduct is found to be reckless. However, in the majority of comparative negligence jurisdictions, P's contributory negligence will reduce his recovery even against D's reckless conduct. Assumption of the risk was formerly a defense to reckless conduct, but in many jurisdictions it is now merely a damage-reducing factor.

Punitive Damages. In most jurisdictions, reckless conduct will support an award of punitive damages.

G. Duty Concepts and General Limitations

1. In General

In negligence law, D's duty can best be analyzed as a general principle with exceptions and limitations, rather than as a collection of specific duties. In general, D has a duty to exercise reasonable care to avoid subjecting others (and their property) to unreasonable risks of physical harm. Specific limitations on that duty are sprinkled throughout the law of torts. The most common general duty limitations include the following.

2. Relationship Between P and D

Negligence law has traditionally held that D is not subject to liability to P unless D breached a duty owed to P and not to someone else. Cf. *Palsgraf v. Long Island R. Co.* (N.Y. 1928). "Negligence in the air, so to speak, will not do." No simple formula exists for determining when this duty exists. The most important factors include (a) a pre-existing relationship between P and D, (b) foreseeability of harm, (c) the nexus between D and P's injury, and (d) reliance by P upon D to protect him.

3. Nature and Scope of the Risk

Conduct may be negligent because it foreseeably threatens property damage, but it actually causes some unforeseen personal injury. Or conduct may be negligent because it foreseeably threatens one type of harm to P, but it actually causes another type of harm, as to which the risk was not unreasonable. Some courts will hold that there was no duty to protect against the harm which actually resulted. Other courts will reach the same result under proximate cause principles.

4. Interest Invaded

Certain types of interests are given less than full protection against negligent invasion, such as (1) pecuniary loss alone, unaccompanied by physical harm, (2) harm to the unborn, and (3) psychic trauma.

5. Misfeasance vs. Nonfeasance

Tort law traditionally distinguished between "misfeasance" (tortious conduct consisting of an affirmative act) and "nonfeasance" (inaction which results in, or allows, harm to P). As a general rule, D is not liable for harm to P resulting from his mere failure to intervene to aid or protect P unless there is some pre-existing relationship between P and D sufficient to create the duty, or unless D is responsible for P's situation.

Rescue. Absent a pre-existing relationship between P and D or a duty to act arising from some other source, D has no duty to protect or aid P, who D realizes is in a position of danger.

First Aid. Absent a pre-existing relationship between P and D, or unless D was responsible for P's injury, D has no duty to render aid or assistance to an injured or otherwise needy P.

Relationships Creating Duty. Pre-existing relationships which will support a duty to aid or protect another include carrier-passenger, innkeeper-guest, landowner-lawful entrant, employer-employee, jailer-prisoner, school-student, parent-child, husband-wife, store-customer, and host-guest. A duty has even been found as to friends engaged in a joint social outing.

Responsible for Peril or Injury. The duty arises when D is responsible for P's injury or position of peril, whether or not D was negligent.

Aid to Helpless. One who undertakes to render aid or to protect P, who is helpless to adequately aid or protect himself, must do so with reasonable care. And, having undertaken this duty, he may not abandon P and leave him worse off. This rule has led to "Good Samaritan" statutes in many states which relieve physicians (and others) who render emergency medical aid from all liability for negligence.

Services. When D (gratuitously or otherwise) undertakes to render services which he knows or should know are for P's protection, D must perform those services with reasonable care, at least if (a) his failure to do so increases the risk of harm to P or (b) P's injury results from his reliance on D.

Duty Arising Ex Post Facto. If D does an act, not tortious at the time, and later discovers that his act creates an unreasonable risk of harm to P, D must exercise reasonable care to prevent the risk from taking effect.

Statutory Duty of Protection. When a statute requires one to act for the protection of another, the court may (or may not) use the statute as a basis for an affirmative duty and its scope. This is different from using a statute to establish the standard of care when a duty already exists, or statutes that expressly or impliedly create a cause of action.

Duty to Control Conduct of Another. Certain relationships carry with them a duty by D, the dominant or custodial member, to use reasonable care to regulate the conduct of (1) the person within his custody or control so as to protect third persons or (2) third persons so as to protect the person in his custody or care.

Parent-Child. A parent must exercise reasonable care to prevent tortious conduct by his child, provided the parent knows or has reason to know he has the ability, and knows or should know of the necessity and opportunity to exercise such control.

Master-Servant. A master has a similar duty with respect to a servant; this even extends to one acting outside the scope of his employment, if the servant is on the master's premises or is using his chattel.

Person on D's Land. D has a similar duty with respect to a person using his land or his chattel in his presence and with his permission.

Custodian of Dangerous Person. If D has custody of a person D knows to have dangerous propensities, D must exercise reasonable care to prevent that person from doing harm.

Duty to Protect Person in Custody. If D has custody of P under circumstances such that (a) P is deprived of his normal power of self-protection or (b) P must associate with persons likely to harm him, then D has a duty to exercise reasonable care to prevent tortious conduct against P.

H. Duty: Tort and Contract

1. Parties to the Contract

One possible source of D's duty to P is a contract between them under which D agrees to perform certain services. If D breaches that contract and as a result P sustains physical or other harm, special rules apply to determine whether that breach may give rise to tort liability.

General Rule: Misfeasance vs. Nonfeasance. Where D's duty to act arises because of a contractual relation between D and P, D is not liable in tort for harm caused by his breach of that contract where the breach consists merely of his failure to commence performance at all. But once having begun to perform, he will be liable for his tortious misperformance, whether consisting of acts or omissions to act.

Exceptions: Liability for Nonfeasance

Public Callings. Those engaged in the public or "common" callings—common carriers, innkeepers, public warehousemen, public utilities, and public officers—are subject to tort liability for nonperformance.

Other Relationships. Other relationships, which may or may not be based on contract, impose a duty of affirmative action.

Fraud. A promise made without any intent to perform it may be fraud for which a tort action in deceit will lie.

2. Third Persons Not Parties to the Contract

Common Law Rule. The general common law rule was that P, not a party to a contract between D and another, had no cause of action in tort for harm sustained as a result of D's misperformance or nonperformance. P was not in "privity of contract" with D.

Exceptions: Nonfeasance. In the case of nonfeasance, various exceptions to the privity rule have developed, such as (1) the failure of a telegraph company to transmit a telegram; (2) the nonperformance by an agent of his contractual duty to supervise property or persons over which he has been given control, or to take certain precautions for the safety of third persons; (3) nonperformance of a contract to maintain, inspect, or repair an instrumentality which foreseeably creates a substantial risk of harm to third persons; (4) nonperformance by a landlord of his contract to repair the premises; and (5) in some cases, where D undertakes to render services to reduce the risk of harm to a third person if (a) the failure to exercise reasonable care increases the risk of harm beyond that which existed without the undertaking, (b) D has undertaken to perform a duty owed by the other to the third person, or (c) the person to whom the services are rendered, the third party, or another relies on D's exercising reasonable care in the undertaking.

Exceptions: Misfeasance. Where D's negligence consists of misperformance after having begun to perform, the privity rule is now obsolete, and the overwhelming majority of courts will subject D to liability to P.

V. DEFENSES TO NEGLIGENCE AND OTHER LIABILITY

A. Contributory and Comparative Negligence

1. Rule

Contributory negligence is conduct by P which creates an unreasonable risk of harm to P, and which combines with D's negligence to cause P's injury.

2. Burden of Proof

Contributory negligence is an affirmative defense.

3. Applicable Rules

In general, contributory negligence uses the same rules and tests as negligence.

4. Effect of Plaintiff's Contributory Fault

Complete Bar vs. Mitigation of Damages. Contributory negligence was once a complete defense that totally barred P's recovery. Now, in most jurisdictions it merely reduces his damages pro tanto, although it can still be a complete bar.

Comparative Negligence. All but four states and the District of Columbia have finally accepted the doctrine of comparative negligence. Under this rule, P's contributory negligence is not a complete bar to his recovery. Instead, P's damages are calculated and then reduced by the proportion which P's fault bears to the total causative fault of P's harm.

Types of Comparative Negligence. Under the pure form (minority rule), P may recover a portion of his damages no matter how great his negligence in comparison to that of D. Under the modified form (most jurisdictions), P recovers nothing if his negligence was "as great as" (50%) or "greater than" (51%) that of the defendant (or defendants collectively).

Factors for Assigning Shares. In deciding how to assign percentage shares of responsibility, the trier of fact should consider (1) the duty owed by each person, (2) the extent to which each person's conduct deviated from that duty, and (3) the extent to which the tortious conduct of each person caused the injury in question.

Intentional or Reckless Conduct. Traditionally, ordinary contributory negligence was not a defense to an intentional tort or to reckless conduct (but contributory reckless conduct was a defense to the latter). In most comparative negligence jurisdictions, P's contributory negligence will reduce his recovery even though D's conduct was reckless, but not if it was intentional.

Strict Liability. Prior to the adoption of comparative negligence, mere contributory negligence was not a defense to a strict liability action. Some comparative negligence jurisdictions permit P's ordinary contributory negligence to reduce his damages; others reduce his damages only for assumption of the risk.

Safety Statutes. Contributory negligence is not a defense to actions founded upon certain types of safety statutes intended to protect a class of persons from dangers against which they are incapable of protecting themselves. Some statutes expressly prohibit this defense.

Serious Misconduct. In some jurisdictions, if P's contributory fault was seriously unlawful or immoral conduct, he will be barred from recovery altogether.

5. Causal Relation

The same rules of causation apply as in the case of negligent conduct. And the defense is not available unless P's harm results from the risk which made P's conduct negligent.

6. Imputed Contributory Negligence

General Rule. With three exceptions, the negligence of a third person will not be imputed to P so as to reduce or bar P's recovery for injuries caused by D's negligence.

Exception: Master–Servant. A master's recovery against a negligent D is reduced (or barred) by the negligence of his servant acting within the scope of his employment.

Exception: Joint Enterprise. P, a member of a joint enterprise, is injured by the concurrent negligence of D, a third person outside the enterprise, and M, another member of the enterprise. P's recovery against D is reduced by M's negligence.

Exception: Consequential Damages. Where P has a cause of action based upon personal injuries to another (A), P's recovery is reduced by A's contributory negligence.

7. P's Negligent Failure to Exercise Control

In General. If P has a duty to control the conduct of A and negligently fails to do so, A's contributory negligence (combined with that of P) reduces or bars P's recovery against D whose negligence was also a cause of P's injury.

Parent. A parent's (P's) recovery from D for injuries to P's child caused by D's negligence may be reduced or barred by P's negligence in protecting or supervising his child.

B. Last Clear Chance

The doctrine of "last clear chance" is now primarily of historical interest; it survives in a dwindling minority of jurisdictions.

The doctrine applies only when D's negligence is later in time than P's contributory negligence. In essence, P (or P's property) is in a zone of danger from which he cannot escape in time, leaving D with the last opportunity to do something to prevent the harm which otherwise will occur. If D then negligently fails to act to prevent the harm, he is not permitted to use P's prior negligence as a defense.

C. Assumption of Risk

1. Rule

Under the traditional common law rule, if P voluntarily assumes a risk of harm arising from the negligent or reckless conduct of D, P cannot recover for such harm. Assumption of the risk is an affirmative defense.

Until recently, most (but not all) jurisdictions recognized this defense, some by a different name. A few have limited it to (1) master-servant and (2) express assumption cases. Some courts analyze P's assumption of risk as affecting D's duty, e.g., negating D's duty to exercise care for P's safety.

2. Meanings of Term

The term "assumption of risk" can mean different things, some of which are not truly defenses to negligent conduct. The term is used to describe several different situations:

Express. P expressly agrees in advance (usually in a written contract) to relieve D of D's duty to exercise care for P's safety with respect to a known or possible risk.

Inherent Hazards Not Arising From Negligence. P chooses to engage in an activity which has certain inherent and commonly accepted risks, even though the others involved exercise proper care. As to these risks, there is no negligence, and therefore the doctrine does not properly apply. Some courts call this "primary" assumption of risk.

Risk of Future Negligence. P voluntarily enters into a relationship with D knowing that there is a risk that D will act negligently. Here, the true basis of liability is P's unreasonable conduct in entering into the relationship (i.e., contributory negligence).

Assumption of Existing Negligently–Created Risk. P, aware of a risk created by the negligence of D, proceeds or continues voluntarily to encounter it. This is true implied assumption of risk.

3. Contributory Negligence Distinguished

In theory, implied assumption of the risk is P's implied voluntary consent to encounter a known danger created by D's negligence. Contributory negligence is unreasonable conduct. The former is a subjective test; the test for the latter is objective.

4. Express Assumption of Risk

Rule. If P, by contract or otherwise, expressly agrees to accept a risk of harm arising from D's negligent conduct, P cannot recover for such harm, unless the agreement is invalid as contrary to public policy.

Construction. Such agreements are strictly construed against D, and are not enforceable if P reasonably was ignorant of that term. They are unenforceable as to intentional torts, and some courts will not enforce them as to reckless conduct.

Public Policy. Such agreements are unenforceable when contrary to public policy. In general, they will not be enforced in favor of employers, those charged with a duty of public service, and those having a significantly superior bargaining position as compared to P.

5. Implied Assumption of Risk

Rule. If P knows, appreciates, and understands the risk of harm created by D's negligent or reckless conduct, and nevertheless voluntarily subjects himself to the risk by conduct which impliedly manifests his consent to accept the risk, then he is subject to the assumption of risk defense. The effect of the defense varies.

Elements: Manifestation of Consent. The essence of the defense is consent to accept the risk, and therefore P's conduct must impliedly manifest that consent.

Elements: Knowledge and Appreciation of Risk. The consent must be an informed one, and therefore D must show that P knew of the existence of the risk, and understood and appreciated its unreasonable character.

Elements: Voluntariness. P's assumption of the risk must be voluntary. However, P's conduct in proceeding into the zone of danger, even reluctantly or under protest, ordinarily may be deemed voluntary. Even if P has no reasonable alternative but to encounter the risk, his doing so is voluntary unless D's tortious conduct is responsible for P's predicament and other conditions are met. Additionally, many courts have held that mere economic duress does not make encountering the risk involuntary.

Violation of Statute. P's assumption of risk bars or reduces his recovery based on D's violation of a statute, unless this result would defeat a policy of the statute. Some statutory torts expressly exclude the defense.

Modern Status of the Defense. There is a strong trend to abolish the defense of implied assumption of risk as a separate defense in negligence cases on the ground that it overlaps completely with the doctrine of contributory negligence. In particular, jurisdictions adopting comparative negligence frequently merge the defenses of contributory negligence and assumption of risk under a general "comparative fault" concept.

Participation in Sporting Events. In many jurisdictions, those who participate in professional or amateur sporting events assume the risk of injuries resulting from other players' misconduct, even when violations of rules of the game having a safety purpose, unless the violation was more than carelessness incident to the play of the game. But D may be liable if he intentionally or recklessly injures P. This may also be analyzed as a limited duty rule.

D. Statutes of Limitations and Repose

1. Statutes of Limitations

In General. A statute of limitations is a statutory time period within which P must file his lawsuit.

Classification. Since there are different time periods for different causes of action, the courts must classify actions for purposes of determining which time period applies. P's characterization in his complaint is not controlling.

Procedural Effect. A statute of limitations is usually an affirmative defense that is waived if not asserted.

Commencement of Running: General Rule. The statute of limitations begins to run on the date the cause of action "accrues," usually the date on which the injury occurs. In wrongful death cases, this is the date of death.

Concealment. D's fraudulent concealment or nondisclosure of the existence of the cause of action from P tolls the running of the statute.

Continuing Duty or Negligence. In some contexts, the courts will extend the available time by finding a continuing duty to disclose or continuing negligence or other tort. In medical negligence cases, some courts hold that the statute does not begin to run until P's course of treatment has been concluded. If D's conduct constitutes a continuing nuisance, the statute may not start to run until D's conduct in creating the nuisance ceases, or it may not start to run as long as the harm continues.

Discovery Rule. Most jurisdictions have adopted a "discovery" rule whereby tort statutes of limitations do not begin to run until P discovers (or by the exercise of reasonable care should discover) that (a) he is injured and (b) the injury is the result of someone's tortious conduct.

Minors and Others Under Disability. A statute of limitations normally does not run against a minor or person under some other legal disability.

Death Cases. In wrongful death cases, the statute begins to run on the date of death, even though the fatal injury occurred earlier.

Latent Potential Harm. Where P may have been exposed to a toxic material resulting in no present symptoms or minor symptoms but a measurable risk that P may contract a serious or fatal illness at some uncertain time in the future, some courts will allow recovery now for the present symptoms or medical monitoring and either (1) damages for the potential future harm times the probability of its occurrence or (2) allow a later suit if and when the potential future harm actually occurs.

Repressed Childhood Sexual Abuse. Some courts have permitted the statute of limitations to be tolled during the time when P has repressed her memory of childhood sexual abuse (assuming the repression began before the applicable statute expired). Others have rejected the defense, holding that whatever "repression" is, it does not toll the statute of limitations. Some legislatures have adopted extended statute of limitations in such cases.

Estoppel. If D actively induces P not to take timely legal action on a claim, and P reasonably relies on D's inducement, D may be estopped to assert the statute of limitations defense.

2. Statutes of Repose

Statutes of repose are special limitation periods which supplement and override statutes of limitations, the discovery rule, and other similar rules and exceptions. They set an outer limit beyond which D can no longer be held responsible for a completed activity, irrespective of whether an injury has occurred.

3. Notice of Claim Statutes

In suits against state or local governments, statutes sometimes require P to give notice to the potential D within a certain time period.

E. Immunities

1. Government and Its Employees: Sovereign Immunity

Prior Common Law. At one time, all levels of government were entirely immune from tort liability.

U.S.: Federal Tort Claims Act. The United States has waived its tort immunity for damages "caused by the negligent or wrongful act or omission of any employee of the Government while acting within the scope of his office or employment, under circumstances where the United States, if a private person, would be liable to the claimant in accordance with the law of the place where the act or omission occurred." 28 U.S.C.A. § 1346(b).

FTCA Exceptions. In addition to exceptions for specified activities, there are two important general exceptions:

Specified Torts. The U.S. is not liable for (1) assault, battery, false imprisonment, false arrest, or malicious prosecution, except in the case of investigative or law enforcement officers; or (2) abuse of process, libel, slander, misrepresentation, deceit, or interference with contract rights. Nor is it subject to strict tort liability in any form.

Discretionary Acts. The U.S. is not liable for acts done with due care in the execution of a statute or regulation (even though invalid), or for "an act or omission . . . based upon the exercise or performance or the failure to exercise or perform a discretionary function or duty . . . , whether or not the discretion be abused."

Current Rule: State and Local Government. Most states have largely abolished state and local governmental sovereign immunity. However, there is limited liability for certain governmental functions. Judicial and legislative functions and executive policy decisions remain immune.

Governmental Officers and Employees. Governmental officers and employees are immune when exercising a judicial or legislative function. The highest executive officers are absolutely immune except when acting clearly beyond the bounds of their authority. Lower level executive and administrative employees have a qualified immunity for the good faith exercise of a discretionary function, but are liable for their tortious ministerial acts.

2. Charities

The common law tort immunity of charitable, educational, religious, and benevolent organizations is no more, except in a few jurisdictions that retain vestiges. However, legislation is recreating immunities for particular charitable activities or for individuals engaged in certain charitable activities.

3. Spouses, Parents and Children

Husband and Wife. At one time, the general common law rule was that husband and wife were each immune from tort liability to the other spouse for torts committed during coverture. The majority of states have now abolished this immunity; most of the rest recognize exceptions.

Parent and Child. At common law, a parent and his unemancipated minor child were each immune from suit by the other for a personal tort, whether intentional or negligent. Some states have largely abolished this immunity. The remainder increasingly recognize exceptions, such as for (a) intentional or reckless conduct, (b) torts occurring during D's business activity, (c) breach of a duty external to the family relationship, and (d) suits after the parent-minor child relationship has ended, as by emancipation of the child or the death of either party. Some states have abolished the immunity in certain classes of cases (e.g., auto). Among the states that have abolished the immunity, some hold that the parent cannot be held liable for negligent supervision, or the exercise of parental authority, or where the negligent act involves the exercise of parental discretion with respect to the provision of food, clothing, housing, medical and dental services, and other care.

4. Infants and Incompetents

Infants. Assuming that the requisite mental state (if any) can be proved, an infant or minor is not ordinarily immune from tort liability.

Incompetents. One with deficient mental capacity is not for that reason alone immune from tort liability. Particularly in torts involving physical harm, the incompetent D is held to the same standard as a normal person. However, D's mental condition may sometimes be relevant in determining whether any tort has been committed.

F. Preemption

Under the supremacy clause of the U.S. Constitution, when a federal statute or regulations expressly or impliedly preempt a particular field, state tort law either cannot regulate the field at all or cannot impose a higher standard than the applicable federal law. Whether (and the extent to which) a federal statute or regulation is preemptive is a question of statutory interpretation for the court.

■ PART FOUR: CAUSATION

VI. CAUSATION

A. Overview of Causation Issues

Causation problems may be analyzed in two categories:

1. **Proximate cause,** also called "legal cause" or scope of liability. Some courts and writers use these terms to encompass all causal relation

issues. Others distinguish between (a) proximate or legal cause and (b) cause in fact. Many now categorize proximate cause issues under the term "scope of liability," completely separating proximate cause issues from the issue of factual causation. This is the preferred approach.

2. **Cause in fact** exists when the "cause-and-effect" chain of events leading to P's injury includes D's tortious conduct.

Proximate (legal) cause (scope of liability) concepts may be used to cut off D's liability when the court decides that it would be unjust under the circumstances, despite the fact that D's tortious conduct was a cause in fact of P's injury. Courts sometimes treat the same or similar scope of liability problems as *duty* issues or *fault* issues.

B. Cause In Fact

1. General Rule

Cause in fact is a question of fact, requiring that the injury would not have occurred "but for" D's conduct (the "sine qua non" rule).

Earlier, many courts added a second element: that D's tortious conduct was a "substantial factor" (or sometimes "a material element [and] [or] a substantial factor") in bringing about P's injury. Increasingly, this factor has been discredited, and many courts now reject the "substantial factor" element as part of the definition of factual causation, while retaining it as a scope of liability issue.

2. Proof

Most cause in fact problems are nothing more than fact questions involving the adequacy of P's circumstantial evidence linking P's injury and D's tortious conduct.

3. Multiple Causes

Concurrent Tortfeasors, Indivisible Injury. If the tortious conduct of Dl and D2 concur and both are causes in fact of P's injury, either or both are subject to liability in full for all of P's damages. It does not matter that Dl and D2 did not act in concert, or that neither's conduct by itself would have caused P's injury.

Concurrent Tortfeasors, Divisible Injury

General Rule. If D1 and D2 each cause separate parts of P's harm, each will be liable only for the part he caused if it is even theoretically possible to determine who caused which part.

Exception: Concert of Action. Both D1 and D2 are liable for all of P's damages, even though divisible, if they were acting in concert or engaged in a joint enterprise.

Exception: Risk of Further Injury. If D's tortious conduct injures P and also foreseeably exposes P to the risk of further injury by another, D is liable both for the injury he caused and also for such further injury.

Burden of Proof. Traditionally, the burden was on P to prove which part of his injury was attributable to which defendant, at the risk of failing to recover against any. Today, in some circumstances defendants may have the burden of proof on apportionment.

Concurrent Independent Tortfeasors, One Cause. Suppose the tortious conduct of D1 and D2 (acting independently) occurs so that either D1 or D2 (but not both) was the cause in fact of P's injury, but P cannot prove which one. Traditionally, P would lose. Today, each defendant may be required to prove that he was not the cause.

Enterprise Liability. Courts may impose "enterprise liability" when: (1) the injury-causing product was manufactured by one of a small number of defendants in an industry; (2) the defendants had joint knowledge of the risks in inherent in the product and possessed a joint capacity to reduce those risks; (3) each defendant failed to take steps to reduce this risk, delegating this responsibility to a trade association; and (4) most, if not all, of the manufacturers are joined as defendants. Liability is joint and several. A manufacturer can escape liability only by proving that its product could not have been the one that injured the plaintiff.

Market Share Liability. A few courts permit "market share" liability when a person was injured by a product (such as a drug) that was produced and sold by multiple manufacturers, but the plaintiff cannot now identify the particular manufacturer that sold the product that caused her injury. Manufacturers representing a substantial share of the relevant market at the time the product was used or consumed can be sued jointly and held severally liable for a proportional part of the plaintiff's damages. The operative details vary among jurisdictions, but in general the plaintiff must join enough manufacturers to encompass the great majority of the relevant market, and prove their relevant market shares. A manufacturer can then escape liability by proving that its product could not have been the one that injured the plaintiff.

Liability for Reduced Chance. Some courts will permit recovery for tortious conduct that did not cause P's harm but merely reduced P's chances of a favorable outcome. Some deny all recovery unless the victim's chances were initially over 50%; some allow damages based on the jury's determination that the defendant's negligence was a "substantial factor" in hastening or precipitating the adverse result; and some allow damages based on the percentage difference attributable to the defendant's negligence times the plaintiff's total damages.

C. Scope of Liability (Proximate Cause)

1. General Principle

Rules of proximate or legal cause limit D's liability to persons and consequences that bear some reasonable relationship to D's tortious conduct. Whether and how proximate cause rules shall be applied is a question of law for the court. However, in some instances the jury is allowed to decide whether the scope of liability in a particular case extends to P's harm.

Proximate cause rules can be grouped into two categories: (1) unforeseeable or remote or indirect consequences; and (2) intervening causes.

2. Unforeseeable Consequences

Majority View: The Risk Principle. Under the majority view, sometimes called the "risk principle" or the "foreseeable-risk rule," D's liability is limited (1) to those consequences, the foreseeability of which made D's conduct tortious in the first place, and (2) to persons within that foreseeable zone of danger.

Minority View: The Direct Consequences Rule. Under the minority view, D is subject to liability for consequences which are a direct result of his tortious conduct, whether or not foreseeable. The result is direct if it follows in an unbroken natural sequence from the effect of D's act upon conditions existing and forces already in operation at the time, without the intervention of any external forces which were not then in active operation. The Restatement (Second) of Torts § 435 adopted a modified direct consequences rule. D is subject to liability if he could have foreseen any harm from his tortious conduct, even though the manner or extent of the harm was unforeseeable, unless the court finds it "highly extraordinary" that the conduct should have brought about the harm.

The Duty–Risk Rule. Some have proposed that all questions of scope of liability or "proximate cause" should be treated as duty issues, to be decided by the court based on a variety of factors: social policy, fairness, expediency, etc. This approach, known as the "duty-risk rule," has won few adherents in principle, but it is not uncommon for courts to rule against plaintiffs on the ground that D had no "duty" to protect P against a particular risk or that D owed no "duty" to P. See, e.g., Judge Cardozo's opinion in the *Palsgraf* case.

Current Status of the Risk Principle. Although most courts follow Cardozo's approach in the *Palsgraf* case and limit D's liability to the foreseeable risks which made his conduct negligent, many tend to allow juries to determine when the harm realized is too remote from D's negligence. They tend to see *all* causation issues as for the jury, and questions as to whether the risk realized is too disproportionate or different from the risk that made D's conduct tortious as questions of duty for the court.

Elasticity of "Foreseeable." Under the majority view, courts can expand or contract the bounds of D's liability by expansive or constrictive rulings on the foreseeability question.

Elasticity of "Hazard." The bounds of D's liability may also be expanded or contracted depending on how the court defines the hazard or risk that makes D's conduct tortious.

Rescuers. The intervention of would-be rescuers is usually deemed foreseeable.

Physical Consequences. Under the so-called "'thin-skulled" or "egg-shell" plaintiff rule, D is liable for the full consequences of P's injury even though, due to P's peculiar susceptibility (of which D was unaware), those consequences were more severe than they would have been in a normal person.

Intentional Torts; Strict Liability. Courts tend to expand the limits of foreseeability when D's conduct amounts to an intentional tort, and conversely confine liability to foreseeable consequences when liability is strict.

3. Intervening Cause

Definition. An intervening cause is conduct by some third person (or an event which occurs) after D's tortious conduct, and operates with or upon D's conduct to produce P's injury.

General Rule. If (1) an intervening cause was foreseeable, or (2) the intervening cause was not foreseeable but the consequences were of the type which D could foresee, the intervening cause will not operate to relieve D of liability. But if both the intervening cause and the resulting consequences were not foreseeable, it is called a *superseding* cause and D's tortious conduct is not deemed a proximate cause of P's injury.

Types of Intervening Causes. An intervening cause may consist of either human conduct or any other natural force or event.

Foreseeable Intervening Causes. Foreseeable intervening causes may include (1) foreseeable weather conditions; (2) negligence by third persons; (3) criminal conduct or intentional torts by third persons, provided D's conduct exposes P to a greater-than-normal risk of such conduct, or if the exposure to such risks is what makes D's conduct tortious; (4) P's self-inflicted harm while insane; (5) acts by rescuers; (6) efforts by P to mitigate the effects of his injury; and (7) disease or subsequent injuries resulting from the impairment of P's health caused by the original injury.

Foreseeable Consequences. If the result is foreseeably within the risk created by D's tortious conduct, then even an unforeseeable intervening cause does not supersede D's liability, unless (1) the unforeseeable intervening cause is the criminal act of a third person, or (2) a third person, who has a duty to act, discovers the danger and has sufficient time and opportunity to prevent the harm but fails to do so.

4. Substantial Factor

The "substantial factor" requirement has been eliminated as part of the definition of cause in fact, but it may be relevant as a scope of liability issue. When D's negligent conduct makes only a trivial contribution to multiple factual causes of P's harm, the harm is not within the scope of D's liability. However, this rule does not apply if the trivial contributing cause is necessary for the outcome; it only applies when the outcome is overdetermined.

■ PART FIVE: SPECIAL LIABILITY RULES FOR PARTICULAR ACTIVITIES

VII. OVERVIEW

Certain activities are governed by special tort liability rules. In some cases, these rules are merely special applications of the general principles of tort liability previously discussed. In other cases, these rules expand or contract the duty which D would otherwise have had under those general principles. These special duty rules often have the effect of taking issues that under the general rules of tort liability would have been issues for the jury and making them issues for the court.

VIII. OWNERS AND OCCUPIERS OF LAND

A. Persons Liable

Certain special duty rules apply to claims against possessors of land for injuries resulting from either a condition of the premises or an activity being conducted on the premises.

B. Persons Outside the Premises

1. Rule

As a general rule, a possessor must exercise reasonable care to see that activities and possessor-created conditions on the land do not harm his neighbors or passers-by on adjacent ways.

2. Adjacent Public Ways

On Ways. D is subject to liability to persons traveling on public ways adjacent to his property if he negligently creates or maintains an artificial condition or activity which subjects those persons to an unreasonable risk of harm.

Deviations From Public Way. If D can foresee that persons using an adjacent public way may deviate from it onto his property as a normal incident of their travel, he must exercise reasonable care to protect them from unreasonable risks of harm which they may encounter as a result of activities or artificial conditions created or maintained on his land.

Intentional Deviations. D's duty extends to (a) unintentional deviations and (b) intentional deviations which are a normal incident to travel on the public way in the exercise of reasonable care, and (c) foreseeable intentional deviations by children.

Distance. Foreseeable deviations will normally be only a short distance (a few feet or yards), but in a proper case may be a greater distance.

3. Neighboring Land

D's duty of ordinary care extends to persons lawfully using adjacent land.

4. Natural Conditions

Rule. D is not liable for physical harm to persons outside the premises or to adjoining land resulting from a natural condition of D's land.

Limitation. This rule is increasingly applied only to rural land. Even there, it applies only to unaltered natural conditions. If D or any one else has ever altered the natural condition of the land so as to create or aggravate the risk, D is subject to liability for unreasonable risks thereby created.

C. Trespassing Adults

1. Trespasser Defined

A trespasser (T) is one who enters or remains upon D's land without a privilege to do so.

2. General Rule

D is under no duty to exercise reasonable care (1) to make the premises reasonably safe for T (or to warn T of hidden dangers) or (2) to carry on activities on the premises so as not to endanger T.

3. Exception: Intentional and Reckless Misconduct

D's immunity from liability to T does not extend to intentional torts. And many jurisdictions hold that D is liable to T for harm caused by D's reckless ("wilful and wanton") misconduct. Others (and the Restatement) do not recognize this latter rule, but achieve somewhat the same result by the following two exceptions.

4. Exception: Frequent Trespassers on Limited Area

When D knows or should know that trespassers constantly intrude upon a limited area of his premises, D owes a duty of reasonable care to such a T (1) in the conduct of active operations on the premises, and (2) to warn T of a dangerous artificial condition on the land (created or maintained by D) which D has reason to believe T will not discover, provided the risk to T is one of serious bodily harm.

5. Exception: Discovered Trespassers

Rule. Once D discovers the presence of a T on his land, D must exercise reasonable care to (1) conduct his activities with regard to T's safety, (2) warn T of an artificial condition which poses a risk of serious bodily harm, if D knows or has reason to know that T is in dangerous proximity to it and that T will probably not discover the danger or realize the risk, and (3) control those forces within his control which threaten T's safety, or give T an adequate warning of them.

Duty to Rescue. D may have to exercise reasonable care to come to the aid of a discovered T who is injured or in peril on D's premises, even though D is not responsible for T's situation.

D. Trespassing Children ("Attractive Nuisance" Doctrine)

1. Discussion

Most jurisdictions have special rules applicable to child trespassers, sometimes called the "turntable" or "attractive nuisance" doctrine.

2. Rule

A possessor of land is subject to liability for physical harm to trespassing children caused by an artificial condition upon the land if the following requirements are met, and D fails to exercise reasonable care to eliminate the danger to such children or otherwise to protect them.

Knowledge of Child Trespassers. D must know or have reason to know that the place where the condition exists is one where children are likely to trespass.

Attraction of Condition. The child need not be attracted onto the premises by the condition that injures him. It is enough that children who do foreseeably trespass can be expected to encounter the condition.

Knowledge of Condition. D must know or have reason to know of the condition, and D must realize or should realize that it involves an unreasonable risk of death or serious bodily harm to such children. D need not have created the condition, but merely maintain it or permit it to exist.

Type of Condition. The doctrine applies only to artificial conditions (not activities or natural conditions) upon the land. In addition, some courts have created categories of "'common hazards" as to which D is not liable, such as fire, falling from a height, drowning in water, visible machinery in motion, piles of lumber, etc. However, the better view is that whether the risk is unreasonable depends on the facts and circumstances of each case.

Risk of Harm. The condition must create a risk of serious bodily harm or death; but if it does, D is subject to liability for any lesser injury.

Child's Awareness of Risk. The child, because of his youth, did not (a) discover the condition or (b) realize the risk.

Reasonableness of D's Conduct. The utility to D of maintaining the condition and the burden of eliminating the danger were outweighed by the risk to the children.

E. Licensees and Invitees

1. Licensee

A licensee is a person who has a privilege to enter or remain on D's land, but is not an invitee.

2. Invitee

An "invitee" is either a public invitee or a business visitor.

Public Invitee. A public invitee is a person who is invited to enter or remain on land as a member of the public for a purpose for which the land is held open to the public.

Business Visitors. A business visitor is a person who is invited to enter or remain on D's land for a purpose directly or indirectly connected with business dealings with the possessor of the land. This includes potential or future business.

Express or Implied. The invitation may be either express, or implied from D's conduct, prior dealings, usages in the community, etc.

Incidental Visitors. Invitees include persons whose visit is for the convenience, or arises out of the necessities of, others who are on the land for a business purpose.

Social Guests. Traditionally, a social guest in D's home is a licensee, despite incidental services performed by the guest or an incidental business motive behind the invitation. However, some courts and legislation now classify social guests as invitees.

Scope of Invitation. The invitation may be expressly or impliedly limited, as to (a) duration, (b) purpose, or (c) the portion of the premises to which the invitation extends. If P exceeds the scope of the invitation, he becomes a trespasser or licensee, depending upon whether or not D consents to his remaining.

3. Duty to Licensees

D's duty to a licensee is similar (but not identical) to that owed a discovered trespasser. Specifically:

Intentional and Reckless Conduct. D is subject to liability to a licensee for intentional and reckless ("wilful and wanton") conduct.

Active Operations (Latent Dangers). In conducting his activities on the premises, D must exercise reasonable care for the safety of licensees, provided (a) he should expect that they will not discover or realize the danger and (b) they do not know or have reason to know of D's activities and the risk involved.

Latent Conditions. As to dangerous conditions, D is subject to liability to a licensee if (a) D knows or has reason to know of the condition and the risk it creates, (b) the licensee does not, (c) D should expect that the licensee will not discover or realize the danger, and (d) D fails to exercise reasonable care to make the condition safe, or to warn the licensee of the condition and the risk involved.

4. Duty to Invitees

Rule. As to invitees, there is no duty limitation; D must exercise reasonable care for their safety.

Open and Obvious Dangers. Until recently, it was commonly held that even as to invitees, D was not liable for "open and obvious" dangers. The emerging and better view is that the obviousness of the danger is merely one fact bearing on whether D was negligent or on P's contributory fault or assumption of risk.

Acts of Third Persons. D must exercise reasonable care to protect his business invitees against foreseeable harm by third persons on the premises, and to discover that such acts by third persons are being done or are likely to occur. Some courts have held that, on particular facts, D's duty does not extend to protection against criminal violence by third persons, but the prevailing view is that in such cases D's negligence is a question of fact for the jury.

5. Other Privileged Entrants; Public Employees

General Rule. One who enters D's land by virtue of a privilege other than that created by D's consent is ordinarily classified a licensee.

Public Employee, Economic Nexus. Public employees who are required by law regularly to enter D's premises to make inspections, deliveries, or collections necessary to D's operations are invitees.

Firemen, Policemen. Firemen and policemen traditionally were classified as licensees. However, there is a trend to make them invitees, at least when upon those parts of the premises held open to the public or when their presence at the place of injury was foreseeable.

6. Recreational Entrants

Most states now have statutes which deny invitee status to persons invited or permitted to come upon D's land without charge for recreational purposes (e.g., hunting, fishing, swimming).

F. Rejection of Categories

1. General Duty of Ordinary Care

Some jurisdictions have abolished or merged the traditional categories, either completely or as to licensees and invitees, substituting a general duty of ordinary care under the circumstances.

2. Expansion of Invitee Status

In jurisdictions retaining the traditional categories, there is a trend to expand the scope of invitee status. In some, all social guests are invitees.

G. Lessors

1. General Rule

A lessor of real property is not liable to his lessee (or anyone on the premises with the lessee's consent) for physical harm sustained by such persons during the term of the lease as a result of a condition of the leased premises.

2. Exception: Latent Hazards

When the lessor knows or has reason to know of a concealed unreasonably dangerous condition (artificial or natural) existing on the premises at the time the lessee takes possession, but fails to warn the lessee about it, the lessor is subject to liability to the lessee and his guests for physical harm caused by that condition.

3. Exception: Persons Outside the Premises

Pre-existing Conditions. The lessor remains liable for a condition (existing at the time the lessee takes possession) which the lessor realizes or should realize unreasonably endangers persons outside the premises.

Conditions and Activities During Lease. A lessor is generally not liable for conditions which come into existence after the lessee takes possession or for the lessee's activities on the premises. But the lessor is subject to liability to persons off the premises if he knows when the lease is executed that the lessee intends to conduct an activity on the premises dangerous to such persons and nevertheless consents to that activity or fails to require proper precautions.

Contract to Repair. In some jurisdictions, negligent failure to perform the lessor's contract to repair the premises subjects him to liability to persons off the premises.

4. Exception: Public Admission

If the lease is for a purpose which involves the admission of the public, the lessor must exercise reasonable care to inspect the premises and remedy unreasonably dangerous conditions which exist when possession is transferred, if he has reason to expect that the public will be admitted before the lessee has remedied the condition.

Lessee's Agreement. The lessee's agreement to make the repair does not exonerate the lessor unless the lessor could reasonably expect him to perform in time.

5. Exception: Retained Control

The lessor is subject to liability for physical harm caused by a dangerous condition located on a part of the premises which the lessee is entitled to use and over which the lessor has retained control, provided the lessor by the exercise of reasonable care could have (1) discovered the condition and the unreasonable risk and (2) made it reasonably safe.

Liability extends to the lessee, members of his family, employees, and all lawful visitors on the premises. It does not extend to areas where tenants and their guests are forbidden.

The fact that the danger is open and obvious does not affect D's duty, but may be relevant on P's contributory fault.

Lease Exculpatory Clause. A clause in the lease exonerating the lessor from this liability may or may not be effective as to the tenant, but is always ineffective as to third persons not parties to the lease.

Criminal Violence. The cases are divided on whether a landlord is subject to liability to his tenants for criminal violence by third persons occurring in common areas of the building, based on his failure to provide adequate security.

6. Exception: Agreement to Repair

In most jurisdictions, the lessor's contractual promise to repair or maintain the leased premises subjects him to tort liability for negligence in failing to perform his contract resulting in an unreasonable risk of physical harm, whether the disrepair existed before or after the lessee took possession. The contract to repair must be supported by consideration.

The lessor's liability extends to the tenant and all others on the premises with the tenant's consent. The extent of D's duty is defined by the contract.

Notice. Unless otherwise provided by the lease, the lessor's duty is only to exercise reasonable care to make the repairs after he has notice of the need for them. He need not inspect the premises.

Services. The lessor may be liable for failure to provide a service required by the lease (e.g. heat, light) where the premises cannot be safely used without it.

7. Exception: Negligent Repairs

A lessor who undertakes (or purports to undertake) repair of the leased premises is subject to liability for physical harm resulting if (a) he increases the danger which existed before he undertook the repairs, or (b) a concealed danger remains and his repairs create a deceptive appearance of safety, or (c) the danger is a latent one and the lessor assures the lessee that the repairs have been made when in fact they have not, provided the danger (or enhanced danger) is such that the lessee neither knows nor should know that the repairs were not made or were made negligently.

8. Independent Contractors

The lessor is liable for the negligence of an independent contractor in performing these duties to the same extent as if the contractor were his employee.

9. General Duty of Reasonable Care

Several states have abandoned this scheme and substituted the rule that the lessor is under a general duty of reasonable care under the circumstances.

10. Statutes

Statutes and ordinances often impose specific requirements on lessors, for example, to keep the premises in repair. Violation of these statutes can subject the lessor to tort liability for resulting physical harm.

H. Vendors and Vendees

1. Vendors and Grantors

General Rule. A transferor of land is not subject to liability to his transferee for physical harm resulting from a dangerous condition of the premises (natural or artificial), whether existing when, or arising after, the transferee took possession.

Exception: Latent Hazards. A transferor (D) is subject to liability to his transferee (P) (or others on the premises with his consent) for physical harm resulting from a concealed dangerous condition, provided (1) P did not know or have reason to know of the condition or the risk involved, (2) D knew or should have known of the condition, realized or should have realized the risk it created, and could anticipate that P would not discover the condition or appreciate the risk, and (3) the risk is an unreasonable one.

Exception: Persons Outside the Premises. A transferor who has created or negligently permitted to remain on the land an artificial condition which involves an unreasonable risk of harm to persons outside the premises is subject to liability for physical harm to such persons caused by that condition after the transferee has taken possession. This liability continues for a reasonable time after transfer, until the transferee has had a reasonable opportunity to discover the condition (or actually discovers it, if it was actively concealed by the transferor) and a reasonable time to correct it.

2. Builder–Vendors

Courts are increasingly subjecting persons who build and market new buildings to tort liability for unreasonably dangerous conditions in them, via (1) ordinary negligence principles, (2) strict liability for breach of warranty, or (3) in a few cases, strict liability analogous to strict product liability, at least where the builder-vendor is a mass-producer of homes.

3. Vendees and Other Transferees

A transferee of land thereby becomes its possessor and is subject to a possessor's duties and liabilities, but not until he discovers or should have discovered any dangerous conditions and has had a reasonable time to remedy them.

IX. PRODUCTS LIABILITY

Liability for physical harm caused by an unsafe product may be based on one or more of three legal theories: negligence, breach of warranty, or strict tort liability.

A. Negligence

In general, ordinary negligence principles apply to product liability actions brought on a negligence theory.

1. Privity Limitations

At one time, the general rule was that the manufacturer or other seller of an unsafe product was not liable in negligence to the user or consumer absent privity of contract between P and D (*Winterbottom v. Wright*)—that is, unless P had bought the product directly from D. Exceptions arose and expanded, and eventually *MacPherson v. Buick Motor Co.* (N.Y.1916) held that lack of privity is not a defense when it is foreseeable that the product, if negligently made, can cause injury to a class of persons which includes P. This effectively abolished the privity limitation.

2. Persons Protected

D is subject to liability not only to the ultimate purchaser or lessee of the product but also to all foreseeable users or consumers, and to all other persons foreseeably exposed to the risk.

3. Types of Negligent Conduct

Manufacturers. Negligence in the manufacturing process includes negligent design; errors or omissions during production; failure to properly test or inspect; unsafe containers or packaging; inadequate warnings or directions for use; and misrepresentation. A subsequent seller's failure to inspect does not relieve the manufacturer of liability for his negligence.

Subsequent Sellers. Subsequent sellers (distributors, retailers) may be negligent in failing to warn of the existence of an unsafe condition or otherwise protect the user. Under the majority view, such seller is liable only for dangers of which he knew or had reason to know; he has no duty to inspect or test the product to discover latent dangers.

Other Suppliers. Lessors and others who furnish chattels commercially are liable for negligence in furnishing an unsafe chattel; their duty includes a duty to inspect. Other suppliers—e.g., donors, gratuitous bailors—are subject to liability if they knew or had reason to know that the product was unsafe. And D may be liable for furnishing a chattel to one who he knows or has reason to know is incompetent to use it safely.

Independent Contractors. Contractors who make, rebuild, or repair a chattel are subject to similar rules.

Ostensible Suppliers. One who puts out as his own a chattel manufactured by another is subject to the same liability as though he were its manufacturer.

B. Breach of Warranty

1. Types of Warranties

Warranty is not a tort concept, but breach of certain (usually, U.C.C.) warranties gives rise to an action for resulting physical harm which is part of the law of "products liability." Liability is strict.

Express (§ 2–313). Express warranties are promissory assertions of fact or descriptions which are part of the basis of the bargain.

Implied Warranty of Merchantability (§ 2–314). The implied warranty of merchantability implies minimum standards of quality including safety. (D must be a "merchant" with respect to goods of that kind).

Implied Warranty of Fitness for a Particular Purpose (§ 2–315). This warranty arises when the buyer relies on the seller to furnish goods suitable for a particular specified use.

2. Limitations

The principal limitations on breach of warranty liability are (1) the seller must be given prompt notice of the breach, (2) the buyer must have relied upon the warranty, and (3) the seller in certain cases can limit or disclaim these warranties (but see U.C.C. § 2–719(3)).

3. Privity

As in the case of negligence, liability for breach of warranty was once limited to the parties to the contract of sale, but that limitation has been modified.

C. Strict Tort Liability for Defective Products

Strict tort liability for defective products was first adopted in *Greenman v. Yuba Power Products, Inc.* (Cal. 1963). Shortly thereafter this principle was codified in R.2d § 402A, and it is now the law in most jurisdictions.

1. Rule

D is strictly liable for physical harm to P or his property caused by a defective condition of a product which renders it unreasonably danger-ous, if (1) D sold the product in that condition and (2) D is engaged in the business of selling such products. R.2d § 402A.

2. Products

The term "product" includes all forms of tangible personal property (chattels). In addition to manufactured products, it includes products which undergo little or no processing, (e.g., mineral water). The doctrine has not been extended to transactions which, although incidentally involving a product, are essentially the rendition of a service.

3. Defect Unreasonably Dangerous

In most jurisdictions, D is subject to liability only if the product contains a "defect" which renders it "unreasonably dangerous" to the user or consumer. These include (1) design defects, such as the use of inadequate materials or the absence of feasible safety devices; (2) defects which occur in a particular product unit because of errors or omissions in manufacturing, assembly or processing; and (3) inadequate warnings or directions for use. The defect may be in the product itself or in its container or packaging.

4. Unreasonably Dangerous

Most jurisdictions require a showing that the product was "unreasonably dangerous." Jurisdictions differ as to the test or tests to be applied in resolving this issue. In some jurisdictions, more than one of these tests are available, sometimes in a single case.

Consumer Expectation Test. One popular test is the "consumer expectation" test, requiring the product to be dangerous "to an extent beyond that which would be contemplated by the ordinary consumer who purchases it, with the ordinary knowledge common to the community as to its characteristics."

Presumed Seller's Knowledge Test. Would the seller have been negligent in marketing the product if the seller had known of its harmful or dangerous condition?

Risk-Benefit Balancing Test. The "risk-benefit" test requires the trier of fact to balance (1) the safety risks of the product as designed, and (2) the utility and other benefits of the product as designed, against (3) the safety risks and benefits of the product if it had been designed as the plaintiff claims it should have been. The factors most often used in this test are: (1) the usefulness and desirability of the product as designed; (2) the likelihood and probable seriousness of injury from the product as designed; (3) the availability of an alternative product or design that would meet the same need and not be as unsafe; (4) the manufacturer's ability to eliminate the danger without impairing the product's usefulness or making it too expensive; (5) the user's ability to avoid the danger; (6) the user's anticipated awareness of the danger; and (7) the feasibility of the manufacturer's spreading the risk of loss by pricing or insurance.

Unavoidably Unsafe Products. Under comment k to § 402A, some highly useful products (e.g., certain drugs and vaccines) may be "unavoidably unsafe" because of inherent dangerous side effects which "in the present state of human knowledge" cannot be eliminated. Such products, "properly prepared, and accompanied by proper directions and warnings," are not defective or unreasonably dangerous.

Crashworthiness. A product such as a vehicle may be defective and unreasonably dangerous because it is insufficiently crashworthy.

Food Products. In the case of food products that contain a harm-causing ingredient, most courts hold that the ingredient constitutes a defect if a reasonable consumer would not expect the food product to contain that ingredient, regardless whether the ingredient is foreign (a piece of glass) or natural (a chicken bone in a chicken pie). A minority of courts allow strict products liability if the ingredient is foreign but not if it is natural, but permit recovery for natural ingredients on a negligence theory.

5. Type of Harm

In most jurisdictions, strict tort liability is limited to physical harm and consequential damages resulting from such harm. Pecuniary loss caused by a defect in the product without an accidental injury to the product or to other persons or property is recoverable only under a breach of warranty theory.

6. Plaintiffs

Liability extends not only to the purchaser or lessee of the product but to all foreseeable users or consumers. Most jurisdictions also allow recovery by "bystanders" whose exposure to the risk of injury was foreseeable.

7. Proof of a Defect

In a strict products liability case, the existence of an unspecified manufacturing defect may be shown by circumstantial evidence, analogous to the use of res ipsa loquitur in a negligence case.

8. Defenses

Contributory Negligence. Prior to the adoption of comparative fault, most jurisdictions held that ordinary contributory negligence was not a defense to strict product liability. Today, some of the jurisdictions adopting comparative negligence permit P's ordinary contributory negligence to reduce P's damages; others do not.

Implied Assumption of Risk. Prior to the adoption of comparative fault, in most jurisdictions implied assumption of the risk was a complete bar to recovery under strict product liability. Today, in most comparative fault jurisdictions implied assumption of the risk is only a damage-reducing factor. It remains a complete bar in a few states.

Misuse. D is not liable for an injury caused by an unforeseeable misuse of his product. But a product may be found defective because it was not designed so as to be reasonably safe in light of an unintended but foreseeable misuse.

Statute of Limitations and Repose. In some jurisdictions, there is an additional limitation period, called a "statute of repose," which runs from the date of the product's manufacture or first sale.

Disclaimer. A purported disclaimer of strict product liability is ineffective.

State of the Art. In some jurisdictions, D can defend by showing that the product was designed in accordance with the "state of the art" when it was manufactured and first sold.

Learned Intermediaries and Sophisticated Users. A prescription drug manufacturer oridinarily has no duty to provide a warning directly to the ultimate user. And where products are sold in bulk, or to sophisticated users, the manufacturer can rely on the intermediate buyer to use the product properly and pass on any appropriate warnings.

9. Defendants

Strict product liability extends to (1) the producer (manufacturer, processor, assembler, packager, or bottler) of the product, and of the component part which was defective, and (2) all downstream vendors and commercial lessors and bailors. D must be "engaged in the business" of dealing in that product, but such product need not be D's principal business. Courts usually refuse to extend strict liability to dealers in used products.

10. Nondelegable Duties

Although the manufacturer is usually not liable unless the product was defective when it left his control, an exception exists when the manufacturer places in the stream of commerce an unfinished or unassembled product which must be assembled or finished by his dealer, who in doing so creates the defect. And a manufacturer cannot delegate to his purchaser the duty to select and purchase optional safety devices, without which the product is not reasonably safe.

11. Post–Sale Duties

In some jurisdictions, a manufacturer may be subject to liability for failure to "retrofit" a previously marketed product with safety devices (or to provide appropriate warnings) when locating current users and furnishing such devices or warnings is not an unreasonable burden compared to the risk of injury inherent in the product without them, even though the product was arguably not unsafe when it was first marketed.

12. Misrepresentation

A similar form of strict liability is imposed on one who misrepresents a material fact to the public concerning the character or quality of a chattel sold by him, and the purchaser relies upon such misrepresentation and thereby sustains physical harm.

D. The Restatement (Third) of Torts: Products Liability

1. New Standards for Different Types of Product Defects

The new product liability provisions, which supersede § 402A, now explicitly recognize the three categories of product defects: manufacturing defects, design defects, and informational defects (warnings and directions for use). Sellers remain strictly liable for manufacturing defects, but the Restatement's proposed liability for design defects is close to a negligence standard, imposing liability only for "foreseeable risks of harm" that could have been avoided by the adoption of a "reasonable alternative design or by reasonable instructions or warnings." Similarly, there is no duty to warn under this provision unless P can prove that the manufacturer knew or should have known of the risk about which P claims she should have been warned. However, if the product's design is "manifestly unreasonable" because of its negligible utility and high risk of danger, defectiveness can be found even without proof of an alternative design (e.g., a dangerous toy gun).

As an alternative, P can recover if she can prove that the product as designed, or the warning, failed to comply with an applicable safety statute or administrative regulation. On the other hand, as evidence that the product was not defective, D can prove the product's compliance with an applicable safety statute or administrative regulation, although such compliance is not conclusive on the issue of defectiveness.

2. Prescription Drug and Medical Device Liability

Under the Restatement (Third), a prescription drug or medical device is not defective in design unless the foreseeable risk of harm is so "great in relation to its foreseeable therapeutic benefits that reasonable health-care providers, knowing of such foreseeable risks and therapeutic benefits, would not prescribe the drug or medical device for any class of patients." Warnings need only be given to "health care providers" unless the manufacturer "knows or has reason to know that health-care providers will not be in a position to reduce the risks of harm in accordance with the instructions or warnings." In that case, but only in that case, an adequate warning is owed to the patient.

Strict liability will still apply to drugs and medical products for manufacturing defects.

X. VICARIOUS LIABILITY

A. Introduction

1. General Rule

One (D1) who, while acting on behalf of another, commits a tortious act and thereby subjects himself to tort liability to P may also thereby subject the person on whose behalf he is acting (D2) to tort liability to P It is said that D2 is vicariously liable to P.

2. Relationships Giving Rise to Vicarious Liability

The forms of relationships which potentially give rise to vicarious liability are (1) master-servant, (2) principal-agent, and (3) employer-independent contractor. For purposes of tort law, there is little distinction between the liability rules governing master-servant and principal-agent relationships. However, the vicarious liability of one who employs an independent contractor is significantly different.

B. Employers and Employees (Master–Servant)

1. Vicarious Liability

If, at the time of his negligent or reckless act, the servant was acting in the course and scope of his employment, then his employer is vicariously liable to P for his servant's tort.

2. Scope of Employment

Whether the employee was acting in the scope of his employment is a question of fact, which depends upon (a) the employee's job description and assigned duties, (b) the time, place and purpose of the employee's act, (c) the similarity of his conduct to the things he was hired to do, or which are commonly done by such employees, and (d) the foreseeability of his act.

3. Intentional Torts

An employer is vicariously liable for his employee's intentional torts committed in the scope of his employment and in furtherance of his employer's business, at least if the employee's act was foreseeable. And where there is some special relationship between the employer and P such that the employer owes P a duty of protection, the employer is subject to vicarious liability for his servant's intentional torts even if committed for personal reasons.

4. Employer's Liability

An employer may be directly (not vicariously) liable for torts committed by his employee based upon the employer's own negligence or other conduct. Thus, the employer may have been negligent in selecting, instructing, or supervising the employee; or he may have commanded, authorized or ratified the employee's tortious act.

5. Partnerships, Joint Ventures

A partner or joint venturer acting in the scope of the business subjects his other partners and joint venturers to vicarious tort liability to third persons.

C. Independent Contractors

1. General Rule

An employer is not vicariously liable for physical harm caused by the tortious conduct of his independent contractor or his contractor's employees.

2. Exception: Employer's Own Negligence

Negligent Selection. An employer is subject to liability for physical harm resulting from his failure to exercise reasonable care to select a reasonably competent, experienced, careful, and properly equipped contractor.

Negligent Instruction. An employer is subject to liability for the negligence of an independent contractor acting in accordance with the employer's instructions.

Failure to Inspect Completed Work. An employer has a duty to inspect his contractor's completed work, at least where he has a duty to third persons to maintain the land or chattels for their protection.

Failure to Require Precautions. If the work will create a foreseeable danger to third persons, the employer must require (in the contract or otherwise) that appropriate precautions be taken for their safety.

Retained Supervision and Control. To the extent that the employer retains or exercises supervision or control over the work of the contractor, he must do so with reasonable care.

Duty as Possessor of Land. A possessor of land held open to the public must exercise reasonable care to protect that public from unreasonably dangerous conditions or activities of an independent contractor on the land.

3. Exception: Nondelegable Duties

Where the safe performance of some duty is of sufficient importance to the community, an employer is vicariously liable for the negligence of his independent contractor in performing that duty which results in physical harm. In other words, these duties are personal to D, and are not "delegable" to an independent contractor so as to relieve D of tort liability if they are negligently performed.

4. Exception: Inherently Dangerous Work

When the contracted work involves a special, greater-than-ordinary danger to others which the employer knows or has reason to know is inherent in, or normal to, the work, or which is contemplated at the time of the contract, the employer is vicariously liable for physical harm caused by the independent contractor's failure to take reasonable precautions against such danger.

5. Collateral Negligence

As a general rule, the employer's vicarious liability is limited to the particular risk(s) which gave rise to the exception.

6. Liability to Contractor's Employees

The authorities are divided on whether the employer's liability extends to employees of the contractor whose injuries result from those risks created by the conditions upon which the contractor was hired to work.

D. Apparent Agency

If a principal creates the appearance that someone is his agent or employee, he is not permitted (i.e., he is "estopped") to deny the agency if a third party, who does not know otherwise, reasonably relies on the apparent agency. A principal can be held vicariously liable in tort for an injury caused by the negligent acts of his apparent agent if the injury would not have occurred but for P's justifiable reliance on the apparent agency. Some states have enacted statutes abolishing such vicarious liability against certain health care providers.

XI. EMPLOYER'S LIABILITY TO EMPLOYEES

A. Common Law Duties of Employer to Employee

1. Safe Place to Work

The employer must provide his employee with reasonably safe working conditions and warn him of unsafe conditions which he should anticipate will not be discovered by the employee.

2. Defenses

The employer's defenses include assumption of risk, contributory negligence, and the fellow servant rule (an employer is not vicariously liable for an injury to an employee caused solely by the negligence of a fellow servant in the performance of the operative details of the work).

B. Workers' Compensation

1. Workers' Compensation Acts

Introduction. The employee's common law tort action against his employer has been replaced in all states and several other jurisdictions by workers' compensation acts, which make the employer strictly liable to pay scheduled benefits for most accidental injuries occurring "in the course of" and "arising out of" the employment.

Exclusive Remedy Against Employer. If an employee's injury occurs in the course of, and arises out of, an employment covered by a workers' compensation act, his remedy under the act is usually his exclusive remedy against his employer, even if for some reason the particular injury is not compensable.

Compensation. In exchange for strict liability and a relatively speedy remedy, the employee's compensation is limited to a statutory schedule of limited benefits, usually a percentage of P's average weekly wage for a specified number of weeks which varies according to the severity of the injury.

Third Party Actions. In most jurisdictions, the workers' comp act does not bar the employee from bringing a tort action and recovering his full damages, even though his injury is compensable under the act, if he can find a third party (other than his employer) whose tort contributed to P's injury. If P is successful against the third party, he must ordinarily repay the workers' compensation he has received.

2. Railroad and Maritime Employees

Employees of common carriers by rail and "seamen" have a special common law negligence action against their employer under the Federal Employers' Liability Act and the Jones Act, respectively. Seamen also have other remedies under admiralty law.

C. Retaliatory Discharge

Under a new tort cause of action known as retaliatory discharge, an at-will employee who is fired for conduct protected by an important, well-defined public policy can sue his former employer for wrongful discharge.

XII. AUTOMOBILES

A. Joint Enterprise

A joint enterprise is an express or implied agreement among two or more persons to use an automobile for a common (usually, business) purpose, with all participants having a mutual and equal right of direction and control over its operation. All participants are vicariously liable to third persons for the negligence of the driver. A participant injured by the driver's negligence may recover from the driver, but not from any other participants.

B. Owner–Passenger

An auto owner who is a passenger in his own vehicle is not vicariously liable for the negligence of the driver, but may be directly liable for his own negligence in failing to exercise control over the driver.

C. Owner–Bailor

Absent a statute or some other tort theory, an owner-bailor (not a passenger) who merely permits another to use his auto is not per se vicariously liable for the driver's negligence.

D. Family Purpose Doctrine

In about half the states, the owner of an auto which he makes generally available for personal (noncommercial) use by members of his immediate household is vicariously liable for its negligent operation by such persons within the scope of the express or implied permission.

E. Consent Statutes

In about one-fourth of the states, an auto owner is vicariously liable for the negligence of anyone operating it on a public highway with his consent, within the scope of the express or implied permission. However, the bailee's negligence is ordinarily not imputed to bar or reduce the owner's damages in an action against a third person.

F. Guest Passengers

Statutes in some states limit a driver's liability for injuries to "guests" in his vehicle to situations where (1) the driver's conduct was more than ordinary negligence, or (2) the driver's intoxication caused the injury, or (3) the injury was caused by a defect in the vehicle of which the driver had knowledge and failed to warn. There is a trend to repeal such guest statutes, and some courts have held them unconstitutional.

G. "No–Fault" Auto Compensation Plans

About half the states have some form of "no-fault" compensation legislation under which mandatory insurance compensates the less seriously injured victims of auto accidents, and in most cases restricts or eliminates such victims' tort cause of action.

XIII. MEDICAL AND OTHER PROFESSIONAL NEGLIGENCE ("MALPRACTICE")

A. Standard of Care

1. Customary Practice = Standard of Care

In most jurisdictions, the standard of care of medical doctors (and sometimes other professionals) is conclusively established by the customary or usual practice of reasonably well-qualified practitioners in that field.

2. Specialists

Physicians or others who are certified specialists, or who hold themselves out as specialists, are held to the standards of that speciality, but again, in most cases the customary conduct of reasonably well-qualified specialists conclusively sets the standard of care.

3. Locality Rule

Until recently, the standard of care of medical professionals (and, occasionally, other professionals as well) was further limited by the "locality rule," under which the standard of care is the customary or usual practice of reasonably well-qualified similar professionals in that geographic locality, or alternatively, in the same or similar localities. Today, almost all jurisdictions have abandoned the locality rule as applied to board-certified specialists, and most jurisdictions have also rejected the rule generally.

B. Proof of Negligence, Standard of Care, and Causation

1. Expert Testimony

In most cases involving a claim of professional negligence, P will be unable to establish a submissible case without expert testimony establishing (1) the relevant standard of care, (2) that D's conduct did not conform to that standard, and (3) that there was a causal relationship between D's breach and P's injury. Although some states have adopted statutes regulating expert testimony in medical negligence cases (e.g. by requiring that the expert not be a mere testifying consultant, or requiring that the expert have the same license and certification as the defendant), the common law applies the usual qualifying tests to such expert testimony.

2. Substitutes for Expert Testimony

Standard of Care. In addition to proof by expert testimony, the standard of care in medical negligence cases can sometimes be established in other ways, such as by (1) admissions by the defendant, (2) authoritative medical literature, (3) standards adopted by government or trade groups, such as hospital licensing rules, (4) hospital by-laws and rules, and (5) literature accompanying medical products that contains warnings and directions for use.

Proof of Negligence: Res Ipsa Loquitur
Common knowledge res ipsa. Occasionally, the facts will be such that the ordinary layperson can determine that the defendant's conduct did not conform to the standard of care. In such "common knowledge" cases, no expert testimony is required to prove the defendant's negligence.

Expert res ipsa. Sometimes an expert witness cannot testify to an opinion as to exactly what the defendant did that was negligent, but can testify that the adverse result would not have occurred if the defendant had exercised ordinary care.

C. Informed Consent

1. Rule

Under the doctrine of informed consent, a patient's/client's consent to a particular treatment, procedure, or other professional conduct must be based on the professional's disclosure of the material risks and alternatives to the proposed conduct so that patient/client can make an informed decision as to whether to consent.

2. Standard

Professional Rule. In medical cases, at one time the prevailing standard only required the doctor to inform the patient of those risks and alternatives that doctors customarily chose to disclose. This has become known as the "professional rule."

Reasonable Patient or "Material Risks" Rule. The professional rule is being replaced by one which gives greater autonomy to the patient: the doctor must disclose those risks and alternatives of which a reasonable patient would want to be informed so as to be able to make an intelligent choice—in other words, all risks material to the decision of the ordinary patient in the plaintiff's position.

Distinguished From Consent to a Battery. In medical negligence cases, violation of this standard does not negate the patient's consent (so as to give rise to a battery) but rather is simply another instance of negligent conduct.

Proof of Causation. Some courts require an objective standard for proof of causation—that a reasonably prudent patient in the plaintiff's position would not have consented if he had been furnished the required information—as opposed to a subjective standard under which the plaintiff is allowed to prove that he would not have consented, regardless of what anyone else would have done.

D. The "Medical Malpractice Crisis" and Tort Reform

Many states have adopted special rules governing medical malpractice cases. These include modifications to the medical standard of care and medical res ipsa loquitur rules; partial abrogation of the collateral source rule; statutes of repose; restrictions on expert testimony; arbitrary limits on the amount recoverable in a medical malpractice action, either generally or for non-economic losses; and mandatory submission of the case to a screening panel prior to taking the case to court.

XIV. NUISANCE

A. Introduction

"Nuisances," public and private, are two distinct fields of tort liability that provide remedies for particular types of harm. It is the interest of P which has been invaded, and not the conduct of D, which determines whether an action for nuisance will lie.

B. Private Nuisance

1. Definition

A private nuisance is a thing or activity which substantially and unreasonably interferes with P's use and enjoyment of his land.

2. Relation to Trespass

A trespass is an invasion of P's interest in the exclusive possession of land. A nuisance is an interference with P's interest in the private use and enjoyment of the land. Unlike trespass, the interference must be unreasonable and cause substantial harm.

3. Basis of Liability

Fault. Liability is not absolute. Absent a statute, D's interference with P's protected interest must be intentional, reckless, negligent, or the result of an abnormally dangerous activity such that principles of strict liability will apply.

Substantial Interference. Nuisance liability requires substantial harm, of a type which would be suffered by a normal person in the community, or by property in normal condition and used for a normal purpose.

Continuing or Recurring Interference. There is no requirement that the interference be continuing or recurring, although some interferences will not be sufficiently substantial unless they are.

Unreasonable Interference. The interference must be unreasonable, which generally means that either (a) the gravity of P's harm outweighs the utility of D's conduct, or (b) if intentional, the harm caused by D's conduct is substantial and the financial burden of compensating for this and other harms does not render unfeasible the continuation of the conduct.

Gravity. In determining the gravity of the harm, the important factors include (i) its extent, (ii) its character, (iii) the social value of P's use or enjoyment it affects, (iv) the suitability of that use or enjoyment to the locality, and (v) the burden to P of avoiding the harm.

Utility. In determining the utility of D's conduct, important factors include (i) its social value, (ii) its suitability to the locality, (iii) the practicability of preventing or avoiding the interference, and (iv) the practicability of continuing D's activity if it is required to bear the cost of compensating for the interference.

4. Remedies

Damages. The usual remedy is damages. If the nuisance is permanent, all damages must be recovered in one action. If the nuisance can be abated, P recovers all damages to the time of trial. If D then fails to abate, future invasions give rise to a new cause of action.

Injunction. If the nuisance threatens to continue and P has no adequate legal remedy, equitable relief may be sought. The court then will undertake a further balancing.

Self–Help. There is a limited privilege to trespass to abate a private nuisance.

5. Persons Liable

Liability for nuisance includes not only one who carries on or participates in a nuisance-creating activity, but in some cases a lessor or possessor who fails to prevent or abate one carried on by third persons on his land.

6. Defenses

Contributory Negligence, Assumption of Risk. P's contributory negligence or assumption of risk is a defense to the same extent as in other tort actions.

Coming to the Nuisance. The fact that P has acquired or improved his land after a nuisance has come into existence is not itself sufficient to bar his action, but is a factor to be considered in determining whether the nuisance is actionable.

Others Contributing to the Nuisance. Except as it may affect the character of the locality, the fact that others contribute to a nuisance is not a bar to D's liability for his own contribution.

Legislation. Legislation authorizing a particular activity or use of land may be used to establish that it is not a nuisance, but such authority is usually narrowly construed to include only reasonable conduct.

C. Public Nuisance

1. What Constitutes

A public nuisance is an unreasonable interference with a right common to the general public. It includes interference with the public health, safety, morals, peace, comfort, or convenience.

2. Public Right

The right interfered with must be common to the public as a class, and not merely that of one person or even a group of citizens.

3. Remedies

A private citizen has no civil remedy for the harm he has sustained as a result of a public nuisance if that harm is of the same kind as that suffered by the general public, even though he has been harmed to a greater degree than others. The remedy is a criminal prosecution or suit to enjoin or abate the nuisance by public authorities or others on behalf of the public. A private citizen may sue for harm caused by a public nuisance only if his harm is different in kind from that suffered by other members of the public.

XV. NEGLIGENT INFLICTION OF EMOTIONAL DISTRESS

A. Introduction

As to liability for negligently-caused emotional distress, the law distinguishes three different fact situations—impact, zone of danger, and bystander.

B. Impact Rule

If D's negligent conduct results in any impact, however slight, with P's body, all courts will allow that impact to support liability for P's emotional distress resulting from the same negligent conduct.

C. Zone of Danger Rule

If D's negligent conduct threatens (but does not result in) bodily harm (impact) to P, most courts will allow P to recover for bodily harm resulting from the fear, shock or other emotional disturbance caused by his presence in the zone of danger.

D. Bystander Rule

1. General Rule

If P is not himself in the zone of danger, but suffers emotional distress as a result of witnessing a shocking event in which D's negligent conduct threatens or causes physical harm to a third person, most courts have refused to hold D liable to P.

2. Exception

A few courts, following *Dillon v. Legg* (Cal. 1968), have allowed P to recover in such situations, provided (a) the threatened injury is a serious one, (b) P is a member of the immediate family of the person in peril, (c) the shock results in bodily harm to P, (d) the event is of short duration, and (e) P actually witnesses the event or its immediate aftermath.

3. Zone of Danger, Fear for Another's Safety

Even before Dillon, some courts would allow P to recover for bystander shock under the facts stated in the preceding paragraph if P was also within the zone of danger.

E. Proximate Cause Limitations

1. Physical Illness Requirement

Absent impact, in most jurisdictions P may recover under the foregoing rules only if his emotional distress results in physical illness or comparable objective bodily consequences.

2. "Eggshell Plaintiff" Rule Inapplicable

Unless D has actual knowledge of some special sensitivity of P, D will be liable only to the extent that P's physical response to the emotional trauma was within the normal range of ordinarily sensitive persons.

F. Direct Victims

A line of cases is emerging allowing recovery where there is no contact or threat of physical harm, but the plaintiff is a "direct victim" of negligent conduct whose only consequence is emotional distress.

G. Fear of Future Harm From Toxic Exposure

Where P has been exposed, or fears he has been exposed, to a toxic substance due to D's negligence, but P has no present symptoms or diagnosis of the feared disease, P may be allowed to recover for the mental distress resulting from the fear of future harm, or for medical monitoring, until such time as it can be established that the risk of such future harm is zero

1. Parasitic to Actual Physical Injury

If P can prove that he sustained any immediate physical harm, however slight, as a result of an actual exposure, the case fits within the traditional "impact" rule, and P can recover emotional distress damages parasitic to that injury.

2. Actual Exposure But No Physical Harm

If P can show actual exposure to the toxic substance but no immediate physical injury, many courts will allow P to recover for medical monitoring and emotional distress, but some courts require P to prove a greater-than–50% chance that he will contract the feared disease at some time in the future. If P can show actual exposure to HIV, he can usually recover for emotional distress between the time of exposure and the time when testing determines that P will not be infected with AIDS.

3. Possible Exposure and No Physical Harm

If P can only establish a possibility or fear of exposure and no present physical harm, almost all courts will deny recovery for emotional distress damages or medical monitoring. Some courts will allow emotional distress damages in HIV/AIDS cases even if P cannot establish actual exposure and there is no physical harm, so long as a channel of exposure exists and P's fear is reasonable.

XVI.   PRENATAL HARM

A.   Child Born Alive

One who tortiously causes harm to an unborn child is subject to liability to the child for such harm if the child is subsequently born alive. The prevailing view is that the fetus need not have been viable at the time of the injury. If the child is born alive but then dies from the injury, a wrongful death action can be maintained. A few recent decisions have extended recovery to include pre-conception as well as post-conception negligence, at least where the pre-conception negligence created a foreseeable risk of the harm to the child that later resulted. Even in those jurisdictions where the parent-child immunity is abolished, the prevailing view is that a mother cannot be held liable for her negligent conduct that results in an injury to her then-unborn child.

B.   Child Not Born Alive

As to the wrongful death of an unborn child, most courts allow the action if the fetus was viable at the time of the injury.

C.   Unwanted Children

1.   Wrongful Conception

When D's negligence fails to prevent conception resulting in the birth of an unwanted but healthy child, most courts allow the parents to recover, but their damages are limited to the cost of pre-natal care and delivery and the associated pain and other general damages. Some courts have allowed, in addition, child-rearing expenses, most (but not all) requiring that such expenses be offset by the accompanying financial and emotional benefits to the parents.

2.   Wrongful Birth and Wrongful Life

Description. Another category of claims arises when D's negligence results in the birth of an unwanted child who is physically or mentally defective. Actions brought by the parents of such children for their damages (including damages for the ordinary and extraordinary costs of caring for such children and their mental distress) are usually referred to as wrongful birth claims. Actions brought by the deformed child for his damages (e.g., pain, suffering, disability, disfigurement) are called wrongful life actions.

Wrongful Birth. Most courts now allow recovery for wrongful birth. Some courts limit damages to the parents' pecuniary losses, but others now award damages for their emotional distress as well.

Wrongful Life. So far, almost all jurisdictions have rejected wrongful life claims. A few courts have allowed such claims, the damages being limited to the child's extraordinary medical expenses (to the extent not recovered by the parents).

XVII. ALCOHOLIC BEVERAGES

A. Commercial Vendors of Alcohol

1. Common Law Liability

The common law rule in most jurisdictions is that one who sells intoxicating beverages is not liable to third persons injured by the person thereby intoxicated, even when the sale is in violation of a statute or ordinance or is negligent.

2. Dram Shop Acts

A number of states have enacted statutes (called "dram shop acts") which impose civil liability on commercial sellers in favor of third persons injured by an intoxicated person. Some statutes require that the sale have been illegal, others merely that the beverage sold have caused or contributed to the intoxication.

B. Social Hosts

So far, most courts have refused to impose negligence liability on persons who are not licensed dram shops for serving alcohol or for failing to control their intoxicated guests. A few jurisdictions have, based on (1) violation of a liquor control statute as negligence per se, or (2) common law negligence principles such as negligent entrustment or negligent supervision or ordinary duty rules.

XVIII. INTERFERENCE WITH FEDERAL CONSTITUTIONAL RIGHTS

A. Persons Acting Under Color of State Law

42 U.S.C.A. § 1983 creates a tort cause of action against one who "under color of" state law interferes with a federal constitutional right of another.

B. Federal Officers and Employees

One whose federal constitutional rights have been violated by a federal officer or employee may have an action against him for damages under the doctrine of Bivens v. Six Unknown Named Agents of Federal Bureau of Narcotics (U.S. 1971).

XIX. ACTIVITIES CAUSING ONLY ECONOMIC HARM

A. In General

Tort law has been reluctant to extend liability for negligent conduct that results solely in economic harm to P (in contrast to the freedom with which economic losses are recoverable in tort actions based on physical harm to P).

B. Economic Loss Caused by Physical Harm to Another

Rule. In general, P cannot recover in negligence for economic loss resulting from physical harm to another or to property in which P has no proprietary interest. A fortiori, unless there is some specific tort cause of action allowing recovery, P cannot recover for any other negligent conduct that results solely in economic loss.

C. Negligent Misrepresentation

Rule. In general, P may not recover for economic loss caused by reliance on a negligent misrepresentation that was not made directly to P or specifically on P's behalf.

D. Exceptions

A number of cases have allowed recovery for pure economic loss, usually in situations in which there is either privity or some "special relationship" between P and D.

1. Negligent Performance of a Service

In the case of negligence in the rendition of certain professional or business services (accountants and auditors, surveyors, termite inspectors, engineers, attorneys, notaries public, architects, weighers, and telegraph companies), liability has been extended in favor of clients (and sometimes others) who foreseeably relied on the service or who were its intended beneficiaries. Liability extends only to the person (or one of a limited, specific and identifiable group of persons) for whose benefit and guidance the furnisher intends to supply the information, or where the furnisher knows that the recipient intends to rely on it. If D has a public duty to furnish the information, D's liability extends to pecuniary loss suffered by any member of the class of persons for whose benefit the duty is created.

2. Exercise of Public Right

In a few cases, a plaintiff whose business is based on the exercise of a public right has been allowed to recover for economic loss caused by D's negligent interference with that right.

■ PART SIX: STRICT LIABILITY

XX. STRICT LIABILITY

A. Strict Liability for Animals

1. Trespassing Animals

Possessors of all animals, including domesticated ones (excluding cats and dogs), are strictly liable for harm resulting from the trespass of their animals on the property of another.

2. Other Harm Caused By Animals

Domestic Animals. One who possesses or harbors an animal customarily domesticated in that region is strictly liable for other harm only if (a) he knew or had reason to know that the animal had a harmful or dangerous propensity or trait and (b) that particular trait or propensity was the cause of the harm. Otherwise he is liable only if he was negligent.

Wild Animals. One who possesses or harbors animals not customarily domesticated in that region is strictly liable for all harm done by the animal as a result of a harmful or dangerous propensity or characteristic of such animals.

Scope of Strict Liability. P cannot recover if he "knowingly and unreasonably" subjects himself to the risk, or if he makes contact or comes into proximity to D's animal for the purpose of securing some benefit from that contact or that proximity, or if D maintains ownership or possession of the animal pursuant to an obligation imposed by law.

Comparative Fault. If P was contributorily negligent in failing to take reasonable precautions, P's recovery is reduced in proportion to P's comparative fault.

Watchdogs. One is privileged to use a watchdog to guard his property only if and to the extent that he would be privileged to use a mechanical protection device.

B. Strict Liability for Abnormally Dangerous Activities

1. *Rylands v. Fletcher:* Original Rule

Strict liability for abnormally dangerous activities originated in the 1868 English case of *Rylands v. Fletcher*, which held D strictly liable for damage to P's mine caused by water which escaped from D's reservoir because a reservoir was a "non-natural use"' of land in that area.

2. *Rylands v. Fletcher:* Modern Rule

General Rule. The doctrine has evolved to one of liability for harm resulting from the conduct by D of "abnormally dangerous activities" (formerly called "'ultrahazardous" activities). It is not necessary that the activity be conducted on D's land, or that the harm be caused by something which "escapes."

Abnormally Dangerous. Several factors may be considered in determining whether an activity is "abnormally dangerous" including (1) the magnitude of the risk, (2) D's inability to eliminate the risk by the exercise of reasonable care, (3) the abnormality of the activity in that area, (4) the appropriateness of the activity in that location, and (5) the social utility of the activity balanced against its dangerous attributes.

Abnormally Dangerous: The New Test. According to the new formulation in R.3d PH § 20(b), an activity is abnormally dangerous if (1) the activity creates a foreseeable and highly significant risk of physical harm even when all actors exercise reasonable care; and (2) the activity is not one of common usage. Under this formulation, the location at which the activity is conducted does not independently determine if is is abnormally dangerous, but could be relevant under either or both criteria. The social utility of the activity is no longer a separate factor.

Candidates for Strict Liability. Activities that are good candidates for strict liability include blasting, crop dusting, pest control and fumigation, the escape of hazardous wastes, other high-energy activities (e.g., rocket testing, pile driving, oil well blowouts), and perhaps large fireworks displays. However, much depends on the facts and circumstances, and few activities are always abnormally dangerous.

Ground Damage From Aircraft. Subject to statutory variations, some jurisdictions impose strict liability for ground damage caused by "the ascent, descent or flight of aircraft, or by the dropping or falling of an object from the aircraft." Other jurisdictions impose liability only for negligence. And state law rules may be affected by federal aviation statutes and regulations.

3. Liability Limitations

Scope of Liability. The harm must result from the abnormal danger, but it is no defense that it was precipitated by an unforeseeable intervening cause. D is not strictly liable to one who intentionally or negligently trespasses on his land where the activity is being conducted. And D is not strictly liable to the extent that P's harm results because P's activity is abnormally sensitive.

Defenses. Assumption of the risk is a defense, but contributory negligence is not except when P "knowingly and unreasonably subjects himself to the risk." The effect of comparative fault principles has not yet been settled.

Legislative and Public Duty Privileges. When legislation expressly authorizes or imposes a duty to carry on an activity, strict liability is usually not imposed. There is no strict liability under the FTCA.

■ PART SEVEN: DAMAGES FOR PHYSICAL HARM

XXI. DAMAGES FOR PHYSICAL HARM

A. Compensatory Damages

1. General vs. Special Damages

General Damages or "Noneconomic Loss." Traditionally, "general" damages are compensatory damages for a type of harm which so frequently results from the tort involved that such damages are normally to be anticipated and hence need not be specifically alleged. Today, such damages are more often categorized as "noneconomic loss" because they are losses not directly measured in dollars.

Special Damages or "Economic Loss." Special damages are those awarded for all other compensable harms (for example, medical expenses or lost wages). Historically, special damages had to be specifically pleaded in order to be recoverable. Modernly, such damages are usually called "economic loss," but sometimes are referred to as "specials." Today, the practice is to specifically allege all types of damages.

2. Nominal Damages

Nominal damages are a trivial sum awarded to a litigant who has proved a cause of action but has not established that he is entitled to compensatory damages.

3. Damages for Personal Injury

When P proves a compensable personal injury, he may recover for all adverse physical and mental consequences of that injury.

4. Pre-Existing Conditions

D is responsible in damages for all the consequences of P's injury, including those caused or aggravated by some pre-existing condition, predisposition, or vulnerability of P which a normal person would not have sustained, even if that condition was unknown to D.

5. Present Value

If P is awarded damages for pecuniary losses which he will incur in the future, the amount of such damages must ordinarily be reduced to present cash value. Certain general damages are not so reduced.

6. Inflation

Some jurisdictions still do not allow the jury to take into account the effects of future inflation in calculating damages for future economic losses.

7. Taxation

Although a growing minority of jurisdictions disagree, the prevailing rule is that the nontaxability of compensatory damages may not be the subject of evidence, argument or instructions to the jury.

8. Collateral Source Rule

Payments made to, or benefits conferred on, the injured party from sources other than D are not credited against D's liability.

9. Limitation or "Caps"

As a result of recent tort reform legislation, a growing minority of jurisdictions place caps or other limits on the amount of general damages recoverable, either in personal injury actions generally or in medical malpractice cases only.

10. Mitigation (Avoidable Consequences)

Under the doctrine of avoidable consequences, P is required to make reasonable efforts to mitigate the consequences of his injury and to take reasonable steps to prevent further harmful consequences from developing.

11. Seat Belts

In some jurisdictions, P cannot recover to the extent that his injuries, sustained in an auto crash, were the result of his failure to make use of an available seat belt.

B. Consequential Damages

1. Spouse

In most jurisdictions, if D's tort has injured one spouse, the other spouse has a separate cause of action for the damages resulting from his or her loss of the injured spouse's society, companionship, and consortium.

2. Parents

A parent can recover damages for loss of services resulting from a tortious injury to his minor child. Some courts permit, in addition, damages for loss of the child's society, companionship and affection.

3. Medical Expenses

A spouse or parent can recover medical and other expenses incurred as the result of an injury to his spouse or child.

4. Children

Except in a few jurisdictions, a child has no action for loss of his parent's care, support, training, guidance, companionship, love, and affection resulting from a tortious injury to the parent.

5. Nature of Action

Such actions by a spouse or parent are independent of the injured spouse's or child's action, but are derivative from it. Thus, D may invoke any defense which would have been available in a suit brought by the injured person, as well as defenses available against P.

C. Punitive Damages

1. Basis

In most jurisdictions, the trier of fact in its discretion may award punitive damages when D's misconduct is sufficiently serious, to punish him and deter him and others from similar conduct in the future.

2. Conduct Required

D must have acted from a wrongful motive, or at least with gross or knowing indifference to the rights or safety of another. In addition to the intentional torts, most jurisdictions also allow them in all cases of reckless or "wilful and wanton" misconduct; others require, in addition, a kind of "malice", which here means a conscious and deliberate disregard of a high probability of harm.

3. Limitations

Several states do not allow punitive damages at all, except where authorized by statute. Typically they are not allowed in wrongful death or survival actions, and may not be awarded in F.E.L.A. or Jones Act cases. And usually they may not be awarded unless P has proved some actual damages. There is a trend to limit further by statute the recovery of punitive damages.

4. Amount

The amount of punitive damages awarded is largely within the discretion of the trier of fact, subject to review for excessiveness. Many courts, particularly in personal injury cases, require that they bear some reasonable relation to the compensatory damages awarded, or at least to the seriousness of the injury. Evidence of D's wealth is ordinarily admissible. Punitive damages are not reduced by P's comparative fault.

5. Vicarious Liability

Many jurisdictions allow punitive damages against an employer for any tort committed by his employee for which the employer is vicariously liable, provided the employee's tort will support them. Other jurisdictions refuse to allow them against the employer unless (a) the employer authorized the doing and the manner of the act, or (b) the employee was unfit and the employer was reckless in employing him, or (c) the employee was working in a managerial capacity, or (d) the employer or one of his managerial agents ratified or approved the act.

6. Constitutional Limitations

Recent decisions by the United States Supreme Court have established due process limits on awards of punitive damages. Under these cases, review of punitive damages by the trial and reviewing courts is constitutionally required, using three guideposts: (1) the degree of reprehensibility of D's misconduct; (2) the disparity between P's actual or potential harm and the punitive damages award; and (3) the difference between the punitive damages awarded and any applicable civil penalties for similar misconduct. And D cannot be punished for conduct that bears no relation to P's harm, such as similar conduct that occurred elsewhere or similar conduct that occurred in other cases. However, such evidence may be relevant as to D's culpable state of mind.

D. Allocation Among Tortfeasors

1. Multiple Tortfeasors

P may join in a single action all tortfeasors responsible for a single injury (or closely related injuries) and obtain judgments against all who are found liable. Depending on the nature of the injury and other factors, the judgments may be (a) joint and several or (b) several. However, P is entitled only to one satisfaction.

Concert of Action. Two or more persons who, in pursuance of a common plan or design to commit a tortious act, actively take part in it, or further it by cooperation or request, or who lend aid or encouragement to the wrongdoer, or ratify or adopt the wrongdoer's acts done for their benefit, are equally (jointly and severally) liable to P for the resulting tort.

Joint Tortfeasors. Joint tortfeasors are those whose fault combined to produce P's injuries, or who are vicariously liable for another such tortfeasor.

2. Divisible Damages

If different persons are each responsible for separate, identifiable parts of P's harm, absent concert of action, each is liable only for the harm traceable to him.

3. Indivisible Harm

Traditional Rule: Joint and Several Liability. Traditionally, two or more persons responsible for the same harm are jointly and severally liable for all of P's damages, together with anyone else who is vicariously liable. P may sue one, some, or all, obtain judgments for the full amount of his damages against as many as he can, and collect his judgment from one or any combination of them, as he chooses. As long as his judgment is not satisfied in full, he can continue to bring further suits or collection proceedings. About one-quarter of U.S. jurisdictions have retained pure joint and several liability.

Several Liability. With the advent of comparative fault, some jurisdictions now make a joint tortfeasor only "severally" liable to P, i.e., his liability is limited to his proportional share of the total liability. About one-quarter of U.S. jurisdictions now have pure several liability.

Hybrid Liability and Reallocation of Damages. About half of U.S. jurisdictions have adopted a mixture of joint and several and several liability. The schemes vary widely and resist simple categorization, and some systems have characteristics of more than one category. Categories include:

Reallocation of Uncollectible Shares. This category begins with joint and several liability for independent tortfeasors who cause an indivisible injury to P. It then places the risk of a T's uncollectibility on all parties who bear responsibility for P's damages, including P. An insolvent tortfeasor's comparative share of responsibility is reallocated to the other parties in proportion to their comparative responsibility. A very similar result is obtained by starting with a rule of several liability but then providing for reallocation in the event a share is uncollectible.

Joint and Several Liabilty Threshhold. In this category, all tortfeasors whose percentage of comparative responsibility exceeds a specified threshold are jointly and severally liable. Tortfeasors whose percentage falls below that threshold are only severally liable.

Type of Harm. In this category, the variable that determines joint and several liability or several liability is the type of harm suffered by P. Independent tortfeasors are jointly and severally liable for damages for certain harms but are severally liable for compensatory damages for other types of harm.

Type of Defendant. In some jurisdictions, joint and several (or several) liability is restricted to certain categories of defendants.

Whether P Was Free From Contributory Fault. In some cases, P gets the benefit of joint and several liability only if P was free from contributory fault.

Intentional Tortfeasors. Regardless of the scheme in a particular jurisdiction for nonintentional torts, joint and several liability is the norm for intentional joint tortfeasors. If D1 is negligent because of D1's failure to take precautions to protect P against the specific risk created by D2, an intentional tortfeasor, then D1 is jointly and severally liable for the share of comparative responsibility assigned to D2 as well as the share assigned to D1.

Vicarious Liability. If D1's liability is entirely vicarious, or imputed, based on the tortious conduct of D2, D1 is jointly and severally liable for whatever share the law of that jurisdiction assigns to the fault of D2. In other words, D1 and D2 are jointly responsible for a single share. If D1 pays that share to P, D1 ordinarily can obtain indemnity from D2.

4. Settlement of P's Claim(s)

P may enter into a settlement agreement with D (or more than one D) by which P settles his claim(s) against D for a fixed sum. The agreement may take the form of a release, covenant not to sue, or loan receipt agreement. Ordinary rules of contract interpretation apply. Settlement agreements may be set aside for fraud, duress, incapacity, or mutual mistake. A dispute may arise as to whether the settlement should be set aside due to mutual mistake when it later develops that P's injuries are much more serious, or of a different type, than the parties believed when the settlement was entered into, particularly if the release by its terms extended to "unknown" injuries.

Release. A release is a form of settlement agreement whereby P completely surrenders his claim against one or more potential defendants. At one time, the general rule was that a release executed in favor of any one tortfeasor released all other tortfeasors potentially liable for the same harm. The modern rule is that if the release is not intended as a full satisfaction, the release does not ipso facto discharge their potential liability to P.

Covenant Not to Sue. A covenant not to sue (or not to execute) is a settlement device designed to avoid the former effects of a release. It is a contract by which P does not release his claim against D, but merely promises to forego any further attempts to enforce it. It does not discharge other potential defendants, even if it contains no reservation of rights against them, unless it is expressly intended as a satisfaction of all P's claims.

Loan Receipt Agreement. Some courts have approved settlement with one potential defendant by a loan receipt agreement (sometimes called a "Mary Carter" agreement), whereby D "loans" P a sum, without interest, to be repaid only if and to the extent that P is successful in his claims against other joint tortfeasors, and only from the proceeds of any amount which P eventually collects from the others.

Effect of Partial Settlement on Amount Recoverable from Non–Settling Tortfeasors in a Joint and Several Liability Situation. If P settles with one tortfeasor (T1) prior to obtaining a judgment against the remaining joint tortfeasor(s), reserving P's right to proceed against the others, and P then succeeds in his remaining claim(s), the tortfeasor(s) against whom P obtains a judgment receive a credit based on the settlement with T1. The amount of that credit varies.

Dollar Credit. In some jurisdictions, the credit is the dollar amount of the settlement with T1. This is called the "pro tanto" or dollar credit rule. In most pro tanto or dollar credit jurisdictions, T1 will be immune from contribution, but only if the court finds that the settlement was in "good faith."

Proportional or Percentage Credit. In some jurisdictions, the credit is the settling tortfeasor's (T1's) proportional share of the common liability, regardless of the dollar amount of the settlement with T1. This is called the proportional or percentage credit rule.

Pro Rata Credit. A third, little-used approach, the "pro rata" method, gives a nonsettling tortfeasor a credit against the judgment equal to the settling tortfeasor's share of damages, which is determined by dividing the recoverable damages by the number of liable parties.

Effect of Partial Settlement on Amount Recoverable from Non–Settling Tortfeasors in a Several Liability Situation. If a settling tortfeasor (T1) is only subject to several liability, any nonsettling tortfeasors simply pay their proportional share(s) as determined by applicable apportionment rules. T1 has settled her several liability, and it matters not whether her settlement is more or less than the amount of her proportional share as later determined.

5. Contribution

Common Law Rule. When P obtains a judgment against two or more tortfeasors, he can collect that judgment from any one, all, or any combination of Ds in any proportion he desires. The common law rule in most jurisdictions was that D1, who paid P more than D1's proportionate share of the judgment, was not entitled to obtain contribution from the other joint tortfeasors. The "no contribution" rule originally applied only to intentional torts, but the majority of U.S. jurisdictions extended it to negligence and strict liability actions.

Modern Status. Contribution among (negligent or strictly liable) joint tortfeasors in some form is now the rule in most jurisdictions. Contribution is only available if and to the extent that parties are jointly and severally liable. There is no right to contribution by or against a party who is only severally liable.

Amount. In most jurisdictions, the damages are allocated among the joint tortfeasors in proportion to their relative fault as determined by the trier of fact, and those shares determine contribution liability.

Absence of Judgment. D can seek contribution against other joint tortfeasors, including those not sued by P. There is a split of authority as to whether contribution can be obtained against a D who is immune from suit by P. A tortfeasor who settles prior to trial can obtain contribution, provided he settles for all tortfeasors and he can prove the others' liability, the amount of the damages, and the reasonableness of his settlement. The prevailing view is that a tortfeasor who settles only his own liability cannot be sued for contribution nor can he obtain contribution from others.

Intentional Tortfeasors. Courts are split as to whether intentional tortfeasors can seek contribution.

Immune Tortfeasors. Jurisdictions are split, but most require D to prove that T was subject to liability to P, so D cannot seek contribution if T is immune with respect to P.

6. Non–Party Tortfeasors.

If a particular tortfeasor is not joined as a defendant or third-party defendant (T), the courts are split as to whether that tortfeasor's proportional share of the total fault can be found by the factfinder and included in the responsible fault calculation. Whether T is included or not may depend on the purpose of the calculation.

Joint and Several Liability. If all tortfeasors are subject to joint and several liability and there is no contribution claim, then there is no reason to allocate fault among multiple tortfeasors, whether joined or not. However, whether T is included could still make a difference in determining P's share of the fault, if P is found contributorily at fault. For purposes of calculating P's share, the total fault should include all tortfeasors, whether joined as a defendant or not.

Several Liability. If some or all defendants are potentially subject only to several liability, then the factfinder must allocate fault proportionally, and it makes a difference whether T's fault is included in the fault calculation. Jurisdictions are split; some require T to be included if there is enough evidence from which the factfinder can assess fault against T. In others, no one who is not a party to the lawsuit can be included in the fault calculation.

Contribution. Where contribution is available to some or all of the defendants (or in a separate action for contribution), it becomes necessary to allocate fault among tortfeasors. For this purpose, the calculation is restricted to the tortfeasors who are parties to the action in which contribution is being sought. In most cases, contribution may not be sought from settling tortfeasors.

7. Indemnity

Distinguished From Contribution. Contribution is an equitable sharing of the loss among joint tortfeasors. Indemnification is a shifting of the entire loss from one tortfeasor to another, by operation of either (1) a prior agreement of the parties, or (2) law, based on equitable considerations.

Indemnity by Agreement. A contract in which T2 agrees to indemnify T1 if T1 is held liable to P is frequently enforceable, although in some instances agreements to indemnify for T1's own negligence may be void by statute or as against public policy. Agreements to indemnify T1 for T1's liability for reckless or intentional misconduct are usually unenforceable.

Indemnity by Operation of Law. Indemnity by operation of law (often called "implied indemnity") is based on the concept of unjust enrichment. It is available when T1 and T2 are both liable for the same harm to P, and (1) T1's liability is based entirely on T1's vicarious liability for the tort of T2, or (2) T1 is the seller of a product (e.g., a retailer), the product was supplied to T1 by T2 (e.g., the manufacturer), and T1 is held liable to P solely because he sold the product to P (i.e., T1 was not independently culpable). If T1 satisfies P's judgment, T1 is entitled to indemnity from T2 for the amount paid to P plus reasonable legal expenses.

■ PART EIGHT: SURVIVAL AND WRONGFUL DEATH

XXII. SURVIVAL AND WRONGFUL DEATH

A. Survival of Tort Actions

1. Rule

At common law, all causes of action for personal torts abated with the death of either the tortfeasor or the person injured. That rule has been changed so that today, most tort actions survive the death of either P or D, regardless of the cause of death.

2. Damages

The measure of compensatory damages in a survival action is generally the same as if no one had died, except that P's death terminates the accrual of future damages which P otherwise could have recovered based on his life expectancy. In most jurisdictions, D's death terminates P's right to seek punitive damages, and in some states so does the death of P. In some cases, funeral and burial expenses and the decedent's last medical expenses may be an element of damages in the survival action, or may be recovered separately.

Punitive Damages. In most jurisdictions, D's death terminates P's right to seek punitive damages. In some states, P's death does also, but in many jurisdictions, P's estate can seek punitive damages in a survival action.

Medical, Funeral and Burial Expenses. In some cases, funeral and burial expenses and the decedent's last medical expenses may be an element of damages in the survival action, or, in the alternative, in the wrongful death action (if there is one). In some jurisdictions, medical, funeral and burial expenses are a separate claim altogether.

B. Wrongful Death

1. Types of Statutes

Any tort theory which would have supported a personal injury action will support an action for wrongful death. There are two basic types of wrongful death acts.

Lord Campbell's Act (most states) creates a new cause of action for the benefit of specified near relatives of P when P would have had a cause of action had he been merely injured and not killed.

A minority of jurisdictions have a "**survival**"-type statute which preserves the cause of action which was vested in P at the moment of his death and enlarges it to include the damages resulting from the death itself.

Statutory Torts. Most statutory tort actions have their own provisions for recovery in the event of death. If not, then an appropriate general death act will be held to apply.

2. Concurrence of Remedies

If P survived his injuries for a time before dying from them, in most jurisdictions either a survival action or a wrongful death action or both may be brought.

3. Beneficiaries

The beneficiaries are the relatives or classes of relatives designated in the statute.

4. Damages

Pecuniary Loss. Many statutes are phrased in terms of "pecuniary loss," which includes at the very least loss of support, services and contributions.

Nonpecuniary Loss. Nonpecuniary loss of P's society, companionship, love and affection is recoverable in some jurisdictions, either by specific statutory language or by judicial construction of the term "pecuniary loss."

Medical and Other Expenses. Medical and other expenses, such as funeral and burial costs, ordinarily may be recovered by the survivor paying them.

Loss to the Estate. A minority of jurisdictions measure damages by the loss to the estate.

Punitive Damages. Jurisdictions are split on whether punitive damages may be recovered in a wrongful death action.

5. Defenses

The same defenses are available as if P had lived. In addition, a beneficiary's contributory negligence bars or reduces that beneficiary's recovery.

6. Procedure

Survival Actions. In a survival action, the plaintiff is the executor or administrator of the decedent's estate, and the surviving cause of action is an asset of the estate. Any recovery in the survival action goes to the estate and is distributed in accordance with the applicable estate law.

Wrongful Death Actions. A wrongful death cause of action is an independent claim by the beneficiaries. It is not an asset of the decedent's estate and does not pass through the estate. The plaintiff may be the executor or administrator of the estate, but it is brought on behalf of the beneficiaries and any recovery goes directly to them and does not pass through the estate. In some jurisdictions, the plaintiff is one of the beneficiaries or their representative who sues on behalf of all the beneficiaries. If there is more than one beneficiary for whom damages are awarded, the recovery is divided in accordance with applicable local procedure.

■ PART NINE: NON–PHYSICAL HARM: MISREPRESENTATION, DEFAMATION, AND PRIVACY

XXIII. MISREPRESENTATION

A. Introduction

1. In General

Misrepresentation is often an element of different torts and other causes of action. However, there is a tort action called "misrepresentation" (formerly deceit), where D in the course of some transaction makes a false statement to P (or another), P acts in justifiable reliance on the statement, and thereby sustains pecuniary loss. (If P sustains physical harm, then one of the other tort actions will lie.)

2. Basis

At common law, this action was called "deceit," and would lie only if D's misrepresentation was *fraudulent*—i.e., was made with "scienter." Today, liability is recognized for some types of negligent misrepresentations.

B. Deceit

1. Elements

The elements necessary to establish a prima facie case in an action for deceit are: (a) D's false representation, ordinarily of a fact; (b) D knew that his statement was false, or else he made it in conscious ignorance or reckless disregard of whether it was true or false; (c) D intended that P act in reliance upon the representation; (d) P acted in justifiable reliance upon the representation; and (e) P sustained actual damage.

2. Scienter

A misrepresentation is "fraudulent" if D (1) knows or believes that the matter is not as he represents it to be, or (2) does not have the confidence in the accuracy of his representation that he states or implies, or (3) knows that he does not have the basis for his representation that he states or implies.

3. Form of Representation

Fact. In general, the representation must be of a fact. It may be by words or conduct.

Ambiguous. A representation capable of two interpretations, one true and the other known to be false, is actionable if made with the intent that it be understood in the false sense or with reckless indifference as to how it will be understood.

Opinion. Statements which represent only D's opinion or prediction are generally not actionable. However, an opinion may be understood as an implied representation concerning its underlying facts.

Quantity, Quality and Value. Statements of quantity ordinarily may be taken as statements of fact. But statements of quality and value are usually opinions upon which no reliance can justifiably be placed, unless sufficiently specific.

Law. Some specific representations as to the state of law may be representations of fact, and even if opinion, may be actionable if reasonably understood as implying a statement of fact.

Intent. A statement that the speaker or another person presently intends to do (or not do) something in the future is generally regarded as a statement of fact which is actionable if untrue.

Incomplete Statements. A representation stating the truth so far as it goes, but which D knows or believes to be materially misleading because of his failure to state additional or qualifying matter, is actionable.

Concealment. If D conceals or otherwise prevents P from acquiring material information, he is liable as though he had stated its nonexistence.

Nondisclosure. At one time, mere silence could not amount to a misrepresentation. Today, there are several significant exceptions. Fiduciary or confidential relations require disclosure of all material facts. Incomplete statements may be actionable. Subsequently acquired information which makes the prior statement untrue or misleading must be disclosed if D knows or believes that P is still acting on the basis of the original statement. If D makes a statement without expecting that P will rely upon it (therefore, not actionable) and D later discovers that P, in a transaction with him, is about to rely upon it, he has an affirmative duty to disclose its falsity. There is a growing trend to find an affirmative duty to disclose essential facts known to D when D has special access to those facts which P does not, and in other cases where there is some reason why non-disclosure would be unconscionable or very unfair.

4. Scope of Liability

Persons. D is liable to the person(s) or class of persons whom he intends or has reason to expect to act in reliance upon his representation. If D intends or has reason to expect that his representation will be communicated to a third person, and that it will influence his conduct in the type of transaction involved, he is subject to liability to that third person.

Proximate Cause. D's representation must have been a substantial factor in influencing P's conduct, and P's loss from the reliance must have been reasonably foreseeable.

5. Contributory Negligence

If P justifiably relies upon a fraudulent misrepresentation, he is not barred from recovery by his contributory negligence in doing so.

6. Justifiable Reliance

P can recover only if he relied upon the representation, and his reliance was justifiable.

Materiality. Reliance is not justifiable unless the matter misrepresented is material.

Duty to Investigate. At one time, persons dealing at arm's length could not justifiably rely on the other's statements if a reasonably independent investigation would have revealed the truth. Today, P may rely on fact representations without further investigation even when their falsity could have been easily and quickly discovered, unless something known to him or apparent in the situation at hand should have warned him that the statement ought not to be accepted without further inquiry.

Opinion of Adverse Party. P cannot justifiably rely on D's statement in the form of an opinion, unless the fact to which the opinion relates is material and D (1) purports to have special knowledge, or (2) stands in a fiduciary or confidential relation to P, or (3) has some other special reason to expect that P will rely on his opinion.

Opinion of Apparently Disinterested Person. P can justifiably rely on the opinion of an apparently disinterested person if the fact that he holds the opinion is material.

7. Damages

Damages for fraudulent misrepresentations are measured by P's pecuniary loss, including the difference between the value of what he paid and the value of what he actually received, consequential damages, and (if a business transaction) the benefit of his bargain.

C. Negligent Misrepresentation

1. Discussion

Even though D honestly believed his erroneous statement to be true, he may have been negligent in (a) failing to exercise reasonable care to ascertain the true facts, or (b) failing to possess or apply the skill and competence required by his business or profession, or (c) the manner in which he expressed his assertion. Most courts, following *Derry v. Peek*, have refused to extend the traditional deceit action to merely negligent misrepresentations which cause only pecuniary loss. However, most jurisdictions now recognize a limited form of liability for such negligent misrepresentations as a separate tort action.

Physical Harm. If D's negligent misrepresentation proximately causes physical harm, ordinary negligence principles apply, not the rules in this section.

2. Scope of Liability

Interest in Transaction. D is not liable for his negligent misrepresentation (causing only pecuniary loss) unless made in the course of his business, profession or employment, or other transaction in which he has a pecuniary interest.

Third Persons in Known Class. At first, D was liable only to the specific person or persons for whose benefit and guidance he intended to supply the information. Today, many courts have extended D's liability to include persons in a limited group, even though not specifically known to D, if D knows that one or more persons in that group will receive and rely upon that information.

Foreseeable Harm to One Remote User. Some courts have extended liability to the case where D knows that the information he furnished will be used by a succession of persons whose specific identity is presently unknowable, but only one such person will suffer loss.

Public Duty to Furnish. Certain kinds of statutes require D to furnish, file or publish information for the protection of a class of persons. If such information is negligently erroneous, a member of that class who relies upon it to his injury may recover.

3. Contributory Negligence

P's contributory negligence in relying upon a negligent misrepresentation is a defense. Comparative negligence rules do not apply.

4. Damages

Damages for negligent misrepresentation include P's out-of-pocket loss and consequential damages, but not the benefit of the bargain.

D. Innocent Misrepresentation

1. Physical Harm: Products

If D is engaged in the business of selling products, he is subject to strict liability for physical harm resulting from a misrepresentation made to the public concerning the character or quality of a product sold by him.

2. Pecuniary Loss: Sale, Rental or Exchange Transaction

The Restatement (Second) § 552C proposes a limited form of strict liability for pecuniary loss sustained as the result of a misrepresentation made by D in a sale, rental or exchange transaction with P.

XXIV. DEFAMATION

A. General Rules

1. Elements of Cause of Action

The elements of a defamation action are: (1) a false and defamatory statement concerning another; (2) an unprivileged, intentional or negligent publication to a third party; (3) in some cases (depending on the status of the defendant), D's fault in knowing or failing to ascertain the statement's falsity; and (4) in some cases (depending upon the type of statement), actual damages.

2. What Is Defamatory?

Rule. A communication is defamatory if it tends to harm P's reputation in the community, either by (1) lowering others' estimation of him, or (2) deterring others from associating or dealing with him.

Standard. A communication is defamatory if a substantial and respectable minority of P's community or associates would so regard it, unless the minority's views on that subject are so anti-social or extreme that it would not be proper for the courts to recognize them.

3. Truth

A defamatory statement is not actionable unless it is false. Traditionally, truth has been regarded as an affirmative defense. Today, in cases involving issues of public interest P must prove falsity; and in many cases P must also prove actual malice.

4. Who May Be Defamed

Deceased Persons. Except as otherwise provided by statute, no action lies for the defamation of a deceased person. Whether the action survives P's death (where P was defamed while alive) depends on the local survival statute.

Entities. Corporations, partnerships and unincorporated associations may be defamed.

5. Meaning of Communication

Understanding of Recipient. The recipient must understand it in a defamatory sense, and understand that it was so intended. If he reasonably so understood it, it does not matter that he was mistaken.

Extrinsic Circumstances. Extrinsic facts and circumstances known to the recipient are taken into account in determining its meaning.

Pleading. If the statement is not facially defamatory, P may have to plead the extrinsic circumstances which gave it a defamatory meaning ("inducement"), set forth the communication verbatim, and explain the defamatory meaning he claimed to have been understood ("innuendo").

6. Application to P

The communication must have been understood by the recipient (correctly, or mistakenly but reasonably) as intended to refer to P. The applicability of the defamatory matter to P may depend upon extrinsic facts or circumstances known to the recipient. If so, such facts and the manner in which they connect the defamatory matter to P ("colloquium") may have to be pleaded.

7. Group Defamation

As a general rule, no action lies for the publication of defamatory words concerning a large group or class of persons. But a member of a small group may recover if the statement may reasonably be understood as applying to him. And so may a member of any size group if the circumstances indicate that it is intended to apply to him.

8. Types of Defamatory Communications

Fact. A defamatory communication (typically, a fact) may be direct or indirect, as where words or pictures imply a defamatory meaning.

Opinion. At common law, a defamatory statement of opinion (if not privileged) was actionable the same as one of fact. This rule appears to have been modified by recent constitutional law interpretations.

Based on Known or Stated Facts. If the defamatory opinion is based entirely on facts (a) known to those making and receiving the statement, or (b) stated as a predicate to the opinion, recent cases indicate that the first amendment permits one to express one's opinion, however misguided or debatable, without defamation liability. However, to the extent that the opinion implies the allegation of undisclosed defamatory facts, it may be actionable.

Ridicule. Humorous or satirical writings, verses, cartoons, or caricatures which may be understood as making a statement about P are similarly protected, at least to the extent that they represent merely negative opinions not implying false facts.

Verbal Abuse. Profanity and similar statements, directed at P in anger and obviously intended as mere vituperation or abuse, ordinarily cannot be taken literally and therefore are not defamatory.

Fabricated Quotation. To attribute a fabricated quotation to P may be defamatory.

B. Libel and Slander

1. Distinguished

Libel is the publication of defamatory matter by (1) written or printed words, or (2) embodiment in physical form, or (3) any other form of communication that has potentially harmful characteristics comparable to those of written or printed words. Radio and television publications are regarded in most jurisdictions as libel, unless otherwise provided by statute.

Slander is the publication of defamatory matter by spoken words, transitory gestures, or other form of communication not amounting to a libel.

Factors to Be Considered. The factors to be considered in distinguishing libel and slander are the area of dissemination, the deliberate and premeditated character of the publication, and the persistence or permanency of the publication.

2. Defamation Actionable Without Proof of Special Damage

Libel. In most jurisdictions, any libel is actionable without proof that P sustained any special harm or damage ("per se"). In a minority, a libel which is not defamatory on its face but requires reference to extrinsic facts to establish its defamatory meaning ("libel per quod") is not actionable without proof of special harm.

Slander. Publication of a slander is not actionable without proof of special damages unless it imputes (1) conduct that constitutes a crime punishable by imprisonment or involving moral turpitude; (2) that P has a venereal or other loathsome and communicable disease; (3) conduct, characteristics or a condition that would adversely affect P's fitness for the proper conduct of his business, trade, profession, or office; or (4) unchastity or serious sexual misconduct. If actionable without proof of special damages, it is called "slander per se"; if not, it is "slander per quod."

Special Damage. In this context, special harm or damages refers to the loss of something having economic or pecuniary value.

C. Publication

1. Definition

Publication is the communication of defamatory matter by D to someone other than P.

2. Fault

The publication must have been intentional or the result of D's negligence.

3. Agent

In most jurisdictions, publication to D's agent is sufficient (but may be privileged). If dictated with the intent that it will be reduced to writing, it is libel. And D is liable for a publication by his agent where he directed or procured it.

4. Multiple Publications

General Rule. Each of several communications to a third person by the same D is a separate publication.

Single Communication. A single communication heard at the same time by two or more third persons is a single publication.

Single Publication Rule. One edition of a book or newspaper, or one radio or TV broadcast, one exhibition of a motion picture, or a similar aggregate publication is deemed a single publication.

Effect. For each single publication, only one action can be maintained in which P must claim all damages resulting from that publication.

5. Wills

Generally, an action will lie against D's estate for libelous matter published in his will after his death.

6. Liability of Republisher

General Rule. One who repeats or otherwise republishes a defamation is subject to liability to the same extent as if he had originally published it.

Exception. One who only delivers or transmits defamatory matter published by a third person is subject to liability only if he knows or has reason to know of its defamatory character. This exception does not apply to broadcasters. Information published on the internet or other similar network will probably be treated as published only by the content provider and not by the ISP or one who merely provides the web site.

7. Causation: Liability of Original Publisher for Republication

D is liable for the republication of his defamatory statement by another if (a) the third person was privileged to repeat it, (b) D authorized or intended the repetition, or (c) the repetition was reasonably foreseeable. D is usually not liable for a repetition by P.

D. Fault

1. Common Law

At common law, D's ignorance of the falsity or defamatory character of the statement was no defense. The only fault required was with respect to its publication: D had to intentionally or negligently publish the matter.

2. First Amendment

Today, the first amendment imposes fault requirements, at least in the case of defamatory matter concerning public officials, public figures, or matters of public concern when D is exercising the freedom of the press protected by that amendment. Some states have followed suit and imposed fault requirements as common law rules.

3. Public Official, Public Figure (*N.Y Times* Rule)

One who publishes a false and defamatory communication concerning a public official or a public figure with regard to his conduct, fitness, or role in that capacity is subject to liability only if D (a) knows that the statement is false and that it defames P, or (b) acts in reckless disregard of these matters.

Fault. The requisite fault is "actual malice" (sometimes described as "constitutional malice"), which means nothing more than knowledge of the statement's false and defamatory character or D's reckless disregard of these matters. Proof of D's fault must be clear and convincing.

4. Private Persons (*Gertz v. Robert Welch, Inc.*)

One who publishes a false and defamatory communication concerning a private person, or concerning a public official or public figure with regard to a purely private matter is subject to liability only if D (a) knows that the statement is false and that it defames P, or (b) acts in reckless disregard of these matters, or (c) acts negligently in failing to ascertain them.

Effect of *Gertz*. After *Gertz*, strict liability for defamation published in the press, media, and possibly books is unconstitutional, regardless of the status of P. However, the states are free to determine the degree of fault required for defamation actions by private persons, provided at least negligence is required.

Majority Rule. So far, the majority of states passing on the question have followed the *Gertz* criteria, so that in those jurisdictions private persons need only prove that D was negligent in ascertaining the falsity and defamatory character of the statement.

Minority Rule. In some jurisdictions, if the defamation concerns a matter of general or public interest, even private persons are required to prove actual malice.

Burden of Proof. Private persons need only prove falsity and the requisite fault by a preponderance of the evidence.

Private Communications. It remains to be seen whether the *Gertz* rule applies to publications other than in the press, media or books.

E. Defenses to Actions for Defamation

1. Consent

P's consent to the publication of defamatory matter concerning him is a complete defense, except that D may be liable for a republication that results from P's honest inquiry or investigation to ascertain the existence, source, content, or meaning of the defamatory publication.

2. Absolute Privileges

Judicial Proceedings. During the course of performing their functions in judicial proceedings, judges and judicial officers, attorneys, parties, witnesses, and jurors are absolutely privileged to publish defamatory matter which has some relation to the proceeding.

Legislative Proceedings. A member of Congress or a state or local legislative body is absolutely privileged to publish defamatory matter in the performance of his legislative functions. A witness is absolutely privileged to publish defamatory matter as part of a legislative proceeding in which he is testifying or in communications preliminary to the proceeding, if the matter has some relation to the proceeding.

Executive and Administrative Officers. An executive or administrative officer of the U.S., or a governor or other superior executive officer of a state, is absolutely privileged to publish defamatory matter in communications made in the performance of his official duties.

Husband and Wife. A husband or wife is absolutely privileged to publish defamatory matter to the other.

Publication Required by Law. One who is required by law to publish defamatory matter is absolutely privileged to publish it.

3. Conditional or Qualified Privileges In General

At common law, certain defamatory communications are conditionally or qualifiedly privileged. As to these privileges, the chief limitation is that D must (1) believe his statement to be true, and (2) (a) in some jurisdictions, have reasonable grounds for believing it to be true, or (b) in other jurisdictions, not have acted recklessly in failing to ascertain its truth or falsity. But the *N.Y Times* and *Gertz* cases, when applicable, require P to prove that D acted either recklessly or negligently in ascertaining the truth or falsity of the statement. Thus, the following privileges apply only when and to the extent that they are not superseded by the *N.Y Times* or *Gertz* rules.

Protection of the Publisher's Interest. D correctly or reasonably believes that (1) the information affects a sufficiently important interest of D, and (2) the information will be useful to the recipient in the lawful protection of that interest.

Protection of Interest of Recipient of Third Person. D correctly or reasonably believes that (1) the information affects a sufficiently important interest of the recipient or a third person, and (2) the recipient is one to whom (a) D is under a legal duty to publish it or (b) its publication is otherwise within accepted standards of decent conduct.

Protection of Common Interest. D correctly or reasonably believes that another who shares a common interest is entitled to know it.

Family Relationships. D correctly or reasonably believes that: (1) the recipient's knowledge will help protect the well-being of a member of D's immediate family; or (2) the recipient's knowledge will help protect the well-being of a member of the immediate family of the recipient or a third person, and the recipient has requested the information or is a person to whom its communication is otherwise within generally accepted standards of decent conduct.

Public Interest. D correctly or reasonably believes that a sufficiently important public interest requires its communication to a public officer or other person who is authorized or privileged to take action if it is true.

Inferior State Officers. Lower level state or local government employees who are not entitled to an absolute privilege have a conditional privilege for communications required or permitted in the performance of their duties.

"Abuse" (Loss) of the Privilege

Knowledge, Recklessness or Negligence Concerning Falsity. Prior to *Gertz*, in some jurisdictions a conditional privilege was lost if D did not honestly believe the truth of his statement, or if he did not have "reasonable grounds" to believe in its truth. It remains to be seen whether this rule has any purpose after *Gertz*. Other jurisdictions have held that only actual malice destroys a conditional privilege. Where *Gertz* or *NY Times* applies, any conditional privilege will be irrelevant.

Rumor. D may be privileged to publish a defamatory rumor or suspicion, even though he believes or knows that it is untrue, provided: (a) he states the defamatory matter as a rumor or suspicion and not as a fact; and (b) the publication is reasonable.

Purpose. There is no conditional privilege unless D publishes the defamatory matter for the purpose of protecting the interest which gives rise to the privilege and reasonably believes the publication to be necessary for that purpose.

Excessive Publication. There is no conditional privilege to the extent that D knowingly publishes the defamatory matter to a person outside its scope, unless he reasonably believes that such publication is a proper means of communicating it to a proper person.

Unprivileged Matter. The privilege is lost to the extent that D adds unprivileged matter to the communication. If not severable, the entire privilege is lost.

Fair Comment on Matters of Public Concern. At common law, there was a qualified privilege "fair comment" (i.e., publicly expressing one's opinion) on matters of public concern. This privilege appears to have been subsumed under the constitutional right to express such opinions without defamation liability.

4. Special Types of Privilege

Report of Official Proceeding or Public Meeting. D is privileged to publish defamatory matter in a report of an official action or proceeding or of a meeting open to the public that deals with a matter of public concern, provided the report is accurate or a fair abridgment of the occurrence reported. As applied to the press and news media, P must also establish D's actual malice in failing to make a fair and accurate report.

Transmission of Message by Public Utility. A public utility under a duty to transmit messages is privileged unless the utility knows or has reason to know that the message is defamatory and that the sender is not privileged to publish it.

Providing Means of Publication. One who provides a means of publication of defamatory matter published by another is privileged to do so if the other is privileged to publish it.

F. Damages

1. Types Recoverable

Damages which may be recoverable in a defamation action include (a) nominal damages, (b) general (or "presumed") damages for harm to reputation, (c) damages for proved special harm caused by the harm to P's reputation, (d) damages for emotional distress and resulting bodily harm, and (e) punitive damages.

2. General Damages

Rule. At common law, once D's liability was established, the jury could award P general damages for harm to his reputation, whether P proved actual harm or not ("presumed" damages). However, *Gertz* prohibits the states from permitting recovery for presumed damages unless P proves D's actual malice; otherwise, proof of actual harm is required.

Exception. A state can award presumed damages when the plaintiff is a private figure and the speech did not involve any issue of public interest or concern.

3. Special Damages

Special damages (i.e., economic or pecuniary loss) resulting from the defamation may always be recovered. They are a prerequisite to liability for slander per quod (and libel per quod in some jurisdictions).

4. Emotional Distress and Bodily Harm

Once D's liability is established, damages for emotional distress and resulting bodily harm are recoverable.

5. Punitive Damages

The common law generally allows punitive damages in a defamation action when D's conduct involves "actual malice," which in this context means an intent to harm P or a reckless disregard of whether or not he will be harmed. In addition, the first amendment prohibits punitive damages, at least against the press and media defendants, unless P proves D's knowledge of the statement's falsity or his reckless disregard for its truth.

6. Mitigation

In most jurisdictions, D's retraction is not a complete defense, but may be considered with other circumstances in mitigation of P's damages.

XXV. PRIVACY

A. Introduction

The tort action for invasion of privacy encompasses four distinct wrongs:

1. **Appropriation** of one's name or likeness;

2. **Intrusion** upon another's privacy or private affairs;

3. **Public disclosure of private facts** about P; and

4. Placing P in a **false light in the public eye**.

The action for invasion of privacy is recognized in most jurisdictions, but not in all forms. It is sometimes affected by statute.

B. Appropriation

D is subject to liability for appropriating P's name or likeness for his own use or benefit, for the *purpose* of taking advantage of P's reputation, prestige or other value associated with his name or likeness. Unless otherwise required by statute, the use need not be for business or commercial purposes, but many states do impose such a requirement.

C. Intrusion

1. Rule

D is subject to liability for intrusion (physical or other) upon the solitude, seclusion, or private life and affairs of another, provided the intrusion would be highly offensive to a reasonable person.

2. Form

The forms of intrusion are varied—unpermitted entry into P's home or hospital room; an illegal search of P's person or property; tapping P's telephone; using mechanical aids to observe P's private activities in his home; opening P's personal mail; and persistent and unwanted communications or close physical presence.

3. Publication

The tort is complete when the intrusion occurs. No publication or publicity of the information is required.

4. Private Matters

The intrusion must be into what is, and is entitled to remain, private. Photographing or watching P in a public place, or inspecting or copying nonprivate records, is not actionable.

5. Substantial Interference

The intrusion must be highly offensive to the ordinary person, resulting from conduct to which the reasonable person would strongly object.

6. Governmental Intrusion

The courts are beginning to recognize a constitutional right of privacy, to be free from excessive or unreasonable governmental intrusion.

D. Public Disclosure of Private Facts

1. Rule

D is subject to liability for giving publicity to some private fact about P, provided the fact publicized would be highly offensive to a reasonable person and is not a matter of legitimate public concern.

2. Publicity

The information about P need not be "published." It is sufficient if it is disclosed so as to be likely to become public knowledge.

3. Private Facts

Since the facts disclosed are true, there is no liability for facts which are already known by, or available to, the public. The facts must be intimate or at least private details of P's private life, the disclosure of which would be embarrassing, humiliating or offensive. And P's right to keep these facts private is balanced against the public's legitimate interest. There are fewer "private facts" of the famous and those in high positions.

4. Legitimate Public Concern or Interest

Constitutional Limitations. The first amendment is a further limitation. It permits (to a certain extent) publication of private facts that are matters of legitimate public concern or interest—i.e., "news."

Public Figures. Persons who have voluntarily become public figures, and even those involuntarily in the public eye by being part of a newsworthy event, cannot complain of the publication of facts, otherwise private, which are of legitimate public concern or interest in connection with that person, activity, or event. This legitimate concern may even extend to the family and close friends of the public figure, and to some facts about persons who were public figures at some time in the past.

E. False Light in the Public Eye

1. Rule

D is subject to liability for giving publicity to a matter which places P before the public in a false light, provided (a) the false light would be highly offensive to a reasonable person, and (b) D had knowledge of the falsity of the matter and the false light it created, or acted in reckless disregard of these matters.

2. Relation to Defamation

In this case, the information is false, and so if it is also defamatory, an action for libel or slander may be an alternative remedy. However, P need not be defamed. It is enough that he is given unreasonable and highly objectionable publicity that attributes to him characteristics, conduct or beliefs that are false.

3. Highly Offensive

The matter must be highly offensive to a reasonable person.

4. Constitutional Limitations

Under *Time, Inc. v. Hill* (U.S. 1967), as to press and media defendants, P must prove by clear and convincing evidence that D knew of the statement's falsity or acted in reckless disregard of its truth or falsity. Whether the *Gertz* case has modified this rule (to include negligence in the case of private individuals), and the extent to which this limitation applies to others than the press and media, has yet to be decided.

F. Privileges

The absolute, conditional and special privileges to publish defamatory matter also apply to the publication of any matter that is an invasion of privacy.

G. Damages

In an action for invasion of privacy, P can recover damages for (1) harm to his interest in privacy; (2) mental distress, if of a kind that normally results from such an invasion; and (3) special damages.

H. Persons Who May Sue

Unless otherwise provided by statute, and except for appropriation, only a living individual whose privacy is invaded can maintain an action for invasion of privacy. Whether an action survives P's death depends on the local survival statute.

*

Perspective

■ A. THE TORTS COURSE

Most of you reading this book are first year law students enrolled in a course called "Torts." This perspective is addressed primarily to you, although parts of it will be useful to persons who may be reading it for a purpose having nothing to do with that course.

Torts is a "core" law school course; it is fundamental and always required. As far as I know, it is always taught in the first year, usually as a four-, five-, or six-hour package typically spread over two semesters. You probably already realize that this subject is of immense practical importance to lawyers and to the law.

Most law students like the subject and find it interesting. I believe that this is due in large part to a combination of (1) its obvious importance and relevance, and (2) the fact that its basic concepts and the fact situations in which they arise are readily understood by persons with no special training in any particular field (e.g., first year law students). Students can relate to the cases and the people in them.

For these (and perhaps other) reasons, tort law is thought by some to be "easy." This appearance is deceptive; don't be fooled! True, some parts of tort law (like any other subject) are easily grasped and learned, but others are conceptually difficult. Some of my students' difficulty with concepts such as duty and "proximate cause" (i.e., scope of liability) stems, I believe, from their unpreparedness for that complexity.

Some students are also surprised when they discover, late in the semester, that tort law encompasses a large number of rules, principles, and concepts. The subject to be mastered is bigger than they thought.

Perhaps they are misled by the pace of the course. Torts, like most other first-year courses, is intended to teach much more than tort law. To some extent it teaches legal method; and one of its primary purposes is to teach an elusive skill—legal analysis and reasoning. In addition, it requires that we teach a little of civil procedure, evidence, trial advocacy, and appellate litigation skills so that we can understand the cases and the law. It's no wonder that the course often starts at a relatively slow pace (in terms of the number of casebook pages covered per day). But sooner or later, the pace quickens as we make progress on these matters and the need for coverage looms relatively larger.

The moral of this story is, don't give your torts course any less effort than you give to your other courses on the theory that you can "cram" for torts in your spare time. Remember—to the extent that some tort concepts are relatively easy to grasp, more will be expected of you. But much of tort law is no less difficult than anything else you are taking. It just seems so.

■ B. ORGANIZATION OF THE TORTS COURSE AND THIS BOOK

Although based on limited observation, I believe that there is a wide variation among torts professors in the way in which they organize their torts courses. An analysis of the nearly 20 torts casebooks currently in print provides additional circumstantial evidence for this thesis. There are vast differences in the order in which they cover the different parts of the subject, and there are philosophical differences as well. Some casebooks seem to be predominantly "practice" oriented, organized around the specific torts themselves. Others use other themes in whole or in part (e.g., fault concepts, economics, jurisprudential issues).

Despite this variety, I believe that books such as this can be useful across the whole range of courses, professors, and casebooks. However important the jurisprudential or economic issues to a particular torts course—and I do not minimize their importance at all (I use some myself)—the bottom line is the application of tort law to specific fact situations. This is what lawyers and judges do. Jurisprudence, economics, psychology, sociology, and other disciplines influence lawmakers (judges and legislators) in making rule choices, and influence lawyers in their selection of arguments and approaches. But in the end, a rule must be selected and applied. Law students—like lawyers, judges, and legislators—must start with, and build upon, the existing framework of rules. Therefore, whatever else a torts course may do, it must also teach the student much about where tort law is, where it has come from, and what are the justifications for these rules. Books such as this are intended to help with that basic task.

There are various ways to subdivide this vast subject. For example, we could divide it according to the type of fault involved—torts which are based on intentional conduct, negligence, or strict liability. One of the most common divisions is between physical harm (injuries to persons and property) and non-physical harm (injuries to relations). Examples of the latter include defamation, misrepresentation, business torts, and injuries to family relations.

This book reflects the coverage of the typical first-year torts course, which emphasizes the torts involving injuries to persons and property. It includes all the topics that are ordinarily covered in the first year torts course, which includes all of that subcategory and sometimes defamation and misrepresentation. There are other torts in the subcategory of "non-physical harm" which I have omitted on the ground that they are almost never taught in the first-year torts course: misuse of legal procedure (Dobbs' Hornbook, Chapter 30); interference with family relations (Dobbs' Hornbook, Chapter 31); and injuries to economic relations, sometimes called "business torts" (Dobbs' Hornbook, Chapters 32 and 33).

The organization of this book is one which I have evolved over the years. There are many other possible ways to organize this material, as is reflected in the various casebooks. My outline may not track your casebook's very well. However, each chapter should be self-sufficient, and should more or less correspond to some identifiable part of your casebook. I have included a text correlation chart (Appendix E) to assist you in identifying these relationships.

On the other hand, you may find that there are one or two parts of your casebook which do not have a corresponding section in this book. You may also find that, even within sections which do correspond, your casebook and other torts books include issues not mentioned here. This should not be a cause for any concern when you appreciate the proper uses and limitations of this and other similar books. Remember—this book is only one tool. The final product must be a synthesis of several sources. Only when that synthesis is your own will you be able to truly learn and understand the subject.

■ C. APPROACH TO TORTS

1. STUDYING TORT LAW IN LAW SCHOOL

No doubt you have already been told how you should approach a law school course such as torts. Briefly, the steps I recommend are:

(1) Prepare for each class by briefing the cases and attempting to answer the note questions. This advice may seem trite, but there is no substitute for this kind of intensive preparation.

(2) Attend class and take good notes.

(3) Soon after each class, review the material covered, clear up any remaining questions or uncertainties about the material, and revise your briefs and note answers.

(4) At the end of each chapter or major section of the casebook, synthesize everything in some useful form. I strongly recommend a written outline in a form similar to that used in this book. This synthesis should include outside readings such as this book. The basic elements of your outline should be as close as possible to the outline which is the table of contents of your casebook.

(5) Use that outline as your primary study source. Supplement your study with practice questions and practice exams. For some of you, a small study group can be useful, but be careful not to allow this to substitute for any step in your own preparation.

You can see, then, that this book must not be a substitute for your own personal course outline. Rather, it should be used as an aid to the preparation of your own outline. It should be consulted the same as any other reference.

This book is structured to provide several tools to aid your study. The first section, "Capsule Summary of Tort Law," is an outline of the outline. It is the type of outline you might use in an open book examination, or for intensive final review just before the examination. Ideally, you could reproduce this outline (or at least the major headings) from memory if called upon to do so.

At the end of each chapter are some questions to test your knowledge. Appendix A contains the answers (don't peek). Appendix B offers a more comprehensive practice exam, much like the final examination itself, Appendix C is a possible analysis of the practice exam.

Appendix D is a glossary of terms. Two of the major mistakes that I see on students' examination papers are (1) the misuse of important legal terms basic to the course, and (2) a total failure to use these terms. Either of these errors is very prejudicial. Conversely, students who know and use the subject's terms correctly create a strong favorable impression. Do not restate basic concepts in your own words. Learn and use the correct vocabulary.

2. THE IMPORTANCE OF CIVIL PROCEDURE

As previously noted, torts professors necessarily teach some civil procedure. Tort law cannot properly be understood except in the context in which it operates. Tort rules are born of litigation in the context of the American version of the adversary system. This may seem obvious, but its consequences are not.

The law student (not to mention the lawyer and judge) must appreciate the manner in which the lawsuit reached the point at which we examine it. Was the complaint dismissed at the pleading stage? Did a party win summary judgment? If there was a trial, did the case go to the jury or was there a directed verdict? If there was a jury verdict, what errors does appellant claim? How are tort law issues raised in appeals from jury verdicts? What are the general differences between the roles of judges and juries in civil cases?

Therefore, the beginning law student would be wise to learn some civil procedure as quickly as possible.

In addition, be sure that your case briefs include a section, "procedural history."

3. OTHER COLLATERAL SUBJECTS

In addition to civil procedure, other subjects have an important relationship to tort law. Be alert to these relationships. For example, the institution of insurance, and especially liability insurance, has had a major impact on tort law. The law of agency is often used in determining rules of vicarious tort liability—sometimes when it doesn't fit. And the law of evidence can have a significant bearing on certain fact issues which may be critical to the resolution of tort law issues. Obviously you should not attempt to study these topics in any depth, but pay attention when they come up in your torts course and try to understand as much as is necessary to see the relationship.

■ D. TORTS EXAMINATIONS: ANALYZING TORT PROBLEMS

No doubt you have already received lots of advice on how to analyze legal problems and write law school essay examinations (these are similar tasks, by the way). If not, there are good references available. Ask your professors or fellow students. Valuable suggestions are also contained in some other Black Letter books. The following comments are intended only to supplement the ample general advice available elsewhere.

My model for a good essay exam answer is a good judicial opinion, minus the fact statement. But first, before you write anything, you *MUST* outline your answer.

Start with scratch paper. You're not ready to write in your examination booklet (or begin typing your answer) yet!

Your first step is to identify the issues and subissues and put them in outline form. Use headings and subheadings. These can be copied directly to your exam. Law professors LOVE headings and subheadings on exam answers. Then flesh out your outline with an outline of the answer to each issue or subissue.

Budget your time carefully. It is usually better to put down *something* on each question than to do an outstanding job on some questions and not answer others at all. Keep careful track of your time, and stick to your budget as closely as you can.

Don't be afraid to spend a significant part of the time allocated for a question on this scratch-paper outline. Your goal is a comprehensive, thoughtful answer. Shotgun answers done with little advance thought don't score very highly. If you are a slow writer (or if your handwriting is bad), learn to type and type your exams. *PLEASE!* And if you are permitted to use a computer to write your exam, you should do so. As you already know, there are significant advantages to composing on a computer. You can rearrange, delete, add, and modify text much more easily and quickly, you should be able to type faster than you can write, and your answer will be legible. I tell my students, if I can't read it, you don't get credit for it.

Your answer to each issue or subissue should track a good judicial opinion (without the statement of facts). First state (briefly) the issue you are addressing. Then state the applicable rules of law. (Don't put down every rule you can think of that's even remotely related.) Then apply the law to the facts of this case, and finally state your conclusion as to that issue.

If possible, as soon as you sit down to begin the examination, make an outline (from memory) of the entire course. This outline should resemble the table of contents of your casebook, or the basic elements of the Capsule Summary of this book, or some combination of the two. This will serve as a checklist of possible issues. It is vital that you identify and discuss as many issues as possible. Most law professors grade examination papers against their own outline of the issues and subissues. Most of us, I believe, assign points to each. No matter how well you do on the issues you do discuss, it can damage your grade severely to get zero points for important issues that you fail to discuss at all.

When you analyze a torts problem, you must first identify all possible tort theories that may arguably support P's cause of action. Then, test each theory by applying the *ELEMENTS* of that tort to the facts. If there is some factual support for each element of the cause of action (arguably sufficient to raise a jury question), then you will conclude that P can establish a *PRIMA FACIE CASE* as to that theory. Then, and only then, consider any applicable *DEFENSES,* and do the same thing with them. Don't make the mistake of starting with the discussion of an obvious defense, omitting any discussion of the tort cause of action itself.

Should you discuss a possible tort theory if there is an element which is clearly missing? This is a judgment call, and it depends on which element. For example, in an auto accident case, you would not discuss battery if there is no evidence of intent. As a general rule, however, if the facts seem to suggest a particular tort, you will probably want to discuss that tort even if you conclude that P will not succeed on that theory due to the lack of a key element.

Finally, it is vital in tort law to learn the distinction between issues which are issues for the court and those which are for the jury. On my examinations—just as in real life—it is not always necessary to conclude that "P wins" or "defendant wins." It is sometimes a sufficient answer to say, there is enough evidence of, e.g., negligence, to permit submission of the case to the jury. I do not require you to predict what the jury will in fact do.

■ E. OTHER SOURCES

In tort law, the three most important reference works are:

1) **Dan B. Dobbs, The Law of Torts (West Group 2000).** Now this is the current West Hornbook on torts, superseding the Hornbook which for decades was the standard one-volume work in the field—Dean William L. Prosser's The Law of Torts. The latest edition of that work was Prosser and Keeton on The Law of Torts, Fifth Edition (1984), edited by W. Page Keeton, Dan B. Dobbs, Robert E. Keeton, and David G. Owen. After Page Keeton's death, Professor Dobbs set out to update this book, but in the process decided that an entirely new book was necessary. The Prosser Hornbook was quite influential in the courts, and it may safely be predicted that its successor, the Dobbs Hornbook, will be as well.

2) **Fowler Harper, Fleming James & Oscar Gray, The Law of Torts.** Now in its Second/Third Edition, published by Aspen Law & Business. This six-volume treatise was first published in 1956 in two principal volumes, authored by Professors Harper and James, two giants in tort law. Professor Gray, also an eminent torts scholar, has become the sole author. The second edition, published in 1986, is kept current with semi-annual supplements, and is being replaced, volume by volume, with the third edition. Volume 1 of the Third Edition was published in 1996.

3) **Restatement (Second) of Torts; Restatement (Third) of Torts.** Now one of the most significant projects of the American Law Institute—a national organization made up of distinguished judges, lawyers, and law professors—is to promulgate the various "Restatements" of the law. The Restatements are drafted by knowledgeable committees, and are intended to represent the best thinking as to the state of the law in each of the areas covered. They consist of "black letter" statements of the rules, followed by explanatory comments and illustrations.

The Restatement (Second) of Torts, like the original version, has been very influential in the courts. It was completed in 1977, but it is still largely current. Work has begun on the Restatement (Third) of Torts, of which two units are finished—Products Liability (1998) and Apportionment of Liability (2000). A third unit—Liability for Physical Harm—is in preparation but still incomplete. A handy reference for students (and others) is A Concise Restatement of Torts, published by the American Law Institute. A single softbound volume, it includes some of the important provisions of both the second and third restatements.

In addition to these, there are other good one-volume references and study aids dealing with tort law generally and specific tort topics.

There are several current Nutshells covering torts, including: (1) Kionka, Torts in a Nutshell (4th ed. 2005); (2) Elias & Moes, The Law of Medical Liability in a Nutshell (2d ed. 2003); (3) Owen & Phillips, Product Liability in a Nutshell (7th ed. 2005); (4) Eggen, Toxic Torts in a Nutshell (2d ed. 2000); and (5) Hood, Hardy & Lewis, Workers' Compensation and Employee Protection Laws in a Nutshell (4th ed. 2004).

■ F. ABBREVIATIONS

As used in this book:

P = plaintiff or a person who is a potential plaintiff—i.e., the victim of tortious conduct. It also includes (where appropriate) deceased victims, where the lawsuit would be brought by a personal representative for the benefit of P's survivors.

D = defendant or a person who is a potential defendant—i.e., the alleged tortfeasor or one who is vicariously liable for his tort. The Restatement uses the term "actor." See R.2d § 3.

Dobbs = Dobbs Hornbook

R.2d = Restatement (Second) of Torts.

R.3d PL = Restatement (Third) of Torts: Products Liability

R.3d AL = Restatement (Third) of Torts: Apportionment of Liability

R.3d PH = Restatement (Third) of Torts: Liability for Physical Harm. We will cite only to those parts of this unit that have been completed and approved.

*

PART ONE

Introduction

■ **ANALYSIS**

I. General Considerations

A. Overview of Tort Law

"Torts" is the general legal classification encompassing a number of different civil causes of action providing a private remedy, almost always in the form of money damages, for an injury to P caused by the tortious conduct of D. Each tort is separately named and defined, and each tort action has its own rules of liability, defenses, and damages. Thus, the injured person must find a tort action or theory which fits the facts of his case in order to pursue this remedy. Some rules or principles are common to various torts or groups of torts, but there is no universal formula for tort liability. The law of each tort must be separately examined.

B. The Definitional Dilemma

1. What is a Tort? —no definition

The concept "tort" is elusive. The word is not used in common speech. Yet tort law is one of the most important parts of our modern legal system. Although it describes one of the major pigeon-holes of the law, the concept "tort" cannot be usefully defined. Any definition which is sufficiently comprehensive to encompass all torts is so general as to be almost meaningless.

• civil wrong
where the remedy is damages
• ∃ a duty

2. No General Principle of Tort Liability — no general principle

Is there a general principle of tort liability? Or are there only the laws of the individual "torts," a miscellaneous and more or less unconnected collection of nominate civil actions grouped together merely for convenience of reference? So far, no such general principle has been recognized, except insofar as the concept "negligence" can be so characterized. The law remains as it developed through case-by-case evolution, a system of more or less independent named torts, each with its own more or less unique rules.

3. Definition — ∃ a harm

The only common element of all torts is that someone has sustained a loss or harm as the result of some act or failure to act by another. In general, a tort is a civil wrong, wherein one person's conduct causes a compensable injury to the person, property, or recognized interest of another, in violation of a duty imposed by law.

4. Fault — ∃ a fault (not all the time)

Sometimes it is suggested that a common element of tort liability is *fault*, that tortious conduct is that which falls below accepted community

—fault

standards of behavior. Some sort of fault is common to many torts, although it might more accurately be described as conduct that creates an unreasonable or unacceptable risk of harm. But even in this sense, fault is not a universal principle of liability. Various kinds of blameworthy conduct resulting in damage do not give rise to tort liability. Conversely, the law sometimes imposes tort liability simply because a particular activity can and should bear the cost of damage associated with it, regardless of the fact that the conduct of the "tortfeasor" was morally blameless.

fault —

C. Bases, Purposes and Functions of Tort Law

1. Where Does Tort Law Come From?

Tort law, of course, comes from case law and legislation. But where do judges and legislators get the ideas that result in tort law rules? There are at least four ways in which tort law rules can be derived, individually or in combination.

a. Morality or corrective justice

Morality or corrective justice attempts to hold defendants liable, and to compensate plaintiffs, only when it seems fair or "right" to do so. One criterion of justice is current community standards of fairness.

b. Social utility or policy

Social utility or policy can support a rule. For example, if we impose liability for conduct we wish to discourage, people will be deterred from engaging in that conduct. Conversely, if we immunize certain conduct from liability, that conduct will be encouraged, but immunity breeds carelessness.

c. Process or procedural considerations

Process considerations motivate us to create rules that can be fairly, efficiently, and effectively administered.

d. Formal reasoning

Formal reasoning is the mechanical application of preexisting rules of law without regard to justice, policy, or procedural considerations. Lower courts typically have no discretion to make or modify rules; their task is merely to discover and apply the appropriate rule by application of formal reasoning.

2. Functions or goals of tort law

Tort law has three main purposes or functions:

a. Compensation

The most important function of tort law is to restore P, so far as money damages can do so, to his status prior to the injury caused by D.

b. Justice and Promotion of Desired Policies

Tort law also seeks to impose the cost of compensating P upon the person or persons who caused P's injury, or who in justice or for policy reasons ought to be financially responsible for it, but only upon such persons.

c. Deterrence

The threat of tort liability is intended to regulate human behavior by deterring tortious conduct, thereby preventing at least some injuries and making society safer. This is a function shared with the criminal law.

Other secondary functions include vindicating P, providing a substitute for private retaliation, and preventing resort to self-help remedies.

D. Sources of Tort Law *CL, no codification*

The rules and principles of tort law have been created and developed almost entirely through judicial decisions—what we call "case law" or "common law." So far it remains largely common law, but it is increasingly affected by legislation. However, no jurisdiction has attempted a codification of tort law. The Civil Codes of California and Louisiana contain some general principles of tort liability.

E. Historical Development of Tort Law

1. Evolution of Tort Remedies

English law in its earliest stages did not differentiate between tort and crime; indeed, such terms were unknown. When one person was harmed by another, the remedy was a private war or "feud" in retaliation, the object being to cause an equivalent harm to the wrongdoer.

In their earliest form, English courts were local and applied local laws. After the Norman Conquest (1066), the royal courts were created and gradually took limited jurisdiction over a specified list of "wrongs"— primarily felonies where there was a breach of the "king's peace," and disputes involving land.

[handwritten margin notes: justice v policy — · protect free exchange of goods · property rights & owners]

At first, all prosecutions for "wrongs" in the king's courts were brought by the individual harmed. Plaintiff accused defendant in open court and offered the appropriate form of trial (combat, ordeal, or oaths), but even if P was successful, no compensation was awarded. This procedure was known as the "appeal of felony."

As time went on, royal writs became the grant of jurisdiction to a royal court to adjudicate a case. Gradually, a formal system of named writs evolved, and it became necessary for the plaintiff to purchase an appropriate writ from the king's chancellor to commence his action. The writs became crystallized into certain forms and contents, and if plaintiff could not fit his case into one of the prescribed writs, he had no action in the royal courts. By the fifteenth century, it had become possible, and common, to commence an action by bill (complaint) instead of royal writ, but plaintiff's declaration still had to state a cause of action in the recognized form, corresponding to the writs that could have been selected.

The most important personal civil action was trespass. Its great significance lay in the fact plaintiff recovered his actual damages, if any. For many years it also retained a quasi-criminal character in that a vanquished defendant was usually imprisoned or fined. It became immensely popular and largely supplanted the "appeal" in felony cases except for homicide. No civil action was permitted in the king's court for wrongful death until the passage of Lord Campbell's Act in 1846.

The three common forms of the writ were (1) trespass *vi et armis* (with force and arms) for assault, battery, and false imprisonment; (2) trespass *de bonis asportatis* (taking of goods) for trespass to chattels; and (3) trespass *quare clausum fregit* (breach of the "close") for trespass to land.

Concurrent with the growth of trespass there developed a practice of issuing and honoring writs for wrongs which did not fit within the confines of the designated trespass actions. Such writs eventually became classified as an action of trespass on the case or, more correctly, "action on the case." Unlike the trespass writs which had been developed into inflexible forms, the "case" writs set forth the facts of plaintiff's particular case. By the sixteenth century, case had become a distinct and generic form of action.

As time went on, certain of the recurring case actions crystallized and were separated into named actions having rules and writs of their own.

Trespass, together with case and its progeny, account for almost all of the actions which we now refer to as the law of torts. The most important case-spawned action was negligence.

2. Evolution of Theories of Liability

In the final stages of their evolution, there were three basic differences between trespass and case so far as tort remedies were concerned:

(1) **Trespass** was applicable when the defendant committed some affirmative act which caused a direct and immediate injury to the plaintiff; case was the remedy for indirect or consequential harm. *Scott v. Shepherd* (K.B. 1772).

> *Example:* D throws a log onto the highway. P1, struck by the log as it fell, can maintain trespass. P2, hurt when he stumbles over it as it lay in the road, must sue in case.

(2) **Case** required proof of actual damages; trespass actions did not.

(3) At one time, it was thought that trespass liability was **strict**, or nearly so. It was said that the plaintiff did not have to prove the defendant's fault. More recent analyses, however, suggest that the situation may have been more complicated than we thought, and to some extent may be beyond our knowledge because of the applicable rules of procedure and the limited reports available. It may be that if the defendant pleaded the general issue, under that defense he could prove his lack of fault. But whatever the true rule may have been, it is clear that fault was not a part of the plaintiff's case; absence of fault, if relevant at all, was a defense, and it was not an absolute defense because the jury could decide for the plaintiff anyway.

[handwritten margin note: Is it fair to blame someone who is not at fault (social policy)]

Negligence was until relatively recently merely one basis for liability in a number of different civil actions for which case was the appropriate writ. Gradually, during the nineteenth century, negligence emerged as a separate action.

In the United States, fault quickly became a necessary element of plaintiff's case in a trespass action. Thus, in *Brown v. Kendall* (Mass. 1850), D, attempting to beat two fighting dogs with a stick, accidentally struck P in the eye. In P's suit against D, even though trespass was the proper form of the action (direct injury), P lost because he failed to prove fault (intentional or negligent misconduct).

F. The Roles of Judges and Juries

In the United States, the vast majority of tort cases are settled prior to trial, but they are settled largely on the basis of counsel's predictions as to what a jury verdict in the case is likely to be. This book briefly outlines the rules of tort law, but you should remember that for the most part, these rules do not decide actual cases. The pre-eminent power in resolving tort cases lies with the "trier of fact," in most tort cases a jury.

jury – fact; law – court (t which)

It is commonly said that questions of law are for the court and questions of fact are for the jury. This is not entirely true, and can be a little misleading, since judges possess the ultimate power to decide which is which. But through well-established rules and customs, and by use of the general verdict, juries are given wide latitude to decide these controversies without court interference.

jury: ① what happened ② consequences ③ was there damage

Jury questions are of three kinds. R.2d § 328C. First, the jury must determine what in fact occurred. Then, in most cases, the jury is required to make one or more decisions as to the legal consequences of these facts—was plaintiff or defendant negligent, were the words defamatory, was plaintiff a trespasser, licensee, or invitee, etc.—usually on the basis of some general legal definition given by the court. R.3d PH § 8. Finally, the jury must determine whether plaintiff was damaged by defendant's tortious act and the dollar value of plaintiff's compensable damages.

① duty / right ② elements / measure ③ imposes / excuses AMOL

court:

Questions of law for the court are also of three kinds. R.2d § 328B. First, certain issues are invariably issues of law, such as (1) whether defendant owed plaintiff any recognized legal duty, or, conversely, whether plaintiff has a legally protected right; (2) the elements of proof necessary to establish liability (or nonliability) and the measure of damages; and (3) whether, on the facts, some particular rule of law imposes or excuses liability as a matter of law—for example, the rule that violation of a certain safety statute is negligence per se, or that false statements of intent are not actionable misrepresentations. The last are sometimes stated in terms of duty or "proximate" cause, but they are more particularized standards of conduct than the broad general rules usually associated with the term "duty," such as the duty to exercise reasonable care in operating a motor vehicle.

By embodying particular standards of conduct in rules of law, courts take from the jury the power to determine the legal consequences of certain facts, and thereby transform questions of fact into questions of law and enable the court to decide the case instead of the jury.

[handwritten: determine what's law/fact]

Second, all issues which are ordinarily questions of fact for the jury become questions of law for the court if the judge decides that the evidence on that issue so overwhelmingly favors one conclusion that reasonable persons jurors) could not reach the opposite conclusion. R. 3d PH § 8.

[handwritten: apply Procedure]

Third, judges alone apply rules of procedure which may have an important effect upon the outcome of the case, especially rules concerning the admission and exclusion of evidence, burden of proof, presumptions, and the applicability of res ipsa loquitur.

However, juries do render the ultimate judgment in a substantial proportion of tort cases, particularly where the controlling issues involve disputes as to what occurred or mixed questions of law and fact such as breach of duty, status, damages, causation, and the like.

Tort law is not merely a system of rules of actionable or nonactionable conduct, but also of rules which determine when the law will not decide cases and instead will leave the decision whether to impose liability to the more or less unfettered discretion of the jury. In fact, one scholar has suggested that "nearly all legal theory in negligence cases is designed to serve the ends of allocating the power of judgment respectively to judge and jury." (L. Green, Judge & Jury 261). In many—perhaps even most—tort cases, rules of law take one only so far, and the lawyer or judge cannot determine the ultimate liability question. In such cases, it is necessary and entirely appropriate to say that beyond a certain point, the remaining issues are jury questions, and therefore whether or not the particular defendant is liable to the particular plaintiff is merely an educated guess.

See generally R.2d 328B, 328C; Harper, James & Gray ch. 15; Dobbs §§ 17–19.

G. Tortious Conduct *[handwritten: no definition but 3 a duty]*

Almost any imaginable conduct may, in the right circumstances, be a source of injury to another and therefore is potentially tortious. But not every injury is actionable in tort. It is commonly said that conduct is tortious if, but only if, that conduct violates some duty imposed by law. But this test is meaningless, since it is tort law that determines which duties are actionable in tort. Therefore, no meaningful definition of "tort" or "tortious conduct" is possible, apart from the specific liability rules of the individual torts themselves.

H. Tort Duties and Contractual Duties

When D enters into a contract with P, he voluntarily assumes an obligation to take certain action (or, occasionally, to refrain from some action). Since this duty arises from the contract, its breach is actionable in contract and not in tort. However, some contractual undertakings are held to create, in addition to contractual duties, duties which may be actionable in tort if breached. See IV.H., infra.

I. Tort Law and Criminal Law

In a very general sense, tort law is the private or civil counterpart of criminal law. Indeed, in the early stages of the common law, tort and crime were not separate concepts. There was one law of "wrongs." Today they are entirely distinct, but there are tort actions which roughly correspond to many crimes. However, the principles of liability of analogous torts and crimes are not necessarily the same, and should not be confused.

J. Terms

Appendix D contains a glossary of terms with which you should be familiar. However, a few terms are so important that they must be agreed upon between us at the outset.

1. Injury

An "injury" means the invasion of an interest which is protected by tort law. R.2d § 7(1). It is not limited to physical harm, or even harm that is directly measurable in monetary terms.

2. Harm

"Harm" refers to an injury to a person or property which is measurably detrimental. R.2d § 7(2). Thus, it is narrower in scope than "injury," which includes merely technical invasions of a protected interest having no measurable detrimental effect.

3. Physical Harm

"Physical harm" refers to an injury that physically impairs in any way the human body, or physically impairs the condition of land or a chattel. R.2d § 7(3); R.3d PH § 4. Emotional distress, without resulting physical impairment, is not physical harm. R. 3d PH § 4, comment *b*.

Example: D trespasses upon P's land and strikes him with his fist. The trespass is an injury, since it invades P's legally protected interest, but the trespass itself causes no actual harm. The assault and battery cause both harm (the assault producing fear and anxiety, but no physical harm) and physical harm (the battery). See R.2d § 7.

4. Conduct

"Conduct" includes both acts and omissions to act. R.2d § 6.

5. Subject to Liability

"Subject to liability" is used to refer to the situation where the actor has engaged in conduct which is (or may be found to be) tortious, without regard to whether the other conditions to a finding of liability are present. It is used when it would be inaccurate to say that D is "liable." For example, one who manufactures and markets a product which contains a defect unreasonably dangerous to the user or consumer is subject to liability (but may or may not be, in fact, liable) to one injured as a result of that defect. R.2d § 5.

6. Had Reason to Know

"Had reason to know" means that D had information from which a person of reasonable intelligence (or of D's actual intelligence, if superior) would infer that the fact exists, or that such person would govern his conduct on the assumption that the fact exists. R.2d § 12(1).

7. Should Have Known

"Should have known" means that a person of reasonable intelligence (or of D's superior intelligence) and of reasonable prudence would have ascertained the fact, or would govern his conduct on the assumption that the fact exists. R.2d § 12(2).

Example: A cookie manufacturer would have "reason to know" that his product will be eaten by children who cannot read, even if he successfully denies actual first-hand knowledge of that fact. An absentee landlord arguably "should have known" that the common stairway in his apartment building was in disrepair (because he had a duty to inspect and ascertain that fact), even though he successfully proves that he had no "actual knowledge" or "reason to know" because he never visited the premises and no one ever notified him of that fact.

*

PART TWO

Intentional Torts

■ ANALYSIS

C.   Assault
  1.   Rule
  2.   Intent Required
  3.   Apprehension
      a.   Threat Against Another
      b.   D Apparently Intends Only Assault
      c.   Reasonableness of Apprehension
  4.   Imminent
      a.   Words
      b.   Apprehension of Future Battery
      c.   Apparent Ability to Consummate
  5.   Conditional Threat
D.   False Imprisonment
  1.   Rule
  2.   Intent
  3.   Confinement
      a.   What Constitutes
      b.   Direct or Indirect
      c.   Means
          1)   Physical Barriers
          2)   Physical Force
          3)   Other Duress
          4)   Legal Authority
          5)   Refusal to Release
  4.   P's Knowledge
  5.   Shoplifters
  6.   Accessories
  7.   Malicious Prosecution Distinguished
E.   Intentional or Reckless Infliction of Emotional Distress
  1.   Rule
  2.   D's Conduct
      a.   General Rule
      b.   Exception: Public Utility
      c.   Intent
  3.   P's Response
  4.   Abuse of Power
  5.   Conduct Directed at Third Persons
  6.   Proximate Cause
  7.   Transferred Intent
  8.   Public Official and Public Figure Plaintiffs
  9.   Mishandling of Corpse

II. Liability Rules for Intentional Torts

A. Intent
(Dobbs §§ 24–26, 40–41; R.2d § 8A; R.3d PH § 1)

1. Rule

In tort law, conduct is intentional if the actor (a) desires to cause the consequences of his act ("purpose" intent), or (b) knows or believes the consequences are substantially certain to result from it ("knowledge" intent). R.2d § 8A; R.3d PH § 1.

2. Proof of Intent

'circumstential evidence

Ordinarily, D's intent must be proved circumstantially—that is, inferred from his conduct. D will be presumed to have intended the natural and probable consequences of his acts in light of the surrounding circumstances of which he may be assumed to be aware.

Example: D throws a bomb into a room, knowing that both A and P are present. The bomb is powerful enough to kill everyone in the room. D will be found to have intended to kill both A and P, no matter what D claims to have been his actual intent, and even if his only purpose was to kill A.

3. Intent Distinguished From Motive

Intent is the desire to cause certain immediate consequences. Motive is the actor's reason for having that desire—revenge, protest, punishment, self-defense, defense of another, or even to be of help. So far as liability for intentional torts is concerned, the actor's motive is irrelevant on the issue of intent. However, motive may sometimes aggravate or mitigate the damages, or be part of an affirmative defense (e.g., self-defense).

4. Intentional Conduct Distinguished From Negligent or Reckless Conduct

Certainty of harmful consequences is the basis on which we distinguish intentional torts from negligent or reckless conduct. If the harmful result is intended or certain to occur, the tort is intentional. If D's conduct merely creates a foreseeable risk of harm, which may or may not be realized, his conduct is either negligent or reckless depending upon the magnitude and probability of the risk.

5. Children

Since intent is the desire to cause certain immediate consequences, very young children may be held liable for intentional torts even though so young as to be incapable of negligence.

6. Mentally Incompetent Persons

In most jurisdictions, a mentally incompetent or insane person is liable for his intentional torts, even when incapable of forming a purpose or understanding the consequences of his conduct. *Accord*: R. 896J. In effect, if he committed the act, his mental incapacity is ignored and he is treated as if he were sane. In a minority, such persons may be liable if the trier of fact finds that they in fact formed the necessary intent, even though their reasons and motives were entirely irrational.

7. Transferred Intent

Transferred intent is an expanded rule of proximate cause applicable to and among the five intentional torts which are the progeny of the parent trespass action—assault, battery, false imprisonment, trespass to land, trespass to chattels. D's intent to commit any one of these torts automatically "transfers" and supplies the intent necessary to any of the other torts in this group. It also transfers from X (D's intended victim) to P (D's actual but unintended victim). E.g., assume that D acts with the intent to injure A, but at the same time (or instead) injures P. D is deemed to have committed an intentional tort upon P, even though D was unaware of P's existence or presence or of any risk of harm to P. R.3d PH § 33, comment *c.*; R.2d §§ 16(2), 21(1)(a), 35(1)(a).

Example: D intentionally shoots at A and wounds or misses him. The bullet strikes P, who was hidden from view and not known to be in the vicinity. D is subject to liability to P for battery.

8. Scope of Liability (Proximate Cause)

Broader scope of liability rules apply to intentional torts. A tortfeasor who intentionally causes physical harm is subject to liability for that harm even if it was unlikely to occur. R.3d PH § 33.

B. Battery

(Dobbs §§ 28–32; R.2d §§ 13–20)

1. Rule

Battery is a harmful or offensive contact (direct or indirect) with Ps person, caused by D who has the required intent. R.2d §§ 13, 18.

2. Intent Required

D must have acted intending to cause a harmful or offensive contact with P (or another), or an imminent apprehension of such a contact. R.2d §§ 13, 14, 16, 18, 20.

3. P's Person

P's "person" includes his body and those things in contact with it or closely connected to it and identified with it, such as clothing, an object held in his hand, or an object so closely associated or identified with P that, considering the nature of the contact, a normal person would deem it an offense against his person.

Example: D swings his arm at P and forcefully knocks off P's hat, or forcibly grabs a plate that P is holding in his hand. D shoots a horse which P is riding. All may be batteries.

4. P's Awareness

The tort is the contact, and therefore P need not have been aware of it at the time.

5. No Harm Intended

It is only required that D intend the contact which is in fact harmful or offensive; it does not matter that he intended no harm or offense.

Example: An unwanted kiss or fondling may be battery, even though D (erroneously) assumed consent. So may be harmful or offensive contact where D intended only a practical joke. Even surgery performed without P's consent is battery, even though D had only the best of motives and the result was beneficial to P.

6. Harmful Contact

A harmful contact is actionable only if it produces some bodily harm. This includes any physical damage, however slight, to any part of P's body (such as a cut, bruise, or burn), even if the "damage" is ultimately beneficial (e.g., a surgical procedure); illness; and physical (but not emotional) pain. R.2d § 15.

7. Offensive Contact

An offensive contact is one which offends a reasonable sense of personal dignity, such as by being hostile, insulting, loathsome, or unduly personal. R.2d § 19.

Example: D flicks a glove in P's face, or angrily grabs his lapels, or drops a quantity of offensive matter in his lap. D puts his arms around P, a stranger, and kisses her. D has committed a battery.

Example: P is about to undergo a cesarean section for delivery of her baby. She informs the hospital personnel through her physician that her religious beliefs prohibit her from being seen unclothed by a male. During the cesarean section, while she is unconscious, a male nurse observes and touches her naked body. She learns of this touching later. The touching is a battery.

8. Consent

If P consents to the contact, D is privileged to make it and there is no tort. (This is generally true of all intentional torts.) Consent may sometimes be assumed. In a crowded society, some unpermitted contact is inevitable and customary. And consent may be assumed because of some pre-existing relationship between P and D.

[handwritten margin notes: Surgery is battery unless consent. — cut off wrong e.g. — battery b/c not consented to · feud to assure consent an certain contacts]

C. Assault

(Dobbs §§ 33–35; R.2d §§ 21–34)

1. Rule

Assault is an act by D which arouses in P a reasonable apprehension of an imminent battery, caused by D who has the required intent. R.2d § 21.

2. Intent Required

D must have acted intending to cause a harmful or offensive contact with P (or another), or to cause an imminent apprehension of such a contact. R.2d §§ 21, 32.

However, D's conduct need not have been motivated by hostility. An assault emanating from a practical joke, or even an attempt to be helpful (e.g. medical treatment), is nonetheless an assault. R.2d § 34.

3. Apprehension

The essence of the tort is P's *apprehension*, so P must have been aware of D's threatening act *at the time*, before it is terminated. R.2d § 22. Note that *apprehension* of the contact is all that is required; it is not necessary that P experience the emotion of *fear*.

a. Threat Against Another

It is not necessary that D direct his act against P; it is sufficient that P reasonably perceives the threat of a battery to P. R.2d § 32. But P's apprehension of a battery only to a third person, and not to P, is not an assault against P, no matter how concerned P may be for the third person's safety. R.2d § 26.

Example: D aims his gun at S, P's son. There is no assault of P unless P is located so as reasonably to apprehend a .battery to P

b. **D Apparently Intends Only Assault**
D's conduct may be an assault even if it is apparent to P that D intended only an assault and not a battery, provided P apprehends that the battery may occur. R.2d § 28.

Example: D aims his gun in P's direction and shoots, saying, "This is only a warning shot." There is an assault if P apprehends that the bullet, although intended to miss him, may in fact strike him.

c. **Reasonableness of Apprehension**
If D's assault is directed against P, D is subject to liability to P even though a person of normal courage would not have apprehended a battery if P, being unusually sensitive, does in fact apprehend it. R.2d § 27.

4. Imminent

The contact must be perceived as imminent. There must be an apparent intent and ability to carry out the threat immediately. R.2d §§ 24, 29.

a. **Words**
Mere words, unaccompanied by a physical act, are not an assault. But words may give a sufficiently threatening character to an otherwise innocuous or inoffensive movement. R.2d § 31.

b. **Apprehension of Future Battery**
If D's words or other circumstances are understood by P as threatening only a battery at some time other than the present, there is no assault.

c. **Apparent Ability to Consummate**
D must have an apparent present ability to carry out the battery. If D is so located or confined or otherwise under some restriction or disability so as to be incapable of immediately carrying out the threat, and P is aware of this, there is no assault. On the other hand, if it appears to P that D has the present ability to commit the battery, it does not matter that, in fact, D does not have or believe he has that ability. R.2d § 33.

Example: D aims an unloaded gun at P; the fact that it is unloaded is not apparent. D is subject to liability for assault.

5. Conditional Threat

Even though D gives P an option to avoid the battery by obeying D's command, there is still an assault unless under the circumstances D is privileged to enforce the command by means of the threatened contact. R.2d § 30.

Example: D says to P, a trespasser in D's home, "Leave immediately or I'll throw you out." Since D is privileged to use this force, there is no assault.

D. False Imprisonment

(Dobbs §§ 36–39; R.2d §§ 35–45A, 120A)

1. Rule

False imprisonment occurs when D, intending to confine P (or another) within boundaries fixed by D, so confines P, and P is conscious of the confinement or is harmed by it. R.2d § 35.

2. Intent

The requisite intent is merely the intent to confine P, or another where P is confined instead or in addition. A mistake of identity is no excuse. And no personal malice, hostility, or desire to harm is necessary. A good faith belief that the confinement is justified is no excuse. R.2d §§ 43, 44.

3. Confinement

a. What Constitutes

The place of confinement may be broader than the term "imprisonment" implies. It is enough that P is prevented from leaving a given area, such as a room, an automobile, a building, or perhaps even a larger area. Within that area, however, the confinement must be complete, and P must have no reasonable or safe avenue of exit or escape known to him. Merely to block P's path in one direction is not sufficient. R.2d §§ 36, 38.

b. Direct or Indirect

So long as the requisite intent is present, it is immaterial whether D's act directly or indirectly causes the confinement. R.2d § 37.

c. **Means**

The confinement may be by means of:

1) **Physical Barriers**

Actual or apparent physical barriers. R.2d § 38.

2) **Physical Force**

Physical force, or credible threats of physical force, to which P submits. R.2d §§ 39, 40.

3) **Other Duress**

Duress sufficient to vitiate P's consent, as where D threatens to harm another or P's valuable property, or restrains such property. R.2d § 40A. However, merely moral or social pressure is not sufficient.

> *Example:* P remains confined to clear his name, or to avoid attracting attention or public humiliation. There is no false imprisonment.

4) **Legal Authority**

Color of legal authority, sometimes called false arrest. R.2d § 41. If D *has* or *purports to have* legal authority to take P into custody, exercises it, P believes that D has or *may have* such authority, and P submits against his will, there is confinement. False arrest is merely one form of false imprisonment, not a separate tort.

5) **Refusal to Release**

D's refusal to release P from a once-valid confinement, or to aid in such release by providing a means of escape, when D was under a duty so to act. R.2d § 45.

4. **P's Knowledge**

Ordinarily P must be aware of the confinement. However, if P suffers some *physical harm* from the confinement, it is immaterial that, due to some mental or sensory defect or other circumstance, P did not know that he was confined. R.2d § 42.

5. **Shoplifters**

When D in good faith detains a suspected shoplifter, courts tend to deny liability, such as by finding that P voluntarily consented to remain or by creating a special privilege to detain him on the premises, without arrest. R.2d § 120A. And most states have enacted statutes which give the shopkeeper a limited privilege to detain such persons in a reasonable manner for a reasonable time to investigate, based on a reasonable suspicion.

6. Accessories

D must have been an *active* and *knowing* participant in *procuring* or *instigating* the confinement, including its wrongful aspect. R.2d § 45A. It is not sufficient that D merely gives information to others who independently decide whether and how to confine R.2d § 45A comment *c*. Nor is D liable when he requests a proper arrest and some one else performs an improper one. *Id.*

7. Malicious Prosecution Distinguished

Malicious prosecution is the tort of instituting a groundless criminal proceeding against P for an improper purpose. As a part of that proceeding, there may be a false arrest (false imprisonment) of P, for which D will be liable only if he participated personally in the manner described in 6., above, and the arrest was not privileged. Thus, if D complies with the proper formal requirements in procuring P's arrest and confinement, D is liable, if at all, only in malicious prosecution for misuse of legal process to effect a valid arrest for an improper purpose, and not for false imprisonment.

E. Intentional or Reckless Infliction of Emotional Distress

(Dobbs §§ 303–07; R.2d §§ 46–48)

1. Rule

When D, by extreme and outrageous conduct, intentionally or recklessly causes severe emotional distress to P, D is subject to liability to P for that emotional distress and for any resulting bodily harm. R.2d § 46.

2. D's Conduct

a. General Rule

D's conduct must be extreme, outrageous, intolerable, and not merely insulting, profane, abusive, annoying, or even threatening. Unless D knows of some special sensitivity of P, mere verbal abuse, name calling, rudeness, insolence, and threats to do that which D has a legal right to do are generally not actionable, absent circumstances of aggravation.

b. **Exception: Public Utility**

Common carriers, innkeepers, and other public utilities may be liable to their patrons for profane, grossly insulting, or indecent language or conduct by their employees acting within the scope of their employment. R.2d § 48. This rule is under attack.

c. **Intent**

In most decided cases, the emotional distress was inflicted intentionally. However, some cases (and the Restatement (Second), § 46) will allow recovery where D knew or had reason to know that there was a high probability that emotional distress would follow from his conduct and D acted in conscious disregard of that risk.

3. **P's Response**

P's emotional distress must be severe. If P merely becomes unhappy, humiliated, or despondent for a short time, he cannot recover. But if P's anguish is great, and especially if prolonged, most courts will allow the action even absent any physical manifestation of the mental suffering, or bodily harm (e.g. physical illness, heart condition, miscarriage) caused by it. A few jurisdictions apparently require such bodily harm.

4. **Abuse of Power**

A common fact situation resulting in liability involves an abuse by D of some *relation* or *status* which gives him actual or apparent power to damage P's interests e.g., threats by bill collectors, insurance adjusters, landlords, school officials, police and those posing as police, and officials of a trade association, where such threats go beyond the ordinary means of persuasion or demands which they have a right to make and become flagrant abuses of power.

5. **Conduct Directed At Third Persons**

Even though D's distress-producing conduct is directed at a third person (T), if D's conduct intentionally or recklessly causes severe emotional distress in P, recovery may sometimes be allowed.

a. The Restatement rule limits recovery by such persons to cases where *either* (i) P is present and witnesses D's conduct, T knows of P's presence, and T is a member of P's immediate family, *or* (ii) P's severe emotional distress results in *bodily harm*. R.2d § 46(2).

Example: D shoots and kills T, P's husband, knowing that P is a witness. D is subject to liability for P's severe emotional distress which results.

b.   The requirement of presence has been relaxed by some courts in particularly compelling circumstances.

> *Example:*   D sexually molests or kidnaps P's child; D, an agent of a foreign government, kidnaps and tortures P's parent, child, or sibling.

6.   Proximate Cause

In the case of most other torts, D must take P as he finds him, and is liable for all of P's physical consequences in fact resulting from D's conduct, however unforeseeable. With respect to this tort, however, D is not liable to the extent that P's emotional response is beyond the bounds of normal human reactions to that conduct. In other words, the distress must be such as a reasonable person of ordinary sensitivity would experience. And where D intended to inflict only severe emotional distress, he is not liable for greater harm (e.g. illness or other bodily harm) unless his conduct created a foreseeable risk of such aggravated harm. R.2d § 312. But if D *knew* that P was peculiarly or specially sensitive, he may be liable for conduct which is extreme and outrageous in light of that special vulnerability, even though the same conduct would not be expected to produce a severe response in a normal, healthy adult.

7.   Transferred Intent

The doctrine of transferred intent does not apply, at least so far as D's intent was only to commit some other intentional tort. R.2d § 47.

8.   Public Official and Public Figure Plaintiffs

"Public officials" and "public figures" (for purposes of First Amendment law) may not recover for the tort of intentional infliction of emotional distress resulting from a media publication unless the publication contains a false statement of **fact** that was made with "actual malice"— i.e., with knowledge that the statement was false or with reckless disregard as to whether or not it was true. *Hustler Magazine v. Falwell* (U.S.1988).

9.   Mishandling of a Corpse

Intentional or reckless mishandling of a corpse may give rise to a cause of action in the next of kin who are thereby emotionally distressed. R.2d § 868.

F. Trespass to Land
(Dobbs §§ 50–58; R.2d §§ 157–166)

1. Rule

D is subject to liability for trespass to land in the possession of P if he intentionally (a) himself enters the land or causes a thing or third person to do so, (b) remains on the land after his privilege to be there has expired, or (c) fails to remove from the land a thing which he is under a duty to remove. R.2d § 158.

2. Possession

Liability for trespass extends only to the person(s) (P) in possession. P is in "possession" (a) when he occupies the land with the intent to control it, or (b) if no one else is in possession, he was the last occupier or he has the right to immediate occupancy. R.2d § 157.

3. Intent

The intent required is merely to enter upon the land, cause the entry, or remain. D's good faith (but erroneous) belief that he has a right to be there, or his reasonable mistake concerning title, right to possession, consent, or privilege, is no defense. R.2d § 164.

4. Manner

The trespass may be directly or indirectly caused.

a. Vertical Boundaries
The boundaries of land extend above and below the surface, and therefore the trespass may be by an intrusion at, above or beneath the surface. R.2d § 159.

b. Exception: Aircraft
Aircraft flights over private property present a special problem. Several theories are used to balance the possessor's rights against the needs of aviation.

1) "Zone" Theory
P owns only so much of the airspace as is in his "effective possession," i.e., the altitude up to which he might in the *future* make effective use of the airspace.

2) "Actual Use" Theory
P owns only so much of the airspace as he is actually using; there is no tort absent interference with his present use and enjoyment.

3) Privilege Theory
P's ownership of the airspace is unlimited, but subject to a privilege of flight.

4) Nuisance Theory

"Ownership" of the airspace is ignored. P has an action in nuisance (or negligence) only if flights interfere with his use and enjoyment of the land.

5) Restatement

Compare R.2d § 159(2): Overflight is a trespass only if it (a) enters into the "immediate reaches" of the airspace next to the land, and (b) interferes substantially with P's use and enjoyment.

6) Federal Aviation Laws

Under the supremacy clause, federal aviation laws and regulations may make privileged flights which would otherwise be a trespass.

c. Causing Trespass by Things

It is no less a trespass if D does not personally enter the land but merely causes some thing to do so.

Examples: Dust, smoke and other particles released into the air by D knowing that they will invade P's property (cf. nuisance); a shot fired by D from adjoining land across P's property, though never touching P's surface; erecting a structure which overhangs P's property line; damming a stream so as to flood P's land; utility wires.

5. Damages

If the trespass is intentional, the tort is complete without proof of any actual harm. Of course, P may recover for all harm resulting to his property, and persons and things upon it, and a broad range of consequential damage. R.2d §§ 162, 163.

6. Reckless or Negligent Intrusions

An intrusion upon P's land may result from D's negligent conduct or abnormally dangerous activity. In such cases liability is determined in the usual fashion by the rules of those other torts. R.2d § 165. Actual harm must be shown. D is not liable for intrusions which are not intentional, negligent, reckless, or the result of an abnormally dangerous activity. R.2d § 166.

G. Chattels
(Dobbs §§ 59–67; R.2d §§ 21–244)

1. Trespass to Chattels and Conversion
Trespass to chattels and conversion are the two principal intentional torts against Ps personal property.

2. Trespass to Chattels

a. Rule
D commits a trespass to P's chattel when he intentionally interferes with it, either by physical contact or by dispossession. R.2d § 217.

b. Possession
At one time, only the person then in possession (or entitled to immediate possession on demand) could maintain an action for trespass to a chattel. The modern view is that both the person in possession and one entitled to future possession may bring a trespass action. R.2d §§ 216, 21–220.

c. Intent
No wrongful motive is necessary. The intent required is merely to act upon the chattel. Thus, D's good faith, reasonable (but mistaken) belief that he owns the chattel or for some other reason is privileged to deal with it is no defense. And D need not know that his conduct is a violation of the possessory rights of another. R.2d §§ 217, 244.

d. Interference by Physical Contact
One form of trespass is interference by physical contact, which may be direct or indirect, and consists of any impairment of the chattel's condition, quality or value. R.2d §§ 218, 219.

e. Dispossession
A dispossession consists of taking a chattel from P's possession without his consent, or by fraud or duress, or into custody of the law; barring P's access to the chattel; or destroying it while it is in P's possession. R.2d § 221. Dispossession even for a short time is still a trespass.

f. Damages
In the case of *physical contact*, P must prove *actual damages*. Thus, if D merely handles the chattel or moves it or perhaps even uses it, without harming or affecting it or impairing its usefulness, he has committed no tort. But any *dispossession* is a trespass for which at

least nominal damages may be awarded. Given a trespass, the same broad damage rules apply as in the case of trespass to land, and D will be liable for all resulting damages to the chattel and to P, however innocently caused, including bodily harm.

3. Conversion

a. Rule

Conversion is an intentional exercise of dominion or control over a chattel which so seriously interferes with Ps right to control it that D may justly be required to pay P its full value. In other words, it is a trespass to the chattel which is so serious, aggravated, or of such magnitude as to justify forcing D to purchase it. R.2d § 222A.

b. Test

There is no simple test for determining when the interference is so aggravated as to constitute a conversion. The important factors are (R.2d § 222A):

1) the *extent* and *duration* of D's exercise of dominion or control;

2) D's *intent* to assert a right which is in fact inconsistent with P's right of control;

3) D's *good faith*;

4) the extent and duration of the resulting interference with P's right of control;

5) the *harm* done to the chattel; and

6) the *inconvenience* and *expense* caused to P.

In other words, it is a matter of degree, measured by the nature, extent and duration of the interference and D's motives and intentions.

c. Intent

While D's beliefs, motives and intentions may be relevant in assessing the seriousness of his interference, the only intent required for the tort is an intent to exercise dominion or control over the chattel. Thus, D's good faith or honest mistake is no defense if the interference is sufficiently great (e.g., destruction). R.2d §§ 224, 244.

Example: D1 steals P's hat from a hat rack. Five minutes later he is apprehended and the hat tendered back. D2, justifiably mistaken, takes P's hat, promptly discovers his error, and is about to replace it when the wind catches it and blows it down a sewer. D3, justifiably mistaken, takes P's hat, promptly discovers his error, and returns it unharmed 5 minutes later. D1 and D2 are subject to liability for conversion; D3 is not.

d. Ways in Which Conversion May Occur
A conversion may occur when D (1) acquires possession, (2) moves the chattel, (3) makes an unauthorized transfer, delivery, or disposal, (4) withholds possession, (5) destroys or materially alters the chattel, or (6) under certain circumstances, merely uses the chattel. See R.2d § 223.

e. Possession
Either the person in possession or the person entitled to immediate possession may maintain the action. R.2d §§ 224A, 225. And to the extent not recovered by one of the former, a person entitled to future possession may recover his loss. R.2d § 243.

f. Types of Chattels
Originally, conversion was available only with respect to tangible chattels. Today, most courts have extended it to include intangible personal property represented by, or merged into, a document. R.2d § 242; U.C.C. § 3419. It may even extend to intangibles represented by documents which do not embody the right but are merely important to its exercise (e.g., a bank deposit book).

g. Damages
Damages include the full value of the chattel at the time of conversion, plus interest. Under the prevailing view, P is never required to (but may) accept a tender of the chattel's return in mitigation of damages. Compare R.2d § 922.

4. **Trespass and Conversion Distinguished**
A conversion is merely a trespass to a chattel that is so serious that D can be forced to buy it. In such cases, P may choose either action, depending on whether or not he wants the chattel back and perhaps also on the preferred measure of damages. Thus, virtually all conversions are also trespasses, but minor trespasses are not conversions.

H. Review Questions

[Answers Provided in Appendix A, pages 391–92]

1. T or F   P is driving through a parking lot and almost hits D who in anger slams his fist on the hood of P's car. D is liable for battery.

2. T or F   D shoots an arrow in P's direction, 110 yards away. The bow and arrow have a maximum range of 100 yards, but P does not know that. P, who was facing the opposite direction when D shot, turns around just in time to see the arrow land 10 yards away. D is liable for assault.

3. T or F   D aims an apparently loaded gun at S, P's son, and threatens to shoot the son. P is standing a few feet away and believes that D is about to shoot S but figures that he can disarm D before D can shoot him (P). D is liable for assault to both S and P.

4. T or F   D locks P in his second floor dormitory room while P is sound asleep and stands outside the only door with the intent to confine P in the room until 6:00 p.m. At 5:50 P wakes up and pushes on the door. Feeling the pushing, D changes his mind and yanks open the door, and P falls forward breaking his wrist. D is liable for false imprisonment but not for battery.

5. T or F   D aims an apparently loaded gun at S, P's son, and threatens to shoot the son. The son knows the gun is a toy but P, standing a few feet away, believes the gun and threat are real. P suffers severe emotional distress as a result. P can recover from D for the intentional or reckless infliction of emotional distress.

6. Short essay: Discuss the difference between trespass to chattels and conversion. *conversion to a higher degree — might as well purchase it*

7. Multiple Choice: D builds a garage on what he and his neighbor both believe to be D's land. Later a resurvey of the land establishes that the garage extends 2 inches into P's land.

   a. D is not liable to P for trespass because he does not live in the garage and thus is not occupying P's land.

   b. D is not liable to P for trespass because the invasion of P's land is de minimus.

c. D is not liable to P for trespass because he had no intent to enter onto P's land.

d. D is liable to P for trespass because he built on P's property.

e. D is liable to P for trespass because he was negligent in not searching the title and surveying the land before building.

III. Defenses to Liability for Intentional Torts: Privileges

A. Privilege
(Dobbs §§ 68–69)

1. Introduction
"Privilege" is the general term applied to various defenses in which special circumstances justify conduct which would otherwise be tortious. In other words, even though P proves facts that establish prima facie the elements of some tort, D can prove other facts which establish some privilege that renders D's conduct nontortious. There are recognized privileges to many different torts; but the most important and commonly used ones apply to the intentional torts.

2. Other Defenses Distinguished
Privileges differ from other defenses such as contributory negligence and immunities which operate to reduce or bar P's recovery but do not negate the tortious character of D's conduct. Privileges do.

3. Types
Privileges may be divided into two general categories: (a) consent, and (b) privileges created by law irrespective of consent.

4. Burden of Proof
With one exception, privileges are affirmative defenses which must be pleaded and proved by D. In the case of the intentional torts against P's person (assault, battery, false imprisonment), absence of consent has been regarded as an element of the prima facie case, and therefore would not be a defense. However, it is doubtful that this distinction has much vitality any longer.

5. Mistake
As a general rule, D's mistaken belief that he has a privilege—however innocent or justified—is per se no defense to an intentional tort, nor does

it negate the requisite intent. However, mistake may be relevant in determining the existence of a privilege; certain privileges are based on D's reasonable belief concerning some fact(s), even though it later turns out that he was mistaken.

B. Consent

(Dobbs §§ 95–106; R.2d §§ 49–62, 167–175, 252–256, 892, 892D)

1. In General

Consent is a defense to virtually any tort, but it is applied most frequently to the intentional torts. In negligence and strict liability cases, a similar defense goes by the name "assumption of risk," but that defense is now largely fault-based and not consent-based.

2. Existence

There is consent when one is, in fact, willing for conduct to occur. It is a matter of Ps subjective state of mind. It is valid whether or not communicated to D. R.2d § 892.

3. Apparent Consent

P's words or conduct manifesting consent are sufficient to create a privilege to D to act in light of the apparent consent, even if P's actual (but undisclosed) state of mind was to the contrary. R.2d §§ 50, 892(2).

4. Conduct

Conduct (a nod, gesture, or movement) can manifest consent. Even silence and inaction may indicate consent, provided such conduct would ordinarily be so interpreted, as where a reasonable person would be expected to speak or move if he objected. R.2d § 892.

5. Custom, Prior Relationship

Consent may be inferred from custom and usage, from prior dealings between the parties, or from the existence between them of some relationship.

6. Capacity to Consent

The consent must be given by one having the capacity to do so, or one authorized to consent for him. Infancy, intoxication, or mental incapacity normally will vitiate effective consent. R.2d § 892A. In addition, some statutes render any purported consent ineffective—for example, consent by a patient to sexual contact with his or her mental health professional.

7. Implied Consent

When an emergency actually or apparently threatens death or serious bodily harm and there is no time or opportunity to obtain consent, consent will be implied. R.2d § 892D. Some courts will construe a surgical consent broadly to include closely related conditions discovered during surgery while the patient is anesthetized and no one with authority to consent for him is immediately available.

8. Scope of Consent

The consent is to D's *conduct*, and once given, P cannot complain of the consequences of that conduct, however unforeseen. But D's privilege is limited to the conduct consented to or acts substantially similar. The consent may be conditioned or limited as to time, place, duration, area, and extent. R.2d § 892A.

9. Mistake, Ignorance, Misrepresentation

Even though given pursuant to P's material mistake, misunderstanding or ignorance as to the nature or character of D's proposed conduct or the extent of the harm to be expected from it, P's consent is effective as manifested unless D knows of the mistake or induced it by his misrepresentation. R.2d § 892B. If the misrepresentation goes to the essential nature or character of the act, the consent is invalid. For example, P's consent to sexual contact based on the misrepresentation that it is medical treatment is invalid. But consent to such contact is not invalid if it was obtained by collateral fraud. Thus, P's consent is valid even though fraudulently induced by D's false representation that he is a wealthy lawyer who will take P on a European vacation.

10. Informed Consent

Under the doctrine of informed consent, if D (e.g., a physician) misrepresents or fails to disclose to P the *possible consequences* or *risks* of D's proposed conduct (e.g., a medical procedure), P's consent is not an *informed* one and therefore is not valid. Under the prevailing view, such risks or possible consequences are deemed *collateral*, and therefore failing to properly disclose them is a matter of negligence only. The failure to disclose does not vitiate the consent and thus there is no battery.

11. Duress

Consent given under duress is not effective. Duress includes threats of *immediate* harm directed against P, his family or valuable property, but usually not threats of *future* harm or of economic duress. R.2d § 892B.

12. Consent to Crime

Under the majority view, the consent is *not* effective if the conduct consented to is a crime, at least in battery cases. For example, two persons who consent to an illegal boxing match could each sue the other for battery. The minority view (and R.2d §§ 60, 61, 892C) is that consent to criminal conduct is valid *unless* in violation of a statute making conduct criminal to protect a class of persons irrespective of their consent (e.g., statutory rape).

C. Self–Defense and Defense of Others

(Dobbs §§ 70–75; R.2d §§ 63–76, 156, 261)

1. Self–Defense

a. Rule

D has a privilege to use so much force as reasonably appears to be immediately necessary to protect himself against imminent physical harm threatened by the intentional or negligent conduct of another. R.2d §§ 63, 65, 66–68, 7075.

b. Threatened Harm

Self-defense is normally invoked against an assault. However, it may also be privileged as to false imprisonment (including false arrest), the threat of negligently-caused harm (R.2d §§ 66, 68) and trespass or conversion (R.2d § 261).

c. Excessive Force

1) Privilege Limited to Defensive Force

D may use only so much force as reasonably appears to be necessary for his defense. If he becomes the aggressor, or continues to use force after P has become subdued, disarmed, or helpless or has clearly withdrawn from the fray, D is subject to liability for harm to the extent that it results from the excessive force. R.2d §§ 70, 71.

2) Deadly Force

D may use force likely to inflict death or serious bodily harm only when (a) he reasonably believes that he is in danger of similar harm, and (b) he is not required to retreat or escape. R.2d § 65.

3) Duty to Retreat

Some jurisdictions never require D to retreat. Others (and R.2d § 65) hold that D is not privileged to use deadly force if there is a safe and expedient means of retreat or escape. However, retreat is never required in one's dwelling.

4) Negligently–Created Threats

The foregoing rules apply if the threatened harm is battery or false imprisonment. If the threat arises from conduct which is merely negligent, D may use deadly force only if he reasonably believes that is the only way to prevent his own death or serious bodily harm. R.2d §§ 64, 66.

d. Form of Defensive Conduct

D's self-defensive conduct may take the form of an assault, battery, or false imprisonment, as appropriate to the situation. R.2d § 67.

e. Effect of D's Mistake

The privilege exists even when D reasonably but mistakenly believes that self-defense is necessary. The reasonableness of D's belief is judged by the objective standard of the reasonable person of average courage. Relevant factors include the circumstances of the event and the past history of the relationship, if any, between the parties. R.2d § 63.

f. Injuries to Third Persons

In the course of defending himself against the conduct of A, D injures P. If the injury to P was:

1) Unintentional, then ordinary negligence rules apply and D is liable or not depending on the reasonableness of D's conduct under the circumstances. R.2d § 75.

2) Intentional, then D is subject to liability to P for compensatory damages, unless the harm to P was relatively minor and substantially less than that with which D was threatened. R.2d §§ 73, 74.

2. Defense of Third Persons

a. Rule

D is privileged to come to the defense of any other person under the same conditions and by the same means as he would be privileged to defend himself. R.2d § 76.

b. **Effect of Mistake**

Under the majority view, D's privilege exists only if and to the extent that the third person in fact had a right of self-defense. If D is wrong, his mistake, however reasonable, is irrelevant. Under the minority view (and R.2d § 76), D's reasonable mistake does not negate the privilege.

3. **Duty to Protect**

If D is under a duty to protect another or his land or chattels, he is privileged to use reasonable force or confinement to do so. R.2d § 156.

Example: A railroad is under a duty to protect its passengers from harm by drunken ruffians on board its train, and therefore may use reasonable force to do so.

D. **Defense and Recovery of Property**

(Dobbs §§ 76–81; R.2d §§ 77–111, 260)

1. **Defense of Property**

a. **Rule**

A possessor is privileged to use reasonable force to expel another or a chattel from his land, or to prevent another's imminent intrusion upon or interference with his land or chattels, or to prevent his dispossession, even though such conduct would otherwise be an assault, battery, false imprisonment, or trespass to the chattel. R.2d §§ 77, 80, 87, 260.

b. **Request**

The possessor must first request that the intruder desist, unless it appears that the request would be useless or cannot be made before substantial harm is done. R.2d § 77.

c. **Amount of Force**

D may then use force or the threat of force, but only such actual force as is minimally required to prevent or terminate the intrusion. Force likely to cause death or great bodily harm is not privileged. Of course, the intruder is not privileged to resist, and if he does the possessor's privilege of self-defense applies, under which deadly force could be justified. R.2d §§ 77, 79, 81, 82.

d. **Watchdogs, Spring Guns**

Spring guns, concealed traps, and other mechanical devices, and vicious animals, used to defend D's property are used at D's risk. D is subject to liability for harm caused an intruder by them which he would not have been privileged to inflict himself if present. R.2d §§ 84, 85.

e. **Privileges to Intrude**
There are a number of rules which govern privileges to enter upon land and to invade interests in chattels. Such rules are normally beyond the scope of law school and bar examinations. See R.2d §§ 167–215, 252–278.

f. **Effect of Mistake**
If the intruder in fact has one of these privileges, D has no privilege to defend his property, even though D through ignorance or mistake reasonably believes that the intruder has no privilege, unless the intruder himself was responsible for that mistake. Conversely, the intruder's mistake does not defeat D's privilege unless the mistake was caused by D's fault. R.2d §§ 77, 78.

g. **Property of Others**
There is a similar privilege to defend the property of others, at least if the third person is a member of D's immediate family or household or is one whose possession D has a duty to protect. R.2d § 86.

2. **Forcible Retaking of Chattels**

a. **Rule**
There is a limited self-help privilege to use force or threats of force to recapture D's chattel, wrongfully and forcibly taken from D's possession, even under claim of right, or obtained by fraud or duress. R.2d § 100.

b. **Fresh Pursuit**
D must begin his recapture efforts promptly after his dispossession, or immediately upon learning of it, and continue them without interruption. R.2d § 103.

c. **Demand**
Unless it would be futile, D must first demand his chattel's return. R.2d § 104.

d. **Force**
Only reasonable force (short of that likely to cause serious bodily harm) may be used. R.2d §§ 106, 107.

e. Effect of Mistake
Same as above (§ D.1.f.). R.2d § 101.

f. Chattel Rightfully Acquired
If the chattel was rightfully acquired but is merely being tortiously withheld from D, this privilege does not exist. R.2d § 108.

g. Entry Upon Land
Under certain circumstances, there is a privilege to enter upon another's land in pursuit of the chattel. R.2d §§ 198, 200.

3. Possession of Land

a. Peaceful Repossession
D, who is entitled to the immediate possession of land, may, if he can, peacefully enter and retake possession without liability for trespass, and thereafter defend his possession as outlined in part 1. above. R.2d §§ 97, 185.

b. Forcible Repossession
In most jurisdictions, the rules for forcibly reacquiring possession of land are set forth in "forcible entry and detainer" statutes. In the absence of such a statute, see R.2d §§ 88–99.

E. Necessity
(Dobbs §§ 107–109; R.2d §§ 19–197, 262–263)

1. Rule
The privilege of necessity may be invoked when D, in the course of defending himself or his property (or others or their property) from some threat of imminent serious harm for which P is not responsible, intentionally does some act reasonably deemed necessary toward that end, which results in injury to P's property and which would otherwise be a trespass or conversion.

2. Public Necessity
If the danger affects an entire community, or so many persons that the public interest is involved, the privilege is complete and D's tort liability is entirely excused. This is the case whether D is a public official or a private citizen. R.2d §§ 196, 262.

Example: D intentionally dynamites P's house to stop the spread of a fire which threatens a substantial part of the town. P's house and all of its contents are destroyed. D is not subject to liability to P.

3. Private Necessity

If the danger threatens only harm to D or his property (or to a third person or his property), D is privileged to commit the act which causes the trespass or conversion, but he is subject to liability for compensatory damages for any resulting *actual physical harm.* R.2d §§ 197, 263.

> *Example:* D intentionally keeps his boat moored to P's dock during a storm to save the boat. The dock is extensively damaged. D is privileged to moor his boat (i.e., P may not resist or refuse), but D is subject to liability to P for the resulting damage.

4. Scope of Privilege

D's reasonable belief that his act is necessary is sufficient; but his conduct must be reasonable considering the extent of the threatened harm in relation to the foreseeable damage to P's property.

F. Authority of Law

(Dobbs §§ 82–87; R.2d §§ 112–145, 20–215, 265–266, 273, 278)

1. Rule

One acting under authority of law is privileged, under certain circumstances, to commit acts which would otherwise constitute an assault, battery, false imprisonment, trespass, or conversion. The scope of the privilege varies according to the type of authority being exercised and other factors.

2. Scope: Ministerial vs. Discretionary Acts

In general, if D must exercise significant judgment or discretion in determining whether or how to act (e.g., to seek an indictment or close a public street), the act is privileged if done in good faith. Ministerial acts are not privileged if done improperly, regardless of D's good faith.

3. Scope: Jurisdiction

Acts done without jurisdiction are not privileged. But acts merely "in excess of" D's jurisdiction (i.e., within the general subject matter of his power but outside his authority of the particular facts) are privileged if done in good faith.

4. Types of Acts

The most common types of such acts are arrest and prevention of a crime (R.2d §§ 112–144, 20–207), execution of civil process, writs, or court orders (R.2d §§ 145, 208–210, 266), and acts required or authorized by legislation (R.2d §§ 211, 265, 273). In addition, the constitution and certain public accommodations laws require that persons cannot be denied access to certain designated areas open to the public based solely on race, gender, speech content, etc.

5. Use of Force

Whether D is privileged to break and enter an enclosure or building, or to use force against P's person, and the amount of such force permitted, depend upon the source and nature of the privilege being exercised. See R.2d §§ 212, 213.

6. Trespass *ab Initio*

At common law, if D lawfully and properly proceeded to act under authority of law, but at some point acted unlawfully and committed a tort, D's abuse of his authority "related back" and he was deemed a wrongdoer, without privilege, from the very beginning—*ab initio*. This doctrine is now generally repudiated. See R.2d §§ 136, 214(2), 278(2).

G. Discipline

(Dobbs §§ 93–94; R.2d §§ 14–155)

1. Children

a. Parents

A parent is privileged to apply such reasonable force or to impose such reasonable confinement upon his child as he reasonably believes to be necessary for the child's proper control, training, or education. R.2d § 147.

b. Loco parentis

The privilege extends to persons (e.g. school officials) having responsibility for the custody, control, training or education of the child, except so far as the parent has restricted their authority to do so. Public officials (including public schools) are not bound by the parent's restrictions so far as the child's education and training are concerned. R.2d §§ 147, 152, 153, 154.

c. Reasonableness

The reasonableness of the force or confinement depends upon:

1) whether D is a parent;

2) the age, sex, physical and mental condition of the child;

3) the nature of the offense and the child's apparent motive;

4) the influence of the child's example;

5) its necessity and appropriateness to compel obedience to a proper command; and

6) whether disproportionate to the offense, unnecessarily degrading, or likely to cause serious or permanent harm. R.2d § 150.

d. Purpose
It must be administered in good faith, for proper purpose, and without malice. R.2d § 151.

2. Military
Military superiors are privileged to use force, confinement or threats thereof to enforce orders and commands, provided they are (a) lawful or (b) believed by D to be lawful and not obviously unlawful. R.2d § 146. This privilege is now largely governed and administered by military law.

3. Ship Captain
The master of a ship may exercise reasonable discipline over his crew and passengers.

H. Review Questions
[Answers Provided in Appendix A, pages 392–394]

1. (T) or F Traveler is en route to a business meeting when he comes upon a detour that would take him miles out of his way. He can see that the road construction necessitating the detour doesn't continue very far and decides to drive onto adjacent land to avoid the barricade. Owner sees Traveler drive upon his land. Owner has the right to stop Traveler and demand that he leave the way he came.

2. (T) or F Owner shouts to Traveler and tells him to leave. Traveler continues to drive across Owner's land. Owner's shooting out Traveler's tires to stop him is impermissible.

3. T or (F) While stopped at the detour, Traveler observes Owner whipping a small child. Traveler believes that Owner is putting the child in danger and, therefore, goes onto Owner's land to stop Owner. Owner can successfully sue Traveler for trespass, assault and battery.

4. (T) or F   Owner sees Traveler stopped at the detour sign. He gestures, intending to show Traveler the route he should take. Traveler reasonably believes that Owner is gesturing his consent for Traveler to cross his property to reach the road beyond the construction. Traveler waves his thanks and enters Owner's property. Owner sues Traveler for trespass, and Traveler defends by arguing that Owner consented to his actions. Traveler will be successful.

5. (T or F)   Owner gestures to allow Traveler to enter upon his land a short distance to reach the road beyond the construction. Traveler shifts into four wheel drive and tears up Owner's hillside en route to the highway. Owner may successfully sue for trespass.

6. (T) or F   Owner sees Traveler about to enter his land and moves his tractor to block Traveler's progress. Traveler pulls a gun from his back seat and aims it at Owner. Owner moves the tractor out of Traveler's way, then sues for trespass. Traveler's defense that Owner consented to his conduct will not be successful.

7. (T) or F   Doctor tells Patient she must undergo risky surgery or she will die. Patient consents to surgery, which results in her permanent disability. Patient then discovers that surgery was not necessary. Patient's battery action against Doctor will be successful.

8. (T) or F   In a suit for battery (arising out of a boxing match) D defends on the ground that plaintiff consented to the battery. D must plead and prove that P consented.

9.   Short essay: Officer and Girlfriend were leaving a bar. Hood drapes himself across the doorway barring their exit. Officer asks Hood to move, but Hood refuses and insults Officer, making threatening gestures. Officer responds physically, knocking Hood to the floor and breaking his nose and jaw. Discuss whether Officer's conduct was privileged.

10.   Short essay: Hood comes up fighting mad, and charges Officer frothing at the mouth. Officer grabs Girlfriend and shoves her into Hood's path to slow him down. Girlfriend does her best, but is injured in the process. Hood ricochets off Girlfriend and crumples on top of Bystander. Discuss Officer's liability to Girlfriend and Bystander.

11. Short essay: Welch buys a car from Fast Eddie, the sleazy used car salesman, and agrees to make timely payments. Shortly thereafter, Welch discovers Eddie in the process of hotwiring his newly purchased car. Welch shoves Eddie aside, beats him severely, and ties him to a fence post, while he calls the police. Fast Eddie tells the police that Welch had failed to make two payments, so he was entitled to retake the car. In the resulting lawsuit, what result?

PART THREE

Negligence

■ ANALYSIS

IV. **Negligence Liability Rules**
    A.   The Elements of the Negligence Cause of Action
    B.   Characteristics of Negligent Conduct
        1.   Definition
        2.   Objective Test
        3.   Care Required
        4.   Attributes of the Reasonable Person
            a.   Knowledge, Experience and Perception
            b.   Knowledge Common to Community
            c.   Activities Requiring Skill
            d.   Physicians
            e.   Physical Characteristics
            f.   Mental Capacity
            g.   Minors
            h.   Is a Minor Too Young to be Negligent?
        5.   Conduct in Emergencies
        6.   Sudden Incapacity
        7.   Anticipating Conduct of Others
        8.   Failure to Warn or Instruct
        9.   Other Types of Negligent Conduct
       10.   When Is a Risk "Unreasonable"?

7. P's Negligent Failure to Exercise Control
   a. In General
   b. Parent
B. Last Clear Chance
   1. Discussion
   2. Operative Variables
      a. Helpless Plaintiff
      b. Inattentive Plaintiff
      c. Observant Defendant
      d. Inattentive Defendant
   3. Rules
      a. Helpless Plaintiff vs. Observant Defendant
      b. Helpless Plaintiff vs. Inattentive Defendant; Inattentive Plaintiff vs. Observant Defendant
      c. Inattentive Plaintiff vs. Inattentive Defendant
      d. Doctrine Rejected
   4. Limited to Subsequent Negligence
   5. Effect of Comparative Negligence
C. Assumption of Risk
   1. Rule
   2. Discussion
   3. Meanings of Term
      a. Express Assumption of Risk (Release)
      b. Inherent Hazards Not Arising From Negligence
      c. Risk of Future Negligence
      d. Assumption of Existing Negligently–Created Risk
   4. Contributory Negligence Distinguished
   5. Express Assumption of Risk
      a. Rule
      b. Construction
      c. Public Policy
   6. Implied Assumption of Risk
      a. Rule
      b. Elements: Manifestation of Consent
      c. Elements: Knowledge and Appreciation of Risk
      d. Elements: Voluntariness
         1) Reluctance
         2) Economic Duress
         3) Public Policy

IV. Negligence Liability Rules

A. The Elements of the Negligence Cause of Action
(Dobbs §§ 110–115)

"Negligence" is both (1) the name of a tort *cause of action*, and (2) the term given to *conduct* which falls below the standard which the law requires. The elements of a *negligence* cause of action (prima facie case) are:

(1) A *duty* by D to act or refrain from acting;

(2) A *breach* of that duty by D's failure to conform his conduct to the required standard (i.e., "negligence");

(3) A sufficient *causal connection* between the negligent conduct and P's injury (i.e., *cause in fact* or *actual cause*); and

(4) *Actual* (provable) *harm*—i.e., harm which the law says is measurable and compensable in money damages.

Cf. R.2d § 281; R.3d PH § 6.

It is sometimes said that there is a fifth element—the harm must be within the *scope of liability* as defined by the rules traditionally referred to as "proximate cause" rules. See R.3d PH § 6, comment b, R.3d PH ch. 6. Strictly speaking, this is not an element of the negligence cause of action but a liability limitation that cuts off recovery, similar to a duty limitation, even when the four traditional elements are established. In some cases, the court determines the scope of D's liability as a matter of law. But in some cases, the jury determines whether D's negligence was a "proximate cause" of P's harm.

B. Characteristics of Negligent Conduct
(Dobbs §§ 116–131; R.2d §§ 281–284, 289–309) .

1. Definition
"Negligence" is *conduct* which falls below the standard established by law for the protection of others against unreasonable risks of harm. R.2d § 282. A person is negligent when his or her conduct, given all the circumstances, is determined to fall short of *reasonable care*. R.3d PH § 3.

2. Objective Test
Since negligence is conduct which fails to conform to the legal standard, the test for negligence is objective—not whether D intended to exercise

due care, nor whether D did the best he could to be careful (subjective), but whether D's conduct was that of a hypothetical "reasonably prudent (or careful) person" placed in the same or similar circumstances. R.2d §§ 283, 297.

3. Care Required

The standard is "reasonable care" (sometimes called "ordinary care" or "due care") under the circumstances. The law does not require D to be perfect, but only to behave as a reasonably prudent person would behave. And he need only protect others against unreasonable risks of harm. R.2d § 298.

4. Attributes of the Reasonable Person

a. Knowledge, Experience and Perception

In judging D's conduct, D will be charged with what he actually knew and observed, and also with those things which a reasonable person would have known and perceived. R.2d §§ 289, 290. And if D has superior intelligence, memory perception, knowledge, or judgment, he will be held to that standard. R.3d PH § 12. But if D is deficient in any of these attributes, that is too bad; he is still held to the standard of the reasonable (i.e. normal) person. Moreover, he must be mindful of his own ignorance and act accordingly.

b. Knowledge Common to Community

The reasonable person knows those things which at that time are common knowledge in the community; e.g., commonly known qualities and habits of human beings and animals, and qualities, characteristics and capacities of things. R.2d § 290.

c. Activities Requiring Skill

If D chooses to engage in an activity requiring learned skills or certain knowledge, his conduct is measured against the hypothetical person who is reasonably skilled and knowledgeable in that activity. Beginners are held to the same standard.

Examples: One who drives a car is required to know and apply the laws and techniques necessary to do so with reasonable safety. One who undertakes to render services in the practice of a particular trade or profession (whether D is actually licensed or otherwise certified or not) must exercise the skill and apply the knowledge which a reasonably well-qualified and experienced member of that profession or trade would in similar circumstances. And one who undertakes to manufacture a product is deemed to have and must apply the knowledge and skill which a reasonably prudent manufacturer of that product would have and apply. See R.2d §§ 299, 299A, 300.

d. Physicians

In most jurisdictions, the standard of care of medical doctors (and sometimes other professionals) is conclusively established by the customary practice of reasonably well-qualified practitioners in that field. Thus, the standard differs from that applied to other persons, where the customary practice in a particular trade, business, or other activity is merely evidence of the standard of care but not conclusive, and the jury is free to set a standard higher than that evidenced by the customary conduct.

Physicians or others who are certified specialists, or who hold themselves out as specialists, are held to the standards of that specialty, but again, in most cases the customary conduct of reasonably well-qualified specialists conclusively sets the standard of care.

See section XIII. MEDICAL AND OTHER PROFESSIONAL NEGLIGENCE, infra.

e. Physical Characteristics

The "reasonable person" standard is subjective to the extent that if D has a physical deficiency or disability, his conduct is measured against that of a reasonably prudent person with his physical characteristics. R.3d PH § 11(a).

Example: D is blind. His conduct will be judged against that of a reasonably prudent blind person in the same or similar circumstances.

Similarly, a person with exceptional strength, agility, or other physical prowess is held to the standard of a reasonably prudent person with such exceptional physical abilities.

f.   Mental Capacity

The prevailing rule is that, in judging D's conduct, no allowance is made for deficiencies in D's mental capacity to conform to the "reasonable person" standard of care. The fact that D is mentally deficient (in intelligence, judgment, memory, emotional stability, etc.), voluntarily intoxicated, or even insane or mentally disabled does not matter. His conduct is measured against the reasonably prudent sane, sober, and normal person. R.2d §§ 283B, 897J; R.3d PH § 11(c). A few courts apply a subjective standard to insane or mentally disabled persons.

g.   Minors

Minors are an exception. If D is a minor, the test is what is reasonable conduct for a child of D's age, intelligence and experience under the circumstances. R.2d § 283A; R.3d PH §§ 10, 11(c). But this exception does not apply to minors engaging in "adult" or dangerous activities requiring special skills and training, such as driving a car, flying an airplane, operating a snowmobile or a motorboat, and the like. In those cases, the minor is held to the adult, objective standard of care.

h.   Is a Minor Too Young to be Negligent?

Below a certain age, a young child is incapable of negligence because he or she lacks the mental maturity and experience to assess and respond to risks. In some jurisdictions, the trier of fact determines whether a particular child is capable of negligence. In others, children under the age of seven are incapable of negligence as a matter of law; children between seven and fourteen are presumed incapable but the presumption is rebuttable; and minors over the age of fourteen are presumed capable.

5.   Conduct in Emergencies

The fact that D is confronted with a sudden emergency that requires rapid decision is a factor that may be taken into account in determining the reasonableness of his choice of action. R.2d § 296; R.3d PH § 9. However, D may have been negligent in (a) failing to anticipate the emergency or (b) creating the emergency; as to such negligence, the foregoing rule would not be applicable. The emergency does not change the standard of care, and therefore no special jury instruction on conduct in an emergency is required.

6. Sudden Incapacity

The conduct of D during a period of sudden incapacitation or loss of consciousness resulting from physical illness is negligent only if D ought to have foreseen such an incapacity and was negligent in failing to take reasonable precautions to prevent its occurrence. R.3d § PH 11(b).

7. Anticipating Conduct of Others

The reasonable person will regulate his conduct in light of what he can anticipate, expect or foresee others will do. R.2d §§ 302A, 302B, 303. Thus, in particular circumstances he can expect negligent, or even criminal, conduct by others, or that his conduct will likely trigger conduct by another that will subject someone to an unreasonable risk of harm.

8. Failure to Warn or Instruct

One of the most important types of negligence is a failure to warn or instruct another so that he can take proper precautions for his own safety. R.2d § 301. Conversely, D's exercise of reasonable care to give others an adequate warning of a danger does not necessarily prevent D's conduct (the subject of the warning) from being negligent. Generally, if there is an unreasonable risk of harm inherent in D's conduct, D must reduce that risk so far as reasonably possible; only then will an adequate warning of the remaining risk constitute "reasonable care."

Example: D manufactures a cleaner with explosive ingredients, even though an equally effective and inexpensive cleaner could have been made without using such ingredients. A warning label, "Highly Flammable" would not necessarily prevent D's conduct in manufacturing and selling the cleaner from being found to be negligent.

9. Other Types of Negligent Conduct

Illustrations of types of negligent conduct are virtually limitless. Indeed, rather than try to catalog them, it may be more useful to conclude that, subject to duty and proximate cause limitations, any conduct may be negligent under the circumstances. Negligence may consist of an act or a failure to act (R.2d § 284), lack of competence (§§ 299, 299A), or lack of preparation (§ 300). A misrepresentation may be negligent conduct. R.2d § 304. It may be negligence to prevent protective action by another (R.2d § 305); to use an incompetent, defective or inappropriate instrumentality (R.2d § 307); or to permit another to use a thing or engage in an activity under D's control so as to subject another to an unreasonable risk of harm (R.2d § 308).

10. When Is a Risk "Unreasonable"?

Under the classic formulation, a risk is unreasonable when the *foreseeable* probability and gravity of the harm outweigh the burden to D of alternative conduct which would have prevented the harm. Compare R.2d § 291; R.3d PH § 3. This is sometimes referred to as the "Hand" test (see *United States v. Carroll Towing Co.* (2d Cir. 1947), L. Hand, J.) or the "risk-utility" test.

a. **Magnitude of Risk**

The foreseeable probability or likelihood that the harm will result, in conjunction with the gravity or seriousness of the potential harm, are placed on one side of the scale. The gravity of the harm includes both the extent of the damage and the relative societal value of the protected interest—e.g., people are more valuable than property. See R.2d § 293.

b. **Burden of Alternative Conduct**

The burden of reducing or eliminating the risk by alternative conduct is placed on the other side of the scale. Factors relevant in assessing this cost include:

(1) the importance or social value of the activity or goal of which D's conduct is a part;

(2) the utility of the conduct as a means to that end;

(3) the feasibility of alternative, safer conduct;

(4) the relative cost of safer conduct;

(5) the relative utility of safer conduct;

(6) the relative safety of alternative conduct.

See R.2d § 292.

11. Judge and Jury

Whether conduct was or was not negligent is a question of fact for the trier of fact. R.2d §§ 328B, 328C; R.3d PH § 8. In most cases, a jury is given only a short general definition of negligence and the reasonable person test, leaving it to the jury to apply its common experience to the evidence. R.2d § 285.

However, sometimes the decision is for the trial court. The judge may enter summary judgment, direct a verdict, or otherwise take the case out of the jury's hands because the court decides that the conduct in question so clearly was or was not negligent that no reasonable person could reach any other conclusion. The trial court's decision to take (or not to take) such action is reviewable as an issue of law.

C. Sources of Standards of Care
(Dobbs §§ 133–142; R.2d §§ 285–288C)

1. Rules of Law
Appellate courts, reviewing fact situations and deciding that there was or was not sufficient evidence of negligence, often state that given conduct is or is not negligent. Such statements may be either:

*a.   Guidelines for the review of jury determinations of an issue of **fact**; or*

b.   Fixed rules of law that given conduct is or is not negligent as a matter of law.

Some such rules of law may be desirable and lend stability to the law, so long as they are not immutable and admit exceptions. But in general, experience has shown that better results are achieved if negligence is treated as a question of fact for the jury, and such "rules" are merely regarded as guidelines for the courts in determining that certain conduct in certain recurring situations so clearly is (or is not) negligent that the question may be taken from the jury. See R.2d § 285.

Example: *Baltimore & Ohio Ry. Co. v. Goodman* (U.S. 1927) (Holmes, J.) attempted to lay down a fixed standard requiring motorists approaching a railroad crossing to stop, look, listen, and if necessary leave the vehicle to determine if a train was approaching. This rule proved unjust and unworkable and had to be overruled in *Pokora v. Wabash Ry. Co.* (U.S. 1934) (Cardozo, J.)

2. Legislation

a.   In General (R.3d PH § 14)
Legislation (federal and state statutes, municipal ordinances, administrative regulations) often prescribe standards of conduct for the protection of others from harm. For tort law purposes, two types may be distinguished:

(1) legislation which (a) expressly or (b) by necessary implication creates a civil remedy for damages for violation (e.g., F.E.L.A., F.S.A.A.); and

(2) legislation which does not (limited to criminal penalties or fines).

*Courts routinely use legislation of the second type in negligence cases as evidence of, or as establishing, the **standard of care** which D was required to meet, provided the court finds the appropriate **legislative purpose**.*

b. **Legislative Purpose**

Legislation is relevant on the standard of care in a negligence case only if the statute was intended, at least in part, to protect a class of persons which includes P against the particular hazard and kind of harm which resulted. R.2d §§ 286, 288; R.3d PH § 14.

> *Example:* A statute requiring separate pens for animals transported by ship, intended to prevent the spread of disease, was not admissible in action where P's sheep were washed overboard at sea, even though the required pens (which were not provided) would have prevented the loss.

> *Caveat:* Legislative purpose may be broadly construed where the purpose is human safety. E.g., *De Haen v. Rockwood Sprinkler Co.* (N.Y. 1932) (statute requiring fence around open elevator shaft).

c. **Licensing Statutes**

Most courts hold that violation of a statute requiring a license to engage in a particular trade, profession or activity (e.g., physician, physical therapist, auto driver) is not negligence *per se* and therefore the fact that D did not have a valid license is not admissible to show that D was negligent on a particular occasion.

d. **Effect of Violation**

1) **Majority Rule**

*Most courts hold that violation of a relevant statute is **prima facie negligence** or **negligence per se**. This means that if no evidence is introduced by D to excuse the violation, D's negligence is **conclusively established**. R.2d § 288B.*

2) **Minority View**

*In some jurisdictions, violation is merely **evidence** of negligence, which the jury can consider along with all other evidence in determining whether D was negligent. The violation does not **per se** establish negligence.*

3) **Cause**

A violation does not *per se* establish a sufficient causal relation between the violation and P's injury. Proximate cause rules still apply, but some cases have adopted proximate cause rules more favorable to P.

4) **Children**

A minor's violation of a statute does not constitute negligence *per se*, but may be introduced as evidence of the minor's negligence.

5) **Defenses**

Contributory negligence and assumption of risk defenses apply (if and to the extent otherwise available).

Exception: Statutes intended to protect a class of persons against their own inability to protect themselves (e.g., child labor law, factor safety laws, school bus operation laws).

e. **Excused Violations (R.3d PH § 15)**

1) **Certain Safety Statutes**

A few statutes having a strong safety purpose (e.g., F.S.A.A., child labor laws, some factory and construction safety acts, pure food acts, some motor vehicle equipment and maintenance laws) permit no excused violations.

2) **Other Statutes**

As to most other statutes, courts will permit excuses for violations to be shown to rebut the per se or prima facie negligence. These include (a) physical circumstances beyond D's control; (b) innocent ignorance of facts which make the statute applicable; (c) sudden emergencies not of D's making; (d) situations in which it would be more dangerous to comply with the statute than to violate it; (e) violations that are reasonable in light of D's childhood, physical disability, or physical incapacity; and (f) D used reasonable care in attempting to comply with the statute. See R.2d § 288A; R.3d PH § 15. Of course, in jurisdictions where the statute is merely evidence of negligence, any proof tending to excuse or make reasonable the violation would be relevant.

f. Compliance With Statute

D may ordinarily show compliance with a statute as evidence of his reasonable care, but such compliance is not conclusive since a reasonable person might have taken precautions greater than the statutory minimum. R.2d § 288C.

D. Proof of Negligence
(Dobbs §§ 148–165; R.2d §§ 328A–328D)

1. Burden of Proof

a. Elements

P must introduce sufficient evidence to tip the scales of probability in his favor with respect to each element of his cause of action—duty, negligence, cause-in-fact, and damages. R.2d § 328A. Whether a duty exists is usually determined by the court, but in making that determination the court may have to resolve disputed fact issues. In order for P to recover, the trier of fact must find negligence, causation, and damages by a preponderance of the evidence—in other words, the factual basis of each essential element of P's claim must be found to be more probably true than not true.

b. Defenses

Any applicable defenses, such as P's contributory negligence, are affirmative defenses to be pleaded and proved by D by the same standard of proof, more probably true than not true.

c. Circumstantial Evidence

Any fact may be proved by circumstantial evidence (facts that support an inference of the fact sought to be proved) as well as by direct evidence (e.g., eyewitness testimony).

d. Role of Judge and Jury

It is the jury's task to determine, based on the evidence, whether P has proved each element of his or her cause of action by a preponderance of the evidence. But if the evidence on any essential element is so weak that no reasonable person could find that element established, the judge will decide the case and enter judgment for D.

2. Presumptions

Each jurisdiction's tort law has its own set of legal presumptions, which are codified rules of circumstantial evidence.

3. Experts and Opinion Evidence

a. Expert Witnesses

In a large number of tort cases, expert testimony is necessary or desirable to furnish the jury facts beyond its common knowledge. Expert testimony is usually required to establish the standard of care in professional negligence cases.

b. Opinions

Expert witnesses are permitted to testify to opinions or conclusions when they will be helpful to the jury. This even extends to opinions on an "ultimate issue"—i.e., an element of P's prima facie case (e.g., that the product was "unreasonably dangerous," causal relation). See Fed. Rules of Evid. 702–704.

4. Res Ipsa Loquitur

Like presumptions, *res ipsa loquitur* ("the thing speaks for itself") is basically a rule of circumstantial evidence.

a. Rule

If P can establish a prima facie res ipsa loquitur case, he need not prove by direct or other evidence the specific conduct of D which was negligent. If P makes a prima facie showing that:

(1) his injury was caused by an instrumentality or condition which was under D's exclusive management or control at the relevant time(s);

(2) in the ordinary course of events, P's harm would not have occurred unless D was then and there negligent;

then the jury is instructed on res ipsa loquitur and may infer that D was negligent and that D's negligence was the cause of P's injury without any more specific proof of what really happened. See R.2d § 328D.

b. **Control by D**

Although courts formerly required that D be in "exclusive" control of the instrumentality, it is now regarded as sufficient if D had the right to control and the opportunity to exercise it at the relevant time. In addition, D need not have been in control of the injury-causing instrumentality at the time of P's injury. P need only establish that D's negligence, if any, must have occurred while the instrumentality was in D's control. Thus, D's control need only be "exclusive" in the sense that the negligence must have occurred, if at all, when D was in control or responsible for the instrumentality.

c. **Multiple Defendants**

The control requirement ordinarily precludes use of RIL against multiple defendants, because if more than one D could have been the responsible cause of P's injury, the inference of negligence does not point to the culpable D. However in a few cases (e.g., *Ybarra v. Spangard* (Cal. 1944)), the courts have applied a variation of the doctrine and shifted the burden of proof, requiring each D to prove that he was not the one who was negligent. In that case, all the defendants who failed to prove they were not negligent were held jointly and severally liable.

If there are multiple defendants but their relationship was such that they were jointly responsible for the instrumentality at the relevant time, or one would be vicariously liable for the conduct of the other, then the doctrine may be applied.

d. **Inference of Negligence**

P need not show that D's negligence is the only possible explanation for the injury-causing occurrence, but only that the inference that it was D's negligence outweighs the sum of the other possible causes.

e. **P's Conduct**

At one time there was a third element. P was required to prove that his injury was not due to any "voluntary act" by P, or that P's own conduct was not a significant causative factor, or, most recently, that P was not contributorily negligent. However, with the adoption of comparative negligence, this requirement has been eliminated in most jurisdictions. In comparative negligence jurisdictions, comparative fault applies to the same extent as in other negligence cases.

f. Procedural Effect

Once the court determines that P has established a prima facie res ipsa case, the issue becomes one for the jury to determine whether or not to draw the inference, taking into consideration D's contrary evidence (if any). The jury will be given a res ipsa instruction, but in most cases res ipsa is a permissible inference and not a presumption, so the jury is free to find against P even if it finds that P has proved the res ipsa elements. Both res ipsa and specific negligence theories may be submitted to the jury, so long as the two are not inconsistent.

g. Products Liability Cases

There is an analogous circumstantial evidence rule in strict product liability cases. P need not prove the specific defect in the product, so long as the evidence tends to show that the product malfunctioned in such a way that the existence of a defect may be inferred and also tends to exclude possible causes other than a product defect.

5. **Custom, Character**

a. Custom and Usage

1) General Rule

In determining whether conduct is negligent, the customary conduct of the community, industry, trade, business, or profession in similar circumstances is relevant but not conclusive. R.2d § 295A; R.3d PH § 13; *The T.J. Hooper* (2d Cir. 1932). A typical use of such evidence is industry-wide practices introduced to show that D's method of doing the same or a similar thing was or was not negligent.

Example: D, a bottler, uses type X glass. P introduces evidence that all other bottlers use type Y glass.

Such evidence might show that a risk is foreseeable, or that D knew or should have known of the risk, that the risk is an unreasonable one unless the customary precaution is taken, or that a particular safety precaution is feasible.

2) Exception

In professional negligence cases involving physicians and certain other professionals, the customary conduct of such professionals may conclusively establish the standard of care. See section XIII, MEDICAL AND OTHER PROFESSIONAL NEGLIGENCE, *infra*.

b. Character
Evidence that D or P was or was not a careful person is generally not admissible to prove that he acted carefully or negligently on the occasion in question.

6. Trade Rules and Standards

In some jurisdictions, rules and standards for the conduct of an activity promulgated by authoritative groups (e.g., accrediting agencies, trade associations, safety organizations), if relevant and recognized as authoritative, are similar to custom and are often admitted as some evidence of the standard of care.

7. D's Own Rules and Standards

D's own rules and standards are admissible but not conclusive as evidence of the appropriate standard of care.

E. Degrees of Negligence
(Dobbs § 147)

1. Degrees of Care

The duty of those who conduct certain dangerous activities is sometimes stated as greater than "ordinary" or "reasonable" care.

a. Some courts have held that common carriers (operators of airplanes, ships, buses, trains, taxicabs, and even elevators, escalators and amusement devices) are said to owe their passengers the "highest degree of care consistent with the mode of conveyance used and the practical operation of their business."

b. Some courts have held that persons responsible for certain dangerous instrumentalities (e.g., high-voltage electricity, explosives) must exercise a "high degree of care," commensurate with the danger, to protect others from harm.

Analytically, such special duties are unsound. The standard negligence duty—"ordinary" or "reasonable" care under the circumstances—achieves the same result, since the "circumstances" include the high danger or special responsibility. There is a trend away from such special degrees of care.

2. Degrees of Negligence

Occasionally, efforts have been made to subdivide the negligence concept into finer gradations—"slight," "ordinary," and "gross" negligence.

a. *Slight negligence* is the failure to exercise great care.

b. *Gross negligence* is the failure to exercise even slight care. It shades into, and is usually indistinguishable from, reckless conduct. However, it will not support punitive damages, and contributory negligence is a defense to it.

These distinctions have proved unworkable, and are rarely used.

F. Reckless Conduct ("Willful and Wanton Misconduct")

(Dobbs § 147; R.2d §§ 500–503)

1. Definition

Conduct is in "reckless disregard of the safety of another" (also called "willful and wanton misconduct") when D knows or has reason to know that (1) it creates an unreasonable risk of harm and (2) the risk is relatively high, either in degree or in the probability that harm will occur. See R.2d § 500.

According to the R.3d PH § 2, D's conduct is reckless if (1) he knows that his conduct creates a risk of harm (or knows facts from which it should be obvious) and (2) the precautions that would reduce or eliminate the risk are so slight relative to the magnitude of the risk that D's conduct (in failing to take those precautions) shows a conscious indifference to the risk.

2. Distinguished From Negligent Conduct

Negligent conduct merely creates an unreasonable risk; no awareness of that risk is required. For conduct to be reckless, D must be *conscious* (or a reasonable person in D's situation would have been conscious) that it creates a *relatively high* risk of harm to another.

3. Distinguished From Intentional Torts

Conduct is intentional when D either intends to bring about the consequences or knows that they are substantially certain to occur. Reckless conduct lacks that certainty of result.

Example: D, intoxicated, drives his car 60 m.p.h. on a city street. His conduct is probably reckless, even though he drives as carefully as possible, because he knows or has reason to know that his conduct is creating a high risk of harm. But it is not intentional, because he does not intend to cause any harmful consequences nor does he know that they are substantially certain to occur.

4. When Required

Certain statutes (e.g., automobile and airplane guest statutes, governmental immunity acts, "Good Samaritan" laws) exempt D from liability for ordinary negligence, thereby requiring proof of reckless conduct for liability. It is also required by some common law rules—e.g., in some jurisdictions a possessor of land is liable to a trespasser or licensee injured on the premises only for reckless conduct.

5. Effect

a. Proximate Cause

Broader rules of proximate cause may be applied if D's conduct is reckless. R.2d § 501(2); R.3d PH § 33.

b. Defenses

In some jurisdictions, ordinary contributory negligence is not a defense or damage-reducing factor if D's conduct is found to be reckless. However, in the majority of comparative negligence jurisdictions, P's contributory negligence will reduce his recovery even against D's reckless conduct. Assumption of the risk was formerly a defense to reckless conduct (R.2d §§ 502, 503), but in most jurisdictions it is now merely a damage-reducing factor.

c. Punitive Damages

In most jurisdictions, reckless conduct will support an award of punitive damages, the same as intentional torts.

G. Duty Concepts and General Limitations

(Dobbs §§ 225–230; R.2d §§ 314–324A)

1. In General

*In negligence law, D's duty can best be analyzed as a general principle with exceptions and limitations, rather than as a collection of specific duties. In general, D has a duty to exercise reasonable care to avoid subjecting others (and their property) to unreasonable foreseeable risks of physical harm. **Specific*** *limitations on that duty are sprinkled throughout the law of torts. The most common **general** duty limitations are as follows:*

2. Relationship Between P and D

Negligence law has traditionally held that D is not subject to liability to P unless D breached a duty owed to P and not to someone else. Cf. *Palsgraf v. Long Island R. Co.* (N.Y. 1928). "Negligence in the air, so to speak, will not do." The catch is that no workable criteria exist for determining when this duty arises. Generally, D's duty arises (a) out of a pre-existing relationship between P and D or (b) because D could have foreseen that his conduct, if creating an unreasonable risk of harm, would endanger P or P's property.

3. Nature and Scope of the Risk

Conduct may be negligent because it foreseeably threatens property damage, but it actually causes some unforeseen personal injury. Or conduct may be negligent because it foreseeably threatens one type of harm to P, but it actually causes another type of harm, as to which the risk was not unreasonable. Or conduct may be negligent because it creates a risk of injury to A, but unexpectedly injures B. Some courts will hold that there was no duty to protect against the harm that actually resulted. Other courts will reach the same result under proximate cause (scope of liability) principles.

Example: D entrusts a loaded gun to A, an infant. A drops the gun on P's foot. (Assume that the entrustment did not create an unreasonable risk of the latter harm.) Some courts would rule that D had no duty to P with respect to the injury to his foot; others would apply a proximate cause analysis.

4. Interest Invaded

Certain types of interests are given less than full protection against negligent invasion. For example:

a. Pecuniary Loss

Pecuniary loss alone, unaccompanied by physical harm—e.g., the right to have a contract performed, the expectation of financial advantage, misrepresentation.

b. Harm to the Unborn

See section XVI, infra.

c.   Psychic Trauma

See sections II.E., supra, and XV, infra.

5.   Misfeasance vs. Nonfeasance

Throughout its history, Anglo–American tort law has distinguished between "misfeasance" (tortious conduct consisting of an affirmative act) and "nonfeasance" (inaction which results in, or allows, harm to P). As a general rule, D is not liable for harm to P resulting from his mere failure to intervene to aid or protect P unless there is some pre-existing relationship between P and D sufficient to create the duty, or unless D is responsible for P's situation. R.3d PH § 37. As Cardozo said, the question is whether D has gone so far in what he has actually done, and has got himself into such a relation with P, that he has begun to affect the interests of P adversely, as distinguished from merely failing to confer a benefit upon him. *H.R. Moch Co. v. Rensselaer Water Co.* (N.Y. 1928). In practice, however, the distinction between misfeasance and nonfeasance is elusive at best, and often arbitrary.

a.   Rescue

Absent a pre-existing relationship between P and D or a duty to act arising from some other source (e.g. contract, statute), D has no duty to protect or aid P, who D realizes is in a position of danger. R.2d § 314; R.3d PH § 37.

Example: D sees P, a blind person, about to step into the path of an approaching auto. Although he could do so easily, and with no risk to himself, D has no duty to warn or restrain P so as to prevent P's injury.

b.   First Aid

Absent a pre-existing relationship between P and D, or unless D was responsible for P's injury, D has no duty to render aid or assistance to an injured or otherwise needy P. R.3d PH § 37.

c.   Relationships Creating Duty

Courts are eager to find a pre-existing relationship that will support a duty to aid or protect another when the risk arises within the scope of that relationship. Examples of such relationships include carrier-passenger, innkeeper-guest, landowner-lawful entrant, landlord-tenant, employer-employee, jailer-prisoner, school-student, parent-child, husband-wife, store-customer, and host-guest. R.2d §§ 314A,

314B; R.3d PH § 40. A duty has even been found as to friends engaged in a joint social outing. *Farwell v. Keaton* (Mich. 1976).

d. **Responsible for Peril or Injury**
The duty arises when D is responsible for P's injury or position of peril, whether or not D was negligent. R.2d § 322; R.3d PH § 39.

e. **Duties Voluntarily Assumed (R.3d PH § 42–44)**

1) **Aid to Helpless**
One who undertakes to render aid or to protect P, who reasonably appears to be imperiled and helpless or unable to adequately aid or protect himself, must do so with reasonable care. And, having undertaken this duty, he may not abandon P and leave him worse off. R.2d § 324; R.3d PH § 44. (Of course, if D was the one responsible for P's predicament, then D has a duty of care arising from that.) This rule has led to "Good Samaritan" statutes in many states, which relieve physicians (and others) who render emergency medical aid from all liability for negligence.

2) **Services**
When D (gratuitously or otherwise) undertakes to render *services* which he knows or should know are for P's protection, D must perform those services with reasonable care, at least if (a) his failure to do so *increases* the risk of harm to P, or (b) D has undertaken to perform a duty owed by another to P, or (c) P's injury results from his *reliance* on D. R.2d §§ 323, 324A; R.3d PH § 43. Even a *gratuitous promise* to render such services may make D subject to liability if there is reasonable detrimental reliance by P.

Example: Workers' compensation insurers who voluntarily and gratuitously undertake safety inspections of a factory or work site have been held liable for doing so negligently.

f. **Duty Arising Ex Post Facto**
If D does an act, not tortious at the time, and later discovers that his act creates an unreasonable risk of harm to P, D must exercise reasonable care to prevent the risk from taking effect. R.2d § 321; R.3d PH § 39.

Example: D loans his car to A, reasonably believing it in good repair. Later B informs him that the brakes are dangerously defective. D could easily telephone A and inform him, but does not. A then drives the car; the brakes fail and P is injured. D is subject to liability to P.

g. **Statutory Duty of Protection**

When a statute requires one to act for the protection of another, the court may (or may not) use the statute as a basis for an affirmative duty and its scope. R.3d PH § 38. Note that this is different from using a statute to establish the standard of care when a duty already exists. Such statutes are also to be distinguished from statutes that expressly or impliedly create a cause of action.

h. **Duty Based on Special Relationship With Another**

Certain relationships carry with them a duty by D, the dominant or custodial member, to use reasonable care to regulate the conduct of (1) the person within his custody or control so as to protect third persons or (2) third persons so as to protect the person in his custody or care. See R.2d §§ 315–320; R.3d PH §§ 40, 41.

1) **Parent–Child**

A parent must exercise reasonable care to prevent tortious conduct by his dependent child, provided the parent knows or has reason to know he has the ability, and knows or should know of the necessity and opportunity to exercise such control. R.2d § 316; R.3d PH § 41(b)(1).

2) **Master–Servant**

A master has a similar duty with respect to a servant; this even extends to one acting outside the scope of his employment, if the servant is on the master's premises or is using his chattel, or when the employment facilitates the employee's causing harm to third persons. R.2d § 317; R.3d PH § 40(b)(3).

3) **Person on D's Land**

D has a similar duty with respect to a person using his land or his chattel in his presence and with his permission. R.2d § 318.

4) **Custodian of Dangerous Person**

One who has custody of a person he knows to have dangerous propensities (i.e. likely to cause bodily harm to others if not controlled) (e.g., custodians of criminals, insane persons) must exercise reasonable care to prevent him from doing such harm. R.2d § 319; R.3d PH § 41(b)(2).

5) Duty to Protect Person in Custody

D has custody of P under circumstances such that (a) P is deprived of his normal power of self-protection or (b) P must associate with persons likely to harm him. D has a duty to exercise reasonable care to prevent tortious conduct against P, provided D knows or has reason to know he has the ability, and knows or should know of the necessity and opportunity for exercising such control. R.2d § 320.

Example: Police and other peace officers, jailers, officials in charge of asylums for the criminally insane, hospital administrators, persons in charge of schools.

H. Duty: Tort and Contract

(Dobbs §§ 319–321; R.2d §§ 323, 324A)

1. Parties to the Contract

a. Discussion

One possible source of D's duty to P is a contract between them under which D agrees to perform certain services. If D breaches that contract and as a result P sustains physical or other harm, special rules apply to determine whether that breach may give rise to tort liability.

b. General Rule: Misfeasance vs. Nonfeasance

1) Rule

*Where D's duty to act arises because of a contractual relation between D and P, D is not liable in tort for harm caused by his breach of that contract where the breach consists merely of his **failure to commence performance at all**. But once having begun to perform, he will be liable for his tortious misperformance, whether consisting of acts or omissions to act. Cf. R.2d § 323.*

Example: D contracts to cut down a tree on P's premises. D has not yet begun performance when the tree falls on P's house. D is ordinarily not liable to P in tort, even though D could be found to have been negligent in failing to start work. But once having appeared on the premises and begun performance, D is subject to liability for his negligence in performing or abandoning the work with the same result.

2) Misperformance and Nonperformance Distinguished

It is hard to distinguish the line between misperformance and nonperformance, and any distinction is often illusory. In general, the question is whether D's performance (as distinct from his promise or his preparation) has gone so far that it has begun to affect the interests of P beyond the expected benefits of the contract itself and may be regarded as a positive act assuming the obligation beyond the mere promise to perform. In some cases, although the court finds no liability based on nonperformance, the real basis is a policy decision that liability would impose an unreasonable burden—in other words, a scope-of-liability problem.

c. Exceptions: Liability for Nonfeasance

1) Public Callings

Those engaged in the public or "common" callings—common carriers, innkeepers, public warehousemen, public utilities, and public officers—are subject to tort liability for nonperformance.

2) Other Relationships

Other relationships, which may or may not be based on contract, impose a duty of affirmative action. A bailee must take affirmative action to care for the goods; an employer must provide a safe place for his employee to work; a possessor of land must make the premises reasonably safe for invitees.

3) Fraud

A promise made without any intent to perform it may be fraud for which a tort action in deceit will lie.

2. Third Persons Not Parties to the Contract (*Cf.* R.2d § 324A)

a. Common Law Rule

The general common law rule was that P, not a party to a contract between D and another, had no cause of action in tort for harm sustained as a result of D's misperformance or nonperformance. P was not in "privily of contract" with D. A leading authority on this point is Winterbottom v. Wright (Exch. 1842).

b. **Exceptions: Nonfeasance**

In the case of nonfeasance, various exceptions to the privity rule have developed. Illustrations include:

1) **Telegrams**

The failure of a telegraph company to transmit a telegram.

2) **Agents**

The nonperformance by an agent of his contractual duty (1) to supervise property or persons over which he has been given control (e.g., cattle), or (2) to take certain precautions for the safety of third persons (e.g., a railroad crossing guard).

3) **Dangerous Instrumentalities**

Nonperformance of a contract to maintain, inspect, or repair an instrumentality which foreseeably creates a substantial risk of harm to third persons (e.g., elevator, scaffolding, boiler).

4) **Lessor**

In some jurisdictions, nonperformance by a landlord of his contract to repair the premises.

5) **R.2d § 324A; R.3d PH § 43**

The Restatement (Second) of Torts § 324A provides: "One who undertakes, gratuitously or for consideration, to render services to another which he should recognize as necessary for the protection of a third person or his things, is subject to liability to the third person for physical harm resulting from his failure to exercise reasonable care to [perform] his undertaking, if (a) his failure to exercise reasonable care increases the risk of such harm, or (b) he has undertaken to perform a duty owed by the other to the third person, or (c) the harm is suffered because of reliance of the other or the third person upon the undertaking."

R.3d PH § 43, which replaces R.2d § 324A, provides: "An actor who undertakes to render services to another that the actor knows or should know reduce the risk of physical harm to which a third person is exposed has a duty of reasonable care to the third person in conducting the undertaking if: (a) the failure to exercise reasonable care increases the risk of harm beyond that which existed without the undertaking, (b) the actor has undertaken to perform a duty owed by the other to the third person, or (c) the person to whom the services are rendered, the third party, or another relies on the actor's exercising reasonable care in the undertaking."

This provision broadens the scope of liability to third persons of persons undertaking to render services, and applies to both gratuitous and contractual undertakings.

c. Exceptions: Misfeasance
Where D's negligence consists of misperformance after having begun to perform, the privity rule is now obsolete, and the overwhelming majority of courts will subject D to liability to P.

I. Review Questions
[Answers Provided in Appendix A, pages 394–396]

D, an experienced paralegal suffering from an advanced case of alcoholism, moved to a small community and opened a law office. P, who is being sued by A, comes to D for legal advice on a simple matter. P follows D's advice and fails to appear or answer A's complaint. A default judgment is entered against P.

1. T or F In P's malpractice action against D, D's failure to be licensed is inadmissible.

2. T or F Because of D's mental deficiency, she will not be held to the standard of a reasonably prudent lawyer.

3. T or F P must introduce expert testimony.

4. T or F D seeks to show that members of the local legal community customarily give clients the same advice as she gave B. This evidence is inadmissible.

5. T or F This evidence, if admitted, is conclusive proof of D's freedom from fault.

6. T or F Evidence that D was not a careful person generally would be admissible, but not conclusive proof of D's negligence here.

7. **T or F** D gratuitously advises the checkout clerk at the local market on a speeding ticket problem. As a result, the clerk's license is suspended. D is not liable because the service was volunteered and gratuitous.

8. **T or F** P is injured when the brake system recently repaired by D fails to perform adequately. D may not be found liable under *res ipsa loquitur*, because he was not in exclusive control of the brake system at the time of the accident.

9. **T or F** Same facts as 8. E worked on the brake system after D had made his repairs. P can successfully sue both D and E under a *res ipsa loquitur* theory.

10. **T or F** Under *res ipsa loquitur*, P need not prove that there is no other possible cause of his injuries except D's negligence.

11. **T or F** Arnold, a customarily well-mannered and respectful child, attacks and injures Patti, who is shopping with Arnold's mother, D. D is liable to Patti because parents have a duty to exercise reasonable care to control children who are in their custody.

12. **T or F** Patti retaliates for Arnold's attack by spanking Arnold with a paddle. Arnold's mother has no duty to take some action to prevent the spanking.

13. **T or F** Patti retaliates by locking Arnold in her yard where he is attacked by Patti's dog. Ralph, who could easily rescue Arnold from the yard without danger to himself, refuses to get involved, and Arnold is injured. Arnold cannot sue Ralph because Ralph had no duty to rescue Arnold.

14. **T or F** Ralph attempts to rescue Arnold, but does so negligently, thereby placing the helpless Arnold in an even worse position, so that his injuries are greater. Arnold may not sue Ralph, because Ralph had no duty to Arnold in the first place.

15. **T or F** To prevent future attacks upon her person, P wires her clothing to give a severe electrical shock when touched. A cab driver, injured when he attempts to help P from his cab, may successfully claim that P's actions are reckless ("willful and wanton") misconduct.

16. Short essay: City enacts an ordinance requiring all residents to clear snow from their sidewalks within 24 hours of a snowfall. D violates the ordinance,

and P falls on D's sidewalk. P is drunk. Discuss whether, in a suit by P against D, D's violation of the ordinance establishes a prima facie case of liability against D.

17. Short essay: An explosion and the resulting fire damage the kitchen in P's house. At the time of the fire, D (a carpenter) was alone in the house and was using an extremely flammable solvent to remove varnish from the cabinets. Discuss what P must show in order to present a successful *res ipsa loquitur* argument that D's negligence caused the damage to the kitchen.

V. Defenses to Negligence and Other Liability

A. Contributory and Comparative Negligence

(Dobbs §§ 198–210; R.2d §§ 463–496)

1. Rule

Contributory negligence is conduct by P which creates an unreasonable risk of harm to P, and which combines with D's negligence so that both contribute to cause Ps injury. R.2d §§ 463, 466.

2. Burden of Proof

Contributory negligence is an affirmative defense. R.2d § 477.

3. Applicable Rules

In general, the same rules and tests apply to determine whether conduct is contributorily negligent as are used to determine if conduct is negligent. See Chapter IVB., supra; R.2d §§ 464, 469, 476. Prior to the adoption of comparative fault, some courts held that conduct which is negligent is not ipso facto contributory negligence as well, because reasonable care for one's own safety is not necessarily the same as reasonable care for the safety of others. Today, this distinction is largely obsolete, and there is no distinction between P's and D's negligence. R. 3d AL § 3.

4. Effect of Plaintiff's Contributory Fault

a. Complete Bar vs. Mitigation of Damages

Under the traditional common law rule, P's contributory negligence was a complete defense and totally barred any recovery against a negligent D. R.2d § 467. However, the modern rule, comparative negligence, has been adopted in all but four states (Alabama, Maryland, North Carolina, and

Virginia) and the District of Columbia. Under comparative negligence, P's contributory negligence is sometimes not a complete bar but merely reduces P's damages pro tanto.

b. **Comparative Negligence**
By statute in most jurisdictions, and by judicial decision in several others, all but four states (AL, MD, NC, VA) and DC have finally accepted the doctrine of comparative negligence. Under this rule, P's contributory negligence is not a complete bar to his recovery. Instead, P's damages are calculated and then reduced by the proportion which P's fault bears to the total causative fault of P's harm.

Example: D's negligence contributed 75% and P's negligence 25% to P's injury. P sustained $100,000 damages. P will be awarded a judgment against D for $75,000.

c. **Types of Comparative Negligence**

1) **Pure Form**
Under the pure form, P may recover a portion of his damages no matter how great his negligence in comparison to that of D. A minority of jurisdictions adopted this form—AK, AZ, CA, FL, KY, LA, MI, MO, MS, NM, NY, RI, WA—and it applies under the F.E.L.A. and Jones Act.

Example: P was 80% at fault and D 20%. P sustained $100,000 damages. P will be awarded a judgment against D for $20,000.

2) **Modified Form**
In most jurisdictions, P recovers nothing if his negligence was "as great as" (50%) or "greater than" (51%) that of D.

Example: P was 60% at fault and D 40%. P recovers nothing.

d. **Factors for Assigning Shares of Responsibility**
According to R.3d AL § 8, the trier of fact, in deciding how to assign percentage shares of liability, should consider (1) the nature of the risk-creating conduct (including any awareness of the risk or indifference to it, and any intent to harm) and (2) the causal connection between the person's risk-creating conduct and the

harm. Stated another way, the factors are (1) the duty owed by each person, (2) the extent to which each person's conduct deviated from that duty, and (3) the extent to which the tortious conduct of each person caused the injury in question.

e. **Intentional or Reckless Conduct**

Traditionally, ordinary contributory negligence was not a defense to an intentional tort or to reckless conduct (but contributory reckless conduct was a defense to the latter). R.2d §§ 481, 482. In most comparative negligence jurisdictions, P's contributory negligence will reduce his recovery even though D's conduct was reckless, but not if D's conduct was intentional. R.3d AL § 1 calls for application of comparative fault rules to all claims for physical harm, but takes no position on the question whether a plaintiff's comparative fault reduces his recovery against an intentional tortfeasor. Some comparative negligence states do not permit ordinary contributory negligence to reduce P's damages if D's tortious conduct was reckless ("willful and wanton").

f. **Strict Liability**

Prior to the adoption of comparative negligence, contributory negligence was not a defense to a strict liability action, except when that conduct amounted to assumption of the risk. R.2d § 484. Today, some of the jurisdictions adopting comparative negligence permit P's ordinary contributory negligence to reduce P's damages; others do not, the only damage-reducing defense being P's assumption of the risk.

g. **Safety Statutes**

Contributory negligence was traditionally not a defense to actions founded upon certain types of safety statutes intended to protect a class of persons from dangers against which they are incapable of protecting themselves—e.g., child labor laws, statutes prohibiting the sale of certain items to minors, certain acts concerning intoxicated persons, factory acts and other laws for the protection of workmen. R.2d § 483. Certain statutes expressly prohibit this defense. For the most part, the same result has been reached even after the adoption of comparative negligence.

h. **Serious Misconduct**

In some jurisdictions, if P's contributory fault was seriously unlawful or immoral conduct, he will be barred from recovery altogether.

5. Causal Relation

The same rules of causation apply as in the case of negligent conduct. See Chapters VI, VII, infra; R.2d § 465. And the defense is not available unless P's harm results from the risk which made P's conduct negligent. R.2d § 468.

Example: P, who is negligent for standing on an unstable platform, is not contributorily negligent with respect to injuries sustained when an adjacent wall collapses upon him.

6. Imputed Contributory Negligence

a. General Rule

With three exceptions, the negligence of a third person will not be imputed to P so as to reduce or bar Ps recovery for injuries caused by D's negligence, despite the existence of some relationship between P and the third person. R.2d § 485.

Example: The negligence of one spouse is not imputed to the other (P) in a negligence action by P against D. R.2d § 487. The negligence of a parent does not reduce his child's (P's) recovery against D. R.2d § 488. The negligence of the bailee of a chattel does not reduce recovery by the bailor, R.2d § 489—e.g., P loans his car to B and it is wrecked by the combined negligence of B and D. The negligence of a carrier or host is not imputed to his passenger or guest. R.2d § 490. Unless otherwise provided by statute, the negligence of one beneficiary under a death statute does not reduce or bar recovery by another beneficiary. R.2d § 493. The negligence of one parent does not reduce recovery by the other for injuries to their child. R.2d § 494A.

b. Exception: Master–Servant

A master's recovery against a negligent D is reduced or barred by the negligence of his servant acting within the scope of his employment. R.2d § 486.

c. Exception: Joint Enterprise

P, a member of a joint enterprise, is injured by the concurrent negligence of D, a third person outside the enterprise, and M, another member of the enterprise. P's recovery against D is reduced by M's negligence. R.2d § 491. Note that P also has a cause of action against M.

d. **Exception: Consequential Damages**
Where P has a cause of action based upon personal injuries to another (A), P's recovery is reduced by A's contributory negligence. R.2d § 494.

Example: A husband has a cause of action against D for loss of his wife's consortium resulting from personal injuries to the wife caused by D's negligence. The husband's recovery against D is reduced by his wife's contributory negligence.

e. **Auto Financial Responsibility Statutes**
Statutes in some states make the owner of an auto vicariously liable for the negligence of a person he allows to drive it. The better rule is that such statutes do not impute the driver's negligence to the owner when the owner is suing a third person for injuries or damage to the vehicle. A few decisions are contra.

7. **P's Negligent Failure to Exercise Control**

a. **In General**
If P has a duty to control the conduct of A and negligently fails to do so, A's contributory negligence (combined with that of P) reduces P's recovery against D whose negligence was also a cause of P's injury. R.2d § 495.

Example: P, a passenger in his own car, has a duty to control the driving conduct of the driver, A. P negligently fails to do so. As the result of the negligence of D (the driver of another car) and A, a collision occurs and P is injured. P's recovery from D is reduced by A's negligence.

b. **Parent**
A parent's (P's) recovery from D for injuries to P's child caused by D's negligence is reduced by P's negligence in protecting or supervising his child, who was too young to be responsible for his own safety. R.2d § 496.

B. Last Clear Chance
(Dobbs § 207; R.2d §§ 479, 480)

1. Discussion

The doctrine of "last clear chance" is now primarily of historical interest; it survives in a dwindling minority of jurisdictions. It was intended to ameliorate the harsh effects of the contributory negligence bar, and as such it was primarily an intermediate stop on the road to comparative fault. Most jurisdictions adopting comparative fault have also abolished this doctrine.

The doctrine of last clear chance applies only when D's negligence is *later in time* than P's contributory negligence. In essence, P (or P's property) is in a zone of danger from which he cannot escape in time, leaving D with the last opportunity to do something to prevent the harm which otherwise will occur. If D then negligently fails to act to prevent the harm, he is not permitted to use P's prior negligence as a defense.

2. Operative Variables

Jurisdictions vary with respect to the fact situations in which they will permit the rule to be applied. The principal variables are (1) the nature of P's predicament and (2) the state of D's attentiveness to P's peril. The relevant situations may be described as helpless plaintiffs, inattentive plaintiffs, observant defendants, and inattentive defendants.

a. Helpless Plaintiff

The helpless plaintiff is one who has negligently placed himself in a position of peril from which he is now helpless to escape in time.

Example: P is in the path of D's moving vehicle and he cannot move because (a) his foot is stuck, or (b) he is unconscious or sick or in a drunken stupor, or (c) he has been so injured by a third person.

b. Inattentive Plaintiff

The inattentive plaintiff has negligently placed himself in a position of peril and has failed to observe the danger.

Example: P is jogging down the middle of a road, oblivious to the approach of D's auto from behind.

c. Observant Defendant

The observant defendant actually sees P in time to act so as to avoid the harm (assuming that D has a duty to so act under the circumstances), and observes P's helpless or inattentive condition, but thereafter is negligent in failing to act to prevent P's harm. D's conduct need not be the source of P's danger.

The better rule is that P need not prove that D actually perceived P's helplessness or inattentiveness; it is sufficient to show that D saw P and that any normal person in D's situation would have realized that P was helpless or inattentive.

d. **Inattentive Defendant**

The inattentive defendant is one who was under a duty to maintain a lookout such that he would have seen P in time to avoid the harm, and (had he been looking) would have been able to perceive his helpless or inattentive condition, and would have been able by the exercise of reasonable care to avoid the harm. But due to D's negligence in failing to maintain the necessary lookout, he fails to see P in time and the injury occurs.

3. **Rules**

The various possible combinations of these situations are:

a. **Helpless Plaintiff vs. Observant Defendant**

This is the classic last clear chance situation, and all jurisdictions which accept the doctrine will apply it here.

b. **Helpless Plaintiff vs. Inattentive Defendant; Inattentive Plaintiff vs. Observant Defendant**

Most jurisdictions recognizing the rule will apply it in these situations. See R.2d §§ 479, 480.

c. **Inattentive Plaintiff vs. Inattentive Defendant**

No jurisdiction applies the doctrine here.

d. **Doctrine Rejected**

Some jurisdictions rejected the doctrine altogether, but frequently reached the same result under reckless or willful and wanton misconduct rules.

4. **Limited to Subsequent Negligence**

Remember that the doctrine applies only when D's negligence occurs after that point in time when he discovers (or should have discovered) P's peril.

Example: D's negligence was failing to keep his brakes in repair; this was the reason he could not stop in time to prevent P's injury. This is antecedent negligence and the doctrine does not apply.

5. Effect of Comparative Negligence

The better rule is that the doctrine does not survive the adoption of comparative negligence; it is subsumed.

C. Assumption of Risk

(Dobbs §§ 211–215; R.2d §§ 496A–496G)

1. Rule

Under the traditional common law rule, if P voluntarily assumes a risk of harm arising from the negligent or reckless conduct of D, P cannot recover for such harm. R.2d § 496A.

2. Discussion

Prior to the widespread adoption of comparative negligence, most (but not all) jurisdictions recognized this defense, some by a different name. A few have limited it to (1) master-servant cases and (2) express assumption of risk cases. Some courts analyze P's assumption of risk as affecting D's duty, e.g., negating D's duty to exercise care for P's safety.

3. Meanings of Term

Much confusion has arisen because the term "assumption of risk" can be employed to mean different things, some of which are not truly defenses to negligent conduct. The term is used to describe several different situations:

a.   Express Assumption of Risk (Release)

P expressly agrees in advance (usually in a writing) to relieve D of D's duty to exercise care for P's safety with respect to a known or possible risk.

b.   Inherent Hazards Not Arising From Negligence

P chooses to engage in an activity that has certain inherent and commonly accepted risks, even though the others involved exercise proper care—e.g., hazardous employment, spectators and participants in some sporting events. As to these risks, there is no negligence, and therefore no assumption of the risk of negligent conduct; thus, the doctrine does not properly apply. Some courts call this "primary" assumption of the risk. These are "no duty" or "no negligence" cases.

c. Risk of Future Negligence

P voluntarily enters into a relationship with D knowing that there is a risk that D will act negligently. E.g., P agrees to ride with D, an intoxicated or known reckless driver. Here, the true basis of liability is P's unreasonable conduct in entering into the relationship, and hence such cases should ordinarily be restricted to the defense of contributory negligence.

d. Assumption of Existing Negligently–Created Risk

P, aware of a risk created by the negligence of D, proceeds or continues voluntarily to encounter it. This is true implied assumption of risk.

Example: D negligently furnished P, a painter, a scaffold with a frayed rope. P discovers the rope's condition, but decides to use the scaffold anyway and is injured. P may be said to have "assumed the risk" that the rope would break.

4. **Contributory Negligence Distinguished**

In theory, implied assumption of the risk is P's implied voluntary consent to encounter a known danger created by D's negligence. Contributory negligence is unreasonable conduct. The former is a subjective test; the test for the latter is objective.

Example: D negligently offers P a seat in D's chair, which has a defective leg. The chair collapses and P is injured. If P knew the leg was broken, he probably assumed the risk of that defect. He may also have been contributorily negligent if a reasonably prudent person would not have used the chair. If P did not actually know of the defect, he did not assume the risk, even though he may have been contributorily negligent if a reasonably prudent person would have inspected the chair or discovered the defect before using it. Note that these defenses overlap, and given facts may give rise to either or both.

5. Express Assumption of Risk

a. Rule

If P, by contract or otherwise, expressly agrees to accept a risk of harm arising from D's negligent or reckless conduct, P cannot recover for such harm, unless the agreement is invalid as contrary to public policy. R.2d § 496B.

> *Example:* P joins D's health club. P signs a written contract containing a prominent provision by which D is relieved of liability for negligence in the operation of the club. The contract is probably valid.

b. Construction

Such agreements are strictly construed against D, and are not enforceable if P reasonably was ignorant of that term. They are unenforceable as to intentional torts, and some courts will not enforce them as to reckless conduct.

c. Public Policy

Such agreements are unenforceable when contrary to public policy. Generally they will not be enforced in favor of employers, those charged with a duty of public service (e.g. common carriers, innkeepers, health care providers), and those having a significantly superior bargaining position as compared to P. However, those rendering a public service may limit their liability to a fixed sum, provided P is given the option to purchase full protection.

6. Implied Assumption of Risk

a. Rule

If P knows, appreciates and understands the risk of harm created by D's negligent or reckless conduct, and nevertheless voluntarily subjects himself to the risk by conduct which impliedly manifests his consent to accept the risk, then he is subject to the assumption of risk defense. Compare R.2d § 496C, which is broader and covers several meanings of "assumption of risk" (see Part D. 3. b.–d., supra). The effect of the defense varies from one jurisdiction to the next.

b. Elements: Manifestation of Consent

The essence of the defense is consent to accept the risk, and therefore P's conduct must impliedly manifest that consent.

Example: P, a pedestrian, attempts to dash across the street ahead of D's speeding car. P's conduct does not manifest consent to relieve D of his duty to exercise reasonable care for P's safety, and therefore is not assumption of the risk (although it may well be contributory negligence).

c.   **Elements: Knowledge and Appreciation of Risk**
The consent must be an informed one, and therefore D must show that P knew of the existence of the risk, and understood and appreciated its unreasonable character. R.2d § 469D.

Example: P, who installs his TV antenna near D's uninsulated power line, may not have appreciated the risks (1) that it contained 12,000 volts or (2) that current could arc from one to the other. Note that P will be charged with matters of common knowledge or which are readily ascertainable by observation.

Where there are several risks, P is held to assume only the risk(s) he appreciates, and not the one(s) he does not.

d.   **Elements: Voluntariness**
P's assumption of the risk must be voluntary. R.2d § 496E.

1)   **Reluctance**
P's conduct in proceeding into the zone of danger, even reluctantly or under protest, may ordinarily be deemed voluntary. Even if P has no reasonable alternative but to encounter the risk, his doing so is voluntary unless D's tortious conduct is responsible for P's predicament and P must encounter the risk to avert harm to himself or another or exercise or protect a right or privilege of which D has no right to deprive him.

Examples: P, a tenant, does not assume the risk created by D (the landlord) in negligently maintaining a common stairway that P must use for access to his apartment. P, a motorist, does not assume the risks created by D railroad in negligently maintaining a public crossing. Rescuers do not assume the risk of their own injury by attempting the rescue. But P, who must ride in D's car or bleed to death, assumes the risk of the car's defective brakes.

2) Economic Duress

Many courts have held that mere economic duress does not make encountering the risk involuntary. For example, an employee assumes the risk of negligently-created dangers in his work situation, even though his only alternative is to refuse to encounter them and be fired. Other courts (and the better view) hold contra.

3) Public Policy

It has been suggested that the same public policies which negate an express assumption of risk should similarly prevent the finding of an implied assumption. See R.2d § 496C, Comment j.

e. Violation of Statute

P's assumption of risk bars his recovery based on D's violation of a statute, unless this result would defeat a policy of the statute to place the entire responsibility for such harm on D. R.2d § 496F. Some statutory torts (e.g. F.E.L.A., structural work acts) expressly exclude the defense.

f. Limitation to Particular Risk

The assumption is limited to the particular risk which was knowingly and voluntarily encountered.

g. Burden of Proof

Assumption of risk is an affirmative defense. R.2d § 496G.

h. Modern Status of the Defense

There is a strong trend to abolish the defense of implied assumption of risk as a separate defense in negligence cases on the ground that it overlaps completely with the doctrine of contributory negligence. In particular, when jurisdictions adopt comparative negligence, they frequently merge the defenses of contributory negligence and assumption of risk under a general "comparative fault" concept. Whether retained as a separate doctrine or merged with contributory negligence, the two doctrines become functionally the same when the courts treat them both as damage-reducing factors.

i. Participation in Sporting Events

In many jurisdictions, those who participate in professional or amateur sporting events assume the risk of injuries resulting from other players' misconduct, even when violations of rules of the game having a safety purpose, unless the violation was more than carelessness incident to the play of the game. In other words, P, by choosing to participate in the game, assumes the risk of foreseeable injuries incident to the play of the game, even if those injuries result from D's violation of a rule of the game having a safety purpose, when such rule violations are typical of the game and occur during play. But D may be liable if he intentionally or recklessly injures P. This may also be analyzed as a limited duty rule.

D. Statutes of Limitations and Repose

(Dobbs §§ 216–223)

1. Statutes of Limitations

a. In General

A *statute of limitations* is a statutory time period within which P must file his or her lawsuit. There are statutes of limitations for all causes of action. In tort cases, the time period is usually short, typically one to three years. However, property damage actions may be longer, e.g., five years.

Statutes of limitations are designed to promote stability and avoid the uncertainties and burdens inherent in defending stale and possibly fraudulent claims. The price of this protection, however, is the extinguishment of valid claims.

b. Classification

Since there are different time periods for different causes of action, the courts may have difficulty classifying actions for purposes of determining which time period applies. P sometimes resorts to ingenious pleading to avoid the effect of an expired statute—e.g., suing a physician for medical malpractice on the theory that it is a breach of the physician-patient contract, as to which the (longer) contract statute of limitations applies. The courts have held that P's characterization is not controlling, and the court can redetermine the actual basis for the action.

c. Procedural Effect

A statute of limitations does not extinguish the cause of action. It is an affirmative defense which must be asserted or it is waived.

d. Commencement of Running

1) General Rule

The statute of limitations begins to run on the date the cause of action "accrues." In tort cases, this is usually the date on which the injury occurs, since compensable injury is a necessary element of the cause of action. Once the statute of limitations starts to run, no subsequent event will toll it.

2) Concealment

D's fraudulent concealment or nondisclosure of the existence of the cause of action from P tolls the running of the statute.

3) Continuing Duty or Negligence

In some contexts, the courts will extend the available time by finding a continuing duty to disclose or continuing negligence or other tort. In medical negligence cases, some courts hold that the statute does not begin to run until P's course of treatment has been concluded. If D's conduct constitutes a continuing nuisance, the statute may not start to run until D's conduct in creating the nuisance ceases, or it may not start to run as long as the harm continues.

4) Discovery Rule

Strict application of the statute of limitations can be especially harsh in certain cases where P justifiably failed to discover that he even had a cause of action until after the limitation period had expired. In response to this problem, courts (and sometimes legislatures) have created a "discovery" rule whereby the statute is tolled and does not commence to run until P discovers (or by the exercise of reasonable care should have discovered) that (a) he is injured and (b) the injury is the result of someone's tortious conduct. This "discovery" rule was first applied in medical malpractice cases, and is often extended to others such as product liability and other professional negligence cases. Some apply the discovery rule broadly. Whether P meets the requirements for the discovery rule is normally a question of fact for the jury.

5) Minors and Others Under Disability

A statute of limitations normally does not begin to run if P is a minor or person under some other legal disability when the cause of action accrues. It commences when P is no longer under any disability.

6) Death Cases

In wrongful death cases, the statute begins to run on the date of death, even though the fatal injury occurred earlier. In such cases, the statute of limitations is often regarded as an intrinsic part of the cause of action rather than as a mere affirmative defense.

7) Latent Potential Harm

P, as a result of D's negligence, may have been exposed to a toxic material resulting in no present symptoms or minor symptoms but a measurable risk that P may contract a serious or fatal illness at some uncertain time in the future. Some courts will allow recovery now for the present symptoms or medical monitoring and either (1) damages for the potential future harm times the probability of its occurrence or (2) allow a later suit if and when the potential future harm actually occurs.

8) Repressed Childhood Sexual Abuse

Some courts have permitted the statute of limitations to be tolled during the time when P has repressed her memory of childhood sexual abuse (assuming the repression began before the applicable statute expired). Others have rejected the defense, holding that whatever "repression" is, it does not toll the statute of limitations. Some legislatures have adopted extended statute of limitations in sexual abuse cases.

e. Estoppel to Assert

If D actively induces P not to take timely legal action on a claim, and P reasonably relies on D's inducement, D may be estopped to assert the statute of limitations defense.

2. **Statutes of Repose**

Statutes of repose are special limitation periods which supplement and override statutes of limitations, the discovery rule, and other similar rules and exceptions. Their purpose is to set an outer limit beyond which D can no longer be held responsible for a completed activity, irrespective of whether an injury has occurred. Sometimes, particularly in product liability cases, they merely create a presumption of nonliability. The most common forms of these statutes are in the areas of (1) medical malpractice (X years after the allegedly negligent treatment), (2) product liability (Y years after D manufactured the product or placed it in the stream of commerce, and (3) professional negligence of builders, architects and engineers (Z years after completion of the structure). These statutes may have the effect of barring a lawsuit before the cause of action even accrues. Despite this, for the most part they have been held to be constitutional.

3. Notice of Claim Statutes

In suits against state or local governments, statutes sometimes require P to give notice, in a specified form, to the potential D within a certain time period (typically six months or a year, but sometimes as little as 60 or 90 days) after the date of the injury as a further condition on the right to sue.

E. Immunities
(Dobbs § 225; R.2d §§ 895A–895D)

1. Government and Its Employees: Sovereign Immunity (Dobbs §§ 260–278)

a. Prior Common Law
At one time, all levels of government (federal, state, local) were entirely immune from tort liability.

b. United States

1) Federal Tort Claims Act
In the Federal Tort Claims Act, the United States has waived its tort immunity for personal or property damage "caused by the negligent or wrongful act or omission of any employee of the Government while acting within the scope of his office or employment, under circumstances where the United States, if a private person, would be liable to the claimant in accordance with the law of the place where the act or omission occurred." 28 U.S.C.A. § 1346(b). See R.2d § 895A.

2) Exceptions
In addition to exceptions for specific activities (tax collection, failure to deliver mail, military combat in time of war, actions arising in foreign countries), there are two important general exceptions:

a) Specified Torts

The U.S. is not liable for (1) assault, battery, false imprisonment, false arrest, or malicious prosecution, except in the case of investigative or law enforcement officers; or (2) abuse of process, libel, slander, misrepresentation, deceit, or interference with contract rights.

b) Discretionary Acts

The U.S. is not liable for acts done with due care in the execution of a statute or regulation (even though invalid), or for "an act or omission . . . based upon the exercise or performance or the failure to exercise or perform a discretionary function or duty . . . , whether or not the discretion be abused."

c) Strict Tort Liability

The U.S. is not subject to strict tort liability in any form.

d) The *Feres* Rule

The U.S. is not liable for injuries to members of the armed forces on active duty if the injury is "incident to service." The doctrine does not bar recovery by the service member's spouse or child if that person is *directly* injured by government negligence.

c. States

All but a few states have largely abolished state sovereign immunity; the rest provide some limited means of making a claim. Many states have legislation which limits the state's liability for certain governmental functions. Immunity is generally preserved for judicial and legislative acts, and for the exercise of high-level administrative discretion. R.2d § 895B.

d. Local Governments

After a period during which the immunity of local governments was eroded, as by holding them liable for "proprietary" (as opposed to "governmental") functions, where the entity had purchased liability insurance, and for other activities (e.g. operation of vehicles), a strong trend has developed to abolish immunity entirely, usually by judicial decision. Liability is now the rule in a majority of states, subject to limited immunities for certain governmental functions. Both the common law and statutes exempt judicial and legislative functions, and exempt executive and administrative policy or planning decisions. R.2d § 895C. In some cases, the courts hold there is no liability if the duty in question is owed to the public generally and not to P specifically, or if the decision to act or not to act (which P claims was negligently made) is one that implicates the allocation of public resources (for example, when to provide police protection or what level of protection to provide). In some cases, immunity is retained for discretionary acts.

e. Governmental Officers and Employees

Governmental officers and employees are immune from tort liability when exercising a judicial or legislative function. The highest executive officers of state and federal governments are absolutely immune, except where they have so far exceeded the scope of their official discretion as to be acting clearly beyond the bounds of their authority. Lower level executive and administrative employees have a qualified immunity for the good faith exercise of a discretionary function, but are liable for tortious ministerial acts.

Various statutes increasingly alter the scope of governmental officers' and employees' liability.

2. **Charities** (Dobbs §§ 282–83; R.2d § 895E)

At one time, all but one or two states held that charitable, educational, religious, and benevolent organizations and enterprises were immune from tort liability. Today, that immunity has been generally abolished in all but a few jurisdictions, but many retain vestiges of immunity or other liability limitations, such as caps on damages.

Increasingly, legislation is recreating specific immunities for particular charitable activities or for individuals engaged in certain charitable activities.

3. **Spouses, Parents and Children** (Dobbs §§ 279–281; R.2d §§ 895F–895H)

a. Husband and Wife

At one time, the general common law rule was that husband and wife were each immune from tort liability to the other spouse for torts committed during coverture. More than half the states have now abolished this immunity. R.2d § 895F. Many of the remaining states (a few of which have statutes expressly preserving it) recognize exceptions, as for suits brought after the marriage has been terminated, intentional torts, and suits against persons vicariously liable for the spouse's tort.

b. Parent and Child

The general common law rule was that a parent and his unemancipated minor child were each immune from suit by the other for a personal tort, whether intentional or negligent. Today, a substantial minority of the states have abolished this immunity altogether (R.2d § 895G). In the remainder, the number of exceptions is increasing, such as for (a) intentional or reckless conduct, (b) torts occurring during D's business activity, (c) breach of a duty external to the family relationship (e.g., child-driver runs over pedestrian-parent), and (d) suits after the parent-minor child relationship has ended, as by emancipation of the child or the death of either party. Some states have abolished the immunity in certain classes of cases (e.g., motor vehicle accidents). Among the states that have abolished the immunity, some hold that the parent cannot be held liable for negligent supervision, or the exercise of parental authority, or where the negligent act involves the exercise of parental discretion with respect to the provision of food, clothing, housing, medical and dental services, and other care.

The immunity is personal, and does not protect one vicariously liable; and it does not extend to persons who only stand in loco parentis. The courts are divided as to whether foster parents are entitled to the same immunity as parents.

c. Siblings and Other Kin

Brothers, sisters, and other kin are not, by reason of their relationship, immune from tort liability to one another. R.2d § 895H.

4. Infants and Incompetents (Dobbs § 120; R.2d § 895I, 895J)

a. Infants

Assuming that the requisite mental state (if any) can be proved, an infant or minor is not immune from tort liability, unless the liability depends upon the enforceability of a contract which the infant is privileged to disaffirm. R.2d § 895I.

b. Incompetents

One who has deficient mental capacity is not for that reason alone immune from tort liability. R.2d § 895J. Particularly in torts involving physical harm, the incompetent D is held to the same standard as a normal person. However, D's mental condition may be relevant in determining whether any tort has been committed.

F. Preemption

Under the supremacy clause of the U.S. Constitution, federal law is supreme over state law. Thus, when a federal statute or regulations expressly or impliedly preempt a particular field (e.g., regulations governing railroad crossing warnings, statutes governing cigarette warnings), state tort law either cannot regulate the field at all or cannot impose a higher standard than the applicable federal law. Whether (and the extent to which) a federal statute or regulation is preemptive is a question of statutory interpretation for the court.

G. Review Questions

[Answers Provided in Appendix A, pages 396–398]

1. Name and briefly describe the situations in which the defense of contributory negligence has limited or no application. *reckless* *intentional* *strict liability* *per se*

2. Contributory negligence will *not* be imputed in which of the following circumstances:

    a. A child's negligence to his parent.

    b. An employee's negligence to his employer.

    c. One member of a joint enterprise to another.

    d. A wife's negligence to her husband, in his suit for loss of consortium.

    e. A parent's negligence to his child.

    f. A husband's negligence to his wife in her negligence action against D.

3. P, a tightrope walker, signs a contract with her employer, a circus owner, in which she expressly relieves the employer of liability for negligence in the operation of the circus. That contract provision is unenforceable under which of the following circumstances:

    a. The tightrope breaks because of negligent maintenance.

    b. The tightrope breaks because the strong man cuts it in a fit of jealousy.

c.   The tightrope breaks because the maintenance crew used substandard materials, which they should have known presented an unreasonable risk of great harm.

d.   The language of the provision was so convoluted that P reasonably did not understand it.

e.   In all of the above, because such agreements are generally held unenforceable in favor of employers as contrary to public policy.

4.   Short essay: P accepts a ride home from an office party with D, who has been drinking heavily and is unsteady on his feet. On the way home, D drives his car into a large tree severely injuring P. In a jurisdiction that permits the defense of assumption of the risk in negligence cases, P sues D and D claims that P impliedly assumed the risk that D's negligence would injure him. What result in the following cases:

a.   P was not near D at the party and did not observe his drinking or unsteadiness. *no assumption — no knowledge*

b.   P had no money with him and could not have paid cab fare. *assumption — because unreasonable, implied*

c.   P becomes unconscious at the party, and his friends load him into the car. *no assumption*

d.   P believes D when he says that he has had nothing to drink. *depends*

5.   Short essay: Runner is jogging along late at night wearing dark clothing. He cuts across a dark alley to reach his home. Neighbor is backing down the alley from his garage and strikes Runner. Runner sues Neighbor who raises the defense of Runner's contributory negligence. Runner argues that Neighbor had the last clear chance to prevent Runner's harm. The case goes to trial in a comparative negligence jurisdiction. The jury returns a verdict for Runner, but also specifically finds Runner and Neighbor equally negligent. What result?

6.   Short essay: Discuss how the result in the case described above would change under the following circumstances.

a.   If Neighbor was Runner's wife.

b.   If Neighbor was Runner's son.

c.   If Neighbor was Runner's brother.

d. If Neighbor was the Mayor of City and was driving to his office.

e. If Neighbor was incompetent.

PART FOUR

Causation

■ ANALYSIS

VI. Causation

A. Overview of Causation Issues

Causation problems are common to many different torts (and to all torts involving physical harm).

Causation problems are among the most difficult, conceptually, in tort law. They may be analyzed in two categories:

1. *Proximate cause,* also called "legal cause" or scope of liability. Some courts and writers use these terms to encompass all causal relation issues (e.g., R.2d §§ 9, 43–453). Others distinguish between (a) proximate or legal cause and (b) cause in fact (e.g., Dobbs, Chapters 9 and 10). Many now categorize proximate cause issues under the term "scope of liability," completely separating proximate cause issues from the issue of factual causation. This is the preferred approach, and the one used by the Restatement. See R.3d PH § 26, comment *a*.

2. *Cause in fact.* This outline will treat cause in fact as separate from proximate cause.

Cause in fact exists when the "cause-and-effect" chain of events leading to P's injury includes D's tortious conduct. *Proximate (legal) cause* (scope of liability) concepts may be used to cut off D's liability when the court (or, in some cases, the jury) decides that it would be unjust under the circumstances, despite the fact that D's tortious conduct was a factual cause of P's injury. Courts sometimes treat the same or similar scope of liability problems as *duty* issues or *fault* issues.

B. Cause in Fact

(Dobbs §§ 166–179; R.2d §§ 431–434; R.3d PH §§ 26–28)

1. General Rule

Cause in fact is a question of fact, requiring proof that the injury would not have occurred "but for" D's conduct (the "sine qua non" rule). R.3d PH § 26.

Example: D drives his car negligently and collides with A's car, causing A's car to knock down a pole supporting electric wires. The wires break, causing a loss of electric power at a hospital six blocks away. The hospital's auxiliary power system fails, and P, who was connected to an electric-powered life-support device, dies. D's negligence is a cause in fact of P's death.

Example: D's cow kicks over a kerosene lantern, which D negligently placed within her reach. The resulting fire destroys most of the City of Chicago. D's negligence is a cause in fact of all of the fire damage.

In both examples, other rules (duty limitations, scope of liability limitations) may cut off D's liability for these consequences, but D's negligence was still a factual cause of the harm.

Earlier versions of the Restatement, and many courts, added a second element: that D's tortious conduct was a "substantial factor" (or sometimes "a material element [and] [or] a substantial factor") in bringing about P's injury. See, e.g., R.2d §§ 431, 432. Increasingly, this factor has been discredited. Courts and torts scholars have recognized that this factor was more appropriate to scope of liability ("proximate cause") questions. Confusion between factual cause and proximate cause has been the norm, both in the courts and in the earlier Restatements, which conflated the two concepts. In addition, the advent of comparative fault has eliminated the need to screen out factual causes that are insubstantial. For an excellent discussion of this issue, see R.3d PH § 26, comment *j*, and especially the Reporter's Note to comment *j*. Therefore, the current Restatement (and many courts) now reject the "substantial factor" element as part of the definition of factual causation. R.3d PH § 26. However, it has been retained as a scope of liability issue. R.3d PH § 36.

2. Proof

Most cause in fact problems are nothing more than fact questions involving the adequacy of P's circumstantial evidence linking P's injury and D's tortious conduct. The issue is, has P met his burden of going forward with the evidence—in other words, made a submissible case—on the issue? Is P's evidence sufficient to permit a rational factfinder to infer causation?

Example: P's body is found at the bottom of D's stairs, which were poorly lighted and strewn with debris. Whether D's negligence in maintaining the stairs was a cause in fact of P's death is a question of fact.

Where P's injury is closely linked to D's tortious conduct, courts are often lenient in permitting the trier of fact to infer factual causation.

In cases involving injuries by toxic substances, factual cause issues are very complex. See R.3d PH § 28, comment *c* and Reporter's Note to comment *c*.

3. Multiple Causes

In real life, every occurrence has more than one cause in fact. D's conduct need only be "a" cause of P's harm. It need not be the sole cause or even the major or most important cause. See R.3d PH § 26, comments *c* and *d*.

a. Concurrent Tortfeasors, Indivisible Injury

If the tortious conduct of D1 and D2 concur and both are causes in fact of P's injury, either or both are subject to liability for P's damages. It does not matter that D1 and D2 did not act in concert, or that neither's conduct by itself would have caused the injury.

Example: D1 and D2 both drive negligently and collide, and E's car careens into P, a pedestrian. D1 and D2 are both subject to liability to P.

Both D1 and D2 are also subject to liability to P when either's tortious conduct alone would have caused P's harm. R. 3d PH § 27.

Example: D1 and D2, acting independently, negligently set separate fires. Both fires go out of control and combine to destroy P's property. P may sue either D1 or D2 or both for all of his damages, even though either fire alone would have caused the same result. Note that the "but for" rule does not apply here.

This same rule applies even when one cause was tortious and the other was not. R.3d PH § 27, comment *d*.

b. Concurrent Tortfeasors, Divisible Injury

1) General Rule

If tortfeasors D1 and D2 each cause separate parts of P's harm, D1 and D2 will each be liable only for the part he caused if is possible to determine who caused which part. R.3d PH § 28, comment *d*; R.3d AL § 26, and comments.

Example: D1 and D2 each independently make statements defamatory of P. D1 is liable only for that part of P's damages attributable to his statement, and D2 is liable only for the damages attributable to his statement.

2) Exceptions

a) Concert of Action

Both D1 and D2 are liable for all of P's damages, even though divisible, if they were acting in concert or engaged in a *joint enterprise*. For example, D1 and D2 combine to beat P, and D1 breaks P's right leg and D2 his left. P may sue either D1 or D2 to recover for both broken legs.

b) Risk of Further Injury

If D's tortious conduct injures P and also foreseeably exposes P to the risk of further injury by another, D is liable both for the injury he caused and also for such further injury. For example, P's injury, negligently caused by D, is aggravated by the negligence of P's treating physician. D is subject to liability for both the original injury and the aggravation.

3) Burden of Proof

The burden is on P to prove which part of his injury is attributable to which defendant. R.3d AL § 26, comment *h*; R.3d PH § 26, comment *d*. If he cannot, the traditional rule is that he cannot recover against any. The modern and better view shifts the burden of proof on apportionment to defendants. See R.2d § 433B(2); R.3d AL § 26; R.3d PH § 28(b).

4. Concurrent Independent Tortfeasors, One Cause (Alternative Liability)

Suppose the tortious conduct of D1 and D2 (acting independently) occurs so that either D1 or D2 (but not both) was the cause in fact of P's injury, but P cannot prove which one. Traditionally, P would lose. The modern and better view shifts the burden of proof to each defendant to prove that he was not the cause. See R.3d PH § 28(b).

Example: Two hunters (D1 and D2), acting independently, each negligently fire their shotguns at the same time. A pellet from one of the guns strikes a third hunter, P, in the eye. There is insufficient evidence to determine which shotgun's pellet hit P. D1 and D2 each must prove that he did not cause P's injury; if neither can, then both are liable to P.

Example: P's car is rear-ended by a car negligently driven by D1. A car negligently driven by D2 then strikes both cars. P cannot prove which collision caused his sprained neck. The burden is on D1 and D2 each to prove that he did not cause the injury.

Of course, if D1 and D2 were acting in *concert* or engaged in a *joint enterprise*, both are subject to liability for the single harm.

5. Enterprise and Market Share Liability

In product liability cases involving an injury caused by a product from an unidentifiable manufacturer, some courts have been willing to create new rules of causation when the plaintiff can prove that similar products were marketed during the relevant time by a group of manufacturers. The injury must have been caused by a common design feature of the similar products. In such cases, several manufacturers may be held jointly and severally liable to a plaintiff for an injury caused by a product manufactured and marketed by only one.

a. Enterprise Liability

Courts may impose so-called "enterprise liability" when:

1) The injury-causing product was manufactured by one of a small number of defendants in an industry;

2) The defendants had joint knowledge of the risks inherent in the product and possessed a joint capacity to reduce those risks;

3) Each defendant failed to take steps to reduce this risk, delegating this responsibility to a trade association; and

4) Most, if not all, of the manufacturers are joined as defendants.

Liability is joint and several. A manufacturer can escape liability only by proving that its product could not have been the one that injured the plaintiff.

b. Market Share Liability

So-called "market share" liability can sometimes be used when a person was injured by a fungible product (such as a drug) that was produced and sold by multiple manufacturers, but the plaintiff cannot now identify the particular manufacturer that sold the product that caused her injury. In the small number of jurisdictions recognizing this rule, the manufacturers representing a substantial share of the relevant market at the time the product was used or consumed can be sued jointly and held severally liable for a proportional part of the plaintiff's damages. The operative details vary among jurisdictions, but in general the plaintiff must join enough manufacturers to encompass the great majority of the relevant market, and prove their relevant market shares. A manufacturer can then escape liability by proving that its product could not have been the one that injured the plaintiff. There is some variation as to the effect of absent or escaped manufacturers on the shares of the remaining defendants. See R.3d PH § 28, comment *o*; R.3d AL § 26, Reporter's Note to comment *n*.

6. Liability for Reduced Chance

Suppose that defendant's tortious conduct does not "cause" P's harm in a "but for" sense, but merely reduces P's chances of a favorable outcome.

Example: P's decedent, having contracted a form of cancer, had a 40% chance of cure if he had received proper treatment. As a result of defendant's negligence in failing to make a prompt diagnosis, his chance of cure was reduced to 25%, and he died.

Is D liable, and if so, for how much? The courts are divided. Some deny all recovery unless the victim's chances were initially over 50%; some allow damages based on the jury's determination that the defendant's negligence was a "substantial factor" in hastening or precipitating the adverse result; and some allow damages based on the percentage difference (in this case, 15%) attributable to the defendant's negligence times the plaintiff's total damages. See R.3d PH § 26, comment *n*.

C. Scope of Liability (Proximate Cause)

(Dobbs §§ 180–197; R.2d §§ 9, 430, 435–461)

1. General Principle

*Rules of **proximate cause** or **scope of liability** limit D's liability to (a) persons and (b) consequences that bear some reasonable relationship to D's tortious conduct. Whether and how scope of liability rules shall be applied is a question of **law** for the **court**. However, in some instances the jury is allowed to decide whether the scope of liability in a particular case extends to P's harm. Proximate cause rules can be broadly grouped into two categories:*

(a) *unforeseeable* or *remote* or *indirect* consequences; and

(b) intervening causes.

Earlier Restatements (and some courts) use the term "legal cause" to encompass both proximate cause and cause in fact. This usage is now obsolete, although some courts continue to use the term "proximate cause" to include both. To eliminate confusion and error, the better approach is to abandon both terms—"legal cause" and "proximate cause"—in favor of the terms "scope of liability" and "cause in fact." Nevertheless, the term "proximate cause" is still widely used to describe this category.

2. Overview

It is difficult to derive proximate cause rules because different courts will use different approaches, sometimes even in the same jurisdiction and in similar types of cases. Broadly defined, there are three typical approaches to the first category (unforeseeable or remote or indirect consequences): (a) the risk principle; (b) the direct consequences rule; and (c) the duty-risk rule. One of these approaches will be used, unless the case falls into a category (i.e., a fact pattern) in which there is a fixed proximate cause or duty rule. Examples of the latter categories include liability to rescuers, greater-than-foreseeable harm due to P's preexisting condition that make P more vulnerable, and enhanced harm resulting from a third person's efforts to aid the injured P.

Special proximate cause rules have developed in certain situations involving an "intervening cause"—that is, a situation where D's negligence has created a risk of some future harm, but that risk would not have materialized into P's harm but for a later intervening cause which is completely independent of D. These rules determine whether D is liable to P or whether the intervening cause cuts off D's liability (in which case it is called a "superseding cause").

3. Unforeseeable or Remote or Indirect Consequences (Dobbs §§ 187–189; R.2d § 435; R.3d PH § 29)

a. The Risk Principle

*Under the majority view, D's liability is limited (1) to those **consequences**, the **foreseeability** of which made D's conduct tortious in the first place, and (2) to **persons** within that **foreseeable zone of danger**. This is sometimes known as the "risk principle" or the "foreseeable-risk rule."*

Example: D negligently spills a large quantity of gasoline on the ground. D is subject to liability for injuries to persons and property in the vicinity caused by the ensuing fire, even though it occurs hours later and the ignition source is unknown. But D is arguably not liable for the death of P's dog that, before the fire, wandered by and drank some of the gasoline.

Example: D's employees help a passenger board a train pulling out of the station, and in doing so negligently dislodge a package wrapped in newspaper. The train runs over the package which explodes, causing a scale located on the platform some distance away to tip over and injure P. D is arguably not liable to P since an injury to her was not a foreseeable consequence of the employees' negligence.

Under this test, we put ourselves in D's shoes, prior to the occurrence, and ask whether, if we were a reasonable person in D's position, the risk of what happened to P would have been sufficiently foreseeable that D was negligent in not taking sufficient care to obviate that risk. This is a "foresight"-oriented test because we are judging what D ought to have foreseen prior to the occurrence. D may have been negligent with respect to other risks, but if D was not negligent with respect to the risk that resulted in P's harm, D is not liable to P for that harm.

This is the test favored by the Restatement (Third) of Torts. R.3d PH § 29.

b. **The Direct Consequences Rule**
Under the direct consequences rule (a minority view), D is subject to liability for those consequences that are a direct result of D's tortious conduct, whether or not foreseeable. The result is direct if it follows in an unbroken natural sequence from the effect of D's act upon conditions existing and forces already in operation at the time, without the intervention of any external forces which were not then in active operation. Thus the direct consequences rule embodies a hindsight test.

Example: D's stevedores negligently cause a wooden plank to fall into the hold of a ship. Unexpectedly, the plank strikes a spark, which ignites gasoline vapor in the hold, and the ship is destroyed. D is subject to liability for the loss, even if the risk of the plank striking a spark and igniting the vapor was totally unforeseeable.

Under the direct consequences rule, D can be liable to P if she was negligent with respect to any risk, even if that was not the risk that resulted in P's injury, as long as the injury-producing event is not too remote or indirect from D's negligent conduct. This rule is sometimes expressed as a substantial factor test. Courts using this test typically permit the jury to determine whether D's negligence was a "substantial factor" in causing P's harm, or whether P's harm was a "natural and probable" result of D's negligence, subject to the court's right to decide the issue if it concludes that such a finding would be unreasonable. A leading example of this test is Judge Andrews' dissenting opinion in the *Palsgraf* case.

The Restatement (Second) of Torts adopted a modified direct consequences rule. According to R.2d § 435, D is subject to liability if D could have foreseen any harm from her tortious conduct, even though the manner or extent of the harm was unforeseeable, unless the court finds it "highly extraordinary" that the conduct should have brought about the harm. This rule has been superseded and replaced by R.3d PH § 29.

c. The Duty–Risk Rule

Both the risk principle and the direct consequences rule have been criticized as being too easily manipulated to reach a result desired on other grounds. Some—most notably, Dean Leon Green—have proposed that all questions of scope of liability or "proximate cause" should be treated as duty issues, to be decided by the court based on a variety of factors: social policy, fairness, expediency, etc. This approach, known as the "duty-risk rule," has won few adherents in principle, but it is not uncommon for courts to rule against plaintiffs on the ground that D had no "duty" to protect P against a particular risk or that D owed no "duty" to P—an analysis consistent with the duty-risk rule. See, e.g., Judge Cardozo's opinion in the *Palsgraf* case. Note that this approach (duty rules specific to a particular case) is inconsistent with other duty rules, which are rules of more general application.

Example: D, a physician, prescribes a drug for A but negligently fails to warn A that he should not drive a car after taking the drug because it will make him drowsy. A, having taken the drug, is driving his car in which P is a passenger when A passes out. The car crashes and P is injured. Although D's negligence is clearly a cause in fact of P's harm, and injury to P is foreseeable, the court held that D was not liable to P because D owed no duty to P.

d. Current Status of the Risk Principle
Although most courts follow Judge Cardozo's approach in the *Palsgraf* case and limit D's liability to the foreseeable risks that made D's conduct negligent, many tend to allow juries to determine when the harm realized is too remote from D's negligence. They tend to see *all* causation issues as for the jury, and questions as to whether the risk realized is too disproportionate or different from the risk that made D's conduct tortious as questions for the court.

e. Elasticity of "Foreseeable"
Under the majority view, courts can expand or contract the bounds of D's liability by expansive or constrictive rulings on the foreseeability question. Courts may find particular results foreseeable (or not), and thereby reach a decision preferred on policy grounds. Courts sometimes reach a desired outcome by characterizing the result as "not unforeseeable."

f. Elasticity of "Hazard"
The bounds of D's liability may also be expanded or contracted depending on how the court defines the hazard or risk that makes D's conduct tortious. See R.2d § 281, Comments f, g.

Example: Even though D's tortious conduct created a foreseeable risk only of damage to P's property, most courts will hold D liable for P's personal injuries resulting from the same conduct, even if unforeseeable. Thus, if D poisons P's dog and the poison infects and kills P, D is subject to liability for P's death even though any injury to P himself was in fact unforeseeable. See R.2d § 281, Comment j.

g. Rescuers
Rescuers benefit from a fixed scope of liability rule. The intervention of would-be rescuers is usually deemed foreseeable as a matter of

law, and therefore when D's tortious conduct endangers anyone (including himself), he is subject to liability to P who is injured in attempting a rescue, so long as the harm arises from a risk inherent in the effort to provide aid. R.3d PH § 32. Note that professional rescuers are often treated differently under what is known as the "firefighter rule."

h. Physical Consequences

Under another fixed rule, the so-called "thin-skulled" or "eggshell" plaintiff rule, D is liable for the full consequences of P's injury even though, due to P's peculiar susceptibility to harm (of which D was unaware)—P's physical or mental condition or other characteristics—those consequences were more severe than they would have been in a normal person. "You take your plaintiff as you find him." R.3d PH § 31.

Example: D negligently rides his bicycle and runs into P, a pedestrian, knocking him down. Unknown to D, P has an unusually thin skull, which strikes the pavement. P dies from multiple skull fractures. Or, P has hemophilia, as a result of which he bleeds to death. D is subject to liability for P's death, even though a normal person's injuries would have been minor.

Example: D negligently throws a dart, blinding P in his right eye. Unknown to D, P was already blind in his left eye. D is subject to liability for P's total blindness.

i. Intentional Torts; Strict Liability

Courts tend to expand the limits of foreseeability when D's conduct amounts to an intentional tort, and conversely confine liability to foreseeable consequences when liability is strict. See R.2d §§ 435A–B, 504(3)(c), 524A; R.3d PH § 33.

4. **Intervening Cause** (Dobbs §§ 190–96; R.2d §§ 440 461; R.3d PH § 34)

a. Definition

An intervening cause is conduct by some third person, or an event which occurs, after D's tortious conduct, and operates with or upon D's conduct to produce P's injury.

Example: D negligently spills a quantity of gasoline upon the ground and departs. Some time later, a third person negligently discards a cigarette and the gasoline ignites. Or the gasoline is ignited by a bolt of lightning. The act of the third person and the lightning are intervening causes of the resulting injury to P.

b. **General Rule**
If (1) an intervening cause was foreseeable, or (2) the intervening cause was not foreseeable but the consequences were of the type which D could foresee as resulting from his conduct, the intervening cause will not operate to relieve D of liability. But if both the intervening cause and the resulting consequences were not foreseeable, it is called a superseding cause and D's tortious conduct is not deemed a proximate cause of P's injury. R.3d PH § 34.

c. **Types of Intervening Causes**
An intervening cause may consist of either human conduct or any other natural force or event (e.g., action of weather, animals).

d. **Foreseeable Intervening Causes**
Foreseeable intervening causes may include:

1) **Weather**
Non-extraordinary weather conditions or changes.

2) **Negligence**
Negligence by third persons is normally foreseeable. See R.2d § 447.

3) **Criminal Conduct**
Criminal conduct or intentional torts by third persons are deemed foreseeable if D's negligent conduct exposes P to a greater-than-normal risk of such conduct, or if the exposure to such risks is what makes D's conduct tortious.

Example: D negligently leaves P's car unlocked with the keys in the ignition. The criminal act of a thief in stealing the car is not a superseding cause.

Example: D negligently leaves his car unlocked with the keys in the ignition in a neighborhood populated by derelicts and drunks, one of whom steals the car and negligently drives it, injuring P. Neither the theft nor the negligence of the driver is a superseding cause of P's injury.

Example: D negligently spills a large quantity of gasoline. T, an arsonist, seeing the gasoline puddle, throws a match into it for the purpose of causing it to ignite. The ensuing explosion injures P. D is subject to liability to P if the foreseeable risk of T's conduct was one of the things that made D's conduct negligent in the first place.

Example: P is a guest at D's motel. Returning to her room, P is assaulted by X, who was able to gain entrance to P's room because the lock on the door was of the simple residential type that can easily be defeated with a credit card. P sues D claiming negligence in providing inadequate locks for guest rooms. Assuming D is found negligent, X's criminal acts are not a superseding cause of P's harm.

4) Acts While Insane

If D's tortious conduct causes P to become so insane as to lose control of his mind, D is subject to liability for P's self-inflicted harm resulting from that insanity. R.2d § 455.

5) Rescuers

Acts, even negligent ones, by rescuers and others who render aid reasonably required by P's injury. R.3d PH § 35.

6) Efforts by P to Mitigate

Efforts by P to mitigate the effects of his injury.

7) Further Harm

Disease contracted or subsequent injuries sustained because of the impairment of P's health resulting from the original injury caused by D's tortious conduct. R.2d §§ 458, 459.

e. Foreseeable Consequences

If the result is foreseeably within the risk created by D's tortious conduct, then even an unforeseeable intervening cause does not supersede D's liability.

Example: D negligently spills a large quantity of gasoline, which is ignited by fragments of a falling meteor. D is subject to liability.

5. Substantial Factor

As noted above, the "substantial factor" requirement has been eliminated as part of the definition of cause in fact, but it may be relevant as a scope of liability issue. When D's negligent conduct makes only a trivial contribution to multiple factual causes of P's harm, the harm is not within the scope of D's liability. R.3d PH § 36. However, this rule does not apply if the trivial contributing cause is necessary for the outcome; it only applies when the outcome is overdetermined.

D. Review Questions

[Answers Provided in Appendix A, pages 398–399]

A's northbound car crosses the line into the southbound traffic lane. Southbound B, who is driving too fast for weather conditions, swerves to the right to avoid a collision with A. B is injured when his car strikes an electric pole. The resulting power disruption causes P, a patient in a nearby hospital, brain damage when his respirator ceases to work.

1. T or F   Whether A's negligence is a proximate (legal) cause of P's injury is a question of law for the court.

2. T or F   Whether A's negligence was the cause in fact of P's injury is a question of law for the court.

3. T or F   In a joint-and-several liability jurisdiction, if the negligent actions of both A and B are found to have proximately caused P's injury, either can be held liable for the full amount of damages.

4. T or F   If the negligent acts of A and B proximately caused P's damage, A is liable only if P's injury would not have occurred but for his negligence.

5. T or F   A is liable for any aggravation of B's injury resulting from B's negligent medical treatment.

6. T or F   A and B are not liable for P's brain damage, because a normal person would not have been harmed by so brief a deprivation of oxygen, so P's injury was unforeseeable.

7. T or F   Assume P died when his wife, out of pity for his brain-damaged condition, "pulled the plug" on his life support system. A and B are not liable for his death.

8. T or F   C rushes to rescue B from his burning car. C is burned. A is liable for C's injury.

9. T or F   In attempting to rescue B, C exacerbates B's injury. A is liable.

10. T or F   While P is fighting for his breath, robber X enters his room, takes P's money and property, and hits him on the head. A is liable.

*

PART FIVE

Special Liability Rules for Particular Activities

■ ANALYSIS

4. Natural Conditions
   a. Rule
   b. Limitation
   c. Exception: Urban Land
C. Trespassing Adults
   1. Trespasser Defined
   2. General Rule
   3. Exception: Intentional and Reckless Misconduct
   4. Exception: Frequent Trespassers on Limited Area
   5. Exception: Discovered Trespassers
      a. Rule
      b. Duty to Rescue
   6. General Duty of Reasonable Care Distinguished
D. Trespassing Children ("Attractive Nuisance" Doctrine)
   1. Discussion
   2. Rule
      a. Knowledge of Child Trespassers
      b. Attraction of Condition
      c. Knowledge of Condition
      d. Type of Condition
      e. Risk of Harm
      f. Child's Awareness of Risk
      g. Reasonableness of D's Conduct
   3. General Duty of Reasonable Care
E. Licensees and Invitees
   1. Licensee
   2. Invitee
      a. Public Invitee
      b. Business Visitors
      c. Express or Implied
      d. Present or Future Business Dealings
      e. Incidental Visitors
      f. Social Guests
      g. Scope of Invitation
   3. Duty to Licensees
      a. Intentional and Reckless Conduct
      b. Active Operations (Latent Dangers)
      c. Latent Conditions
   4. Duty to Invitees
      a. Rule

VII. Overview

Certain activities are governed by special tort liability rules. In some cases, these rules are merely special applications of the general principles of tort liability, previously discussed. In other cases, these rules expand or contract the duty which D would otherwise have had under those general principles.

Note that these special duty rules often have the effect of taking issues which, under the general rules of tort liability would have been issues for the jury, and making them issues for the court. These rules can best be understood by identifying the policy considerations underlying them.

VIII. Owners and Occupiers of Land

A. Persons Liable

The following special duty rules apply to claims against *possessors* of land for injuries resulting from either a *condition* of the *premises* or an *activity* being conducted on the premises. The benefits and burdens of these special rules apply to (1) the *possessor* of the land, (2) activities carried on by members of the possessor's *household*, and (3) activities conducted and conditions created by another acting *for the possessor*.

1. Possessor

The possessor is the person in actual occupation of the land with the intent to control it, or if there is no such person, the last person to do so. If there are no such persons, then it is the person entitled to immediate possession. R.2d § 328E.

2. Members of Possessor's Household

See R.2d § 382.

3. Persons Acting on Possessor's Behalf

See R.2d §§ 383–385, 387.

4. Others

Persons not within any of the foregoing categories are liable or not according to the usual rules of tort liability. R.2d § 386. The special duty rules described below do not apply.

B. Persons Outside the Premises
(Dobbs § 587; R.2d §§ 363–371)

1. Rule
As a general rule, a possessor must exercise reasonable care to see that activities and possessor-created conditions on the land do not harm his neighbors or passers-by on adjacent ways. R.2d §§ 364, 365, 366, 370, 371.

2. Adjacent Public Ways

a. On Ways
D is subject to liability to persons traveling on public ways (highways, streets, alleys, sidewalks) adjacent to his property if he negligently creates or maintains an artificial condition or activity which subjects those persons to an unreasonable risk of harm. R.2d § 368.

b. Deviations From Public Way
If D can foresee that persons using an adjacent public way may deviate from it onto his property as a normal incident of their travel, he must exercise reasonable care to protect them from unreasonable risks of harm which they may encounter as a result of activities or artificial conditions created or maintained on his land. R.2d § 368, 371.

c. Intentional Deviations
D's duty extends to (a) unintentional deviations and (b) intentional deviations which are a normal incident to travel on the public way in the exercise of reasonable care, and (c) foreseeable intentional deviations by children. R.2d § 369.

Example: P, a pedestrian, stops in D's doorway to tie his shoelace. But when P's departure from the public way is so substantial (in time or distance) as to amount to an interruption of his travel and an entry on D's land not incident to his travel, P ceases to be a traveler and becomes a trespasser.

Example: P leaves the public way and goes upon D's land to rest or to chat with a friend.

d. Distance
Foreseeable deviations will normally be only a short distance (a few feet or yards), but in a proper case may be a greater distance (e.g., where D so maintains part of his land that others will believe it to be a public highway, R.2d § 367).

3. Neighboring Land

D's duty to exercise reasonable care to protect against unreasonable risks of harm arising from activities or artificial conditions on his land extends to persons lawfully using adjacent land. R.2d §§ 370, 371.

4. Natural Conditions

a. Rule

D is not liable for physical harm to persons outside the premises or to adjoining land resulting from a natural condition of D's land.

> *Example:* The natural flow of surface water off the land; natural accumulations of ice and snow on adjacent public ways; D's trees which die and fall off the premises.

b. Limitation

This rule applies only to unaltered natural conditions. If D or anyone else has ever altered the natural condition of the land so as to create or aggravate the risk, D is subject to liability for unreasonable risks thereby created.

> *Example:* A structure on D's land is so erected or maintained that water, snow or ice is discharged or unnaturally accumulates on a public way; the land is landscaped so as to change the natural flow or surface water; trees are planted next to the highway.

c. Exception: Urban Land

Courts are increasingly willing to alter this rule with respect to urban land. For example, an urban land owner may be liable for negligence in failing to inspect and maintain his trees so as to prevent an unreasonable risk of harm to passers-by on adjacent public ways. R.2d § 363(2).

C. Trespassing Adults

(Dobbs § 232; R.2d §§ 329, 333–338)

1. Trespasser Defined

A trespasser (T) is one who enters or remains upon D's land without a privilege to do so. R.2d § 329. Such privilege usually arises from D's consent.

2. General Rule

D is under no duty to exercise reasonable care (1) to make the premises reasonably safe for T (or to warn T of hidden dangers) or (2) to carry on activities on the premises so as not to endanger T. R.2d § 333.

3. Exception: Intentional and Reckless Misconduct

D's immunity from liability to T does not extend to intentional torts. And many jurisdictions hold that D is liable to T for harm caused by D's reckless ("willful and wanton") misconduct. Others (and the Restatement) do not recognize this latter rule, but achieve somewhat the same result by the following two exceptions.

4. Exception: Frequent Trespassers on Limited Area

When D knows (or from facts within his knowledge ought to be aware) that trespassers constantly intrude upon a limited area of his premises, D is subject to liability to such T if he fails to exercise reasonable care (1) in the conduct of active operations on the premises which create a risk of serious bodily harm to T (R.2d § 334) and (2) to warn T of a dangerous artificial condition on the land (created or maintained by D) which D has reason to believe T will not discover and which creates a risk of serious bodily harm (R.2d § 335).

Example: D railroad knows that pedestrians regularly cross its tracks at a certain point. Although the path is on railroad land and is not a designated crossing, and despite warning signs that trespassers at this point will be prosecuted, D must operate its trains past this point in the exercise of reasonable care for T's safety.

5. Exception: Discovered Trespassers

a. Rule

Once D discovers the presence of T on his land, D must exercise reasonable care to (a) conduct his activities with regard to T's safety (R.2d § 336), (b) warn T of an artificial condition which poses a risk of serious bodily harm, if D knows or has reason to know that T is in dangerous proximity to it and that T will probably not discover the danger or realize the risk (R.2d § 337), and (c) control those forces within his control which threaten T's safety, or give T an adequate warning of them (R.2d § 338).

b. Duty to Rescue

D may have to exercise reasonable care to come to the aid of a discovered T who is injured or in peril on D's premises, even though D is not responsible for T's situation.

6. General Duty of Reasonable Care Distinguished

Note that even as to frequent trespassers on a limited area and discovered trespassers, D's duty is not a general duty of reasonable care.

D. Trespassing Children ("Attractive Nuisance" Doctrine)

(Dobbs § 236; R.2d § 339)

1. Discussion

Most (but not all) jurisdictions have special rules applicable to child trespassers, sometimes called the "turntable" or "attractive nuisance" doctrine. The component rules vary among jurisdictions, but the courts have increasingly relied upon R.2d § 339 and it now represents the most widely held version.

2. Rule

*A possessor of land is subject to liability for physical harm to trespassing children caused by an **artificial condition** upon the land if the following requirements are met, and D fails to exercise reasonable care to eliminate the danger to such children or otherwise protect them.*

a. Knowledge of Child Trespassers

D *knows or has reason to know* that the place where the condition exists is one where children are likely to trespass. It is not enough that child T's are merely foreseeable, and D need not inspect the premises to see if children trespass or if such dangerous conditions are present. But D is held to what he actually knows about the premises and what he can reasonably anticipate based on that knowledge.

b. Attraction of Condition

At one time, many courts held that the child must be attracted onto the premises by the condition that injured him (hence the doctrine's name); this is no longer required. It is enough that children who do foreseeably trespass can be expected to encounter the condition. It need not be an open and obvious condition, and the child need not even discover it prior to his injury.

c. Knowledge of Condition

D must know or have reason to know of the condition, and must realize or should realize that it involves an unreasonable risk of death or serious bodily harm to such children. D need not have created the condition, but merely maintain it or permit it to exist.

d. Type of Condition

The doctrine applies only to *artificial conditions* (not activities or natural conditions) upon the land. This is a specific application of the general rule that the risk must be an *unreasonable one*—i.e., the *risk* to the child outweighs the *utility* of the condition and the *burden* to D of reducing or eliminating the danger to the child.

Some courts have codified this rule, creating categories of "common hazards" as to which D is not liable, or limiting D's liability to injuries caused by "dangerous instrumentalities." Under this view, D is not liable for dangers such as fire, falling from a height, drowning in water, visible machinery in motion, piles of lumber, etc., which almost all children are held to appreciate. However, the better view is that whether the risk is unreasonable depends on the facts and circumstances of each case.

e. Risk of Harm

The condition must create a risk of serious bodily harm or death; but if it does, D is subject to liability for any lesser injury in fact sustained.

f. Child's Awareness of Risk

The child, because of his youth, does not (a) discover the condition or (b) realize the risk. While some courts have established arbitrary age limits (e.g. 14), the better (and Restatement) view does not; but the older the child, the fewer the dangers he will not have understood and appreciated.

g. Reasonableness of D's Conduct

The utility to D of maintaining the condition and the burden of eliminating the danger are outweighed by the risk to the children involved.

3. **General Duty of Reasonable Care**

The duty created by R.2d § 339 approximates that which would be imposed by a general duty to exercise reasonable care as to children whose trespasses can be anticipated. A few courts have opted for this approach.

E. Licensees and Invitees
(Dobbs §§ 233–235; R.2d §§ 330, 332, 341–350)

1. Licensee
A "licensee" (as that term is used in this branch of the law) is a person who has a privilege to enter or remain on D's land, but is not an invitee. The Restatement definition (§ 330) limits this term to those whose privilege is based on D's consent, but courts sometimes use the term to encompass persons with other privileges (e.g., public employees).

Examples: (1) A person who enters D's land with consent but solely for his own purpose c.g., to get out of the rain; (2) members of D's household (not paying guests or servants); (3) social guests in D's home.

D's consent may be express or implied from his conduct, or from custom, usages in the community, or prior dealings.

2. Invitee
An "invitee" is either a *public invitee* or a *business visitor*. R.2d § 332.

a. Public Invitee
A public invitee is a person who is invited to enter or remain on land as a member of the public for a purpose for which the land is held open to the public.

Example: Persons attending free public meetings, lectures, church services, free public amusements, or using public or private land held open to the public for a recreational or social purpose.

b. Business Visitors
A business visitor is a person who is invited to enter or remain on D's land for a purpose directly or indirectly connected with business dealings with the possessor of the land.

Example: Customers in stores; patrons of theaters, banks, places of amusement; employees and independent contractors entering to perform their work.

c. Express or Implied
The invitation may be either express, or implied from D's conduct, prior dealings, usages in the community, etc.

d. **Present or Future Business Dealings**

Invitees include persons entering only for the purpose of potential or future business dealings—persons entering a store only to browse, or even to return merchandise.

e. **Incidental Visitors**

Invitees include persons whose visit is for the convenience, or arises out of the necessities of, others who are on the land for a business purpose—e.g., a child taken by its parent to a shop; P going to a hotel to visit a guest; P going to an airport to meet a passenger; P in common areas of an apartment building on his way to visit a tenant.

f. **Social Guests**

Traditionally, a social guest in D's home is a licensee, despite incidental services performed by the guest or an incidental business motive behind the invitation (e.g. the boss invited to dinner). However, a few courts now classify social guests as invitees.

g. **Scope of Invitation**

The invitation may be expressly or impliedly limited, as to (a) duration, (b) purpose, or (c) the portion of the premises to which the invitation extends. If P exceeds the scope of the invitation, he becomes a trespasser or licensee, depending upon whether or not D consents to his remaining.

3. **Duty to Licensees**

D's duty to a licensee is similar (but not identical) to that owed a discovered trespasser. Specifically:

a. **Intentional and Reckless Conduct**

D is subject to liability to a licensee for intentional and reckless ("willful and wanton") misconduct.

b. **Active Operations (Latent Dangers)**

In conducting his activities on the premises, D must exercise reasonable care for the safety of licensees, provided (a) he should expect that they will not discover or realize the danger and (b) they do not know or have reason to know of D's activities and the risk involved. R.2d § 341.

c. **Latent Conditions**

As to dangerous conditions, D is subject to liability to a licensee if (a) D *knows or has reason to know* of the condition and the risk it creates,

(b) the licensee does not, (c) D should expect that the licensee will *not discover or realize the danger,* and (d) D fails to exercise reasonable care to make the condition safe, or to *warn* the licensee of the condition and the risk involved. R.2d § 342. Note that D must have *actual knowledge* of the condition (or of facts which are the equivalent of such knowledge); he has no duty to inspect or discover such conditions.

4. Duty to Invitees

a. Rule
As to invitees, there is no duty limitation; D must exercise reasonable care for their safety with respect to the conduct of activities and the maintenance of the premises. R.2d §§ 341A, 343.

b. Open and Obvious Dangers
Until recently, it was commonly held that even as to invitees, D was not liable for "open and obvious" dangers. R.2d §§ 341A, 343(b), 343A. The emerging and better view is that the obviousness of the danger is merely one fact bearing on whether D was negligent or on P's contributory fault or assumption of risk, and is not per se a duty limitation.

c. Acts of Third Persons
D must exercise reasonable care to protect his business invitees against foreseeable harm by third persons on the premises, and to discover that such acts by third persons are being done or are likely to occur. R.2d § 344. While some courts have held that, on particular facts, D's duty does not extend to protection against criminal violence by third persons, the prevailing view is that in such cases D's negligence is a question of fact for the jury.

5. Other Privileged Entrants; Public Employees

a. General Rule
One who enters D's land by virtue of a privilege other than that created by D's consent is ordinarily classified a licensee. R.2d § 345(1).

b. Public Employees—Economic Nexus
Public employees who are required by law regularly to enter D's premises to make inspections, deliveries or collections necessary to

D's operations—e.g., sanitary and safety inspectors, garbage collectors, meter readers, postmen, revenue collectors—are invitees.

   c. Firemen, Policemen

Firemen and policemen traditionally were classified as licensees. However, there is a trend to classify them as invitees, at least when upon those parts of the premises held open to the public (R.2d § 345(2)), or to the extent that their presence at the place of injury was foreseeable (e.g., after-hours security check of D's business premises).

6. Recreational Entrants

Most states now have statutes which deny invitee status to persons invited or permitted to come upon D's land for recreational purposes (e.g., hunting, fishing, swimming), provided D makes no charge to, or receives no consideration from, the visitor.

F. Rejection of Categories

(Dobbs § 237)

1. General Duty of Ordinary Care

Beginning with *Rowland v. Christian* (Cal. 1968), there are now a number of jurisdictions which have abolished the arbitrary classification of entrants upon land, either completely or as to licensees and invitees, substituting a general duty of ordinary care under the circumstances, one of the circumstances being the status of P on the land. Some states have done so by judicial decision, others by statute.

2. Expansion of Invitee Status

Among the jurisdictions that have retained the traditional categories, there is a trend to expand the scope of invitee status. A few courts have ruled that all social guests are invitees.

G. Lessors

(Dobbs §§ 240–241; R.2d §§ 355–362, 377–379A, 837)

1. General Rule

A lessor of real property is not liable to his lessee (or anyone else on the premises with the lessee's consent) for physical harm sustained by such persons during the term of the lease as a result of a condition of the leased premises, whether that condition arose or existed before or after the lessee took possession. R.2d §§ 355, 356.

2. Exception: Latent Hazards

When the lessor knows or has reason to know of a concealed unreasonably dangerous condition (artificial or natural) existing on the premises at the time the lessee takes possession under the lease, but says nothing to the lessee about it, the lessor is subject to liability for physical harm sustained as a result of that condition. R.2d § 358.

a. Lessor's Knowledge

The lessor need not inspect the premises to discover such conditions. He must know or have reason to know of the condition, and realize or should realize the risk involved.

b. Latent

The danger must be latent, in the sense that it may be expected that the lessee will not discover the condition or the extent of the risk. D's duty is only to disclose the existence of the condition, and thus there is no liability for open and obvious hazards, however dangerous.

c. Persons Protected

D's liability extends to the lessee and all persons on the premises with his consent or by his right.

3. Exception: Persons Outside the Premises

a. Pre–Existing Conditions

If there is a condition on the land existing at the time the lessee takes possession, which the lessor realizes or should realize unreasonably endangers persons outside the premises, the lessor's liability to such persons survives the transfer of possession to the lessee. R.2d § 379.

b. Conditions and Activities During Lease

The lessor is generally not liable for conditions on the premises which come into existence after the lessee takes possession (R.2d § 377) or for the lessee's activities on the premises. But if the lessor knows at the time the lease is executed that the lessee intends to conduct an activity on the premises which will subject persons off the premises to the risk of actionable harm, and nevertheless consents to that activity or fails to require proper precautions, the lessor is subject to liability for foreseeable resulting harm to such persons. R.2d §§ 379A, 837.

c. Contract to Repair

In some jurisdictions, negligent failure to perform the lessor's contract to repair the premises subjects him to liability to persons off the premises. R.2d § 378.

4. Exception: Public Admission

When the lessor leases his premises for a purpose which involves the admission of the public, he must exercise reasonable care to inspect the premises and remedy unreasonably dangerous conditions which exist when possession is transferred, if he has reason to expect that the public will be admitted before the lessee has remedied the condition. R.2d § 359.

a. Lessee's Agreement

The lessee's agreement to make the repair does not exonerate the lessor unless the lessor could reasonably expect him to perform in time.

b. Size

It is not necessary that the parties contemplate admitting large numbers of persons; the rule encompasses any place, however small, where the public may enter.

c. Scope

P need not be a business invitee of the lessee or lessor, nor need there be an admission charge. But D's liability is limited to those parts of the premises open to the public under the lease, and to persons entering for the contemplated purpose.

5. Exception: Retained Control

The lessor is subject to liability for physical harm caused by a dangerous condition located on a part of the premises which the lessee is entitled to use and over which the lessor has retained control, provided the lessor by the exercise of reasonable care could have (1) discovered the condition and the unreasonable risk and (2) made it reasonably safe. R.2d § 360.

Examples: (1) Common areas used by tenants and their visitors, such as approaches, entrances, hallways, common stairways, elevators, yards, garages, common rooms, and basements;

(2) appliances and other appurtenances necessary to the use of the premises, such as heating and air conditioning

systems, water and water heating systems, electrical systems, and common laundry facilities; and

(3) in some cases, structural components of the building, such as foundations.

a. Scope

Liability extends to the lessee, members of his family, his employees, and all lawful visitors on the premises. But it does not extend to areas where tenants and their guests are forbidden, nor to visitors of a tenant who intrude upon areas that have nothing to do with the proper purpose of their visit.

The fact that the danger is open and obvious does not affect D's duty, but may be relevant on P's contributory negligence or assumption of risk. Most courts extend liability to unreasonably dangerous natural, as well as artificial, conditions.

b. Lease Exculpatory Clause

A clause in the lease exonerating the lessor from this liability may or may not be effective as to the tenant, but is always ineffective as to third persons not parties to the lease.

c. Criminal Violence

The cases are divided on whether a landlord is subject to liability to his tenants for criminal violence by third persons occurring in common areas of the building, based on his failure to provide adequate security.

6. Exception: Agreement to Repair

Until recently, the general rule was that there was no tort liability for negligent failure to perform a contract to repair or maintain the leased premises. Today, most jurisdictions follow R.2d § 357 and hold that the lessor's contractual promise to repair subjects him to tort liability for negligence in failing to perform his contract resulting in an unreasonable risk of physical harm, whether the disrepair existed before or after the lessee took possession.

a. Scope

The lessor's liability extends to the tenant and all others on the premises with the tenant's consent. The extent of his duty is defined by the contract.

b. Notice

Unless otherwise provided by the lease, the lessor's duty is only to exercise reasonable care to make the repairs after he has notice of the need for them. He need not inspect the premises.

c. Consideration

The contract to repair must be supported by consideration. As yet, there is no liability for failure to perform a gratuitous promise to repair.

d. Services

The lessor may be liable for failure to provide a service required by the lease (e.g. heat, light) where the premises cannot be safely used without it.

7. Exception: Negligent Repairs

A lessor who undertakes (or purports to undertake) repair of the leased premises is subject to liability for physical harm resulting if (1) *he increases the danger* which existed before he undertook the repairs, or (2) *a concealed danger remains* and his repairs create a *deceptive appearance of safety*, or (3) the danger is a *latent* one and the lessor *assures the lessee* that the repairs have been made when in fact they have not.

This exception applies *only when* the danger (or enhanced danger) is such that the lessee neither knows nor should know that the repairs were not made or were made negligently. R.2d § 362.

8. Independent Contractors

The lessor cannot escape his responsibilities by delegating the work to an independent contractor. He is liable for the contractor's negligence in performing the foregoing duties to the same extent as if the contractor were his employee. R.2d §§ 419–421.

9. General Duty of Reasonable Care

Several states have abolished the foregoing limited rules and substituted the rule that the lessor is under a general duty of reasonable care under the circumstances.

10. Statutes

Statutes and ordinances in many jurisdictions impose duties on lessors which have the effect of expanding their common law tort duties, particularly their duty to keep the premises in repair. Violation of these statutes can subject the lessor to liability for resulting physical harm.

H. Vendors and Vendees
(Dobbs § 239; R.2d §§ 351–354, 372–376)

1. Vendors and Grantors

a. General Rule
A transferor of land is not subject to liability to his transferee for physical harm resulting from a dangerous condition of the premises (natural or artificial), whether existing when, or arising after, the transferee took possession. R.2d §§ 351, 352, 354.

b. Exception: Latent Hazards
The transferor is subject to liability to his transferee (or others on the premises with his consent) for physical harm resulting from a concealed dangerous condition, provided (1) the transferee did not know or have reason to know of the condition or the risk involved, (2) the transferor knew or should have known of the condition, realized or should have realized the risk it created, and could anticipate that the transferee would not discover the condition or appreciate the risk, and (3) the risk is an unreasonable one. R.2d §§ 353, 354.

c. Exception: Persons Outside the Premises
A transferor who has created or negligently permitted to remain on the land an artificial condition which involves an unreasonable risk of harm to persons outside the premises is subject to liability for physical harm to such persons caused by that condition after the transferee has taken possession. This liability continues for a reasonable time after transfer, until the transferee has had a reasonable opportunity to discover the condition (or actually discovers it, if it was actively concealed by the transferor) and a reasonable time to correct it. R.2d §§ 373, 376.

2. Builder–Vendors
Courts are increasingly subjecting persons who build and market new buildings to tort liability for unreasonably dangerous conditions in them, via (1) ordinary negligence principles, (2) strict liability for breach of warranty, or (3) in a few cases, strict liability analogous to strict product liability, at least where the builder-vendor is a mass-producer of homes.

3. Vendees and Other Transferees

A transferee of land thereby becomes its possessor and is subject to a possessor's duties and liabilities, but not until he discovers or should have discovered any dangerous conditions and has had a reasonable time to remedy them. R.2d § 366. If the risk of harm is to persons outside the premises, the rule is the same, except that in certain circumstances he may assume that a private nuisance exists with the consent of those affected by it.

I. Review Questions

[Answers Provided in Appendix A, pages 399–401]

1. T or F   Mort has built a replica castle that is visible from the street and sidewalk. He has told sightseers and neighbors not to go in the yard and has numerous "no trespassing" signs posted, because he has also created authentic defensive devices to protect the castle. Passerby sees the castle and decides to get a closer look. He is injured by a low hanging branch that is actually on Mort's neighbor's land. Mort is not liable.

2. T or F   Child has seen the castle many times and knows that Mort has told people not to go on his property. However, Child decides to go onto Mort's land and falls into the moat Mort erected. Mort is not liable, because he had adequately warned Child of the danger.

3. T or F   Meter Reader decides to deviate from his job and take a closer look at the castle. He is injured when he trips over a barricade. Mort is liable.

4. T or F   Owner owns property adjacent to a stretch of public highway that is closed for repairs. Traveler is driving along the highway unaware that the road ahead is closed, because vandals have defaced the warning and detour signs. Owner assumes that no one will be on the road because of the construction and fells several large trees bordering the highway just before the stretch of closed road. Traveler is injured when one of the trees strikes his car. Owner is not liable.

5. T or F   Owner maintained a paved frontage road alongside the stretch of closed highway. Traveler mistook the frontage road for a public road, and drove across the grass on the roadside and along the frontage road, where he was injured when his car was struck by one

of Owner's falling trees. Owner is not liable, because Traveler was trespassing.

6.   T or F   Traveler is injured when a rotten tree on Owner's property is blown down by the wind into the path of Traveler's car, which is traveling the public highway. Owner is not liable.

7.   T or F   Traveler discovers that the road is closed and enters onto Owner's land, despite the presence of several "private property" signs, in an attempt to detour the construction area. Traveler is injured when his car is struck by one of the trees Owner is felling. Owner is liable.

8.   T or F   Owner knows that many highway travelers have used his frontage road. Traveler is injured when his car is struck by one of the trees Owner is felling. Owner is liable.

9.   T or F   Owner discovers Traveler trespassing. Owner must warn Traveler of the danger of falling trees and cease his activities if Traveler's safety is threatened.

10.   An old treehouse exists in one of the trees on Owner's land bordering the highway. Traveler Jr. (7 years old), who is biking along the bikepath adjacent to the highway, sees the treehouse and decides to inspect it. He climbs over a low fence and ignores the "private property" signs. The ladder leading to the treehouse collapses and Traveler Jr. is injured when he falls from the tree. Owner is liable in which of the following situations?

a.   Owner just bought the land and was unaware of the presence of the treehouse. *no*

b.   Traveler Jr. is 15 years old. *no*

c.   Owner discovers the treehouse and attempts to minimize the danger by mutilating the ladder. *yes*

11.   Which of the following persons are categorized as Owner's "invitees" for the purposes of premises liability?

a.   Members of Owner's household.

b.   Customers.

c.   Social guests. *depends*

(d.) Business visitors.

e.   Children attracted by the treehouse.

(f.) Children accompanying their parents who are customers.

(g.) Meter readers.

h.   Non-paying fishermen.

12. Short essay: When is a lessor of real property liable to his lessee for physical harm sustained during the term of the lease as a result of a condition of the leased premises?

IX. Products Liability

(Dobbs §§ 351–376; R.2d §§ 388–408; R.3d PL; Products Liability Nutshell)

Liability for physical harm caused by an unsafe product may be based on one or more of three legal theories: *negligence, breach of warranty,* or *strict tort liability.* In most cases, a P injured by a product may elect any or all of these theories in the same lawsuit, to the extent the facts support the essential elements of one or more of them.

A. Negligence

In general, ordinary negligence principles apply to products liability actions brought on a negligence theory.

1. Privity Limitations

Prior to *MacPherson v. Buick Motor Co.* (N.Y. 1916), the general rule was that the manufacturer or other seller of an unsafe product was not liable in negligence to the user or consumer absent privity of contract between P and D (*Winterbottom v. Wright*)—that is, unless P had bought the product directly from D. Exceptions arose (1) when the unsafe condition was fraudulently concealed by the seller, and (2) for products "inherently" or "imminently" dangerous to human life or health (e.g., poisons, guns, explosives). Following some expansion of these exceptions, *MacPherson* (per Cardozo, J.) held that lack of privity is not a defense when it is foreseeable that the product, if negligently made, is likely to cause injury to a class of persons which includes P. This effectively abolished the privity limitation. Eventually *MacPherson* was followed in all jurisdictions.

2. Persons Protected

D is subject to liability not only to the ultimate purchaser or lessee of the product but also to all foreseeable users or consumers, and to all other persons foreseeably exposed to the risk it creates. R.2d §§ 395, 406. Usual proximate cause rules apply.

3. Types of Negligent Conduct

a. Manufacturers

Negligence in the manufacturing process includes negligent design (R.2d § 398); errors or omissions during production (R.2d § 395); failure to properly test or inspect; unsafe containers or packaging; inadequate warnings or directions for use; and misrepresentation. A subsequent seller's failure to inspect does not relieve the manufacturer of liability for his negligence. R.2d § 396.

b. Subsequent Sellers

Subsequent sellers—e.g., distributors, retailers—may be negligent in failing to warn of the existence of an unsafe condition or otherwise protect the user. R.2d § 401. Under the majority view, such seller is liable only for dangers of which he knew or had reason to know; he has no duty to inspect or test the product to discover latent dangers. R.2d § 402.

c. Other Suppliers

Commercial lessors, and others who furnish chattels to be used for the supplier's business purposes, are liable for negligence in furnishing an unsafe chattel; their duty *includes* a duty to inspect. R.2d §§ 391–393, 408. Other suppliers—donors, gratuitous bailors—are subject to liability if they *knew or had reason to know* that the product was unsafe. R.2d § 388, 389, 405. And one who supplies a chattel to one who he knows or has reason to know is incompetent to use it safely is subject to liability for resulting physical harm. R.2d § 390.

d. Independent Contractors

Contractors who make, rebuild, or repair a chattel are subject to similar rules. R.2d §§ 403, 404.

e. Ostensible Suppliers

One who puts out as his own a chattel manufactured by another is subject to the same liability as though he were its manufacturer. R.2d § 400.

B. Breach of Warranty

1. Types of Warranties

Warranty is not a tort concept, but breach of certain warranties gives rise to an action for resulting physical harm which is part of the law of "products liability." In most cases the following warranties codified by the Uniform Commercial Code are involved.

a. Express (§ 2–313)

Express warranties are promissory assertions of fact or descriptions that are part of the basis of the bargain.

b. Implied Warranty of Merchantability (§ 2–314)

The implied warranty of merchantability implies minimum standards of quality including safety. (Here, D must be a "merchant" with respect to goods of that kind).

c. Implied Warranty of Fitness for a Particular Purpose (§ 2–315)

This warranty arises when the buyer relies on the seller to furnish goods suitable for a particular specified use.

2. Strict Liability

Liability for breach of warranty is strict; no negligence or other fault need be shown.

3. Limitations

The principal limitations on liability for breach of warranty are (1) the seller must be given prompt *notice* of the breach, (2) the buyer must have *relied* upon the warranty, and (3) the seller in certain cases can *limit* or *disclaim* these warranties (but see U.C.C. § 2–719(3)).

4. Privity

As in the case of negligence, liability for breach of warranty was once limited to the parties to the contract of sale. The first exception was in cases involving products intended for human consumption, and then for intimate bodily use. *Baxter v. Ford Motor Co.* (Wash. 1932) signaled the end of the privity limitation as to express warranties; *Henningsen v. Bloomfield Motors, Inc.* (N.J. 1960) abolished the privity limitation as to the implied warranties.

C. Strict Tort Liability for Defective Products

Urged by legal writers and led by Justice Traynor's concurring opinion in *Escola v. Coca Cola Bottling Co.* (Cal. 1944), strict tort liability for defective products was first adopted in *Greenman v. Yuba Power Products, Inc.* (Cal. 1963). Shortly thereafter this principle was codified in R.2d § 402A, and it is now the law in most jurisdictions.

1. Rule

*D is strictly liable for physical harm to P or his property caused by a **defective condition** of a product which renders it unreasonably dangerous, if (1) D sold the product in that condition and (2) D is engaged in the business of selling such products.* **R.2d § 402A.**

2. Rationales for Strict Products Liability

Various rationales have been advanced in support of strict tort liability for defective products, some stronger than others. Support for such liability is based on some combination of these rationales.

a. *Consumer expectations and reliance.* By placing a product on the market, the seller impliedly represents that it is reasonably safe and healthy, and consumers justifiably rely on that implied representation.

b. *Enterprise liability.* The most economically efficient means of distributing the costs resulting from injuries caused by defective products is to place those costs on the manufacturer or seller, who can spread those costs among all purchasers of their products.

c. *Problems of proof.* Although manufacturers of defective products will often have been negligent, it is difficult and costly for the purchaser or consumer to prove negligence, and therefore too many valid negligence claims will be lost or deterred.

d. *Deterrence.* Strict liability provides the necessary incentive for manufacturers to make their products as safe as reasonably possible.

e. *Practicality I.* Strict liability can already be accomplished by a series of warranty actions, but such extended litigation is wasteful and needless.

f. *Practicality II.* The manufacturer is in a better position than the consumer to protect against harm from defective products, and to insure against such liability.

g. *Fairness.* The manufacturer imposes nonreciprocal risks on the consumer, and reaps a significant economic benefit from placing its products on the market. Therefore, it is fair for the manufacturer to be held responsible for the risks it creates, rather than to impose the costs of those risks on the victim or on society at large.

3. Products

The term "product" includes all forms of tangible personal property (chattels). With rare exceptions, the courts have not extended the concept to sales of other commodities, such as human blood and electricity after it has been delivered to the consumer. In addition to manufactured products, it includes products which undergo little or no processing, (e.g., bottled water). The doctrine has not generally been extended to transactions which, although incidentally involving a product, are essentially the rendition of a service.

4. Defect Unreasonably Dangerous

a. Types of Defects

In most jurisdictions, D is subject to liability to P only if the product contains a "defect" which renders it "unreasonably dangerous" to the user or consumer. The types of defects include:

1) Design Defects

Design defects are those that are inherent in the product's design and thus are common to every unit of the product on the market. Examples include the use of inadequate materials or the absence of feasible safety devices. In design defect cases, the product is exactly as the manufacturer intended it to be; P's argument is that the manufacturer's intended design was flawed and unsafe.

2) Manufacturing Defects

A manufacturing defect is one that occurs in a particular product unit because of an error or omission in manufacturing, assembly, or processing. The product was *not* marketed in the condition the manufacturer intended. Example: An automobile power steering mechanism with (a) metal particles in the steering fluid that clog the mechanism and cause the steering to lock up or (b) a missing bolt that has the same effect.

3) Defects in Warnings or Instructions for Use

A product may be defective and unsafe because of inadequate directions for use or inadequate safety warnings, i.e., information defects. Note that this is also a type of design defect. Warnings and directions for use may be inadequate if they do not adequately and effectively communicate not just that there is a danger but its nature and extent, the possible consequences of encountering the risk, and, if applicable, alternatives that will minimize or negate the risk. A product may not be defective for failure to warn of an open and obvious danger, but if D can anticipate harm despite the obviousness, the product could be found defective if it could have been made safer, or if a warning could be found to have effectively prevented the harm.

P must prove causation—that is, that he would have read, understood, and heeded the warning or instructions that should have accompanied the product if they had been provided.

4) The Defect May Be in the Product Itself or in its Container or Packaging Or in the Documentation Accompanying the Product.

b. "Unreasonably Dangerous"

Most jurisdictions follow the Restatement (Second) of Torts § 402A and require that the product be not only "defective" but also "unreasonably dangerous." (A few states, e.g. California, consider these two concepts synonymous; on this basis, one or two have rejected the "unreasonably dangerous" requirement as redundant.) However, jurisdictions differ as to the test to be applied to determine when a product's design is "unreasonably dangerous." While this issue can apply to all types of defects, it usually arises in design defect cases.

1) Consumer Expectation Test

One popular test is known as the "consumer expectation" test, derived from the language of § 402A comment *i*, requiring the product to be dangerous "to an extent beyond that which would be contemplated by the ordinary consumer who purchases it, with the ordinary knowledge common to the community as to its characteristics." This is similar to the UCC's standard of "merchantability." This test is adequate in many situations, but sometimes the ordinary consumer does not have enough information to have a reasonable expectation as to the product's design safety. In addition, this test sometimes tends to insulate manufacturers from liability for open and obvious design defects.

2) **Presumed Seller's Knowledge Test**

Another test implements the strict liability standard directly: would the seller have been negligent in marketing the product *if the seller had known of its harmful or dangerous condition*? This test, often applied in design defect cases, is actually just another form of the risk-benefit test, since it requires the same kind of "Hand test" balancing of the risks and benefits of the design chosen by D vs. the safer design proposed by P.

3) **Risk–Benefit Balancing Test**

The popular "risk-benefit" test requires the trier of fact to balance (1) the safety risks of the product as designed, and (2) the utility and other benefits of the product as designed, against (3) the safety risks and benefits of the product if it had been designed as P claims it should have been. In practice, this is the same kind of "Hand test" balancing that would occur if the cause of action were based on negligence. The difference is that the focus is on the *product* and not on the *conduct* of the manufacturer. Thus, in theory, it does not matter whether the manufacturer's design choice was objectively reasonable at the time it was made if the trier of fact concludes that the product could have been designed to be safer (and thus have prevented P's injury) without incurring unreasonable additional costs.

The seven factors proposed by Dean John Wade are often used in this test: (1) the usefulness and desirability of the product as designed; (2) the likelihood and probable seriousness of injury from the product as designed; (3) the availability of an alternative product or design that would meet the same need and not be as unsafe; (4) the manufacturer's ability to eliminate the danger without impairing the product's usefulness or making it too expensive; (5) the user's ability to avoid the danger; (6) the user's anticipated awareness of the danger; and (7) the feasibility of the manufacturer's spreading the risk of loss by pricing or insurance. In some jurisdictions, more than one of these tests are available, sometimes in a single case.

c. **Unavoidably Unsafe Products**

Under comment *k* to R.2d § 402A, some highly useful products (e.g., certain drugs and vaccines) may be "unavoidably unsafe" because of inherent dangerous side effects which "in the present state of human knowledge" cannot be eliminated. Such products, "properly prepared, and accompanied by proper directions and warnings," are not defective or *unreasonably* dangerous. Key issues, as to which the courts disagree, include whether this provision applies (1) only to design defects, and (2) to unknowable dangers, or only to known but preventable dangers. As to prescription drugs and medical devices, R.3d PL § 6 goes beyond comment *k*; if a reasonable health care provider, knowing the benefits and risks of the product, would prescribe it, then the manufacturer is not liable.

d. Crashworthiness

A product such as a vehicle may be defective and unreasonably dangerous because it is insufficiently crashworthy.

e. Food Products

In the case of food products that contain a harm-causing ingredient (e.g., a sharp one-inch chicken bone in a chicken enchilada, a piece of glass in a serving of slaw), most courts (and the Restatement) hold that the ingredient constitutes a defect if a reasonable consumer would not expect the food product to contain that ingredient, regardless whether the ingredient is foreign (the glass) or natural (the chicken bone). R.3d PL § 7 thus retains the consumer expectation test for food products. A minority of courts allow strict products liability if the ingredient is foreign but not if it is natural, but permit recovery for natural ingredients on a negligence theory.

5. Type of Harm

Strict tort liability for defective products is almost always limited to damages for physical harm, and consequential damages resulting from physical harm, attributable to the defect. In one or two states, recovery is allowed for pecuniary loss alone, but in all other jurisdictions pecuniary loss caused by a defect in the product without an accidental injury to the product itself, or to persons or other property, is recoverable only under a breach of warranty or contract theory.

6. Plaintiffs

Liability extends not only to the purchaser or lessee of the product but to all foreseeable users or consumers. And most jurisdictions allow recovery by "bystanders" (persons other than the above) whose exposure to the risk of injury was foreseeable (e.g., a third person injured in a crash caused by a defect in an auto).

7. Proof of a Defect

In a strict products liability case, the existence of an unspecified manufacturing defect may be shown by circumstantial evidence, analogous to the use of res ipsa loquitur in a negligence case. R.3d PL § 3, states the rule: It may be inferred that the harm sustained by the plaintiff was caused by a product defect existing at the time of sale or distribution, without proof of a specific defect, when the incident that harmed the plaintiff (a) was of a kind that ordinarily occurs as a result of product defect, and (b) was not, in the particular case, solely the result of causes other than product defect existing at the time of sale or distribution.

8. Defenses

a. Contributory Negligence

Prior to the adoption of comparative fault, most jurisdictions held that P's "ordinary" contributory negligence was not a defense to strict product liability. In other words, if P's fault was only in failing to discover the defect or to guard against the possibility of a defect, such fault was not a defense. Today, some of the jurisdictions adopting comparative negligence permit that type of contributory negligence to reduce P's damages; others continue to hold that such negligence is not a damage-reducing factor.

b. Implied Assumption of Risk

Prior to the adoption of comparative fault, in most jurisdictions implied assumption of the risk—that is, unreasonably proceeding to use the product after discovering the defect—was a complete bar to recovery under strict product liability. Today, in most comparative fault jurisdictions, implied assumption of the risk is only a damage-reducing factor, and in many, it is not even a separate concept, having been merged into contributory fault. It remains a complete bar in a few states. According to R.3d PL § 17, whatever comparative fault system is used generally in a given jurisdiction should also be used in products liability cases.

c. Misuse

P's misuse of the product is not a defense at all, but is relevant on P's prima facie case. If P's injury was caused by an *unforeseeable misuse* of the product, D is not liable, since either the product was not defective or any defect was not a cause in fact of P's harm. But if P's use, even though not an intended use of the product, was a *foreseeable misuse* (e.g., standing on a chair, a child drinking furniture polish), the product may be found defective because it was not designed so as to be reasonably safe in light of the *foreseeable misuse*. On this basis, auto crashes are generally regarded as a "foreseeable misuse" of autos, and autos must be designed so as not to subject occupants to enhanced injuries from unreasonably dangerous design features of the auto during a collision.

d. Statute of Limitations and Repose

The statute of limitations does not begin to run until P is injured. This can result in liability for some very old products. Legislation in some jurisdictions imposes an additional limitation period, called a "statute of repose," which runs from the date of the product's manufacture or first sale.

e. Disclaimer

A purported disclaimer of strict product liability is ineffective. R.3d PL § 18.

f. State of the Art

In some jurisdictions, D can defend by showing that the product was designed in accordance with the "state of the art" at the time it was manufactured and first sold.

g. Learned Intermediaries and Sophisticated Users

When prescription drugs are sold to a physician with physician-appropriate warnings, the manufacturer ordinarily can rely on the physician to protect the ultimate user, and so the manufacturer has no duty to provide a warning aimed at, or communicated to, the consumer. And where products are sold in bulk (so that further processing or distribution is contemplated), or to sophisticated users, the manufacturer can similarly rely on the intermediate buyer to use the product properly and pass on any appropriate warnings.

9. Defendants

Strict product liability extends to (1) the producer (manufacturer, processor, assembler, packager, or bottler) of the product and of the component part which was defective, and (2) all those in its distribution chain—wholesaler, distributor, retailer, and commercial lessors and bailors. D must be "engaged in the business" of dealing in that product, but such product need not be his principal business. Courts usually refuse to extend liability to dealers in used products.

10. Nondelegable Duties

Although the manufacturer is usually not liable unless the product was defective when it left his control, an exception is where the manufacturer places in the stream of commerce an unfinished or unassembled product which must be assembled or finished by his dealer, who in doing so creates the defect. And a manufacturer cannot delegate to his purchaser the duty to select and purchase optional safety devices, without which the product is not reasonably safe.

11. Post–Sale Duties

In some jurisdictions, a manufacturer may be subject to liability for failure to "retrofit" a previously marketed product with safety devices (or to provide appropriate warnings) when locating current users and furnishing such devices or warnings is not an unreasonable burden compared to the risk of injury inherent in the product without them, even though the product was arguably not unsafe when it was first marketed. See R.3d PL § 10.

12. Misrepresentation

A similar form of strict liability is imposed on one who misrepresents a material fact to the public concerning the character or quality of a chattel sold by him, and the purchaser relies upon such misrepresentation and thereby sustains physical harm. R.2d § 402B.

D. The Restatement (Third) of Torts: Products Liability

1. New Standards for Different Types of Product Defects

The new product liability provisions, which supersede § 402A, now explicitly recognize the three categories of product defects: manufacturing defects, design defects, and informational defects (warnings and directions for use). Sellers remain strictly liable for manufacturing defects, but the Restatement's proposed liability for design defects is close to a negligence standard, imposing liability only for "foreseeable risks of harm" that could have been avoided by the adoption of a "reasonable alternative design" (§ 2(b)) or by "reasonable instructions or warnings" (§ 2(c)). Thus, as a general rule, under this provision a product is not defectively designed unless P can prove that there was a feasible alternative design at the time the product was manufactured, and that the risk created by the product as designed was known or should have been known by the manufacturer. Similarly, there is no duty to warn under this provision unless P can prove that the manufacturer knew or should have known of the risk about which P claims she should have been warned. However, if the product's design is "manifestly unreasonable" because of its negligible utility and high risk of danger, defectiveness can be found even without proof of an alternative design (e.g., a dangerous toy gun).

As an alternative, P can recover if she can prove that the product as designed, or the warning, failed to comply with an applicable safety statute or administrative regulation (§ 4(a)). On the other hand, as evidence that the product was not defective, D can prove the product's compliance with an applicable safety statute or administrative regulation, although such compliance is not conclusive on the issue of defectiveness (§ 4(b)).

2. Prescription Drug and Medical Device Liability

The Restatement (Third) further restricts liability for defective prescription drugs and medical devices. Under § 6(c), a prescription drug or medical device is not defective in design unless the foreseeable risk of harm is so "great in relation to its foreseeable therapeutic benefits that reasonable health-care providers, knowing of such foreseeable risks and therapeutic benefits, would not prescribe the drug or medical device for any class of patients." Under § 6(d), warnings need only be given to "health care providers" unless the manufacturer "knows or has reason to know that health-care providers will not be in a position to reduce the risks of harm in accordance with the instructions or warnings." In that case, but only in that case, an adequate warning is owed to the patient.

Strict liability will still apply to drugs and medical products for manufacturing defects.

3. Acceptance by the Courts

It is too early to tell what influence the Restatement (Third) of Torts: Products Liability will have in the courts. Product liability law is now rather well settled, and proof of a feasible alternative design is not a universal requirement in design defect cases. Therefore, it seems possible that the Restatement (Third) provisions dealing with product liability will not have an impact on tort law comparable to that of their predecessor, § 402A of the Restatement (Second). See, e.g., *Vautour v. Body Masters Sports Industries, Inc.* (N.H. 2001).

E. Review Questions
[Answers Provided in Appendix A, pages 401–402]

1.   Short essay: Father buys a riding lawnmower manufactured by the Joe Elk Company and sold by E–Z Rider Lawn Equipment. He allows his six-year-old Son to ride the machine on a hillside, despite warnings that the machine is not to be driven on hills and that no one under the age of 16 should be allowed to drive the machine. Joe Elk expressly disclaims any liability for injuries resulting from the use of its mower. Son is injured when the mower flips over, and the blade cuts his leg. Father sues the Joe Elk Company and E–Z Rider for Son's injuries. Discuss these defendants' potential liability under current products liability law.

2.   Short essay: Discuss Joe Elk's and E–Z Rider's potential liabilities under a negligence theory.

X.   Vicarious Liability

A.   Introduction

1.   General Rule
One (D1) who, while acting on behalf of another, commits a tortious act and thereby subjects himself to tort liability to P may also thereby subject the person on whose behalf he is acting (D2) to tort liability to P. It is said that D2 is *vicariously liable* to P.

2.   Relationships Giving Rise to Vicarious Liability (Dobbs §§ 333–341)
The forms of relationships which potentially give rise to vicarious liability are (1) employer-employee, traditionally called the "master-servant" relationship, (2) principal-agent, and (3) employer-independent contractor. For purposes of tort law, there is little distinction between the liability rules governing master-servant and principal-agent relationships. However, the vicarious liability of one who employs an independent contractor is significantly different.

B.   Employers and Employees (Master–Servant)
(Dobbs §§ 333–335)

1.   Vicarious Liability
If, at the time of his negligent or reckless act, the tortfeasor was acting in the "scope" or "course and scope" of his employment, then his employer is vicariously liable to P for his servant's tort.

2. When is One an Employee?

Typically, the law of agency is used to determine whether the actor is the employee (servant) of another. According to the Restatement (Second) of Agency § 220 (2), in determining whether one acting for another is a servant or an independent contractor, the following matters of fact, among others, are considered:

(a) the extent of control which, by the agreement, the master may exercise over the details of the work;

(b) whether or not the one employed is engaged in a distinct occupation or business;

(c) the kind of occupation, with reference to whether, in the locality, the work is usually done under the direction of the employer or by a specialist without supervision;

(d) the skill required in the particular occupation;

(e) whether the employer or the workman supplies the instrumentalities, tools, and the place of work for the person doing the work;

(f) the length of time for which the person is employed;

(g) the method of payment, whether by the time or by the job;

(h) whether or not the work is a part of the regular business of the employer;

(i) whether or not the parties believe they are creating the relation of master and servant; and

(j) whether the principal is or is not in business.

One can be an employee (or servant) even without payment or the promise of payment for his services, provided the other incidents of the relationship are sufficient. R.2d of Agency § 225.

3. Scope of Employment

Whether the employee was acting in the scope of his employment is a question of fact, which depends upon (a) the employee's job description and assigned duties, (b) the time, place and purpose of the employee's act, (c) the similarity of his conduct to the things he was hired to do, or which are commonly done by such employees, and (4) the foreseeability of his act. See R.2d of Agency §§ 228, 229.

4. Intentional Torts

An employer may be vicariously liable for his employee's intentional torts committed in the scope of his employment and in furtherance of his employer's business, at least if the employee's act was foreseeable. R.2d of Agency § 231. And where there is some special relationship between the employer and P such that the employer owes P a duty of protection, the employer is subject to vicarious liability for his servant's intentional torts even if committed for personal reasons.

5. Employer's Liability

An employer may be directly (not vicariously) liable for torts committed by his employee based upon the employer's own negligence or other conduct. Thus, the employer may have been negligent in selecting, instructing, or supervising the employee; or he may have commanded, authorized or ratified the employee's tortious act.

6. Partnerships, Joint Ventures

Partners and joint venturers acting in the scope of the business subject the other partners and joint venturers to vicarious tort liability to third persons just as if they were employees.

C. Independent Contractors

(Dobbs § 336; R.2d §§ 409–429)

1. General Rule

*An employer is **not** vicariously liable for physical harm caused by the tortious conduct of his independent contractor or his contractor's employees. R.2d § 409.*

An independent contractor is a person who contracts with another to do something for him but who is not controlled by the other nor subject to the other's right to control with respect to his physical conduct in the performance of the undertaking. R.2d of Agency § 2(3).

2. Exception: Employer's Own Negligence

a. Negligent Selection

An employer must exercise reasonable care to select a reasonably competent, experienced, careful, and properly equipped contractor, and is subject to liability for physical harm resulting from his failure to do so. R.2d § 411.

b.   Negligent Instruction
     An employer is subject to liability for the negligence of an independent contractor acting in accordance with the employer's instructions. R.2d § 410.

c.   Failure to Inspect Completed Work
     An employer has a duty to inspect his contractor's completed work, at least where he has a duty to third persons to maintain the land or chattels for their protection. R.2d § 412.

d.   Failure to Require Precautions
     If the work will create a foreseeable danger to third persons, the employer must require (in the contract or otherwise) that appropriate precautions be taken for their safety. R.2d 413, 414A.

e.   Retained Supervision and Control
     To the extent that the employer retains or exercises supervision or control over the work of the contractor, he must do so with reasonable care. R.2d § 414.

f.   Duty as Possessor of Land
     A possessor of land held open to the public must exercise reasonable care to protect that public from unreasonably dangerous conditions or activities of an independent contractor on the land. R.2d § 415.

3.   **Exception: Nondelegable Duties (Dobbs § 920)**
     Where the safe performance of some duty is of sufficient importance to the community, an employer is vicariously liable for the negligence of his independent contractor in performing that duty which results in physical harm. In other words, these duties are personal to D and are not "delegable" to an independent contractor so as to relieve D of tort liability if they are negligently performed. Examples include:

     a.   Work done in a public place (R.2d § 417);

     b.   Construction or maintenance of public highways or other governmental premises held open to the public (R.2d § 418);

     c.   The various duties owed by the possessor or lessor land to lessees and business visitors (R.2d §§ 419–421, 425);

     d.   Construction, repair, or other work on the possessor's land or a structure on the land, if he has possession during the work or after he has resumed possession of the land upon its completion (R.2d § 422);

e. The duty of the lessor or bailor of a chattel, or one furnishing a chattel for his own business purposes (e.g. an employer furnishing tools to his employees) (R.2d § 425);

f. Making or repair or instrumentalities used in highly or abnormally dangerous activities (R.2d § 423, 427A);

g. Precautions required by statute or regulation (R.2d § 424);

h. Work done pursuant to the employer's franchise (R.2d § 428);

i. Work given to the employer in reliance upon the employer doing the work himself (R.2d § 429);

j. And others.

4. Exception: Inherently Dangerous Work

When the contracted work involves a special danger to others which the employer knows or has reason to know is inherent in, or normal to, the work, or which is contemplated at the time of the contract, the employer is vicariously liable for physical harm caused by the independent contractor's failure to take reasonable precautions against such danger. R.2d 416, 427. The risk need not be an inevitable or unavoidable one; merely expectable or foreseeable. And the danger need not be abnormal or extrahazardous; merely special or greater than ordinary.

Example: An independent contractor hired to transport gasoline.

5. Collateral Negligence

As a general rule, the employer's vicarious liability is limited to the particular risk(s) which give rise to the exception; he is not vicariously liable when the contractor's negligence pertains to or creates a risk which is collateral. R.2d § 426.

Example: The employer may be vicariously liable when a bricklayer drops a brick on a passer-by, or negligently constructs a wall. But the negligence of the bricklayer in driving a truck en route to the brickyard is collateral.

6. Liability to Contractor's Employees

The authorities are divided on whether the employer's liability extends to employees of the contractor whose injuries result from those risks created by the conditions upon which the contractor was hired to work.

D. Apparent Agency

Apparent or ostensible agency is based on principles of estoppel. If a principal creates the appearance that someone is his agent or employee, he is not permitted to deny the agency if a third party, who does not know otherwise, reasonably relies on the apparent agency. A principal can be held vicariously liable in tort for an injury caused by the negligent acts of his apparent agent if the injury would not have occurred but for P's justifiable reliance on the apparent agency. Some states have enacted statutes abolishing such vicarious liability against certain health care providers.

E. Review Questions

[Answers Provided in Appendix A, page 402]

1. T or F   D, a pizza delivery man, is rushing to make a late delivery when he runs a stop sign and hits P. P sues D's employer, who is found to be vicariously liable for P's negligence.

2. T or F   D has a community-wide reputation as a bully. He delivers a pizza to X, who refuses to pay because the pizza is cold. D slugs X and takes his money. D's employer is not liable.

3. In which of the following cases is the employer vicariously liable for his independent contractor's tortious conduct?

    a. Employer hires Contractor without checking his references or work experience, basing his selection solely on the low bid. Contractor has a reputation for unsafe practices on the worksite. Contractor's employee drops lumber on a passerby.

    b. Landlord hires Contractor to repair the stairway of an office complex. Contractor's repairs are defective, and Lessee's customer is injured on the stairs.

    c. Storeowner hires Decorator to redesign the lobby of his Store. Decorator sends Helper to the fabric store for samples. While on that errand, Helper negligently injures P.

    d. Landlord hires Contractor, who has a spotless reputation, to repair the porch of a piece of rental property. Contractor does so, but is negligent. Landlord does not discover the negligence until Lessee is injured when he falls through the porch.

e. Lessee of an exhibition booth at the fair hires Carpenter to erect his display case. Carpenter is trying to secure the case when it falls on Fairgoer, injuring him seriously.

f. Manager hires Local Contractor to perform work according to his franchise's specifications.

XI. Employer's Liability to Employees

(Dobbs §§ 392–396)

A. Common Law Duties of Employer to Employee

1. Safe Place to Work

The employer's common law duty to his employees is analogous to the duty of a possessor of land to business invitees. He must provide his employee with reasonably safe working conditions and warn him of unsafe conditions which he should anticipate will not be discovered by the employee. Specifically, this includes, inter alia, a duty:

a. To provide safe premises, tools, equipment, structures, appliances, and instrumentalities for the work;

b. To provide a sufficient number of competent fellow servants;

c. To promulgate and enforce plans and rules for the conduct of the work and of the employees so as to make the work reasonably safe;

d. To provide adequate supervision; and

e. To properly instruct the employee and give him suitable work.

2. Defenses

The employer's defenses include:

a. Assumption of Risk

b. Contributory Negligence

c. Fellow Servant Rule. In most jurisdictions, an employer is not vicariously liable for an injury to an employee caused solely by the negligence of a fellow servant in the performance of the *operative details* of the work (i.e., work which is *not* in furtherance of the employer's duty to provide a safe place to work).

B. Workers' Compensation

1. Workers' Compensation Acts

a. Introduction
The employee's common law tort action against his employer proved inadequate, due mainly to these three defenses. It has been replaced in all states and several other jurisdictions by workers' compensation acts, which make the employer *strictly liable* to pay scheduled benefits for most employee injuries occurring *"in the course of"* and *"arising out of"* the employment.

b. Type of Occurrence
Ordinarily workers' compensation is available only for "accidental" injuries. If P's injury was caused by environmental conditions over a period of time, his remedy is under an occupational diseases act. However, an intentional tort by a fellow employee can be a compensable accidental injury as to P if it arises out of the employment.

c. Exclusive Remedy Against Employer
If an employee's injury occurs in the course of, and arises out of, an employment covered by a workers' compensation act, his remedy under the act is his exclusive remedy against his employer, even if for some reason the particular injury is not compensable. He has no common law tort action against his employer, except in rare instances when (a) the employer's conduct amounts to an intentional tort or certain criminal violations, or (b) P is an illegally employed minor. In such cases P may elect between the workers' comp and tort remedies.

d. Compensation
In exchange for strict liability and a relatively speedy remedy, the employee's compensation is limited to a statutory schedule of limited benefits, usually a percentage of P's average weekly wage for a specified number of weeks which varies according to the severity of the injury.

e. Third–Party Actions
In most jurisdictions, the workers' comp act does not bar the employee from bringing a tort action and recovering his full

damages, even though his injury is compensable under the act, if he can find a third party (other than his employer) whose tort contributed to P's injury—e.g., a product liability action against the manufacturer of the tool that caused the injury. If P is successful against the third party, he must ordinarily repay the workers' compensation he has received.

f. Arbitration

Workers' compensation issues are tried in an arbitration system, rather than through a civil lawsuit.

2. Railroad Employees

Employees of common carriers by rail whose work has a sufficient nexus with interstate commerce are not relegated to the workers' compensation remedy. They may bring a common law negligence action against their employer under the Federal Employers' Liability Act. The assumption of risk and fellow servant rule defenses are abolished, comparative negligence applies, and P may recover if the railroad's negligence played any part, "however slight," in producing the injury or death.

3. Maritime Employees

The remedies of a seaman include (a) maintenance and cure, (b) a common law action for "unseaworthiness," and (c) a common law action under the Jones Act (similar to F.E.L.A.). A harbor worker is covered by the Longshoremen's and Harbor Workers' Compensation Act unless his work was local in nature, in which case the appropriate state workers' compensation law applies.

C. Retaliatory Discharge (Dobbs § 454)

Many courts have recognized a new tort cause of action known as retaliatory discharge. Under this doctrine, an at-will employee who is fired for conduct protected by an important, well-defined public policy can sue his former employer for wrongful discharge. Common examples include employees fired for (1) filing a workers' compensation claim, (2) reporting illegal conduct to appropriate public officials, and (3) refusing to engage in certain kinds of illegal conduct.

D. Review Questions

[Answers Provided in Appendix A, page 403]

1. Short essay: Employer assigns employees Ying and Yang to a window washing job requiring scaffolding. Ying is injured on the job. What arguments might he make in a *common law* tort action against Employer?

2. Short essay: Discuss Employer's possible defenses.

XII. Automobiles

(Dobbs § 340; R.2d §§ 318, 489–491, 495)

A. Joint Enterprise

The doctrine of *joint enterprise* is a unique creation of American tort law, founded upon an express or implied agreement among two or more persons to use an automobile for a common purpose, with all participants having a mutual right of direction and control over its operation.

1. Business Purpose

Most courts require that there be some business, financial or pecuniary interest in the objective of the journey.

2. Mutual Right of Control

All must have an equal voice. Thus, there usually will be no joint enterprise if an employee is riding with his employer. Even joint ownership or possession of the vehicle, or the sharing of expenses of driving, are not conclusive proof of the mutual right of control, although they are some evidence on that fact.

3. Effect

All participants in the joint enterprise are vicariously liable to third persons for the negligence of the driver. A participant injured by the driver's negligence may recover from the driver, but not from any other participants. R.2d § 491.

B. Owner–Passenger

An auto owner who is a passenger in his own vehicle is not vicariously liable for the negligence of the driver, but may be directly liable for his own negligence in failing to exercise control over the driver. R.2d § 495.

C. Owner–Bailor

Absent a consent statute or the family purpose doctrine, an owner-bailor (not a passenger) who merely permits another to use his auto is not vicariously liable for the driver's negligence (unless, of course, the driver was his agent acting within the scope of his employment). Exception: Florida, where a car is deemed a "dangerous instrumentality."

D. Family Purpose Doctrine

In about half the states, the owner of an auto which he makes generally available for personal (noncommercial) use by members of his immediate household is vicariously liable for its negligent operation by such persons within the scope of the express or implied permission.

E. Consent Statutes

By statute in about one-fourth of the states, an auto owner is vicariously liable for the negligence of anyone operating it on a public highway with the owner's consent, within the scope of the express or implied permission.

F. Guest Passengers

Statutes or decisions in some states limit a driver's liability for injuries to "guests" in his vehicle to situations where:

1. The driver's conduct was more than ordinary negligence; or

2. The driver's intoxication caused the injury; or

3. The injury was caused by a defect in the vehicle of which the driver had knowledge and failed to warn.

A "guest" is one who knowingly and voluntarily accepts a ride in the vehicle, absent some direct or indirect pecuniary benefit to the host.

There is a trend to repeal such guest statutes, and some courts have held them unconstitutional.

G. "No–fault" Auto Compensation Plans (Dobbs § 398)

About half the states have some form of "no-fault" compensation legislation under which mandatory insurance compensates the less seriously injured victims of auto accidents, and in most cases restricts or eliminates such victims' tort cause of action.

H. Review Questions

[Answers Provided in Appendix A, page 403]

1. T or F   Employer is driving the business car to a business meeting with his employee as passenger. The employee is not liable for his employer's negligence under the joint enterprise theory.

2. T or F   Son borrows Father's car, with his express permission to use the car on his date with Girlfriend. Son drops off Girlfriend early and

injures Pedestrian while dragracing with the boys. Under the family purpose doctrine, Father is liable because he gave Son permission to use the car.

3. T or F   Driver knew that his passenger door was likely to fly open when the car hit a bump in the road, but failed to warn Passenger, who is injured when he falls from the car into traffic. Even in a guest statute state, Driver is liable.

4. T or F   Owner allows potential Buyer to test-drive his car, while he rides along as a passenger. Buyer hits Pedestrian, who sues Owner. Owner is vicariously liable.

XIII. Medical and Other Professional Negligence ("Malpractice")

(Dobbs §§ 242–259, 484–492)

Negligent conduct by persons practicing a profession or, in some cases, a skilled trade (physician or other skilled health care provider, dentist, optometrist, lawyer, accountant, engineer, architect, clergy, teacher, veterinarian, etc.) is commonly termed "malpractice." Special rules sometimes apply to professional negligence cases.

A. Standard of Care

1. Customary Practice = Standard of Care

As previously noted (section IV.B.4.d., supra), in most jurisdictions, the standard of care of medical doctors (and sometimes other professionals) is *conclusively* established by the customary or usual practice of reasonably well-qualified practitioners in that field. Thus, the standard differs from that applied to other persons, where the customary practice in a particular trade, business, or other activity is merely *evidence* of the standard of care but not conclusive, and the jury is free to set a standard higher than that evidenced by the customary conduct.

2. Specialists

Physicians or others who are certified specialists, or who hold themselves out as specialists, are held to the standards of that speciality, but again, in most cases the customary conduct of reasonably well-qualified specialists conclusively sets the standard of care.

3. Locality Rule

Until recently, the standard of care of medical professionals (and, occasionally, other professionals as well) was further limited by the so-called "locality rule." Where this rule is applied, the standard of care is the customary or usual practice of reasonably well-qualified similar professionals *in that geographic locality*, or alternatively, *in the same or similar localities*. Today, most jurisdictions have abandoned the locality rule as applied to board-certified specialists (where the standard is inherently a national one), and most jurisdictions have also rejected the rule generally. Even in those that still purport to follow the rule, its effect can be avoided by expert testimony that the applicable standard of care is uniform nationally, which it almost always is. Of course, the professional's geographic location, and the facilities and equipment available to her there, are necessarily part of the *circumstances* relevant to the jury's determination whether the conduct of the professional was negligent.

B. Proof of Negligence, Standard of Care, and Causation

1. Expert Testimony

a. Expert Testimony Required

In most cases involving a claim of professional negligence, P will be unable to establish a submissible case without expert testimony establishing (1) the relevant standard of care, (2) that D's conduct did not conform to that standard, and (3) that there was a causal relationship between D's breach and P's injury. Although some courts have purported to adopt an absolute requirement of expert testimony, the rule should be that whether expert testimony is necessary on one or more of those elements must be determined on a case-by-case basis. Most courts now recognize that there can be substitutes for expert testimony.

b. Qualifications of Expert Witness

Although some states have adopted statutes regulating expert testimony in medical negligence cases (e.g. by requiring that the expert not be a mere testifying consultant, or requiring that the expert have the same license and certification as the defendant), the common law applies the usual qualifying tests to such expert testimony.

2. Substitutes for Expert Testimony

a. Proof of Standard of Care: Substitutes for Expert Testimony

In addition to proof by expert testimony, the standard of care in medical negligence cases can sometimes be established in other ways, such as by (1) admissions by the defendant, (2) authoritative medical literature, (3) standards adopted by government or trade groups, such as hospital licensing rules, (4) hospital by-laws and rules, and (5) literature accompanying medical products that contains warnings and directions for use.

b. Proof of Negligence: Res Ipsa Loquitur

The doctrine of res ipsa loquitur (see section IV.D.4., supra) is available in professional negligence cases to establish that the defendant's conduct was negligent. There are two types.

1) Common Knowledge Res Ipsa

Occasionally, the facts will be such that the ordinary layperson can determine that the defendant's conduct did not conform to the standard of care. A common example is the case where a foreign object (sponge, towel, clamp) was left in the patient during surgery. In such "common knowledge" cases, no expert testimony is required to prove the defendant's negligence.

2) Expert Res Ipsa

Occasionally, the facts will be such that an expert witness cannot testify to an opinion as to exactly what the defendant did that was negligent, but can testify that the adverse result would not have occurred if the defendant had exercised ordinary care.

C. Informed Consent

1. Rule

Under the doctrine of informed consent, a patient's/client's consent to a particular treatment, procedure, or other professional conduct must be based on the professional's disclosure of the material risks and alternatives to the proposed conduct so that patient/client can make an informed decision as to whether to consent. Although the rule is most often applied in medical negligence cases, it appears equally applicable to other types of professional negligence.

2. Standard

a. Professional Rule

In medical cases, at one time the prevailing standard only required the doctor to inform the patient of those risks and alternatives that doctors customarily chose to disclose. This has become known as the "professional rule."

b. Reasonable Patient or "Material Risks" Rule

The professional rule is being replaced by one which gives greater autonomy to the patient: the doctor must disclose those risks and alternatives of which a reasonable patient would want to be informed so as to be able to make an intelligent choice in other words, all risks material to the decision of the ordinary patient in P's position.

c. Distinguished From Consent to a Battery; Proof of Causation

In medical negligence cases, violation of this standard does not negate the patient's consent (so as to give rise to a battery) but rather is simply another instance of negligent conduct. The patient still must prove that the lack of proper disclosure caused him to undertake the treatment or procedure with the resulting injury. Some courts require an objective standard for proof of causation— that a reasonably prudent patient in P's position would not have consented if he had been furnished the required information—as opposed to a subjective standard under which P is allowed to prove that he would not have consented, regardless of what anyone else would have done.

D. The "Medical Malpractice Crisis" and Tort Reform

In the recent push for legislative tort reform, many states have adopted special rules to govern medical malpractice cases. These include modifications to the medical standard of care and medical res ipsa loquitur rules; partial abrogation of the collateral source rule; statutes of repose; restrictions on expert testimony; arbitrary limits on the amount recoverable in a medical malpractice action, either generally or for non-economic losses; and mandatory submission of the case to a screening panel prior to taking the case to court. Some of these reform measures have been held unconstitutional, and the mix and type of changes vary from state to state, but one or more of these changes have been adopted in most jurisdictions.

XIV. Nuisance

(Dobbs §§ 462–468; R.2d §§ 821A–840E)

A. Introduction

"Nuisances", public and private, are two distinct fields of tort liability. In essence, nuisance is not a particular kind of tortious conduct. Liability can be based on intentional conduct, negligence, or strict liability. Rather, it is a form of action for particular kinds of harm. It is the interest of P which has been invaded, and not the conduct of D, which determines whether an action for nuisance will lie.

B. Private Nuisance

1. Definition

A private nuisance is a thing or activity which **substantially** *and* **unreasonably** *interferes with Ps* **use** *and* **enjoyment** *of his* **land.** Compare R.2d § 821D. An interference with P personally, but not his use and enjoyment of his land, is not a private nuisance.

> *Example:* (1) Interferences which have a *physical effect* on the land itself, such as by vibration, objects thrown upon it, destruction of crops, flooding, or pollution of its water or soil (see R.2d 832, 833).

> *Example:* (2) Interference with the *comfort, convenience* or *health* of the *occupant,* as by foul odors, smoke, dust, insects, noxious gases, excessive noise, excessive light, high temperatures, repeated telephone calls.

> *Example:* (3) Conditions on *adjoining* land which impair P's mental tranquility by the fear or offensive nature of their mere presence, such as a house of prostitution, a contagious disease hospital, stored explosives, or a vicious animal.

2. Relation to Trespass to Land

A *trespass* is an invasion of P's interest in the *exclusive possession* of land (e.g., by entry upon it). A *nuisance* is an interference with P's interest in the *private use and enjoyment* of the land, which does not require interference with his exclusive possession; but, unlike trespass, the interference must be *unreasonable* and cause *substantial harm.* In a proper case, P may proceed on either or both theories.

3. Basis of Liability

a. Fault

Liability is not absolute. Absent a statute, D's interference with P's protected interest must be intentional, reckless, negligent, or the result of an abnormally dangerous activity such that principles of strict liability will apply. R.2d §§ 822, 824, 825. Many ongoing nuisances can be classified as intentional torts because D knows or has reason to know that his conduct is interfering with P's use and enjoyment of his land but persists in the conduct anyway.

b. Substantial Interference

Nuisance liability requires *substantial harm*, of a type which would be suffered by a normal person in the community, or by property in normal condition and used for a normal purpose. R.2d § 821F. P cannot, by devoting his land to an unusually sensitive use, make a nuisance out of conduct which would otherwise be relatively harmless.

c. Continuing or Recurring Interference

At one time it was thought that a nuisance did not exist unless the interference was continuing or recurring. There is no such requirement, although some interferences will not be sufficiently substantial unless they are.

d. Unreasonable Interference

The interference must be unreasonable, which generally means that either (a) the gravity of P's harm outweighs the utility of D's conduct, or (b) if intentional, the harm caused by D's conduct is substantial and the financial burden of compensating for this and other harms does not render unfeasible the continuation of the conduct. R.2d § 826.

1) Gravity

In determining the *gravity* of the harm, the important factors include (i) its extent, (i) its character, (iii) the social value of P's use or enjoyment it affects, (iv) the suitability of that use or enjoyment to the locality, and (v) the burden to P of avoiding the harm. R.2d § 827.

2) Utility

In determining the *utility* of D's conduct, important factors include (i) its social value, (ii) its suitability to the locality, (iii) the practicability of preventing or avoiding the interference, and (iv) the practicability of continuing D's activity if it is required to bear the cost of compensating for the interference. R.2d § 828.

3) Other Illustrations

Other illustrations of unreasonable conduct include:

(a) conduct inspired solely by *hostility* or a *desire to cause harm* to P, or which is contrary to *common decency* (R.2d § 829);

(b) harm which is *substantial* and *greater* than P should be required to bear without compensation (R.2d § 829A);

(c) harm which is *substantial* and it would be *practicable* for D to *avoid the harm* in whole or in part without undue hardship (R.2d § 830); and

(d) harm which is *substantial*, P's use or enjoyment is *well suited* to the character of the locality, and D's conduct is *unsuited* to the character of that locality (R.2d § 831).

4. Remedies

a. Who Can Recover

Anyone whose use and enjoyment of any interest (possessory or non-possessory) in the land is affected can maintain the action. R.2d § 821E.

b. Damages

The usual remedy is damages. If the nuisance is permanent, all damages must be recovered in one action. If the nuisance can be abated, P recovers all damages to the time of trial. If D then fails to abate, future invasions give rise to a new cause of action.

c. Injunction

If the nuisance threatens to continue and P has no adequate legal remedy, equitable relief may be sought. The court then will undertake a further balancing of (i) the relative economic hardship to the parties from granting or denying the injunction, and (ii) the public interest in continuing D's activity. Thus the court can require D to pay damages but deny injunctive relief

d. Self–Help

There is a limited privilege to enter another's land (or trespass upon his chattel) to abate a private nuisance. R.2d §§ 201, 264.

5. Persons Liable

Not only is one who carries on or participates in a nuisance creating activity liable. In some cases so are lessors and possessors who fail to prevent or abate one carried on by third persons on their land. See R.2d §§ 834, 837, 838, 839, 840, 840A.

6. Defenses

a. Contributory Negligence, Assumption of Risk

In an action for nuisance, P's contributory negligence or assumption of risk is a defense to the same extent as in other tort actions. R.2d §§ 840B, 840C.

b. Coming to the Nuisance

The fact that P has acquired or improved his land after a nuisance has come into existence is not itself sufficient to bar his action, but is a factor to be considered in determining whether the nuisance is actionable. R.2d § 840D.

c. Others Contributing to the Nuisance

Except as it may affect the character of the locality, the fact that others contribute to a nuisance is not a bar to D's liability for his own contribution. R.2d § 840E. And this is true even though no one person's activity, by itself, would have been sufficient.

d. Legislation

Legislation authorizing a particular activity or use of land (e.g., zoning laws, licenses) may be used to establish that it is not a nuisance, but such authority is usually narrowly construed to include only reasonable conduct.

C. Public Nuisance

1. What Constitutes

A public nuisance is an unreasonable interference with a right common to the general public. R.2d § 821B. It is a collection of minor crimes, now mostly statutory.

Examples: (1) Interference with the *public health* (e.g., pollution of a water supply, keeping diseased animals);

(2) Interference with the *public safety* (e.g., storage of explosives, harboring a vicious dog);

(3) Interference with *public morals* (e.g., a house of prostitution, gambling, indecent exhibitions, illegal liquor establishment);

(4) Interference with the *public peace;*

(5) Interference with *public comfort or convenience* (e.g., smoke, dust, vibrations, assembly of large crowds, obstructing a public street or navigable stream).

2. Public Right

The right interfered with must be common to the public as a class, and not merely that of one person or even a group of citizens.

3. Remedies

A private citizen has no civil remedy for the harm he has sustained as a result of a public nuisance if that harm is of the *same kind* as that suffered by the general public, even though he has been harmed to a *greater degree* than others. The remedy is a criminal prosecution or suit to enjoin or abate the nuisance by public authorities or others on behalf of the public. A private citizen may sue for harm caused by a public nuisance only if his harm is *different in kind* from that suffered by other members of the public. R.2d § 821C.

4. Concurrence of Remedies

If a public nuisance also interferes with P's use and enjoyment of his land, P may sue for his damages under either public or private nuisance theories.

D. Review Questions

[Answers Provided in Appendix A, pages 403–04]

1. Short essay: A group of concerned Citizens brings suit against a large chemical company which has a factory located near their residences. Several times over the past few years, the factory has experienced failures of various types, resulting in the release of poisonous gases into the air. These gases have drifted onto Citizens' property, damaging the paint on their cars and homes and causing them discomfort from the noxious odors and smoke. Discuss Citizens' cause of action under private nuisance.

2. Short essay: Discuss Citizens' cause of action under public nuisance.

XV. Negligent Infliction of Emotional Distress

(Dobbs §§ 308–313; R.2d §§ 306, 313, 436, 436A, 456, 905)

A. Introduction

Suppose P's bodily harm results *solely* from his *severe emotional distress*, which was caused by D's negligent conduct. (As to intentional or reckless infliction of emotional distress, see Part II.E., supra.) In such cases, D's duty to P is limited.

The law distinguishes three different fact situations—impact, zone of danger, and bystander.

B. Impact Rule

If D's negligent conduct results in any impact, however slight, with P's body, all courts will allow that impact to support liability for P's emotional distress resulting from the same negligent conduct. R.2d §§ 456, 905.

C. Zone of Danger Rule

If D's negligent conduct threatens (but does not result in) bodily harm (impact) to P, most courts will allow P to recover for bodily harm resulting from the fear, shock or other emotional disturbance caused by his presence in the zone of danger. R.2d § 436(2).

Example: D negligently drives his auto through a red light and narrowly misses P, a pedestrian crossing the intersection. D is subject to liability for P's bodily harm resulting from P's reasonable apprehension of being struck by D's car.

D. Bystander Rule

1. General Rule

If P himself is not in the zone of danger, but merely witnesses a shocking event in which D's negligent conduct threatens or causes physical harm to a third person, most courts have *refused* to hold D liable for P's bodily harm resulting from the shock.

2. Exception

A few courts, following *Dillon v. Legg* (Cal. 1968), have allowed P to recover in such situations, provided (a) the threatened injury is a serious one, (b) P is a member of the immediate family of the person in peril, (c) the shock results in bodily harm to P, (d) the event is of short duration, and (e) P actually witnesses the event, or at least comes upon the scene almost immediately and witnesses its aftermath. R.2d § 436(3).

3. Zone of Danger, Fear for Another's Safety

In jurisdictions that have adopted the zone of danger rule but not the *Dillon* rule, most courts will allow P to recover for bystander shock under the circumstances stated in the preceding paragraph if P was also within the zone of danger.

E. Proximate Cause Limitations

1. Physical Illness Requirement

Absent impact, in many jurisdictions, P may recover under the foregoing rules only if his emotional distress results in physical illness or comparable objective bodily consequences. R.2d §§ 313, 436A. Recently, some jurisdictions have diluted or abolished the physical injury or objective manifestation rule, either generally or in specific fact situations.

2. "Eggshell Plaintiff" Rule Inapplicable

Unless D has actual knowledge of some special sensitivity of P, D will be liable only to the extent that P's physical response to the emotional trauma was within the normal range of ordinarily sensitive persons. D is not liable for unforeseeable physical consequences.

F. Direct Victims

A line of cases is emerging allowing recovery where there is no contact or threat of physical harm, but the plaintiff is a "direct victim" of negligent conduct whose only consequence is emotional distress. Illustrative are cases where a psychotherapist engages in an improper sexual relationship with a patient resulting in severe emotional distress to the patient's spouse, who was participating in the therapy in some way. Another group are misinformation cases (e.g., an erroneous diagnosis that results only in emotional distress) or mishandling of bodies or bodily tissues. These cases tend to require rather clear foreseeability and some sort of preexisting relationship between the tortfeasor and the plaintiff.

G. Fear of Future Harm from Toxic Exposure

Assume P has been exposed, or fears he has been exposed, to a toxic substance due to D's negligence. If, in fact, P was so exposed, there is a risk of serious future harm (AIDS, cancer, etc.) but P has no present symptoms or diagnosis of the feared disease. Can P recover for the mental distress resulting from the fear of future harm, or for medical monitoring, until such time as it can be established that the risk of such future harm is zero?

1. Parasitic to Actual Physical Injury

If P can prove that he sustained any immediate physical harm, however slight, as a result of the exposure, the case fits within the traditional "impact" rule, and P can recover emotional distress damages parasitic to that injury. In most cases, P must show actual exposure to the toxic substance, and not merely a fear (however reasonable) that such exposure occurred.

2. Actual Exposure But No Physical Harm

If P can show actual exposure to the toxic substance but no immediate physical injury, many courts will allow P to recover for medical monitoring and emotional distress, but some courts require P to prove a greater-than–50% chance that he will contract the feared disease at some time in the future. "Actual exposure" means there must be a channel of exposure and also a virus or toxin must be shown to exist. If P can show actual exposure to HIV, he can usually recover for emotional distress between the time of exposure and the time when testing determines that P will not be infected with AIDS.

3. Possible Exposure and No Physical Harm

If P can only establish a possibility or fear of exposure and no present physical harm, almost all courts will deny recovery for emotional distress damages or medical monitoring. Some courts will allow emotional distress damages in HIV/AIDS cases even if P cannot establish actual exposure and there is no physical harm, so long as a channel of exposure exists and P's fear is reasonable.

H. Review Questions

[Answers Provided in Appendix A, page 404]

1. **T** or F   Driver negligently strikes a deer that is crossing a road in an area clearly marked as a deer crossing. Ranger, who is standing near the road, is struck by the deer as it ricochets off Driver's bumper. Driver is liable for Ranger's emotional distress, even if he suffered no significant physical injury.

2. T or **F**   Driver, making a futile attempt to avoid hitting the deer, veers far off of the roadway, striking the deer and coming very close to Ranger, who observes the accident. Driver is liable for Ranger's resulting emotional distress, even absent any bodily harm.

3. T or **F**   Ranger is exceptionally fond of deer, and suffers severe bodily harm as a result of his witnessing Driver's accident. Driver is liable for Ranger's bodily harm.

4.   T or F   Boy Scout witnesses Driver's attempt to avoid the deer and becomes emotionally distressed by the threat of physical harm to Ranger, who is extremely close to the road where Driver veered. Driver is liable for Boy Scout's bodily harm that results from his emotional distress.

XVI.   Prenatal Harm

(Dobbs §§ 288–293; R.2d § 869)

A.   Child Born Alive

1.   Injuries by Third Persons

One who tortiously causes harm to an unborn child is subject to liability to the child for such harm if the child is subsequently born alive. R.2d § 869(1). The prevailing view is that the fetus need not have been viable at the time of the injury. If the child is born alive but then dies from the injury (however briefly the child was alive, and whether or not viable when born), a wrongful death action can be maintained.

A few recent decisions have extended recovery to include pre-conception as well as post-conception negligence, at least where the pre-conception negligence created a foreseeable risk of the harm to the child that later resulted.

2.   Injuries Caused By Mother's Negligence

Even in those jurisdictions where the parent-child immunity is abolished, the prevailing view is that a mother cannot be held liable for her negligent conduct that results in an injury to her then-unborn child.

B.   Child not Born Alive

If D causes harm to an unborn child and the child dies from the injuries prior to birth, the authorities are divided, but most courts now allow the wrongful death action provided the fetus was viable at the time of the injury. See R.2d § 869(2). A few cases even support liability for the death of a fetus that was not viable at the time of the injury.

C.   Unwanted Children

1.   Wrongful Conception

When D's negligent conduct (usually, a negligent attempt to sterilize one parent) fails to prevent conception resulting in the birth of an unwanted but healthy child, the prevailing view is that the parents may recover, but their damages are limited to the cost of pre-natal care and delivery and the associated pain and other general and special damages. Some courts have allowed, in addition, child-rearing expenses, most (but not all) requiring that such expenses be offset by the accompanying financial and emotional benefits to the parents.

2. Wrongful Birth and Wrongful Life

a. Description
Another category of claims arises when D's negligence results in the birth of an unwanted child who is physically or mentally abnormal by reason of a genetic (or other) defect for which D is not responsible.

> *Example:* D, a physician, fails to diagnose or inform the parents that the child might be born deformed, because of a disease contracted by the mother during pregnancy or a genetic condition, in time to permit termination of the pregnancy. P's child is born so deformed. P claims that but for D's negligence, the parents would have obtained an abortion and the child would never have been born.

> *Example:* D negligently performs a sterilization procedure, resulting in the birth of a deformed child.

Actions brought by the *parents* of such children for their damages (including damages for the ordinary and extraordinary costs of caring for such children and their mental distress) are usually referred to as *wrongful birth* claims. Actions brought by the deformed *child* for his damages (e.g., pain, suffering, disability, disfigurement) are called *wrongful life* actions.

b. Wrongful Birth
After initially rejecting wrongful birth claims, most courts now allow recovery. Some courts limit damages to the parents' pecuniary losses, but others now award damages for their emotional distress as well. In some jurisdictions, statutes bar wrongful birth actions.

c. Wrongful Life
So far, almost all jurisdictions have rejected wrongful life claims, the courts finding it impossible to measure the value of life with defects

as compared to no life at all and finding it philosophically difficult to support the child's claim that he should never have been born. A few courts have allowed such claims, the damages being limited to the child's extraordinary medical and care expenses (to the extent not recovered by the parents).

D. Review Questions
[Answers Provided in Appendix A, page 405]

1. Short essay: Doctor negligently fails to inform Parents that they carry a gene which may affect the quality of life of any child born to them. Parents conceive, and a child is born alive. They discover Doctor's negligence and sue him. Discuss the results (1) if the child is healthy, and (2) if the child is defective.

2. Short essay: Driver negligently strikes pregnant Pedestrian. Under what circumstances may Pedestrian sue Driver for the fetus's wrongful death?

XVII. Alcoholic Beverages

(Dobbs § 332)

A. Commercial Vendors of Alcohol

1. Common Law Liability
The general common law rule was that one who sold intoxicating beverages was not liable to third persons injured by the person thereby intoxicated, whether directly (e.g., reckless driving) or indirectly (e.g., his family's loss of support). A few jurisdictions have overturned this rule in cases where the application of ordinary negligence principles would support liability, particularly where the sale was unlawful.

2. Dram Shop Acts
A number of states have enacted statutes (called dram shop acts) which impose civil liability on commercial sellers in favor of third persons injured by an intoxicated person. Some statutes require that the sales have been illegal, others merely that the beverage sold have caused or contributed to the intoxication.

B. Social Hosts
So far, most courts have refused to impose liability on persons who are not licensed dram shops who furnish alcoholic beverages to others with resulting physical harm, even where the application of ordinary negligence principles would justify recovery.

Example: D hosts an after-work beer party for his employees, including a minor, E, who becomes intoxicated with D's knowledge and consent. D permits E to get in his car to drive home, and en route E's intoxication results in a collision in which P is injured. Most courts hold that P has no cause of action against D.

Some jurisdictions are beginning to find liability, based on (1) violation of a liquor control statute as negligence per se, or (2) common law negligence principles such as negligent entrustment or negligent supervision or ordinary duty rules.

C. Review Questions
[Answers Provided in Appendix A, page 405]

1. Short essay: Bartender sells Underage liquor illegally, and Underage becomes intoxicated. On his way home, Underage drives his car up onto a sidewalk and kills Jogger. Discuss Bartender's liability under the common law and dram shop act.

2. Short essay: Host sponsors a holiday party in his home. He provides Guest free liquor. Guest becomes intoxicated and runs down Bicyclist, who dies from his injuries. Discuss Host's liability.

XVIII. Interference With Federal Constitutional Rights

(Dobbs §§ 44–48; R.2d Chapter 42, Introductory Note, and §§ 865, 866)

A. Persons Acting Under Color of State Law
42 U.S.C.A. § 1983 creates a tort cause of action against one who "under color of" state law (i.e., state officers and employees and private citizens acting under the authority or protection of state law) interferes with a federal constitutional right of another.

B. Federal Officers and Employees
One whose federal constitutional rights have been violated by a federal officer or employee may have an action against him for damages under the doctrine of *Bivens v. Six Unknown Named Agents of Federal Bureau of Narcotics* (U.S. 1971).

C. Review Questions
[Answers Provided in Appendix A, pages 405–06]

1. T or F   Marcher is participating in a peaceful protest a lawful distance away from Foreign Embassy. Two uniformed state police officers attempt

to discourage Marcher's activities, telling him that State prohibits protests against foreign countries. Eventually, the officers take Marcher into custody. Marcher claims that the officers interfered with his constitutional rights to free speech and assembly. Marcher may successfully bring a § 1983 action against the officers.

2. T or F   Marcher is peacefully protesting when a group of Hoodlums grabs him and drags him away. Marcher does not have a § 1983 action against the Hoodlums.

3. T or F   Marcher is peacefully protesting when a federal agent tells him he is jeopardizing national security and drags him off. Marcher does not have a § 1983 action against federal agent.

XIX.   Activities Causing Only Economic Harm

(Harper, James & Gray §§ 25.18A–25.18D)

A.   In General

As previously noted (section IV.G.4.a.), tort law has been reluctant to extend liability for negligent conduct that results solely in economic harm to P (in contrast to the freedom with which economic losses are recoverable in tort actions based on physical harm to P). This may be seen as a duty limitation based on a policy consideration—the specter of astronomical liability, out of all proportion to the defendant's fault and beyond all reasonable limits—in effect, an economic death penalty. It has been said that only a limited amount of *physical* damage will ordinarily ensue from a single act, whereas the number of economic interests a tortfeasor may destroy in a brief moment of carelessness is practically limitless.

B.   Economic Loss Caused by Physical Harm to Another

Rule: In general, P cannot recover in negligence for economic loss resulting from physical harm to another or to property in which P has no proprietary interest. A fortiori, unless there is some specific tort cause of action allowing recovery, P cannot recover for any other negligent conduct that results solely in economic loss. R.2d § 766C.

C.   Negligent Misrepresentation

Rule: In general, P may not recover for economic loss caused by reliance on a negligent misrepresentation that was not made directly to P or specifically on P's behalf. See section XXII.C., infra; R.2d § 552.

D. Exceptions

A number of cases have allowed recovery for pure economic loss, but so far these cases defy easy categorization. A common thread, however, is that there is either privity or some "special relationship" between P and D.

1. Negligent Performance of a Service

In the case of negligence in the rendition of certain professional or business services, liability has been extended in favor of clients (and sometimes others) who foreseeably relied on the service or who were its intended beneficiaries. This group includes accountants and auditors, surveyors, termite inspectors, engineers, attorneys, notaries public, architects, weighers, and telegraph companies. Under R.2d § 552 and prevailing case law, such persons are liable for negligence in furnishing false information, but only to the person (or one of a limited, specific and identifiable group of persons) for whose benefit and guidance the furnisher intends to supply the information, or where the furnisher knows that the recipient intends to rely on it. If D has a *public* duty to furnish the information (e.g. a notary public, food inspector), D's liability extends to pecuniary loss suffered by any member of the class of persons for whose benefit the duty is created.

2. Exercise of Public Right

In a few cases, a plaintiff whose business is based on the exercise of a public right (e.g. a commercial fisherman) has been allowed to recover for economic loss caused by D's negligent interference with that right (e.g. by an oil spill).

*

PART SIX

Strict Liability

■ **ANALYSIS**

XX. Strict Liability

A. Strict Liability for Animals
(Dobbs §§ 343–345; R.2d §§ 50–518)

1. Trespassing Animals

a. General Rule

Owners or possessors of all animals, including domesticated ones (except for dogs and cats), are strictly liable for physical harm resulting from the trespass of their animals on the property of another. R.2d § 504; R.3d PH § 21.

b. Exceptions

1) Cats and Dogs

Except where imposed by statute or ordinance, possessors of dogs and cats are not strictly liable for their trespasses.

2) Livestock on Highways

Persons lawfully driving livestock down a highway are not strictly liable for trespasses on property adjoining the road. R.2d §§ 504(3)(b), 505; R.3d PH § 21 comment *i*. Owners or possessors of livestock that stray onto a public highway are not strictly liable when the animals contribute to a highway accident; negligence rules apply. R.3d PH § 21 comment *h*.

3) Fencing Statutes

In some western states, compliance with "fencing in" or "fencing out" statutes avoids strict liability or is a condition to it. R.2d § 504(4).

2. Other Harm Caused by Animals

a. Domestic Animals

One who possesses or harbors animals customarily domesticated in that region is strictly liable for harm (other than harm resulting from trespass) only if (a) he knew or had reason to know that the animal had a harmful or dangerous propensity or trait and (b) that particular trait or propensity was the cause of the harm. R.2d §§ 509, 518; R.3d PH § 23. Otherwise he is liable only if he was negligent.

Exception: Statutes in some jurisdictions impose strict liability for certain kinds of harm (e.g., dog bites), irrespective of the keeper's knowledge of any propensity to cause that harm.

b. **Wild Animals**
One who possesses or harbors animals not customarily domesticated in that region is strictly liable for all harm done by the animal as a result of a harmful or dangerous propensity or characteristic of such animals. R.2d § 507; R.3d PH § 22.

c. **Scope of Strict Liability**
According to the Restatement (Second) of Torts, P cannot recover if he "knowingly and unreasonably" subjects himself to the risk. R.2d § 515. The Restatement (Third) (which does not recognize assumption of the risk as a separate defense) provides that strict liability does not apply (a) if P suffers physical harm as a result of making contact with or coming into proximity to D's animal for the purpose of securing some benefit from that contact or that proximity, or (b) if D maintains ownership or possession of the animal pursuant to an obligation imposed by law. R.3d PH § 24.

d. **Comparative Fault**
According to R.3d PH § 25, if P was contributorily negligent in failing to take reasonable precautions, P's recovery in a strict liability claim for physical harm is reduced in proportion to P's comparative fault.

e. **Watchdogs**
One is privileged to use a watchdog to guard his property only if and to the extent that he would be privileged to use a mechanical protection device. R.2d § 516.

B. Strict Liability for Abnormally Dangerous Activities
(Dobbs §§ 346–351; R.2d §§ 519–524A)

1. ***Rylands v. Fletcher*: Original Rule**
Strict liability for abnormally dangerous activities originated in the 1868 English case of *Rylands v. Fletcher*, which held D strictly liable for damage to P's mine caused by water which escaped from D's reservoir because a reservoir was a "non-natural use" of land in that area, and P's harm was caused by the "escape" of the water from D's land.

STRICT LIABILITY 317

2. *Rylands v. Fletcher*: The Modern Rule

a. General Rule

The doctrine has evolved to one of liability for harm resulting from the conduct by D of "abnormally dangerous activities" (formerly called "ultrahazardous" activities). R.2d § 519; R.3d PH § 20. It is no longer necessary that the activity was conducted on D's land, or that the harm was caused by something which "escapes."

b. Abnormally Dangerous (R.2d § 520)

Several factors may be considered in determining whether an activity is "abnormally dangerous" under R.2d § 520, the formulation usually adopted by the courts:

1) Extent of Risk

Is there a high degree of risk or harm to others, and is it likely that the harm will be great?

2) Ability to Eliminate Risk

Can that risk be eliminated by the exercise of reasonable care? If, despite D's reasonable care, the risk remains, there is greater justification for strict liability.

3) Abnormality

Is the activity not a matter of common usage? The more unusual the activity, the greater the justification for strict liability.

Example: Automobiles are a common usage on streets; moving a two-story house down the road is not.

4) Location

Is the activity inappropriate to the place where it is being conducted?

Example: Oil wells are appropriate to Texas oil fields, but not to downtown Los Angeles.

5) Social Utility

Is the activity's value to the community outweighed by its dangerous attributes?

Example: Water reservoirs are vital in southwestern states, but of much less social value in rainy regions. Query: What about atomic power plants? However, federal statutes or immunities may limit their liability.

c. Minority

A dwindling minority of U.S. jurisdictions rejects the rule by name but usually courts reach the same result via trespass or nuisance theories. For example, in blasting cases some jurisdictions once rejected strict liability for concussion damage because there was no physical trespass; today, such artificial limits generally do not exist.

d. Abnormally Dangerous: The New Test (R.3d PH § 20)

According to the new formulation in R.3d PH § 20(b), an activity is abnormally dangerous if (1) the activity creates a foreseeable and highly significant risk of physical harm even when all actors exercise reasonable care; and (2) the activity is not one of common usage. Under this formulation, the location at which the activity is conducted does not independently determine if it is abnormally dangerous, but could be relevant under either or both criteria. And the social utility of the activity is no longer a separate factor. The social utility of the activity is said to be reflected in its commonness. R.3d PH § 20, comment *k*.

e. Candidates for Strict Liability

Few activities can be said to necessarily give rise to strict liability in all cases. Much depends on the facts and circumstances. However, blasting or the use of explosives are said to be typical examples of such an activity. Other activities that are good candidates for strict liability include crop dusting, pest control and fumigation, the escape of hazardous wastes, other high-energy activities (e.g., rocket testing, pile driving, oil well blowouts), and perhaps large fireworks displays.

f. Ground Damage From Aircraft

Subject to statutory variations, strict liability is imposed in some jurisdictions (and by R.2d § 520A) for physical harm to persons and property on the ground caused by "the ascent, descent or flight of aircraft, or by the dropping or falling of an object from the aircraft."

But other jurisdictions impose liability only for negligence. And federal aviation statutes and regulations may affect state law rules. See also XIII, NUISANCE.

3. Liability Limitations

a. Scope of Liability

The harm must result from the risk that gives rise to the abnormal danger, R.2d § 519(2), but according to some, it is no defense that it was precipitated by an unforeseeable intervening cause. R.2d § 522 (some states *contra*). D is not strictly liable if P intentionally or negligently trespasses on D's land where the activity is being conducted. And D is not strictly liable to the extent that P's harm results because P's activity is abnormally sensitive. R.3d PH § 24 provides that strict liability does not apply if P suffers physical harm as a result of coming into proximity to the abnormally dangerous activity for the purpose of securing some benefit from that proximity, or (b) if D carries on the abnormally dangerous activity pursuant to an obligation imposed by law. See also R.2d § 517. The comments to R.3d PH § 20 make it clear that this form of strict liability applies only when others impose the strict liability risks, so that if P is a participant in the activity, P cannot assert a strict liability claim.

b. Defenses

According to R.2d §§ 523, 524, assumption of the risk is a defense, but contributory negligence is not except when P "knowingly and unreasonably subjects himself to the risk." According to R.3d PH § 25, if P has been contributorily negligent in failing to take reasonable precautions, P's recovery in a strict liability claim for physical harm is reduced by P's proportionate share of comparative fault. R.3d AL (and, by implication, R.3d PH § 25) does not recognize assumption of the risk as a separate defense.

c. Federal Tort Claims Act

There is no strict liability under the FTCA.

C. Review Questions

[Answers Provided in Appendix A, pages 406–407]

A keeps several animals on his property.

1. T or F   In the absence of an applicable statute or ordinance, A is not strictly liable for his cat's trespass on B's property.

2. T or F   A's mailman is injured when he enters A's property to deliver registered mail and is sprayed by one of A's skunks. A is not strictly liable.

3. B, a salesman, enters A's property. Under which of the following conditions is A liable if his dog attacks B?

    a.   If a statute or ordinance imposes strict liability for dog bites.

    b.   If A knew that the dog was vicious.

    c.   If A is negligent and his negligence results in B's injury.

    d.   All of the above.

4. B ignores the "KEEP OUT! DANGEROUS ANIMALS!" signs and enters A's property. He sees a large bear tethered to a tree. Nearby a sign warns of the bear's sharp claws and great strength. In spite of these warnings, B pokes and taunts the bear until the animal pulls loose from its tether and clubs him. Under what circumstances is A strictly liable?

    a.   If B is a child under the age of seven.

    b.   If B is illiterate.

    c.   If A knew that B was cruel and likely to provoke an attack by one of his animals, but A invited him onto his property anyway.

    d.   Under no circumstances. A adequately warned of the bear's dangerous propensity, and B assumed the risk of attack.

5. T or F   As a publicity stunt, A plans to drive cross-country with a 20 feet tall helium-filled balloon shaped like his company's product tethered to his car's bumper. At the first intersection, the balloon tangles with several heavy-duty power lines, which fall to the ground electrocuting B. A is strictly liable.

6. T or F   City has been plagued by mine subsidence. Street cave-ins have caused numerous accidents, and the structural damage to buildings has been both costly and dangerous. Coal Company agrees, pursuant to legislative requirements, to correct the problem by bolstering supports in old tunnels, but this requires a small amount of blasting. A's house is damaged by the blasting. Coal Company is strictly liable.

7. T or F   B, a City resident, knew of the blasting activities and of the potential danger resulting from them, but refused to evacuate when ordered to do so by City officials acting on Coal Company's recommendations. B is injured. Coal Company is not strictly liable.

8. T or F   C, who knows of Coal Company's plans to blast in a particular tunnel, sneaks into that tunnel on Coal Company property to steal some of the blasting equipment. C is injured in an explosion. Coal Company is strictly liable.

9. T or F   B is moving his collection of blown glass animals from one room to another, when he is frightened by an explosion set off in one of the tunnels. Coal Company is not strictly liable for the damage that results to B's collection when he drops it.

*

PART SEVEN

Damages For Physical Harm

■ ANALYSIS

XXI. Damages for Physical Harm

(Dobbs §§ 377, 380–384, 385–390; R.2d §§ 875–886B, 901–932; R.3d AL §§ 10–26)

A. Compensatory Damages

1. General vs. Special Damages (R.2d § 904)

a. General Damages or "Noneconomic Loss"

Traditionally, general damages are compensatory damages for a type of harm which so frequently results from the tort involved that such damages are normally to be anticipated and hence need not be specifically alleged in P's complaint in order for P to prove and recover them (for example, pain and suffering). Today, such damages are more often categorized as noneconomic loss because they are losses not directly measured in dollars.

b. Special Damages or "Economic Loss"

Special damages are those awarded for all other compensable harms (for example, medical expenses or lost wages). Historically, special damages had to be specifically pleaded in order to be recoverable. Modernly, such damages are usually called "economic loss," but sometimes are referred to as "specials." Today, the practice is to specifically allege all types of damages.

2. Nominal Damages

Nominal damages are a trivial sum (e.g., one dollar) awarded to a litigant who has established a cause of action but has not established that he is entitled to compensatory damages. R.2d § 907. Some tort actions (e.g., negligence) do not support nominal damages.

3. Damages for Personal Injury

When P proves a compensable personal injury, he may recover for all adverse physical and mental consequences of that injury, past and future. R.2d § 924. This includes:

a. Economic loss

Past and future pecuniary losses and out-of-pocket expenses, including:

1) Medical, hospital, rehabilitative, and similar costs;

2) Lost wages, earnings or profits;

3) Substitute labor;

4) Custodial care;

5) In some situations, medical monitoring;

6) Any other specifically identifiable pecuniary losses resulting from the injury (e.g., travel to obtain medical care).

b. **Physical pain and suffering (past and future)**

c. **Mental or emotional distress, such as:**

1) Fright and shock;

2) Anxiety about the future;

3) Loss of peace of mind, happiness, mental health;

4) Humiliation, embarrassment, or loss of dignity;

5) Loss of the ability to enjoy a normal life, sometimes referred to as "disability" (not to be confused with loss of earning capacity);

6) Inconvenience.

In some cases, plaintiffs have sought recovery for something called "hedonic damages" as a separate element. The term is ambiguous. To the extent that it means plaintiff's awareness of his or her diminished ability to enjoy life and the pleasures that made life better, this is simply another name for a type of mental suffering (see A.3.c.5, above). To the extent that it refers to a separate element of damages, recoverable even when P is unaware of the loss (such as when P is in a coma), most courts have rejected such a claim. However, in some cases such damages are recoverable under the label "disability."

d. **Physical Impairment**
Physical impairment of some portion of the body, to the extent not recoverable under one of the foregoing. However, this is usually categorized under the term "disability." See A.3.c.5, above.

4. Pre–Existing Conditions

D is responsible in damages for all the consequences of P's injury, including those caused or aggravated by some pre-existing condition, predisposition, or vulnerability of P that a normal person would not have sustained, even if that condition was unknown to D. This is an aspect of the so-called "eggshell" or "thin-skulled" plaintiff rule.

5. Present Value

If P is awarded damages for *pecuniary* losses which he will incur in the future, the amount of such damages must ordinarily be reduced to *present cash value*. R.2d § 913A. Certain general damages (e.g., pain and suffering) are not reduced.

6. Inflation

Some jurisdictions still do not allow the jury to take into account the effects of *future inflation* in calculating damages for future economic losses. A growing number do.

7. Taxation

Damages for personal injuries involving physical harm are generally not subject to federal income taxation. However, other kinds of tort damages are taxable, such as damages for purely emotional injuries and punitive damages.

Although a growing minority of jurisdictions disagree, the prevailing rule is that the nontaxability of compensatory damages may not be the subject of evidence, argument or instructions to the jury. R.2d § 914A. Some courts recognize an exception where P's income loss is very high.

8. Collateral Source Rule

Payments made to, or benefits conferred on, the injured party from sources other than D are not credited against D's liability, even though they cover all or part of the harm for which D is liable. R.2d § 920A(2).

Examples: Private health and accident insurance, workmen's compensation, social security, disability insurance, wage continuation plans, sick leave, veterans' benefits, public aid; free medical or nursing services provided as a matter of professional courtesy.

Exception: Statutes in an increasing number of jurisdictions modify the collateral source rule, allowing D a partial credit in some or all cases. In some cases this credit is offset by the insurance premiums P paid for the collateral source benefit for a specified period of time.

9. Limitation or "Caps"

As a result of recent tort reform legislation, a growing minority of jurisdictions place caps (e.g., $250,000) or other limits on the amount of general damages recoverable, either in personal injury actions generally or in medical malpractice cases only.

10. Mitigation (Avoidable Consequences)

Under the doctrine of avoidable consequences, P is required to make reasonable efforts to mitigate the consequences of his injury and to take reasonable steps to prevent further harmful consequences from developing. R.2d § 918.

11. Seat Belts

In some jurisdictions, P cannot recover to the extent that his injuries, sustained in an auto crash, were the result of his failure to make use of an available seat belt.

B. Consequential Damages

1. Spouse

In most jurisdictions, if D's tort has injured one spouse, the other spouse (husband or wife) has a separate cause of action against D for the damages resulting from his or her loss of the injured spouse's society, companionship, and consortium (marital relations). Dobbs § 310; R.2d §§ 693, 694, 694A.

2. Parents

A parent can recover damages for loss of the services of his minor child resulting from an injury to the child caused by the tortious conduct of D. A few courts permit, in addition, damages for loss of the child's society, companionship and affection. R.2d §§ 703, 704, 704A.

3. Medical Expenses

A spouse or parent can recover medical and other expenses incurred as the result of an injury to his spouse or child.

4. Children

Except in a few jurisdictions, a child has no action for loss of his parent's care, support, training, guidance, companionship, love, and affection resulting from a tortious injury to the parent. R.2d § 707A.

5. Nature of Action

Such actions by a spouse or parent are independent of the injured spouse's or child's action, but are derivative from it. Thus, D may invoke any defense (e.g. contributory negligence) which would have been available in a suit brought by the injured person, as well as defenses available against P. Some courts require actions for consequential damages to be brought in the same lawsuit with the injured person's action for his damages.

C. Punitive Damages (Dobbs §§ 381–384)

1. Basis

In most jurisdictions, the trier of fact in its discretion may award punitive damages when D's misconduct is sufficiently serious, to punish D and deter D and others from similar conduct in the future. R.2d § 908.

2. Conduct Required

D must have acted from a wrongful motive, or at least with gross or knowing indifference to the rights or safety of another. D's conduct must have an element of outrage, similar to that which is a crime. An intentional tort will usually suffice. Most jurisdictions also allow them in all cases of reckless or "willful and wanton" misconduct; others require, in addition, a kind of malice, which here means a conscious and deliberate disregard of a high probability of harm.

3. Limitations

Several states do not allow punitive damages at all, except where authorized by statute. Typically they are not allowed in wrongful death or survival actions. They may not be awarded in F.E.L.A. or Jones Act cases. And usually they may not be awarded unless P has proved some actual damages.

There is a trend to limit further by statute the recovery of punitive damages, such as by establishing caps, requiring a higher level of judicial scrutiny, or setting a higher burden of proof than for other damages.

4. Amount

The amount of punitive damages awarded is largely within the discretion of the trier of fact, subject to review for excessiveness. Many courts, particularly in personal injury cases, require that they bear some reasonable relation to the compensatory damages awarded, or at least to the seriousness of the injury. Evidence of D's wealth is ordinarily admissible as a factor to be considered. Punitive damages are not reduced by P's comparative fault.

5. Vicarious Liability

Many jurisdictions allow punitive damages against an employer for any tort committed by his employee for which the employer is vicariously liable, provided the employee's tort will support them. Other jurisdictions follow the Restatement (§ 909) and refuse to allow them against the employer unless (a) the employer authorized the doing and the manner of the act, or (b) the employee was unfit and the employer was reckless in employing him, or (c) the employee was working in a managerial capacity, or (d) the employer or one of his managerial agents ratified or approved the act.

6. Constitutional Limitations

Recent decisions by the United States Supreme Court have established due process limits on awards of punitive damages. *BMW of North America, Inc. v. Gore* (U.S. 1996) (due process limits amount of punitive damages); *Honda Motor Co. v. Oberg* (U.S. 1994) (due process requires judicial review of punitive damages award); *Cooper Industries v. Leatherman Tool Group, Inc.* (U.S. 2001) (constitutionality of punitive damages award is subject to de novo standard of review); *State Farm Mut. Auto. Ins. Co. v. Campbell* (U.S. 2003) ($145 million award excessive). Under these cases, review of punitive damages by the trial and reviewing courts is constitutionally required, using three guideposts: (1) the degree of reprehensibility of D's misconduct; (2) the disparity between P's actual or potential harm and the punitive damages award; and (3) the difference between the punitive damages awarded and any applicable civil penalties for similar misconduct. And D cannot be punished for conduct that bears no relation to P's harm, such as similar conduct that occurred elsewhere or similar conduct that occurred in other cases. However, such evidence may be relevant as to D's culpable state of mind.

D. Allocation Among Tortfeasors (Dobbs §§ 385–390; R.3d AL, Topics 2–3, 5)

1. Multiple Tortfeasors

P may join in a single action all tortfeasors responsible for a single injury (or closely related injuries) and obtain judgments against all who are found liable. Depending on the nature of the injury and other factors, the judgments may be (a) joint and several or (b) several. However, P is entitled only to one satisfaction.

a.   Concert of Action

Two or more persons who, in pursuance of a common plan or design to commit a tortious act, actively take part in it, or further it by cooperation or request, or who lend aid or encouragement to the wrongdoer, or ratify or adopt the wrongdoer's acts done for their benefit, are equally jointly and severally) liable to P for the resulting tort. R.3d AL § 15.

Example: D1 and D2 drag race their autos down a residential street. D1 negligently skids out of control and strikes P. D2 is liable to P even though his negligence, if any, had no causal relation to P's injury.

Example: Dl and D2 decide to beat P Dl does all the beating. D2 merely stands by and encourages Dl. D2 is liable to P for battery.

b.   Joint Tortfeasors

Joint tortfeasors are those whose fault combined to produce P's injuries, or who are vicariously liable for another such tortfeasor. It is not necessary that their tortious conduct concur in time or place. It includes those who are merely vicariously liable (e.g., master and servant).

Example: Dl negligently installs an electric line. Several years pass, and due to D2's negligent inspection the line short circuits and injures P. Dl and D2 are joint tortfeasors.

2.   **Divisible Damages**

If different persons are each responsible for separate, identifiable parts of P's harm, absent concert of action, each is liable only for the harm traceable to him.

3.   **Indivisible Harm**

a.   Traditional Rule: Joint and Several Liability

Traditionally, if two or more persons are responsible for the same harm, all whose tortious conduct is found to be a legal and factual cause of that harm are *jointly* and *severally* liable for all of P's damages (together with anyone else who is vicariously liable). P may sue one, some, or all, obtain judgments for the full amount of his damages against as many as he can, and collect his judgment from one or any combination of them, as he chooses. R.2d § 882; R.3d AL § 10. As long as his judgment is not satisfied in full, P can continue to bring further suits or collection proceedings. About one-quarter of U.S. jurisdictions have retained pure joint and several liability. Joint and several liability has the effect of placing the risk of uncollectability on the defendants.

b. Several Liability
    With the advent of comparative fault, some jurisdictions now make even a joint tortfeasor only "severally liable" to P—i.e., his liability is limited to his proportional share of the total liability. R.3d AL § 11.Several liability has the effect of placing the risk of uncollectibility on P. About one-quarter of U.S. jurisdictions now have pure several liability.

    Example: D1's proportional share of P's $100,000 damages is found to be 30%. In those jurisdictions, P will be awarded a judgment against D1 for only $30,000. Under the traditional rule, his judgment against D1 would have been $100,000.

c. Hybrid Liability and Reallocation of Damages
    About half of U.S. jurisdictions have adopted a mixture of joint and several and several liability. The schemes vary widely and resist simple categorization, and some systems have characteristics of more than one category. Broadly defined, they can be described as:

    Reallocation of Uncollectible Shares. This category begins with joint and several liability for independent tortfeasors who cause an indivisible injury to P. It then places the risk of a T's uncollectibility on all parties who bear responsibility for P's damages, including P. An insolvent tortfeasor's comparative share of responsibility is reallocated to the other parties in proportion to their comparative responsibility. A very similar result is obtained by starting with a rule of several liability but then providing for reallocation in the event a share is uncollectible.

    Joint and Several Liabilty Threshhold. In this category, all tortfeasors whose percentage of comparative responsibility exceeds a specified threshold are jointly and severally liable. Tortfeasors whose percentage falls below that threshold are only severally liable. The threshold serves to impose the risk of uncollectibility on P as to all tortfeasors below the specified threshold.

Type of Harm. In this category, the variable that determines joint and several liability or several liability is the type of harm suffered by P. Independent tortfeasors are jointly and severally liable for damages for certain harms (e.g., "economic" or "pecuniary" harms, or pollution damage) but are severally liable for compensatory damages for other types of harm.

Type of Defendant. In some jurisdictions, joint and several (or several) liability is restricted to certain categories of defendants.

Whether P Was Free From Contributory Fault. In some cases, P gets the benefit of joint and several liability only if P was free from contributory fault.

d. Intentional Tortfeasors

Regardless of the scheme in a particular jurisdiction for nonintentional torts, joint and several liability is the norm for intentional joint tortfeasors. R.3d AL § 12. In other words, if D1 and D2 are both *intentional* tortfeasors with respect to P's indivisible injury, both are jointly and severally liable.

If D1 is *negligent* because of D1's failure to take precautions to protect P against the specific risk created by D2, an *intentional* tortfeasor, then D1 is jointly and severally liable for the share of comparative responsibility assigned to D2 as well as the share assigned to D1. R.3d AL § 14.

Example: P is a guest at a hotel operated by D1. D1 is negligent in failing to provide adequate door locks and other security, as a result of which D2, an intruder, gains access to P's room, assaults P, and steals P's property. D1 is liable to P for the shares of comparative responsibility assigned to both D1 and D2. If D1 pays more than his share, he can (in theory) obtain contribution from D2.

e. Vicarious Liability

If D1's liability is entirely vicarious, or imputed, based on the tortious conduct of D2, D1 is jointly and severally liable for whatever share the law of that jurisdiction assigns to the fault of D2. In other words, D1 and D2 are jointly responsible for a single share. If D1 pays that share to P, D1 ordinarily can obtain indemnity from D2. R.3d AL § 13.

4. Settlement of P's Claim(s)

a. Settlement Agreements Are Contracts

P may enter into a settlement agreement with D (or more than one D) by which P settles his claim(s) against D for a fixed sum. The agreement may take the form of a release, covenant not to sue, or loan receipt agreement. Ordinary rules of contract interpretation apply. Settlement agreements may be set aside for fraud, duress, incapacity, or mutual mistake. A dispute may arise as to whether the settlement should be set aside due to mutual mistake when it later develops that P's injuries are much more serious, or of a different type, than the parties believed when the settlement was entered into, particularly if the release by its terms extended to "unknown" injuries.

The prevailing view is that a settlement by P during his lifetime (or a judgment during P's lifetime for either party) will bar a wrongful death action by P's survivors when the death results from the same injuries.

b. Release

A release is a form of settlement agreement whereby P completely surrenders his claim against one or more potential defendants. At one time, the general rule was that a release executed in favor of any one tortfeasor released all other tortfeasors potentially liable for the same harm. The modern rule is that if the release is not intended as a full satisfaction and contains a reservation of rights against others, the release does not ipso facto discharge their potential liability to P. Under the Restatement view, no such reservation of rights is required; a release is effective only as to the party released, unless it is intended as a full satisfaction of all of P's claims arising out of the occurrence in question. R.2d § 885; R.3d AL § 24.

c. Covenant Not to Sue

A covenant not to sue (or not to execute) is a settlement device designed to avoid the former effects of a release. It is a contract by which P does not release his claim against D, but merely promises to forego any further attempts to enforce it. It does not discharge other potential defendants, even if it contains no reservation of rights against them, unless it is expressly intended as a satisfaction of all P's claims. R.2d § 885(2); R.3d AL § 24.

d. **Loan Receipt Agreement (R.3d AL § 24, comment *i*)**

Some courts have approved settlement with one potential defendant by a loan receipt agreement (sometimes called a "Mary Carter" agreement), whereby D "loans" P a sum, without interest, to be repaid only if and to the extent that P is successful in his claims against other joint tortfeasors, and only from the proceeds of any amount which P eventually collects from the others. Although such agreements were at one time valid in many jurisdictions, they are now increasingly disapproved as against public policy. If allowed, such an agreement must be disclosed at trial so that D's credibility can be evaluated.

e. **Effect of Partial Settlement on Amount Recoverable from Non–Settling Tortfeasors in a Joint and Several Liability Situation**

Assume that P has a claim against more than one joint tortfeasor in a situation in which all joint tortfeasors are subject to joint and several liability. Assume P settles with one tortfeasor (T1) prior to obtaining a judgment against the remaining joint tortfeasor(s), reserving P's right to proceed against the others. If P then succeeds in his remaining claim(s), the tortfeasor(s) against whom P obtains a judgment receive a credit based on the settlement with T1. What should be the amount of that credit?

1) **Dollar Credit**

In some jurisdictions, the credit is the dollar amount of the settlement with T1. This is called the "pro tanto" or dollar credit rule.

Example: P has a claim against T1, T2, and T3 for an indivisible injury. P settles prior to trial with T1 for $50,000 and proceeds to trial against T2 and T3. P obtains a $300,000 judgment against T2 and T3, and the jury apportions fault one-third each to T1, T2, and T3. The court will enter a joint and several judgment against T1 and T2 for $250,000. T2 and

T3 cannot seek contribution against T1, but can seek contribution between themselves if either pays more than his proportional share, which is $125,000.

In most pro tanto or dollar credit jurisdictions, T1 will be immune from contribution, but only if the court finds that the settlement was in "good faith," i.e., an arm's length bargain and a bona fide (not a collusive) settlement.

2) **Proportional or Percentage Credit**

In some jurisdictions, the credit is the settling tortfeasor's (T1's) proportional share of the common liability, regardless of the dollar amount of the settlement with T1. This is called the proportional or percentage credit rule. This is the rule favored by R.3d AL § 16.

Example: P has a claim against T1, T2, and T3 for an indivisible injury. P settles prior to trial with T1 for $50,000 and proceeds to trial against T2 and T3. P obtains a $300,000 judgment against T2 and T3, and the jury apportions fault one-third each to T1, T2, and T3. The court will enter a joint and several judgment against T1 and T2 for $200,000. T2 and T3 cannot seek contribution against T1, but can seek contribution between themselves if either pays more than his proportional share, which is $100,000. Note that P will recover only $250,000 of his $300,000 verdict, because P settled with T1 for what turned out to be less than T1's share.

Example: P has a claim against T1, T2, and T3 for an indivisible injury. P settles prior to trial with T1 for $150,000 and proceeds to trial against T2 and T3. P obtains a $300,000 judgment against T2 and T3, and the jury apportions fault one-third each to T1, T2, and T3. The court will enter a joint and several judgment against T1 and T2 for $200,000. T2 and T3 cannot seek contribution against T1, but can seek contribution between themselves if either pays more than his proportional share, which is

$100,000. Note that P will recover a total of $350,000, even though his verdict was only $300,000. P is entitled to the benefit of his settlement with T1 even though it turned out to be greater than T1's proportional share.

3) Pro Rata Credit

A third, little-used approach, the "pro rata" method, gives a nonsettling tortfeasor a credit against the judgment equal to the settling tortfeasor's share of damages, which is determined by dividing the recoverable damages by the number of liable parties.

f. Effect of Partial Settlement on Amount Recoverable from Non-Settling Tortfeasors in a Several Liability Situation

If a settling tortfeasor (T1) is only subject to several liability, any nonsettling tortfeasors simply pay their proportional share(s) as determined by applicable apportionment rules. T1 has settled her several liability, and it matters not whether her settlement is more or less than the amount of her proportional share as later determined.

Example: P, a passenger in T1's car, is injured in a collision with T2's auto. P settles with T1 for $25,000. P's case against T2 proceeds to verdict ($170,000), but the jury assesses T1's fault at 99% and T2's fault at 1%. P recovers $1,700 from T2 and nothing further from T1, for a total recovery of $26,700.

5. Contribution

a. Common Law Rule

When P obtains a judgment against two or more tortfeasors, he can collect that judgment from any one, all, or any combination of Ds in any proportion he desires. The common law rule in most jurisdictions was that D1, who paid P more than D1's proportionate share of the judgment, was *not* entitled to obtain contribution from the other joint tortfeasors. The "no contribution" rule originally applied only to intentional torts, but the majority of U.S. jurisdictions extended it to negligence and strict liability actions.

b. Modern Status

Contribution among (negligent or strictly liable) joint tortfeasors in some form is now the rule in most jurisdictions. R.3d AL § 23, replacing R.2d § 886A. Of course, contribution is only available if and to the extent that parties are jointly and severally liable. There is no right to contribution by or against a party who is only severally liable.

c. Amount

In most jurisdictions, the damages are allocated among the joint tortfeasors in proportion to their relative fault as determined by the trier of fact, and those shares determine contribution liability. R.3d AL § 23. (In a few jurisdictions, damages are divided pro rata.) D (having made a successful contribution claim against other tortfeasors) and who then pays P more than D's proportional share of the judgment has a right to recover the excess amount over his proportional share from the other contribution defendants.

Example: P sues D1, D2, and D3 for an indivisible injury sustained in an automobile accident. P obtains a judgment against D1, D2, and D3 whereby they are jointly and severally liable to P for $100,000. The factfinder assigns responsibility 50% to D1, 30% to D2, and 20% to D3. D1 pays P the entire judgment. D1 may recover contribution from D2 or D3 or both for a total of $50,000 ($100,000 x .50), because D1's satisfaction of the judgment extinguished D2's and D3's liability to P.

Example: Same facts, except that D1 pays P $80,000 of the $100,000 judgment, and D2 and D3 pay P the remaining $20,000. P can obtain contribution from D2 or D3 for a total of $30,000 (($100,000 x .50 minus the $20,000 that D1 did not have to pay).

d. Absence of Judgment

D can seek contribution against other joint tortfeasors, including those not sued by P. There is a split of authority as to whether contribution can be obtained against a D who is immune from suit by P. A tortfeasor who settles prior to trial can obtain contribution, provided he settles for all tortfeasors and he can prove the others' liability, the amount of the damages, and the reasonableness of his settlement. He need not prove that he would have been found liable to P, only that there was a potential for such liability. The prevailing view is that a tortfeasor who settles only his own liability cannot be sued for contribution nor can he obtain contribution from others.

e. Intentional Tortfeasors

In some jurisdictions, intentional tortfeasors cannot seek contribution, but R.3d AL § 23, comment *l*, says they can.

f. Immune Tortfeasors

If P is injured by the combined negligence of D (whom P sues) and T (who is immune from liability to P), can D join and seek contribution from T so that, if P obtains (and later collects) a judgment against D, D can recover from T the amount in excess of D's proportionate share? Jurisdictions are split, but most require D to prove that T was subject to liability to P, so D cannot seek contribution if T is immune with respect to P.

6. Non–Party Tortfeasors

If a particular tortfeasor is not joined as a defendant or third-party defendant (T), the courts are split as to whether that tortfeasor's proportional share of the total fault can be found by the factfinder and included in the responsible fault calculation. A tortfeasor may be a nonparty because: (1) T cannot be identified by name, such as a hit-and-run driver; (2) T is immune from suit; (3) T has settled with P before trial; (4) T cannot be served with process; (5) T is P's employer and P's injury occurred in the course and scope of P's employment; or (6) P simply chose not to sue T for some other reason (e.g., T is uncollectible). Whether T is included or not may depend on the purpose of the calculation.

a. Joint and Several Liability

If all tortfeasors are subject to joint and several liability and there is no contribution claim, then there is no reason to allocate fault among multiple tortfeasors, whether joined or not. However, whether T is included could still make a difference in determining P's share of the fault, if P is found contributorily at fault.

Example: P, a factory worker, is injured while working on a machine. She brings a products liability claim against D, the manufacturer of the machine. P's employer, T, could be found negligent in failing to properly maintain the machine. If P is found contributorily negligent, P's share of the fault might vary depending on whether it is compared only to D's fault or to the combined fault of D and T.

For purposes of calculating P's share, the total fault should include all tortfeasors, whether joined as a defendant or not. R.3d AL § 7, comment *g*.

b. Several Liability

If some or all defendants are potentially subject only to several liability, then the factfinder must allocate fault proportionally, and it makes a difference whether T's fault is included in the fault calculation.

Example: P is injured in an automobile accident. She brings a products liability claim against D1, the auto's manufacturer, and joins a negligence claim against D2, the driver of the car. Assume T, the driver of another car involved in the collision, was also negligent and was identified, but has since disappeared and cannot be located. If the jury finds all (P, D1, D2, and T) equally at fault, and P's damages are $100,000, then judgment will be entered for P against D1 and D2 for $25,000 each. But if T's fault is not included, and the jury finds P, D1, and D2 equally at fault, then judgment will be entered for P against D1 and D2 for $33,333 each.

Jurisdictions are split; some require T to be included if there is enough evidence from which the factfinder can assess fault against T. In others, no one who is not a party to the lawsuit can be included in the fault calculation. The Restatement rule is that the calculation may include such nonparties if they can be sufficiently identified. R.3d AL § D19(a) and comment *k*.

c. Contribution

Where contribution is available to some or all of the defendants (or in a separate action for contribution), it becomes necessary to allocate fault among tortfeasors. For this purpose, the calculation is restricted to the tortfeasors who are parties to the action in which contribution is being sought. In most cases, contribution may not be sought from settling tortfeasors.

7. Indemnity (R.3d AL § 22)

a. Distinguished From Contribution

Contribution is an equitable sharing of the loss among joint tortfeasors. Indemnification is a shifting of the entire loss from one tortfeasor to another, by operation of either (1) a prior agreement of the parties, or (2) law, based on equitable considerations.

b. **Indemnity by Agreement**

A contract in which T2 agrees to indemnify T1 if T1 is held liable to P is frequently enforceable, although in some instances agreements to indemnify for T1's own negligence may be void by statute or as against public policy. Agreements to indemnify T1 for T1's liability for reckless or intentional misconduct are usually unenforceable.

c. **Indemnity by Operation of Law**

Indemnity by operation of law (often called "implied indemnity") is based on the concept of unjust enrichment. It is available when T1 and T2 are both liable for the same harm to P, and (1) T1's liability is based entirely on T1's vicarious liability for the tort of T2, or (2) T1 is the seller of a product (e.g., a retailer), the product was supplied to T1 by T2 (e.g., the manufacturer), and T1 is held liable to P solely because he sold the product to P (i.e., T1 was not independently culpable). If T1 satisfies P's judgment, T1 is entitled to indemnity from T2 for the amount paid to P plus reasonable legal expenses.

Example: T2 is T1's employee. T2, driving a company car on company business, negligently injures P. T1, being vicariously liable for T2's negligence, is joined as a defendant in P's lawsuit and P recovers a judgment against T1, which T1 pays. T1 is entitled to indemnity from T2.

Example: Acme Hardware Store (T1) sells a lawn mower manufactured by T2 to P. The mower has a defect that results in an injury to P. P sues Acme and recovers a judgment against Acme, but P did not join T2. Acme pays the judgment. Acme is entitled to indemnity from T2.

d. **"Active–Passive" Implied Indemnity**

Prior to the adoption of comparative contribution, implied indemnity was also available when there was a significant or qualitative difference between the blameworthiness of T1 and T2, both of whom are nevertheless legally liable to P for his injury, such that the primary responsibility for the harm rests upon the defendant against whom indemnity is sought. This was often called "active-passive" indemnity, because the fault of the indemnitor was "active" or major and the fault of the indemnitee was "passive" or minor. In those jurisdictions adopting comparative contribution, contribution is usually deemed to supersede the "active-passive" form of implied indemnity

E. Review Questions

[Answers Provided in Appendix A, pages 407–408]

1. T or F Punitive damages may be awarded whenever the jury feels such damages are appropriate.

2. T or F Consequential damages are those damages which P is due as a consequence of D's negligence.

3. T or F If P suffers a single injury as a result of the actions of two or more persons, all of the persons whose conduct proximately caused the harm are jointly and severally liable for the full amount of P's damage.

4. D negligently injures P and, as a result, P is confined to the hospital for 3 weeks and incurs a hospital bill of $4800. This sum is paid directly to the hospital by P's insurance. In a suit against D,

    a. P cannot recover the $4800 from D because it has been paid by a collateral source.

    b. P cannot recover the $4800 because it was paid directly to the hospital although he could have recovered it if the insurance company had paid the money directly to P

    c. P can recover the $4800 from D even though it has been paid by a collateral source, but only if P specifically alleged this fact.

5. D negligently drove his car over P causing P severe injuries which resulted in P being hospitalized for 20 days and which left him unable to work for 8 months as a result of which he lost 8 months wages. P incurred numerous other medical expenses. P has been billed for some of these expenses but he has not yet been billed for others. In addition, P experienced intense pain and suffering, is now fearful of going out of his home for fear of being struck by another car, and will never be able to work overtime or long hours like he did before the accident because of his injuries. Mark as true those answers which

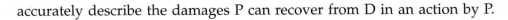

accurately describe the damages P can recover from D in an action by P.

a. P can recover his hospital expenses.

b. P can recover his lost wages, past and future, minus the taxes and social security he would have paid on them.

c. P can recover compensation for his pain and suffering.

d. P cannot recover for his fear of being struck by another car.

e. P cannot recover from D for those medical expenses that have not yet been billed to P.

f. P cannot recover from D for any expenses for which P was compensated by P's own auto or health insurance.

g. Any amounts P recovers for lost future wages or expenses must be discounted to their present value.

h. P can recover punitive damages to punish D for his wrongful conduct.

PART EIGHT

Survival And Wrongful Death

■ ANALYSIS

XXII. Survival and Wrongful Death

(Dobbs §§ 294–301; R.2d §§ 493, 494, 925, 926)

A. Survival of Tort Actions

1. Common Law Rule

At common law, all causes of action for personal torts abated with the death of either the tortfeasor or the person injured, regardless of the cause of death.

2. Statutory Modifications

All jurisdictions have more or less modified the common law rule, almost always by statute. About one-third of the states provide that either (a) all tort actions or (b) all tort actions except defamation survive the death of either P or D. The rest have a wide variety of inclusions and exclusions.

3. Personal Injury Actions

Personal injury actions survive in almost all jurisdictions, but sometimes with limitations on the damages recoverable. In a few states, personal injury actions do not survive the injured person's death except as part of an action for that death. Actions for consequential damages sometimes do not survive. In most states, wrongful death actions survive the death of the tortfeasor.

4. Measure of Damages

The measure of damages in a survival action is generally the same as if no one had died, except that the victim's death terminates the accrual of certain kinds of future damages (pain and suffering, mental distress, medical expense, loss of earnings, disability, etc.) which the victim otherwise could have recovered based on his life expectancy. R.2d § 926. Survival statutes some times contain other limitations.

5. Punitive Damages

In most jurisdictions, D's death terminates P's right to seek punitive damages. In some states, P's death does also, but in many jurisdictions, P's estate can seek punitive damages in a survival action.

6. Medical, Funeral and Burial Expenses

In some cases, funeral and burial expenses and the decedent's last medical expenses may be an element of damages in the survival action, or, in the alternative, in the wrongful death action (if there is one). In some jurisdictions, medical, funeral and burial expenses are a separate claim altogether. Note that a survival action may be brought even when the decedent died from some cause unrelated to decedent's claim against D. Decedent's estate would have no claim for medical, funeral, or burial expenses against D to the extent that these expenses are causally unrelated to P's cause of action against D.

B. Wrongful Death

1. Common Law Rule
Since *Baker v. Bolton* (Eng. 1808), the general common law rule here has been that one whose tortious conduct results in the death of P is not liable to P's survivors (Hawaii alone to the contrary).

2. Statutory and Other Modifications
Beginning in 1846, statutes were passed in England (Lord Campbell's Act) and all American jurisdictions creating a remedy for wrongful death. A few cases have reversed the common law rule e.g., *Moragne v. States Marine Lines, Inc.* (U.S. 1970) (common law wrongful death action recognized in admiralty cases); *Gaudette v. Webb* (Mass. 1972).

3. Basis
Any tort theory that would have supported a personal injury action will support an action for wrongful death. Usual rules of proximate cause apply.

4. Types of Statutes
There are two basic types of wrongful death acts.

a. Lord Campbell's Act
Most states have adopted a wrongful death act patterned after the 1846 English statute that creates a new cause of action for the benefit of specified near relatives of P when P would have had a cause of action had he been merely injured and not killed.

b. Survival
A few jurisdictions have a "survival"-type statute which preserves the cause of action which was vested in P at the moment of his death and enlarges it to include the damages resulting from the death itself.

c. Statutory Torts

Most statutory tort actions (F.E.L.A., dram shop acts) have their own provisions for recovery in the event of death. If not, then an appropriate general death act will be held to apply.

5. Concurrence of Remedies

If P survived his injuries for a time before dying from them, in most jurisdictions either a survival action or a wrongful death action or both may be brought independently or in the same lawsuit. In a few, the causes of action merge; in a few others, P's survivors must elect one or the other; and in a few others, the survival action abates in whole or in part.

6. Beneficiaries

The beneficiaries are the relatives or classes of relatives designated in the statute. P's spouse and children, if any, receive the award to the exclusion of all other surviving relatives. In most jurisdictions, stepchildren and unmarried cohabitants do not qualify as beneficiaries.

7. Damages

A wide variety of rules govern the elements of damages recoverable. See R.2d § 925. The general types of statutes are:

a. Loss to the Survivors

Elements of damages include:

1) Pecuniary Loss

Many statutes are phrased in terms of "pecuniary loss," which includes at the very least loss of support, services and contributions. In some jurisdictions, this includes loss of a probable inheritance.

2) Nonpecuniary Loss

Nonpecuniary loss—loss of P's society, companionship, love and affection—is recoverable in some jurisdictions, either by specific statutory language or by judicial construction of the term "pecuniary loss." A few allow recovery for the survivor's mental anguish (bereavement). In the case of decedents whose earnings are small or zero (children,

3) Medical and Other Expenses

Medical and other expenses, such as funeral and burial costs, ordinarily may be recovered by the survivor paying them, either as part of the death action or separately.

b. **Loss to the Estate**

A minority of jurisdictions measure damages by the loss to the estate—P's future earnings minus his personal expenses, or his probable future accumulations or net savings. A few jurisdictions permit recovery of both the loss to survivors and the loss of to the estate (i.e., loss of inheritance).

c. **Punitive Wrongful Death Acts**

In two states damages are determined without reference to P's earnings or his family's needs, but are based solely on D's fault.

d. **Punitive Damages**

Jurisdictions are split on whether punitive damages may be recovered in a wrongful death action. In a few states, they are expressly allowed by statute.

e. **Limits**

At one time, almost half the states had specific dollar limits on wrongful dea3th awards. Today, all but one or two have removed such limits, but a few jurisdictions limit particular elements of damage, or limit damages as to certain beneficiaries.

8. **Defenses**

The same defenses are available as if P had lived (e.g., P's contributory negligence or assumption of risk can reduce or negate the beneficiaries' claim). R.2d § 494. In addition, a beneficiary's negligence that contributed to the death bars or reduces that beneficiary's recovery. R.2d § 493. Remarriage of P's spouse does not mitigate the spouse's damages. The intra-family immunities generally are not available as defenses in wrongful death actions. As to the statute of limitations, courts are split as to whether beneficiaries are barred from bringing a wrongful death action which otherwise would have been viable if the statute of limitations applicable to decedent's cause of action had expired by the time the decedent died.

C. **Procedure**

1. **Survival Actions**

In a survival action, the plaintiff is the executor or administrator of the decedent's estate, and the surviving cause of action is an asset of the estate. Any recovery in the survival action goes to the estate and is distributed in accordance with the applicable estate law. As such, it is subject to the claims of the estate's creditors.

2. Wrongful Death Actions

A wrongful death cause of action is an independent claim by the beneficiaries. It is not an asset of the decedent's estate and does not pass through the estate. In some jurisdictions, the plaintiff is the executor or administrator of the estate, but it is brought on behalf of the beneficiaries and any recovery goes directly to them and does not pass through the estate. It is not subject to claims of the estate's creditors. In some jurisdictions, the plaintiff is one of the beneficiaries or their representative who sues on behalf of all the beneficiaries. If there is more than one beneficiary for whom damages are awarded, the recovery is divided in accordance with applicable local procedure.

D. Review Questions

[Answers Provided in Appendix A, page 408.]

1. T or F   At common law a person whose tortious conduct resulted in the death of another was not liable to the survivors of the deceased.

2. T or F   At common law any causes of action in tort that a person might have had expired at his death because tort actions are personal. However, a defendant's heirs remained liable for his torts even after his death.

*

PART NINE

Non-Physical Harm: Misrepresentation, Defamation, And Privacy

■ ANALYSIS

XXIII. Misrepresentation

(Dobbs §§ 469–483; R.2d §§ 525–552C)

A. Introduction

1. In General

Misrepresentation is often an element of different torts and other causes of action. However, there is a tort action called "misrepresentation" (formerly "deceit"), where D in the course of some transaction makes a false statement to P (or another), P acts in justifiable reliance on the statement, and thereby sustains *pecuniary* loss. (If P sustains *physical harm*, then one of the other tort actions will lie. Cf. R.2d § 557A).

2. Basis

At common law, this action was called "deceit," and would lie only if D's misrepresentation was *fraudulent*—i.e., was made with "scienter." Today, liability is recognized for some types of negligent misrepresentations.

B. Deceit

1. Elements

The elements necessary to establish a prima facie case in an action for deceit are (R.2d § 525):

a. Representation

D made a *false representation*, ordinarily of a *fact*.

b. Scienter

D must have *known* that his statement was false, or else he must have made it in *conscious ignorance* or *reckless disregard* of whether it was true or false.

c. Intent to Induce Reliance

D must have *intended* that P act (or refrain from acting) in reliance upon the representation.

d. Justifiable Reliance

P must have *justifiably relied* upon the representation in acting or failing to act.

e. Damages

P must have sustained *actual damage* as a result of his reliance.

2. Scienter

a. Rule

A misrepresentation is "fraudulent" (i.e., made with scienter) if D

1) *knows* or *believes* that the matter is not as he represents it to be, or

2) does not have the *confidence* in the accuracy of his representation that he states or implies, or

3) knows that he does not have the basis for his representation that he states or implies. R.2d § 526.

Compare the rule of *Derry v. Peek:* P must prove that "a false representation has been made (1) knowingly, or (2) without belief in its truth, or (3) recklessly, careless whether it be true or false."

Cardozo, J. in *Ultramares Corp. v. Touche, Niven & Co.* (N.Y.1931):

"Fraud includes the pretense of knowledge when there is none."

b. Intent vs. Motive

If D had the foregoing *intent*, his *motive* is irrelevant. It is no defense that he did not intend to harm P, or even that he thought he was benefiting him.

3. Form of Representation

a. Fact

In general, the representation must be of a *fact*. It may be by words or conduct.

b. Ambiguous

A representation capable of two interpretations, one true and the other known to be false, is actionable if made with the intent that it be understood in the false sense or with reckless indifference as to how it will be understood. R.2d § 527.

c. Opinion

As a general rule, statements that represent only D's opinion or prediction are *not* actionable. However, an opinion may be understood as an *implied representation* concerning its underlying facts. R.2d § 539.

d. Quantity, Quality and Value

Statements of *quantity* ordinarily may be taken as statements of fact. But statements of *quality* and *value* traditionally have been classified as opinions upon which no reliance can justifiably be placed, unless sufficiently specific.

e. Law

At one time, statements of *law* were deemed opinions and therefore not actionable. Today, it is recognized that some *specific* representations as to the state of law may be representations of *fact*, and even if *opinion*, may be actionable if reasonably understood as implying a statement of fact.

f. Intent

A statement that the speaker or another person presently intends to do (or not do) something in the future is generally regarded as a statement of fact which is actionable if untrue. R.2d §§ 530, 544.

g. Incomplete Statements

A representation stating the truth so far as it goes, but which the maker knows or believes to be materially misleading because of his failure to state additional or qualifying matter, is actionable. R.2d § 529.

h. Concealment

If D conceals or otherwise prevents P from acquiring material information, he is liable as though he had stated its nonexistence. R.2d § 550.

i. Nondisclosure

At one time, mere silence could not amount to a misrepresentation. Parties to a transaction were free to knowingly take advantage of the other's ignorance of material facts. This rule is now subject to several significant exceptions (R.2d § 551):

1) Fiduciary or Confidential Relations

Fiduciary or confidential relations, such as principal-agent, guardian-ward, executory-beneficiary, bank-depositor, trustee-cestui que trust, attorney-client, physician-patient, majority-minority stockholder, and parties to certain contracts (surety-ship, insurance, partnership), carry with them the duty to make disclosure of all material facts.

2) **Incomplete Statements**
See ¶ B.3.g., above.

3) **Subsequently Acquired Information**
Subsequently acquired information which makes the prior statement untrue or misleading must be disclosed if D knows or believes that P is still acting on the basis of the original statement.

4) **Newly Discovered Reliance**
If D makes a statement without expecting that P will rely upon it (therefore, not actionable) and D later discovers that P, in a transaction with him, is about to rely upon it, he has an affirmative duty to disclose its falsity.

5) **Basic Facts**

There is a growing trend to find an affirmative duty to disclose *essential* facts known to D when D has special access to those facts which P does not, and in other cases where there is some reason why nondisclosure would be unconscionable or at least very unfair. Compare R.2d § 551(2)(e).

4. **Scope of Liability**

The scope of D's liability for a fraudulent misrepresentation is as follows.

a. **Persons**
D is liable to the person(s) or class of persons whom he *intends* or has *reason to expect* to act (or refrain from acting) in reliance upon his representation. R.2d §§ 531, 534.

b. **Third Persons**
If D intends or has reason to expect that his representation will be communicated to a third person, and that it will influence his conduct in the type of transaction involved, he is subject to liability to that third person. R.2d § 533.

c. **Type of Transaction**
P's reliance must ordinarily be in the *transaction* or *type of transaction* in which D intends or has reason to expect that P's conduct will be influenced. R.2d § 531.

d.   Proximate Cause

D's representation must have been a *substantial factor* in influencing P's conduct (R.2d §§ 546, 547), and P's loss from the reliance must have been *reasonably foreseeable* (R.2d § 548A).

5.   Contributory Negligence

If P justifiably relies upon a fraudulent misrepresentation, he is not barred from recovery by his contributory negligence in doing so. R.2d § 545A.

6.   Justifiable Reliance

P can recover only if he relied upon the representation, and his reliance was *justifiable.* R.2d § 537. The standard is a subjective one.

a.   Materiality

Reliance is not justifiable unless the matter misrepresented is *material.* R.2d § 538.

b.   Duty to Investigate

At one time, persons dealing at arm's length could not justifiably rely on the other's statements if a reasonably independent investigation would have revealed the truth. This is no longer true; it is now held, at least as to representations of fact, that P may justifiably rely on them without further investigation even when their falsity could have been easily and quickly discovered, unless something known to him or apparent in the situation at hand should have served as a warning to him that the statement ought not to be accepted without further inquiry. R.2d §§ 540, 541, 541A.

c.   Opinion of Adverse Party

P cannot justifiably rely on D's statement in the form of an opinion, unless the *fact* to which the opinion relates is material and D (1) purports to have *special knowledge,* or (2) stands in a *fiduciary* or *confidential relation* to P, or (3) has some other *special reason* to expect that P will rely on his opinion. R.2d § 542.

d.   Opinion of Apparently Disinterested Person

P can justifiably rely on the opinion of an apparently *disinterested* person if the fact that he holds the opinion is material. R.2d § 543.

7. Damages

Damages for fraudulent misrepresentations are measured by P's pecuniary loss, including the difference between the value of what he paid and the value of what he actually received, consequential damages, and (if a business transaction) the benefit of his bargain.

C. Negligent Misrepresentation

1. Discussion

Even though D honestly believed his erroneous statement to be true (and therefore lacked scienter), he may have been negligent in (a) failing to exercise reasonable care to ascertain the true facts, or (b) failing to possess or apply the skill and competence required by his business or profession (e.g., attorney, accountant, surveyor, product manufacturer), or (c) expressing his assertion as he did (R.2d § 528).

2. Physical Harm

If D's negligent misrepresentation proximately causes physical harm, ordinary negligence principles apply. R.2d § 311. The limitations of the Restatement do not apply to communications that create a risk of physical harm.

3. Pecuniary Loss

Most courts, following *Derry v. Peek*, have refused to extend the traditional deceit action to merely negligent misrepresentations that cause only pecuniary loss. However, most jurisdictions now recognize a limited form of liability for such negligent misrepresentations as a separate tort action. R.2d § 552.

4. Scope of Liability

a. Interest in Transaction

D is not liable for his negligent misrepresentation (causing only pecuniary loss) unless made in the course of his business, profession or employment, or other transaction in which he has a *pecuniary interest.*

b. Actual Knowledge of P

At first, D was liable only to the specific person or persons for whose benefit and guidance he intended to supply the information. *Ultramares Corp. v. Touche, Niven & Co.* (N.Y.1931); *Glanzer v. Shepard* (N.Y.1922).

c. Third Persons in Known Class

Today, many courts have extended D's liability to include persons in a *limited* group, even though not specifically known to D, if D knows that one or more persons in that group will receive and rely upon that information, R.2d § 552(2), even though D had no knowledge of their specific identity or the particulars of the transaction in which it would be used.

d. Foreseeable Harm to One Remote User

Where D knows that the information he furnished will be used by a succession of persons whose specific identity is presently unknowable, but only one such person will suffer loss (the person using the information at the time the error is discovered), some courts have extended D's liability to all who will foreseeably use and rely upon the information.

Examples: Surveyors; title abstracters.

e. Public Duty to Furnish

Certain kinds of statutes (e.g., securities laws, recording acts) require D to furnish, file or publish information for the protection of a class of persons. If such information is negligently erroneous, a member of that class who relies upon it to his injury may recover. R.2d § 552(3).

f. Transaction

Liability is limited to the transaction for which the information was furnished or a substantially similar transaction.

5. Contributory Negligence

P's contributory negligence in relying upon a negligent misrepresentation is a defense. R.2d § 552A. Comparative negligence rules, if any, do not apply.

6. Damages

Damages for negligent misrepresentation include P's out-of-pocket loss and consequential damages, but not the benefit of the bargain. R.2d § 552B.

D. Innocent Misrepresentation (Strict Liability)

1. Physical Harm: Products

If D is engaged in the business of selling products, he is subject to strict liability for physical harm resulting from a misrepresentation made to the public concerning the character or quality of a product sold by him. R.2d § 402B.

2. Pecuniary Loss: Sale, Rental or Exchange Transaction

The Restatement (Second) § 552C proposes strict liability for pecuniary loss sustained as the result of a misrepresentation made by D in a sale, rental or exchange transaction with P Damages would be limited to the difference between the value of what P received and the value of what he gave. So far, only a few cases support this rule. Traditionally, contract, equitable or restitutionary remedies have been applied in this situation.

E. Review Questions

[Answers Provided in Appendix A, pages 408–409]

1. D, a used car salesman, tells P that a car in which P has expressed interest in was owned by the proverbial little old lady, has only been driven 25,000 miles, and was never driven over 30 miles an hour. These statements are all true. However, D also knows that the oil was never changed, and that the car was in 3 major accidents and spent 6 months at the bottom of a lake. D gives P the former owner's phone number, but P does not bother calling. Instead P buys the car and without inspecting it drives off. Three days later, while P is driving the car, the bent and rusted front axle breaks and P has an accident which results in the total destruction of the car and in serious injury to P.

   a. P cannot recover any damages for misrepresentation because D misrepresented nothing.

   b. P cannot recover any damages for misrepresentation because he could easily have discovered the defect by looking or by phoning the proverbial little old lady.

   c. P can recover the difference between what he paid for the car and what it was worth before the accident.

   d. P can recover the difference between what he paid for the car and its value before the accident and, in addition, he can recover for the damage to the car and his injuries from the accident if these were proximately caused by his reliance on D's statements.

2. T or F   Knowing misrepresentations made with an intent to induce reliance are actionable if they are in fact relied on by a person to whom they were made and who was justified in that reliance.

3. T or F   Ordinarily a person who suffers pecuniary loss as a result of another's negligent misrepresentation may recover in an action in tort.

4. T or F   Under some circumstances one can prevail in a tort action for an innocent misrepresentation.

XXIV. Defamation

(Dobbs §§ 399–423; R.2d §§ 558–623)

A. General Rules

1. Elements of Cause of Action
The elements of a defamation action are (R.2d § 558):

a. Statement
A false and defamatory statement concerning another.

b. Publication
An unprivileged publication to a third party, the publication being intentional or at least negligent on the part of D.

c. Fault
Depending on the status of the defendant, P may have to show some degree of fault on the part of D in knowing or failing to ascertain the falsity of the statement.

d. Damages
Some defamatory statements are actionable without proof of special damage (i.e., are actionable "per se"); others are not.

2. What Is Defamatory?

a. Rule
A communication is defamatory if it tends to harm Ps reputation in the community, either by (1) lowering others' estimation of him, or (2) deterring others from associating or dealing with him. R.2d § 559.

Example: Communications that expose P to hatred, contempt, ridicule; which reflect unfavorably on his morality or integrity; which impair his financial reputation; or which impute that P has a disease or other physical or mental attribute or deficiency such that others will be deterred from associating with him.

b.   **Standard**
A communication is defamatory if a substantial and respectable minority of P's community or associates would so regard it; it is not necessary that all or a majority would. However, it is not defamatory if the minority's views on that subject are so anti-social or extreme that it would not be proper for the courts to recognize them.

Example: Calling P a "civil rights activist" is not defamatory, even though a substantial minority of the community in which P resides would so regard it.

3.   Truth

A defamatory statement is not actionable unless it is false. R.2d § 681A. Traditionally, truth has been regarded as an affirmative defense on which D has the burden of proof. In cases involving issues of public interest, however, the first amendment now requires P to bear the burden of proving falsity. Additionally, (as discussed below) the law now requires P to establish D's fault with respect to the falsity of the statement in at least some, if not all, defamation cases.

4.   Who May Be Defamed

a.   **Deceased Persons**
Unless a statute otherwise provides, no libel or slander action lies for the defamation of a deceased person. R.2d § 560. Whether the action survives P's death (where P was defamed while alive) depends on the local survival statute.

b.   **Entities**
Corporations (R.2d § 561), partnerships and unincorporated associations (R.2d § 562) may be defamed.

5.   Meaning of Communication

a.   **Understanding of Recipient**
A communication is defamatory only if the recipient understands it in a defamatory sense, and understands that it was so intended.

R.2d § 563. If he *reasonably* so understood it, it does not matter that he was mistaken. In determining how the recipient understood it, the context of the statement is considered.

b. **Extrinsic Circumstances**

In determining the meaning of a communication, extrinsic facts and circumstances known to the recipient are taken into account.

Example: The statement "Mary Jones today gave birth to twins" may be found to be defamatory if one or more recipients know that she has been married only one month.

c. **Pleading**

At common law, if a statement was not defamatory on its face, P was required to plead the extrinsic circumstances which gave it a defamatory meaning; this was called the *"inducement."* He then had to set forth the communication verbatim, and then explain the defamatory meaning he claimed to have been understood; this explanation was called the *"innuendo."* These terms and requirements are still in effect in some jurisdictions.

6. **Application to P**

The communication must have been understood by the recipient (correctly, or mistakenly but reasonably) as intended to refer to P. R.2d § 564. The applicability of the defamatory matter to P may depend upon extrinsic facts or circumstances known to the recipient. If so, common law pleading rules required such facts or circumstances and the manner in which they connected the defamatory matter to P to be set forth. This portion of the complaint is called the *"colloquium."*

Example: D publishes a novel about the widow of an assassinated U.S. President who marries a Greek shipping magnate. In a libel action, P may show that people who read the story reasonably understood it to be "of and concerning" her, even though the character in the story had a dissimilar name and the work purported to be fiction.

7. **Group Defamation**

As a general rule, no action lies for the publication of defamatory words concerning a large group or class of persons, since they cannot reasonably be understood as applying to any one individual.

Examples: "All the lawyers in this town are shysters" (there being 150 lawyers). But a member of a small group may recover if the statement may reasonably be understood as applying to him.

"That jury was bribed." "Most of the players on that football team are on drugs." And so may a member of any size group if the circumstances indicate that it is intended to apply to him.

"All lawyers are shysters," where P is the only lawyer present and D's remarks may reasonably be understood as directed at P. R.2d § 564A.

8. Types of Defamatory Communications

a. Fact

Typically, a defamatory communication consists of a *statement of fact*. R.2d § 565. It may be direct or indirect, as where words or pictures imply a defamatory meaning about P without so stating directly.

b. Opinion (R.2d § 566)

At common law, a defamatory statement of *opinion* (if not privileged) was actionable the same as one of fact. This rule appears to have been modified by recent constitutional law interpretations.

1) Based on Known or Stated Facts

If the defamatory opinion is based entirely on facts (a) *known* to those making and receiving the statement, or (b) stated as a predicate to the opinion, recent cases (e.g. *Gertz v. Robert Welch, Inc.*) seem to indicate that the first amendment permits one to express one's opinion, however misguided or debatable, without defamation liability. "Under the first amendment, there is no such thing as a false idea." This is analogous to the common law privilege of fair comment.

2) Based on Undisclosed Facts

On the other hand, if and to the extent that the opinion implies the allegation of undisclosed defamatory facts as the basis for the opinion, it may be actionable. *Milkovich v. Lorain Journal Co.* (US. 1990).

c. Ridicule

Humorous writings, verses, cartoons, or caricatures which may be understood as making a statement about P are similarly protected, at least to the extent that they represent merely negative opinions not implying false facts. *Hustler Magazine v. Falwell* (US. 1988).

d. Verbal Abuse

Profanity and similar statements, directed at P in anger and obviously intended as mere vituperation or abuse, ordinarily cannot be taken literally and therefore are not defamatory.

e. Fabricated Quotation

To attribute a fabricated quotation to P may be defamatory. *Masson v. New Yorker Magazine, Inc.* (U.S.1991).

B. Libel and Slander

1. Distinguished (R.2d § 568)

a. Libel

Libel is the publication of defamatory matter by (1) written or printed words, or (2) embodiment in physical form (e.g., photos, cartoons, sculpture, film, videotape, sound recordings), or (3) any other form of communication that has potentially harmful characteristics comparable to those of written or printed words.

b. Slander

Slander is the publication of defamatory matter by spoken words, transitory gestures, or other form of communication not amounting to a libel.

c. Factors to Be Considered

The factors to be considered in distinguishing libel and slander are the area of dissemination, the deliberate and premeditated character of the publication, and the persistence or permanency of the publication.

d. Radio and TV

Radio and television publications are regarded in most jurisdictions as libel, unless otherwise provided by statute.

2. Defamation Actionable Without Proof of Special Damage

a. Libel: General Rule

In most jurisdictions, any libel is actionable per se, that is, without proof that P sustained any special harm or damage from the publication. Even if

P cannot or does not prove actual damages, the trier of fact can infer harm sufficient to support an award of compensatory or nominal damages. R.2d § 569.

b. Libel Per Quod

In a minority of U.S. jurisdictions, a libel which is not defamatory on its face but requires reference to extrinsic facts to establish its defamatory meaning is not actionable without proof of special harm. This is sometimes called libel per quod.

c. Slander

Publication of a slander is not actionable without proof of special damages unless it defames P in one of the following four ways (R.2d §§ 570, 575):

1) Criminal Conduct

It imputes to P conduct that constitutes a crime punishable by imprisonment or involving moral turpitude. R.2d § 571.

2) Communicable Disease

It imputes that P has a venereal or other loathsome and communicable disease. R.2d § 572.

3) Business, Trade, Profession, or Office

It imputes to P conduct, characteristics or a condition that would adversely affect his fitness for the proper conduct of his business, trade, profession, or office. R.2d § 573.

4) Sexual Misconduct

It imputes serious sexual misconduct. Traditionally, this was limited to imputing unchastity to a woman, but today it extends to imputing serious sexual misconduct regardless of gender. R.2d § 574.

If actionable without proof of special damages, it is called "slander per se"; if not, it is "slander per quod."

d. Special Damage

In this context, special harm or damages refers to the loss of something having economic or pecuniary value, which results from the harm to P's reputation. It does not include P's emotional distress and resulting bodily harm (which may, however, be compensated if the defamation is otherwise actionable).

C. Publication

1. Definition

Publication is the communication of defamatory matter by D to someone other than P. R.2d § 577.

2. Fault

Even at common law (i.e., before *Gertz*), and today, D is not liable for unintended or accidental publication. The publication must have been intentional or the result of D's negligence.

3. Agent

In most jurisdictions, publication to D's agent is sufficient (but may be privileged). If dictated with the intent that it will be reduced to writing (a letter, telegram), it is libel. And D is liable for a publication by his agent where he directed or procured it.

4. Multiple Publications (R.2d § 577A)

a. General Rule

Each of several communications to a third person by the same D is a separate publication.

b. Single Communication

A single communication heard at the same time by two or more third persons is a single publication.

c. Single Publication Rule

One edition of a book or newspaper, or one radio or TV broadcast, one exhibition of a motion picture, or a similar aggregate publication is deemed a single publication.

d. Effect

For each single publication, only one action can be maintained in which P must claim all damages resulting from that publication. This raises issues of venue, statute of limitations, and choice of law when the publication is received in more than one state.

5. Wills

Generally, an action will lie against D's estate for libelous matter published in his will after his death.

6.   Liability of Republisher

a.   General Rule
One who repeats or otherwise republishes a defamation is subject to liability to the same extent as if he had originally published it. R.2d § 578.

> *Example:*   Where a libel is published in a newspaper, magazine or book, the author, editor, printer, publisher and owner are all subject to liability as publisher. One who broadcasts defamatory matter by radio or TV is subject to the same liability as an original publisher (R.2d § 581(2)).

b.   Exception
One who only delivers or transmits defamatory matter published by a third person is subject to liability only if he knows or has reason to know of its defamatory character. This exception does not apply to broadcasters. R.2d § 581.

> *Example:*   News dealers and delivery boys, bookstores, libraries, telephone and telegraph companies, mail or message deliverers.

c.   Publication on the Internet
In all likelihood, information published on the internet or other similar network will be treated as published only by the content provider and not by the internet service provider or one who merely provides the web site. See 47 U.S.C.A. § 230(c)(1).

7.   Causation: Liability of Original Publisher for Republication

D is liable for the republication of his defamatory statement by another if (a) the third person was privileged to repeat it, or (b) D authorized or intended the repetition, or (c) the repetition was reasonably foreseeable. Cf. R.2d §§ 576, 662A. D is ordinarily not liable for a repetition by P.

D.   Fault

1.   Common Law
At common law, defamation liability was strict. D did not have to be aware of the falsity or defamatory character of the statement, or even be negligent in ascertaining these things; nor need he have intended or

foreseen any harm, or that the statement could be understood as referring to P. The only fault required was with respect to its publication: D had to intentionally or negligently publish the matter.

2. First Amendment

Recent court decisions have held that the first amendment to the U.S. Constitution imposes fault requirements, at least in the case of defamatory matter concerning public officials, public figures, or matters of public concern when D is exercising the freedom of the press protected by that amendment. These decisions have led some states to impose fault requirements as common law rules, even where not strictly required by constitutional law.

3. Public Official, Public Figure

Under *New York Times Co. v. Sullivan* (U.S. 1964) and its progeny, one who publishes a false and defamatory communication concerning a public official or a public figure with regard to his conduct, fitness, or role in that capacity is subject to liability only if D (a) knows that the statement is false and that it defames P, or (b) acts in reckless disregard of these matters. R.2d § 580A.

a. Public Official

A *public official* is a governmental employee who has (or appears to have) responsibility for or control over the conduct of governmental affairs, and may include even relatively low-ranking personnel, such as police officers. To receive the benefit of this special first amendment protection, the defamatory statement must concern the official's fitness for or performance in the office.

b. Public Figure

A *public figure* is one who has achieved a degree of fame or notoriety, either generally or as to a particular public issue or controversy. The voluntary nature of P's participation is a factor to be considered. The statement must affect P in his public capacity.

Examples: A well-known college football coach; a retired Army general who had taken a prominent controversial position on racial segregation; candidates for public office; but not a socially prominent woman who has done no more than sue her very wealthy husband for divorce.

c. Fault

The requisite fault is "actual malice" (sometimes described as "constitutional malice"). Here, malice does not have its literal meaning. "Actual malice" means nothing more than knowledge of the statement's false and defamatory character or a reckless disregard of these matters, as when a statement is published despite a high degree of awareness of its probable falsity, or with serious doubts as to its truth. Actual ill will need not be proved. The availability of time and opportunity to check the truth of the statement may be relevant. Proof of D's fault must be clear and convincing.

d. Private Communications

The cases that impose the foregoing fault requirement so far have involved public statements in the press, media and books. It remains to be seen whether these fault requirements apply to other forms of communication, though most jurisdictions do not distinguish between media and non-media cases in applying these rules.

4. Private Persons

Under *Gertz v. Robert Welch, Inc.* (U.S. 1974) and its progeny, one who publishes a false and defamatory communication concerning a private person, or concerning a public official or public figure with regard to a purely private matter (i.e. not affecting his conduct, fitness or role in his public capacity) is subject to liability only if D (a) knows that the statement is false and that it defames P, or (b) acts in reckless disregard of these matters, or (c) acts negligently in failing to ascertain them. R.2d § 580B.

a. Effect of Gertz

After *Gertz*, strict liability for defamation published in the press, media, and possibly books is unconstitutional, regardless of the status of P. However, the states are free to determine the degree of fault required for defamation actions by persons described in ¶ 4., above, so long as at least negligence is required.

b. Majority Rule

So far, the majority of states passing on the question have followed the *Gertz* criteria, so that in those jurisdictions *all* those persons described in ¶ 4. above need only prove that D was *negligent* in ascertaining the falsity and defamatory character of the statement.

c. Minority Rule

In some jurisdictions, if the defamation concerns a matter of *general* or *public interest*, even those persons described in ¶ 4. above are required to prove that D either (1) knew that the statement was false and that it defames P, or (2) acted in reckless disregard of these matters (i.e., same as for public officials and public figures).

d. Burden of Proof

Those persons described in ¶ 4. above must prove falsity and the requisite fault by a preponderance of the evidence.

e. Private Communications

It remains to be seen whether the *Gertz* rule applies to publications other than in the press, media or books. Several state courts have held that it does not, and have sustained verdicts based on strict liability for a private libel. In addition, recent Supreme Court rulings appear to indicate that the *Gertz* rule will apply only when the subject matter of the defamation involves an issue of public interest.

E. Defenses to Actions for Defamation

1. Consent

a. Rule

P's consent to the publication of defamatory matter concerning him is a complete defense. R.2d § 583.

b. Exception

D may be liable for a republication that results from P's honest inquiry or investigation to ascertain the existence, source, content, or meaning of the defamatory publication. R.2d § 584.

2. Absolute Privileges

a. Judicial Proceedings

During the course of performing their functions in judicial proceedings, judges and judicial officers, attorneys, parties, witnesses, and jurors are absolutely privileged to publish defamatory matter which has some relation to the proceeding. R.2d §§ 585–589.

b. Legislative Proceedings

A member of Congress or a state or local legislative body is absolutely privileged to publish defamatory matter in the performance of his legislative functions. A witness is absolutely privileged to publish defamatory matter as part of a legislative proceeding in which he is testifying or in communications preliminary to the proceeding, if the matter has some relation to the proceeding. R.2d §§ 590, 590A.

c.   Executive and Administrative Officers

An executive or administrative officer of the U.S., or a governor or other superior executive officer of a state, is absolutely privileged to publish defamatory matter in communications made in the performance of his official duties. R.2d § 591.

d.   Husband and Wife

A husband or wife is absolutely privileged to publish defamatory matter to the other. R.2d § 592.

e.   Publication Required by Law

One who is required by law to publish defamatory matter is absolutely privileged to publish it. R.2d § 592A.

Example: A newspaper required to publish an official notice.

3.   Conditional or Qualified Privileges

a.   In General

At common law, certain defamatory communications are *conditionally* or *qualifiedly* privileged, so that D is not liable provided he meets all the conditions or qualifications. R.2d § 593. As to these privileges, the chief limitation is that D must (1) *believe* his statement to be true, and (2) (a) in some jurisdictions, have *reasonable grounds* for believing it to be true, or (b) in other jurisdictions, not have acted *recklessly* in failing to ascertain its truth or falsity. But the *N.Y. Times* and *Gertz* cases, when applicable, require P to prove that D acted either recklessly or negligently in ascertaining the truth or falsity of the statement. Thus, if and to the extent that *N.Y. Times* and *Gertz* apply, the existence of a conditional privilege is partly or totally irrelevant. Therefore, the following privileges apply only when and to the extent that they are not superseded by the *N.Y. Times* or *Gertz* rules.

b.   Protection of the Publisher's Interest

1)   Rule

D's defamatory communication is conditionally privileged when the circumstances cause D to correctly or reasonably believe that (1) the information affects a sufficiently important interest of D, and (2) the information will be of service to the recipient in the *lawful protection* of that interest. R.2d § 594.

2) Value of D's Interest

Interests of D worthy of protection include, for example (a) any lawful business or pecuniary interest, *other than* his interest in competition for prospective advantage (e.g., defamation to obtain customers), (b) his bodily security, (c) his present interest in land, chattels, or intangible property, (d) his family, and (e) his own reputation. In each case, the value of D's interest is to be balanced against the harm to P's reputation if the defamatory matter is false.

c. Protection of Interest of Recipient or Third Person

1) Rule

D's defamatory communication is conditionally privileged when the circumstances cause D to correctly or reasonably believe that (1) the information affects a sufficiently important interest of the recipient or a *third person,* and (2) the recipient is one to whom (a) D is under a *legal duty* to publish it or (b) its publication is otherwise within *generally accepted standards of decent conduct.* R.2d § 595.

2) Decent Conduct

Important factors in determining whether the publication is within generally accepted standards of decent conduct include whether (a) it is in response to a *request*, rather than volunteered by D, or (b) a *family* or other *relationship* exists between the parties. R.2d § 595.

3) Examples

Fiduciaries discharging their duties; reports to proper authorities that D believes P is about to commit a crime against another; in most states, reports by credit agencies; communications among members of a trade association; reports to an employer about the character or conduct of a present or prospective employee; communications to a close friend about the character or conduct of a member of his family, made in response to a request for such information.

d. Protection of Common Interest

1) Rule

D's defamatory communication is conditionally privileged when the circumstances cause D to correctly or reasonably believe that another who shares a common interest is entitled to know it. R.2d § 596.

2) Examples

Business partners and associates in a business enterprise exchanging information about employees and others; co-owners of real or personal property, concerning their common interest in that property; members of religious, fraternal and charitable organizations discussing the qualifications of officers, other or prospective members, and association activities.

e. Family Relationships

D's defamatory communication is conditionally privileged when the circumstances cause D to correctly or reasonably believe that:

1) the recipient's knowledge will help protect the well-being of a member of D's *immediate family*; or

2) the recipient's knowledge will help protect the well-being of a member of the *immediate family of the recipient or a third person*, and the recipient has requested the information or is a person to whom its communication is otherwise within generally accepted standards of decent conduct. R.2d § 597.

Example: D tells his sister that he has seen P, her husband, in the company of prostitutes. D, a minister, writes an unsolicited letter to F's father telling him that P, F's fiancé, is a felon. The communications are conditionally privileged.

f. Public Interest

D's defamatory communication is conditionally privileged when the circumstances cause D to correctly or reasonably believe that a sufficiently important public interest requires its communication to a public officer or other person who is authorized or privileged to take action if it is true. R.2d § 598.

Example: Reporting a crime or anticipated crime (unless absolutely privileged, see judicial proceedings); reporting misconduct or incompetence by a public official or employee; petitions for legislative action.

g. Inferior State Officers

Lower level state or local government employees who are not entitled to an absolute privilege have a conditional privilege for communications required or permitted in the performance of their duties. R.2d § 598A.

h. "Abuse" (Loss) of the Privilege

1) Knowledge, Recklessness or Negligence Concerning Falsity

a) Negligence

Prior to *Gertz*, in some jurisdictions a conditional privilege was lost if D did not honestly believe the truth of his statement, or if he did not have "reasonable grounds" to believe in its truth. It remains to be seen whether this rule has any purpose after *Gertz*.

b) Recklessness

Other jurisdictions have held that a conditional privilege is lost only if D knows that the statement is false or acts in "reckless disregard" as to its truth or falsity. Where *Gertz* or *N.Y. Times* applies, any conditional privilege will be irrelevant. R.2d § 600 adopts this version of the rule.

2) Rumor

D may be privileged to publish a defamatory rumor or suspicion, even though he believes or knows that it is untrue, *provided:*

a) he *states* the defamatory matter as a rumor or suspicion and not as a fact; and

b) the publication is *reasonable,* considering the relation of the parties, the importance of the interests affected, and the harm likely to be done. R.2d § 602.

3) Purpose

There is no conditional privilege unless D publishes the defamatory matter for the *purpose* of protecting the interest which gives rise to the privilege, R.2d § 603, and reasonably believes the publication to be *necessary* for that purpose, R.2d § 605.

4) Excessive Publication

There is no conditional privilege to the extent that D knowingly publishes the defamatory matter to a person outside its scope, unless he reasonably believes that such publication is a proper means of communicating it to a proper person. R.2d § 604.

5) Unprivileged Matter

The privilege is lost to the extent that D adds unprivileged matter to the communication. If not severable, the entire privilege is lost. R.2d § 605A.

i. Fair Comment on Matters of Public Concern

At common law, there was a qualified privilege for what was called "fair comment" (i.e., publicly expressing one's opinion) on matters of public concern. This former privilege appears to have been subsumed under the constitutional right to express such opinions without defamation liability. See ¶ A.8.b., above; R.2d § 566.

4. **Special Types of Privilege**

a. Report of Official Proceeding or Public Meeting

D is privileged to publish defamatory matter in a report of an official action or proceeding or of a meeting open to the public that deals with a matter of public concern, provided the report is accurate or a fair abridgment of the occurrence reported. R.2d § 611. Although the Restatement omits this limitation, the privilege probably does not extend to matter published solely for the purpose of harming the person defamed. As a matter of constitutional law, as applied to the press and news media, P must also establish D's fault (as defined in *N.Y. Times* and *Gertz*) in failing to make a fair and accurate report.

b. Transmission of Message by Public Utility

A public utility under a duty to transmit messages is privileged unless the utility knows or has reason to know that the message is defamatory and that the sender is not privileged to publish it. R.2d § 612(2). This privilege may apply even when the utility knows that the message is false.

c. Providing Means of Publication

One who provides a means of publication of defamatory matter published by another is privileged to do so if the other is privileged to publish it. R.2d § 612(1).

F. Damages

1. Types Recoverable

Damages which may be recoverable in a defamation action include (a) nominal damages, (b) general (or "presumed") damages for harm to reputation, (c) damages for proved special harm caused by the harm to P's reputation, (d) damages for emotional distress and resulting bodily harm, and (e) punitive damages.

2. Nominal Damages

One who is liable for a libel or slander actionable per se is liable for at least nominal damages. R.2d § 620.

3. General Damages (R.2d § 621)

a. Rule

At common law, once D's liability was established, the jury could award P general damages for harm to his reputation, whether P proved actual harm or not. In most jurisdictions these are known as "presumed" damages. In the absence of such proof, the jury could compensate P for the harm to his reputation that normally would be assumed to flow from a defamatory publication of the nature involved. However, *Gertz* holds that the first amendment prohibits the states from permitting recovery for presumed damages unless P proves D's knowledge of the defamation's falsity or his reckless disregard for its truth; otherwise, proof of actual harm is required. "Actual harm" is not limited to pecuniary loss; it includes such intangibles as harm to P's reputation and emotional distress. No specific dollar value of such harm need be shown.

b. Exception

In *Dun & Bradstreet, Inc. v. Greenmoss Builders, Inc.* (US. 1985), the Supreme Court held that a state could award presumed damages when P was a private figure and the speech did not involve any issue of public interest or concern.

4. Special Damages

Special damages (i.e., economic or pecuniary loss) resulting from the defamation may always be recovered. In the case of slander per quod (and libel per quod in some jurisdictions), such damages are a prerequisite to liability. See ¶ B.2., above; R.2d § 622.

5. Emotional Distress and Bodily Harm

Once D's liability is established, damages for emotional distress and resulting bodily harm are recoverable. R.2d § 623.

6. Punitive Damages

The common law generally allows punitive damages in a defamation action when D's conduct involves "actual malice," which usually means an intent to harm P or a reckless disregard of whether or not he will be harmed. In addition, the constitution prohibits punitive damages, at least against the press and media defendants, unless P proves D's knowledge of the statement's falsity or his reckless disregard for its truth.

7. Mitigation

By statute in some jurisdictions and common law in most others, a retraction by D is not a complete defense, but may be considered in *mitigation* of P's damages. Other mitigating circumstances may also be considered.

8. Right of Reply

Statutes requiring a newspaper to publish P's reply to a defamatory statement previously printed in it are unconstitutional.

G. Review Questions

[Answers Provided in Appendix A, pages 409–410]

1. T or F   If D defames another and then retracts his defamatory statement the person defamed may not recover damages for the defamation.

2. T or F   A communication which is not intended by its maker to be defamatory can nonetheless be found to be defamatory if the hearer reasonably understands it to be so.

3. T or F   The publication of defamatory material over radio or television is slander.

4. T or F   Because attorneys are officers of the court they cannot recover damages from persons who make defamatory statements about them unless the defamatory statements were made with the knowledge that they are false or in reckless disregard of whether it was true or false.

5. **T or F**   D dictates a letter containing defamatory statements about P to his secretary. Before mailing the letter he changes his mind and destroys the letter. There is publication of the defamatory statement.

6. **T or F**   P applies to E for a job and puts down D as a reference. As a result E calls D and asks him about P D states that P is a liar, a thief, and is generally incompetent. In P's suit against D, D can claim a conditional privilege.

7.   While testifying as a witness in court D falsely and gratuitously refers to his neighbor, who is not in court, who is not a witness, and who is not a party to the suit, as a loud, obnoxious, stupid, old fool whose rantings and ravings disturb the neighborhood.

     a.   P cannot recover damages from D because the statement was made in court.

     b.   P cannot recover damages because he did not himself hear the statement.

     c.   P cannot recover damages unless he can show special damages because this is not a slander per se.

     d.   P cannot recover under the Gertz rule unless he shows that D was at least negligent.

XXV.   Privacy

(Dobbs §§ 424–428; R.2d §§ 652A–652I)

A.   Introduction

The tort action for invasion of privacy is a comparatively recent development, stimulated by an 1890 Harvard Law Review article by Warren and Brandeis. At present, the tort encompasses four distinct wrongs (R.2d § 652A):

1. **Appropriation** of one's name or likeness;

2. **Intrusion** upon another's privacy or private affairs;

3. **Public disclosure of private facts** about P; and

4. Placing P in a **false light in the public eye.**

Other forms (or variations on these forms) may develop in the future; these categories are not limitations.

Example: Governmental intrusion as a violation of various personal or civil rights. And there may be overlap between these forms in a particular case.

The action for invasion of privacy is recognized in most jurisdictions (but not in all forms). In some it is affected by statute.

B. Appropriation

1. Rule

*D is subject to liability for appropriating the **name** or **likeness** of P for his own use or benefit.* R.2d § 652C.

> *Example:* Without permission, D uses the name and photograph of P, a famous baseball player, in an advertisement of D's bread.

2. Commercial Use

Unless otherwise required by statute, the use need not be for business or commercial purposes. Many states, however, do impose a business or commercial purpose requirement.

> *Example:* D signs P's name to a telegram to a senator urging him to vote against a particular bill. D has invaded P's privacy.

3. Appropriation

D must use P's name for the purpose of taking advantage of P's reputation, prestige or other value associated with his name or likeness. Merely adopting a name identical to that of another, or using another's name in a communication or publication, is not an invasion of privacy unless the purpose is to appropriate the benefit of its commercial value.

C. Intrusion

1. Rule

*D is subject to liability for intrusion (physical or other) upon the solitude, seclusion, or private life and affairs of another, **provided** the intrusion would be highly offensive to a reasonable person.* R.2d § 652B.

2. Form

The forms of intrusion are varied—unpermitted entry into P's home or hospital room; an illegal search of P's person or property; tapping P's telephone; using mechanical aids to observe P's private activities in his home; opening P's personal mail; and persistent and unwanted communications or close physical presence.

3. Publication

The tort is complete when the intrusion occurs. No publication or publicity of the information is required.

4. Private Matters

The intrusion must be into what is, and is entitled to remain, private. Photographing or watching P in a public place, or inspecting or copying nonprivate records, is not actionable.

5. Substantial Interference

The intrusion must be highly offensive to the ordinary person, resulting from conduct to which the reasonable person would strongly object.

6. Governmental Intrusion

The courts are beginning to recognize a constitutional right of privacy, to be free from excessive or unreasonable governmental intrusion.

D. Public Disclosure of Private Facts

1. Rule

D is subject to liability for giving publicity to some private fact about P, **provided** *the fact publicized would be highly offensive to a reasonable person and is not a matter of legitimate public concern.* R.2d § 652D.

2. Publicity

The information about P need not be "published." It is sufficient if it is disclosed so as to be likely to become public knowledge.

3. Private Facts

In this case, the facts disclosed are true. Thus, there is no liability for facts which are already known by, or available to, the public. The facts must be intimate or at least private details of P's private life, the disclosure of which would be embarrassing, humiliating or offensive. And P's right to keep these facts private is balanced against the legitimate interest of the public. Thus, there are fewer "private" facts of the famous and those in high positions.

4. Legitimate Public Concern or Interest

a. Constitutional Limitations

The first amendment freedoms of the press and speech are a further limitation of this tort, and permit, to an extent yet to be fully developed, publication of private facts which are matters of legitimate public concern or interest—i.e., "news."

b. Public Figures

Persons who have voluntarily become public figures, and even those involuntarily in the public eye by being part of a newsworthy event, cannot complain of the publication of facts, otherwise private, which are of legitimate public concern or interest in connection with that person, activity, or event. This legitimate concern may even extend to the family and close friends of the public figure, and to some facts about persons who were public figures at some time in the past.

E. False Light in the Public Eye

1. Rule

D is subject to liability for giving publicity to a matter which places P before the public in a false light, provided (a) the false light would be highly offensive to a reasonable person, and (b) D had knowledge of the falsity of the matter and the false light it created, or acted in reckless disregard of these matters. R.2d § 652E.

2. Relation to Defamation

In this case, the information communicated about P is false. Thus, if it is also defamatory, an action for libel or slander may be an alternative remedy. However, it is not necessary to this action that P be defamed. It is enough that he is given unreasonable and highly objectionable publicity that attributes to him characteristics, conduct or beliefs that are false.

Example: A photograph of P an honest taxi driver, is used to illustrate a newspaper article on the practices of taxi drivers who cheat the public. P has an action for both libel and invasion of privacy.

Because it largely overlaps defamation claims, some courts have rejected the false light claim.

3. Highly Offensive

The matter must be highly offensive to a reasonable person. Thus, relatively minor inaccuracies or fictions in an otherwise accurate and favorable story about P are not actionable.

4. Constitutional Limitations

Time, Inc. v. Hill (U.S. 1967) extended the *N.Y. Times* rule to this type of invasion of privacy action, requiring P to prove by clear and convincing evidence that D knew of the statement's falsity or acted in reckless disregard of its truth or falsity. Whether the *Gertz* case has modified this rule (to include negligence in the case of private individuals), and the extent to which this limitation applies to others than the press and media, has yet to be decided.

F. Privileges

The absolute, conditional and special privileges to publish defamatory matter (see part XXIV.E, above) also apply to the publication of any matter that is an invasion of privacy. R.2d §§ 652F, 652G.

G. Damages

In an action for invasion of privacy, P can recover damages for:

1. Harm to his interest in privacy;

2. Mental distress, if of a kind that normally results from such an invasion; and

3. Special damages.

H. Persons Who May Sue

Unless otherwise provided by statute, and except for appropriation, an action for invasion of privacy can be maintained only by a living individual whose privacy is invaded. R.2d § 652I. Whether an action survives P's death depends on the local survival statute.

I. Review Questions

[Answers Provided in Appendix A, page 410]

1. Short Essay: List the 4 types of wrongs encompassed within the tort of invasion of privacy.

2. T or F   P is a 32–year-old housewife who lives in Illinois with her husband and two children. When she was 18 she lived briefly in Florida where she was arrested several times for prostitution, petty theft, and possession of marijuana. She was never convicted of any of these offenses and has never been arrested for anything else. She never told anyone about her arrests in Florida and no one else knew

until D came upon a reference to the arrests in an old newspaper. He reproduced the newspaper page and sent copies to P's husband, children, and neighbors. P can recover damages from D for invasion of her privacy.

3. T or F   D, a photographer, constantly follows P, the widow of a former President, wherever she goes and takes her picture at all hours, under all circumstances and from near distances and far. P can recover damages from D for invasion of her privacy.

4. T or F   The same facts as in 3, but D, acting without P's permission furnishes pictures of P to tourists and other persons who will buy them as souvenirs and curios. D is liable to P for appropriation of her likeness.

5. T or F   The same facts as in 3, but D acting without the permission of P, whose deceased husband was a model of propriety, sells some pictures of P to a magazine which uses the pictures to illustrate an article on philandering by ex-Presidents. D is liable to P for placing her before the public in a false light.

APPENDIX A

Answers to Review Questions

■ **PART TWO: INTENTIONAL TORTS**

II. LIABILITY RULES FOR INTENTIONAL TORTS

[Answers to Questions on pages 159–160]

1. **True.** A battery occurs whenever P, without consent and with the intention of causing a harmful or offense contact makes contact with D or with something so closely connected or identified with D that a normal person would deem it an offense against his person. Striking P's vehicle (when P is inside) is likely an offensive contact with something closely identified with P.

2. **True.** Since P does not know that the arrow could not reach him, he could reasonably apprehend a battery; D had the required apparent present ability. Although the arrow fell short, P could properly anticipate that it might reach him.

3. **False.** P's apprehension of a battery to a third person is not an assault on P no matter how concerned P may be for the third person's safety. Since P never really believed that D would shoot him (P), there is no assault on P.

4. **False.** False Imprisonment: Yes. Exiting from a second floor window is not a reasonably safe means of escape. Therefore P was confined. Although P was aware of his confinement for only a few seconds, that is sufficient. Battery: Yes. Although D did not personally strike P, he arguably knew that P was substantially certain to fall when he yanked open the door. This is sufficient intent. A battery can be indirect. In the alternative, P might argue that the intent to confine transfers and supplies the intent necessary to support the battery action.

5. **True.** Even though D's distress-producing conduct is directed toward one other than P, P may recover if D intentionally or recklessly causes P to suffer severe emotional distress provided, as here, P was present and witnessed D's conduct which was directed against a member of his family.

6. A *trespass to a chattel* occurs whenever D intentionally interferes with P's chattel, whether by physical contact or dispossession. *Any* dispossession, or any physical contact which impairs the chattel's condition, quality, or value, is a trespass. If the tort is based on physical contact, there must be some actual damages, but any dispossession is a trespass for which nominal damages may be awarded.

   A *conversion* is a trespass to P's chattel which is so serious that D may properly be required to "buy" the chattel from P It is an aggravated trespass; thus, all conversions are also trespasses. Whether the trespass is serious enough depends on several factors: the extent and duration of D's exercise of dominion or control and of the interference with P's rights; D's intent; D's good faith; the harm done to the chattel; and P's inconvenience and expense.

7. The correct answer is (d). D is liable because in erecting his building D intended to exercise control over the land which the building occupied and intended that the building enter upon and occupy P's land. Good faith is not a defense and D's liability does not depend on any negligence on his part. Moreover, the fact that the invasion is *de minimus* and does no actual harm is irrelevant if, as here, D had the actual intent to enter or to cause his building to enter upon P's land.

III. DEFENSES TO LIABILITY FOR INTENTIONAL TORTS: PRIVILEGES

[Answers to Questions on pages 170–172]

1. **True.** Traveler has a limited privilege to enter upon Owner's land only if it reasonably appears to be necessary. Here, an alternate route was available, and there was no emergency justifying the trespass.

2. **True.** Owner may only use force or threat of force that is minimally necessary to prevent or terminate Traveler's intrusion. Force likely to cause death or serious bodily injury is not privileged.

3. **False.** Traveler is privileged to come to the defense of any other person and may use so much force as reasonably appears to be immediately necessary to protect Child against imminent physical harm. Although Owner may be privileged to apply such reasonable force upon his child or another child entrusted to his care and training as he reasonably believes to be necessary for the child's proper control, training, or education, under the majority view Traveler's mistake will not negate his privilege if he reasonably believed that Child's safety required his intervention.

4. **True.** Owner's gestures ordinarily would be interpreted as consent, even though Owner's actual state of mind was to the contrary.

5. **True.** Traveler's privilege was impliedly limited in scope. Traveler clearly went beyond that to which Owner had consented.

6. **True.** Owner's consent was given under duress and was not effective.

7. **True.** Her consent was obtained by fraud in the inducement, and not merely the failure to disclose risks or alternatives. Hence, her consent was ineffective, and Doctor's conduct constituted a battery. If Doctor had merely failed to mention the risks involved in the surgery, his conduct would have been negligent under the doctrine of "informed consent" but not a battery.

8. **True.** In the case of intentional torts, the absence of consent traditionally was regarded as an element of P's prima facie case. However, today all privileges, including consent, are affirmative defenses.

9. Officer's conduct was privileged, if he used only so much force as reasonably appeared to be necessary for his and Girlfriend's defense. If he became the aggressor or continued to use force after Hood was subdued or had withdrawn, Officer would be subject to liability for harm to the extent that it resulted from his excessive use of force. Some jurisdictions would require Officer to first retreat (if feasible) if deadly force were required to defend himself.

10. In defending himself against Hood, Officer could be found to have intentionally injured Girlfriend. He may be liable to her for compensatory damages, unless her injuries were relatively minor and substantially less than that with which he was threatened. Officer may be found to have unintentionally injured Bystander, and whether he is liable for those injuries will depend upon the reasonableness of his conduct under the circumstances.

11. In the absence of a statute or a provision in the contract of sale, Fast Eddie has no privilege to repossess the car. It was rightfully acquired but is merely being tortiously withheld from Eddie. Since Eddie has no privilege to retake the car by self-help methods, Welch was privileged to defend his own possession of it. He was entitled to use reasonable force to terminate the intrusion. However, his actions in beating and tying up Eddie exceeded the scope of Welch's privilege, and therefore Welch is liable to Eddie for assault, battery, and false imprisonment.

■ PART THREE: NEGLIGENCE

IV. NEGLIGENCE LIABILITY RULES

[Answers to Questions on pages 203–205]

1. **True.** Violation of a statute requiring a license to engage in a particular profession is generally *not* admissible to show that D was negligent on a particular occasion.

2. **False.** In judging D's conduct, D will be charged with those things which a reasonable person would have known and perceived. Her deficiency will not excuse her performance. Since D held herself out as a lawyer, her conduct is measured against the hypothetical reasonably prudent lawyer.

3. **True.** Expert testimony is usually required to establish the standard of care in professional negligence cases.

4. **False.** In determining the standard of care in a professional negligence case, the customary conduct of the other professionals in the community in similar circumstances is relevant.

5. **False.** Although relevant, evidence of this type is usually not conclusive except in *medical* malpractice actions (some jurisdictions to the contrary).

6. False. Evidence that D was not a careful person is generally not admissible to prove that she acted negligently on the occasion in question.

7. False. When D undertook to render services which she knew or should have known were for the clerk's protection, she had to perform those services with reasonable care, at least if her failure to do so increased the risk of harm to the clerk or the clerk's harm resulted from her reliance on D.

8. False. D need not have been in control of the injury-causing instrumentality at the time of P's injury. P need only establish that D's negligence must have occurred while the instrumentality was in D's control.

9. False. The exclusive control requirement ordinarily precludes use of *res ipsa loquitur* against multiple defendants. But see discussion at IV.D.4.c.

10. True. P need only show that the inference that it was D's negligence outweighs the sum of the other possible causes.

11. False. A parent has the duty to exercise reasonable care to prevent tortious conduct by her child, provided the parent knows or has reason to know of the necessity and opportunity to exercise such control and that she has the ability to do so. Here, Arnold's mother had no reason to suspect that she would need to control his behavior. Therefore, she was not negligent in failing to prevent this attack.

12. False. Normally, one person has no duty to rescue another. However, certain relationships carry with them a duty by the custodial or dominant member to use reasonable care to regulate the conduct of third persons so as to protect the person in his custody or care. Parents have such a duty to protect their children.

13. True. Absent a pre-existing relationship between Arnold and Ralph, Passerby has no duty to protect or aid Arnold, even though he realizes that Arnold is in a position of danger from which he could easily and safely be rescued.

14. False. Although Ralph had no duty to rescue Arnold, once he undertook to render aid to him, he voluntarily assumed the duty to do so with reasonable care. Having done so, he cannot abandon Arnold and leave him worse off than he was before.

15. *False.* P's conduct in wiring her clothing is such that she should have been aware that it created more than a relatively high risk of harm to another; she should have known that harm was substantially certain to occur. Hence, her conduct could be found to be a battery.

16. Normally, a violation of this type of ordinance constitutes negligence per se or at least evidence of negligence. However, a violation does not automatically establish a sufficient causal relation between the violation and P's injury. P has the burden of proving that the violation of the statute was a cause in fact of his injury. If he cannot, or if D is able to persuade the trier of fact that the snow did not contribute to P's injury, then the violation of the ordinance would be irrelevant and D would prevail.

17. P must make a prima facie showing that the damage to the kitchen was caused by D's use of the solvent which was under D's exclusive control, and that the occurrence in question was of the type which would not have occurred unless D was negligent. The modern view is that P need not prove that P's conduct did not contribute to the explosion and fire.

■ V. DEFENSES TO NEGLIGENCE AND OTHER LIABILITY

[Answers to Questions on pages 224–226]

1. In some jurisdictions, contributory negligence is not a defense to a strict liability action except when P voluntarily and unreasonably subjects himself to the risk. It is not a defense to intentional torts or reckless conduct (although, in some comparative negligence jurisdictions, it will reduce P's recovery where D's conduct was reckless) or to actions founded upon certain types of safety statutes intended to protect a class of persons from dangers against which they are incapable of protecting themselves.

2. **a, e,** and **f.**

3. **e.** This type of employer-employee contract provision is generally found to be unenforceable as against public policy. However, even if it were enforceable generally, it would not be under b, c, and d. This type of agreement will be enforced in cases of intentional torts (b), and, in some

jurisdictions, reckless torts (c). It is also unenforceable if P was reasonably ignorant of its provisions (d).

4. a. P cannot be said to have assumed the risk in this case. The consent to ride with D was not "informed," because P did not know that D was drunk, and therefore could not have understood and appreciated the risk of accepting a ride with D.

    b. Even though P did not have the funds to pay cab fare, his decision to ride with D cannot be said to have been made under economic duress. (Even if it had, some courts would not recognize this as a factor making P's consent involuntary.) There may have been other alternatives available to P. Since his consent to ride with D was voluntary, he may be found to have assumed the risk *if* that consent was informed, as described in the answer above.

    c. Here P clearly did not assume the risk. Since he was unconscious, he gave no consent, informed or otherwise. No consent, no assumption of the risk.

    d. P will be charged with knowledge of those facts that are readily ascertainable by observation. If D were so drunk that it was clear from observing him that he was in no condition to drive, P could be said to have assumed the risk. If, however, D were able to conceal his drunken state, P would not have assumed the risk.

5. Runner's last clear chance argument will not succeed in a comparative negligence jurisdiction. The amount of damages will depend upon whether the jurisdiction adopted pure or modified comparative negligence. In a pure comparative negligence jurisdiction, Runner will recover his damages reduced by 50%, the proportion that Runner's fault bears to the total causative fault of his harm. If the jurisdiction has adopted modified comparative negligence, Runner will recover either half his damages or nothing, depending upon the particular comparative negligence statute.

6. a. In some jurisdictions, Runner would be unable to bring suit against his spouse. However, if the marriage had terminated before the suit was filed, or if Runner could show that Wife's actions were intentional rather than negligent, he might still be able to bring suit.

    b. In some jurisdictions, this suit, too, would be barred by a common law immunity. Some jurisdictions that still observe this immunity recognize exceptions in the following cases: intentional or reckless conduct, torts occurring during D's business activities, wrongful death actions, and suits after the parent-minor child relationship has ended.

c. There are no common law or statutory immunities for siblings.

d. In most jurisdictions, Mayor would be liable. Mayor's act in driving to work was not an executive or judicial function, so it would not be protected under a common law or statutory immunity.

e. Neighbor's incompetence would not affect his liability in this case.

■ PART FOUR: CAUSATION

VI. CAUSATION

[Answers to Questions on pages 242–243]

1. *False.* Proximate cause ("scope of liability") is a legal concept used to cut off A's liability when the court or jury decides that it would be unjust under the circumstances, despite the fact that A's tortious conduct was a cause in fact of P's injury. In some instances, proximate cause rules are applied by the court, but in other instances the scope of liability issue is left to the jury.

2. *False.* Cause in fact is usually a question of fact for the jury.

3. *True.* Under joint and several liability, when the tortious conduct of A and B concur and both are causes in fact of P's injury, either or both are subject to liability in full for all of P's damages.

4. *False.* Both A and B are subject to full liability when either's conduct alone would have caused P's harm. It does not matter that A's conduct by itself would not have caused the injury.

5. *True.* If A's tortious conduct injures B and also foreseeably exposes B to the risk of further injury by another, A is liable both for the injury he caused and for the further injury.

6. *False.* Under the "eggshell" plaintiff rule, A and B are liable for the full consequences of P's injury even though, due to P's peculiar suscep-

tibility, the physical consequences of the injury were more severe than they would have been in a normal person.

7. *True.* P's wife's conduct was a superseding cause of his death. Both the conduct itself and its consequences were unforeseeable, and therefore the tortious conduct of A and B are not deemed the proximate cause of P's death.

8. *True.* The intervention of would-be rescuers is deemed foreseeable, and therefore when A's tortious conduct endangers B, he is liable to C who is injured in attempting a rescue.

9. *True.* The acts of rescuers, including negligent ones, are usually considered foreseeable intervening causes. A is liable both for the original injury and its exacerbation.

10. *False.* Criminal conduct by third persons is deemed foreseeable only if A's conduct exposed P to a greater-than-normal risk of such conduct or if the exposure to such risks is what made A's conduct tortious. X's conduct in this case was probably not foreseeable.

■ PART FIVE: SPECIAL LIABILITY RULES FOR PARTICULAR ACTIVITIES

VIII. OWNERS AND OCCUPIERS OF LAND

[Answers to Questions on pages 269–271]

1. *True.* Passerby is a trespasser, and Mort is under no duty to make his property reasonably safe for trespassers.

2. *False.* The castle arguably would constitute an "attractive nuisance." Mort is liable for physical harm to children trespassing on his land caused by an artificial condition if (1) he knows or has reason to know that children are likely to trespass; (2) the moat created a risk of serious bodily harm or death; and (3) Child does not realize the risk. However, the jury would also have to find Mort negligent as to Child in maintaining the condition.

3. *False.* Meter Reader does have a privilege to enter Mort's property, but that privilege was exceeded when Reader deviated from the path to

and from the meter. He then became a trespasser, to whom Mort owed a very limited duty.

4. *False.*   Traveler was traveling a public highway and O is liable if he negligently conducted an activity which subjected T to an unreasonable risk of harm.

5. *False.*   Traveler's trespass was a foreseeable deviation, and Owner is liable if he negligently conducted an activity that subjected Traveler to an unreasonable risk of harm.

6. *True.*   This assumes that the tree grew naturally along the roadway. If Owner or any predecessor planted the tree close to the road as part of his landscaping, or if O's land was located in an urban area, he may be liable if he was negligent.

7. *False.*   Traveler is a trespasser, and Owner is under no duty to exercise reasonable care to carry on activities on the premises so as not to endanger him. However, if Traveler's deviation from the public way is minor and foreseeable by O, O could be liable if he was negligent as to T.

8. *True.*   When Owner knows that trespassers constantly intrude upon his premises, he is liable to Traveler if he fails to exercise reasonable care in the conduct of active operations that create a risk of serious bodily harm to Traveler.

9. *True.*   Owner has a duty to Traveler as a discovered trespasser to control those forces within his control that threaten Traveler's safety.

10. a.   No. Owner must know or have reason to know of the condition and realize that it presents a risk of harm to children.

    b.   No. Traveler Jr. should have realized the risk.

    c.   Yes. The utility of maintaining the condition (none) and the burden of eliminating the danger (small) are outweighed by the risk to the children involved.

11. **b, c** (some jurisdictions), **d, f, g.**

12. Where the lessor knows of a concealed unreasonably dangerous condition existing on the premises at the time the lessee takes possession and fails to

warn the lessee, he is liable. However, the lessor need not inspect the premises to discover the condition, and the danger must be latent.

Lessor is also liable for physical harm caused by dangerous conditions in parts of the premises which lessee is entitled to use and over which lessor retains control, provided lessor by the exercise of reasonable care could have (1) discovered the condition, and (2) made it reasonably safe. Liability does not extend to areas where lessees and their guests are forbidden.

In some jurisdictions, a lessor may also be liable for negligent failure to repair the leased premises, or for negligent repairs under certain conditions, where the repair is required by the lease or applicable statute or ordinance.

■ IX. PRODUCTS LIABILITY

[Answers to Questions on page 283]

1. Father will argue that the mower was unreasonably dangerous for two reasons: (1) it was defectively designed, in that it tipped over when used on slopes; and (2) the warnings against using on hillsides and driving by children were inadequate. Joe Elk Co. will deny these allegations and will argue that Father and Son misused the product by using it in a manner expressly proscribed in the directions.

Misuse is not a defense when it is foreseeable. The disclaimer is ineffective as against public policy. The manufacturer can be strictly liable under R.2d § 402A if the product's design is "defective" causing it to be "unreasonably dangerous." However, under modern products liability rules, in most jurisdictions D will be liable for a design defect only if the risk of harm was foreseeable to D, and in some jurisdictions P must prove that there was a feasible alternative design that would have prevented the harm.

Products liability can include inadequate warnings (don't specify consequences) and directions for use, but P must show that D knew of the danger and then failed to provide a warning. P liability, if it is found to exist here, extends also to E–Z Rider, regardless of its knowledge of the mower's alleged defects. The defenses of contributory negligence (if and to the extent applicable in products liability cases) and assumption of the risk may apply to reduce or bar any damages sought by Father but do not reduce Son's recovery.

2. Father will argue that the mower was negligently designed and that the warnings were inadequate. E–Z Rider will defend that it was unaware and

had no reason to know of the alleged defects in the mower. Joe Elk Co. will deny the allegations, and argue that Son was not a foreseeable user. The standard of care for negligent design (including negligent failure to warn) is similar to the "unreasonably dangerous" standard under strict product liability. Joe Elk will also argue that Father's damages must be reduced by his own contributory negligence or assumption of the risk. Son is too young to be subject to those defenses, and Father's fault is not imputable to him.

■ X. VICARIOUS LIABILITY

[Answers to Questions on pages 288–289]

1. *True.* If, at the time of his negligent act, D was acting in the scope of his employment, his employer is liable.

2. *False.* D was acting within the scope of his employment and in furtherance of his employer's business. Because of his reputation, D's act was foreseeable, and the employer may be found vicariously liable. Moreover, the employer may be found directly liable for his own negligence in hiring or supervising D.

3. **a.** Employer is not vicariously liable, but directly liable for his own negligent selection of Contractor.

   b. Landlord has a nondelegable duty to Lessee. Therefore, he is vicariously liable for Contractor's negligence.

   c. Storeowner is not vicariously liable. This risk is collateral. The employer's vicarious liability is limited to the particular risk which gives rise to the exception to nonliability.

   d. Landlord, if he undertakes to have repairs made, has a duty to inspect the completed work. Therefore, Landlord here is directly liable.

   e. Lessee is vicariously liable for Carpenter's negligence, because of Lessee's non-delegable duty with respect to the safety of work done in a public place.

   f. Manager has a non-delegable duty for work done pursuant to his franchise's specifications and is therefore vicariously liable for Local Contractor's negligence.

XI. EMPLOYER'S LIABILITY TO EMPLOYEES

[Answers to Questions on pages 291–92]

1. Ying may argue that Employer failed to provide safe equipment and appliances, to provide a sufficient number of competent fellow servants, to promulgate and enforce safety rules, or to adequately supervise or instruct.

2. Employer might argue that Ying was contributorily negligent or that he assumed the risk. Also, if Ying was injured by Yang while both were performing their jobs, the fellow servant rule applies, and Employer is not liable.

XII. AUTOMOBILES

[Answers to Questions on pages 293–94]

1. *True.* Because his employer is driving, employee cannot be presumed to have a mutual right of control, such as is required in the joint enterprise theory.

2. *False.* Son's use of the car exceeded the scope of Father's permission. Therefore, Father is not vicariously liable. He may be directly liable under a negligent entrustment theory.

3. *True.* Liability to guest passengers often includes injuries caused by defects of which the driver was aware and failed to warn.

4. *False.* However, Owner may be directly liable for his own negligence in failing to exercise control over Buyer.

XIV. NUISANCE

[Answers to Questions on page 302]

1. A private nuisance is an activity which substantially and unreasonably interferes with a Citizen's use and enjoyment of his land. Here the interference affected both the property itself and Citizens' comfort and health. It may also have impaired Citizens' mental tranquility. Liability is not strict, so Citizens must prove that the company's interference with their interest was

intentional, reckless, negligent, or the result of an abnormally dangerous activity such that principles of strict liability will apply. The interference was recurring, substantial, and unreasonable, since the gravity of Citizens' harm was probably greater than the utility of the company's conduct. Citizens may recover damages, and if the nuisance threatens to continue, an injunction may be sought.

2. Company's activities have interfered with the public's rights to health, safety, and comfort. These rights are common to the public as a class, and not merely to the group of Citizens. Their remedy is a criminal prosecution or suit to enjoin the nuisance by public authorities. They can recover under a public nuisance theory only if their harm is different in kind from that suffered by all members of the public as a class.

XV. NEGLIGENT INFLICTION OF EMOTIONAL DISTRESS

[Answers to Questions on pages 305–306]

1. *True.*   If Driver's negligent conduct results in any impact with Ranger, that impact is sufficient "bodily harm" to support liability for Ranger's emotional distress.

2. *False.*   Ranger was within the zone of danger. Driver's negligence threatened bodily harm to Ranger. Driver would be liable to Ranger for bodily harm that resulted from his emotional distress, but in most jurisdictions, absent impact, D would not be liable for mere emotional distress that did not cause some physical illness or comparable physical consequences.

3. *False.*   Driver would be liable for Ranger's physical harm resulting from his emotional distress, but only if such consequences were reasonably foreseeable. Unless Driver has actual knowledge of Ranger's special sensitivity, he will be liable only to the extent that Ranger's physical response to the emotional trauma was within the normal range of ordinarily sensitive persons.

4. *False.*   If Boy Scout were not himself in the zone of danger, he probably cannot recover for his harm. However, if Ranger were Boy Scout's father, some courts would allow Boy Scout to recover.

XVI. PRENATAL HARM

[Answers to Questions on page 308]

1. Generally, D is not liable for all damages resulting from D's negligence which results in the birth of a healthy child. Some courts have allowed recovery for the cost of prenatal care and delivery resulting from negligent sterilization.

    If the child is born with a birth defect, Doctor may be liable for either (1) Parents' extraordinary childcare expenses or (2) Parent's loss of the child's society and companionship, depending on the jurisdiction.

2. (1) If the child is born alive, but dies from its injuries, and (2) if the child dies from the injuries prior to birth (but, in some jurisdictions, only if the fetus was viable at the time of injury).

XVII. ALCOHOLIC BEVERAGES

[Answers to Questions on page 309]

1. Bartender will be liable under the dram shop act, either because the sale was illegal or merely because the liquor sold caused or contributed to the intoxication. However, dram shop liability is usually limited in amount.

    The general common law rule was that one who sold intoxicating beverages was not liable to third persons injured by the intoxicated person, but some states have altered this rule, imposing liability where the sale was unlawful.

2. Traditionally, liability for providing liquor that caused or contributed to a tortfeasor's intoxication applied only to commercial sellers. The dram shop acts apply exclusively to these sellers. However, courts have begun to be willing to impose liability on social hosts for contributing to their guests' intoxication. Therefore, in a minority of states Host could be held liable in this case.

XVIII. INTERFERENCE WITH FEDERAL CONSTITUTIONAL RIGHTS

[Answers to Questions on pages 309–310]

1. *True.* The officers were state employees acting under the authority of state law and did interfere with Marcher's constitutional rights. Therefore, a § 1983 action would be successful.

2. *True.*   Although § 1983 may be applied to private citizens, they must be acting "under color of state law." The Hoodlums were not so acting, so Marcher has no § 1983 cause of action against them.

3. *True.*   Federal agent was not acting "under color of state law," so Marcher has no § 1983 action. However, Marcher may have an action against agent for damages under the doctrine of *Bivens*.

■ PART SIX: STRICT LIABILITY

XX.   STRICT LIABILITY

[Answers to Questions on pages 319–321]

1. *True.*   Except where imposed by statute or ordinance, possessors of dogs and cats are not strictly liable for their trespasses.

2. *False.*   One who possesses animals not customarily domesticated in the region is strictly liable for all harm done by the animal as a result of a harmful or dangerous propensity characteristic of such animals.

3. **d.**   Under either (a) or (b), A would be considered strictly liable for B's injuries. Under (c), A would be found liable under general negligence principles.

4.   a, b, and c. Although assumption of the risk may be a defense to strict liability, that defense does not apply under any of these situations. Therefore, the general rule applies and A is strictly liable for all harm done by the bear. One who possesses animals not customarily domesticated in that region is strictly liable for all harm done by the animal as a result of a harmful propensity characteristic of such animals.

5. *True.*   A was engaged in an abnormally dangerous activity. There was a high risk of harm; it was clearly an abnormal activity, inappropriate to the place it was being conducted; and the activity has no social utility.

6. *False.*   Coal Company's activities were expressly required by legislation. Therefore, strict liability is not normally imposed.

7. *True.* Assumption of the risk is a defense, as is contributory negligence when B "knowingly and unreasonably" subjects himself to the risk.

8. *False.* Coal Company is not strictly liable to one who intentionally or negligently trespasses on its land where the abnormally dangerous activity is being conducted.

9. *True.* Coal Company is not strictly liable to the extent that B's harm results because B's activity is abnormally sensitive.

■ PART SEVEN: DAMAGES FOR PHYSICAL HARM

XXI. DAMAGES FOR PHYSICAL HARM

[Answers to Questions on pages 343–344]

1. *False.* Punitive damages are only appropriate where D's conduct is intentional or, at the very least, reckless.

2. *False.* Consequential damages are damages that a plaintiff can recover as a consequence of an injury to someone such as a parent, spouse, or child, with whom he has a close relationship.

3. *False.* Although pure joint and several liability was once the prevailing rule, it is now a minority rule. Most jurisdictions now have either several liability or some form of modified or hybrid form of joint liability.

4. **(c)** Payments made or benefits conferred on P from sources other than D do not reduce D's liability. Here even though the money was paid directly to the hospital it reduced P's debt to the hospital and thus was a benefit conferred on P. A hospital bill is the type of damage that commonly results from a tort and need not be specifically alleged on P's complaint.

5. **(a)** *True.* Hospital bills are a type of compensable economic loss.

   (b) *False.* The majority rule is that gross lost wages (past and future) are recoverable in a tort action, unreduced by the taxes that would have been paid on those wages.

(c) *True.*   In a tort action physical pain and suffering is a compensable loss.

(d) *False.*   In a tort action mental distress including anxiety about the future is a compensable loss.

(e) *False.*   Future pecuniary losses and expenses are recoverable in a tort action.

(f) *False.*   Under the collateral source rule payments made to or benefits conferred on P from sources other than D do not reduce D's liability nor count against P's recovery.

(g) *True.*   This states the ordinary rule.

(h) *False.*   Punitive damages are recoverable only when D acted intentionally or at the very least recklessly. Negligent conduct is ordinarily not a sufficient predicate for punitive damages.

■ PART EIGHT. SURVIVAL AND WRONGFUL DEATH

XXII.   SURVIVAL AND WRONGFUL DEATH

[Answers to Questions on page 351]

1. *True.*   The cause of action for wrongful death is almost universally a creature of statute.

2. *False.*   At common law, a tort plaintiff's causes of action died with him and a defendant's liability likewise was personal and died with him. Both rules have been modified to a greater or lesser extent in every common law jurisdiction.

■ PART NINE. NON–PHYSICAL HARM— MISREPRESENTATION, DEFAMATION, PRIVACY

XXIII.   MISREPRESENTATION

[Answers to Questions on pages 366–367]

1. (d) Even though D did not make any false statements, liability can be predicated on the fact that D knew his statements were so factually incomplete that they were misleading. It also seems clear that D intended for P to rely on D's representations and that P in fact did so. Under the modern rule P's failure to call the former owner and his failure to check the condition of the car himself are of no consequence even though P could easily have done these things. P can recover the difference between what he paid for the car and its actual value at that time and, in addition, because it was foreseeable that an accident could result, the damage to the car and his personal injuries that proximately resulted from the accident.

2. *False.* To be actionable a misrepresentation must relate to a material fact and must result in actual damages to the person who relied on it.

3. *False.* Ordinarily a person is only liable for negligent misrepresentation made in the course of his business, employment or profession.

4. *True.* Under R.2d § 402B, a person engaged in the business of selling products is strictly liable for physical harm resulting from a misrepresentations made to potential buyers.

XXIV. DEFAMATION

[Answers to Questions on pages 384–85]

1. *False.* A retraction may reduce D's damages, but ordinarily P can still recover for the original defamation.

2. *True.* This statement correctly states the law.

3. *False.* In most jurisdictions such publications are regarded as libel.

4. *False.* Ordinarily attorneys are not public figures because they are neither true public officials nor persons who have achieved a degree of fame or notoriety. Of course, if an individual attorney falls into either of those categories he is a public figure.

5. *True.* Publication to any person other than P is sufficient even if that person is D's agent.

6. *True.* A conditional privilege exists because D reasonably believed the information affected an important interest of the recipient and the

publication was within generally accepted standards of decent conduct in that it was in response to a request and an employer-employee relationship existed between P and D and a potential relationship between E and P.

7.   (c) is the best answer. (d) is wrong because *Gertz* probably applies only to defamation in the press, media, or in books. (b) is wrong as a matter of law. (a) is wrong because the absolute immunity for statements made in the course of judicial proceedings does not apply where the statement has no relation to the proceeding.

XXV.   PRIVACY

[Answers to Questions on pages 389–390]

1.   (1)   Appropriation of P's name or likeness.

     (2)   Intrusion upon P's privacy or private affairs.

     (3)   Public disclosure of private facts about P; and

     (4)   Placing P in a false light in the public eye.

2.   *True.*   In most jurisdictions, a cause of action for the public disclosure of true private facts can be maintained where, as here, the facts are embarrassing or humiliating, were previously unknown to the general public, and are not matters of legitimate public interest.

3.   *False*.   Photographing or watching a person from a public place, even if offensive, is not actionable because there is no intrusion into the person's private life (assuming D does not intrude too closely into P's personal space).

4.   *True.*   In most jurisdictions a person who appropriates the name or likeness of another for his own use or benefit is liable to the other.

5.   *False.*   There is no evidence that D knew or should have known the use to which the pictures would be put or that such a use would place P in a false light; as a matter of constitutional law, P will have the burden of proving these things by clear and convincing evidence.

APPENDIX B

Practice Examination

QUESTIONS

Three practice examination questions that have actually been used on torts examinations are reproduced below. Try to complete each question in the suggested time, including reading, outlining, and writing your answer. Appendix C discusses some of the issues and rules you should have talked about. Don't peek.

GENERAL INSTRUCTION

Assume that the following events (in both questions) take place in the mythical State of Calinois, which generally follows the prevailing common law of torts and the Restatement (Second) of Torts. Specifically, you may assume that Calinois has adopted the pure form of comparative negligence.

QUESTION ONE

(SUGGESTED TIME: ONE HOUR)

Dudley Dunham owns a computer store in Chicago, Calinois. He has been the victim of a number of burglaries and burglary attempts. Finally, he decided, enough is enough. He installed a metal screen door, to which he connected several automobile batteries. According to his research, which is accurate, the batteries as wired together provide enough electricity to cause a severe shock to one touching the door, but not enough to cause serious or permanent bodily harm or death in ordinary human beings. On October 15, Dudley began electrifying his door with this device each evening between 11:00 p.m. and 6:00 a.m. He posted a sign on the door saying, "WARNING! THESE PREMISES PROTECTED BY AN ELECTRICAL ANTI–THEFT SYSTEM."

On November 1, Jonathan Apple purchased a computer system from Dudley's store. The computer turned out to be hopelessly defective. Despite numerous attempts, Apple was unable to get Dudley to repair or replace his unit. Apple finally reached the limit of his frustration. On the evening of November 1, Apple became intoxicated, and went to Dudley's store. He arrived at 11:30 p.m., but he thought it was much earlier and that the store was open. Too drunk to read the sign, he grabbed the door, and received a severe jolt of electricity. The electrical jolt aggravated his already inebriated state. In a stupor, he staggered into the street and collapsed, unconscious. Seconds later, he was run over and severely injured by an automobile being driven by one Garner, who was driving *non-negligently.*

Analyze and discuss the liability of Dudley Dunham to Jonathan Apple.

QUESTION TWO

(SUGGESTED TIME: TWO HOURS)

Luke Skyman is a student pilot taking flying lessons at USI airport from Ace Flying School and Service, a commercial profit-making enterprise. Luke has had 20 hours of the required 40 hours of in-plane instruction. Under Federal Aviation Administration regulations, he is permitted to act as pilot of a single-engine airplane, and he can fly solo for learning purposes. However, under FAA rules, student pilots are permitted to take passengers only if a currently licensed flight instructor is sitting in the co-pilot's seat.

On December 1, Luke decided to go for a spin in an airplane. He went to the USI airport and rented an airplane from Ace. His friend, Fast Eddy Strickland, went with him. Fast Eddy used to be a flight instructor, but his flight instructor license is no longer current. Luke's girlfriend, Lois Lane, also went with him. She knew he was only a student pilot, and knew that student pilots cannot take passengers unless a licensed flight instructor is along, but she thought that Fast Eddy was still licensed.

When he signed up for the flight course, Luke was required as a condition of the course to sign a release which says, in part:

"I, Luke Skyman, hereby release Ace Flying School and Service and its officers and employees from all liability for damages for any injuries I may sustain as a pilot, passenger, or otherwise, as long as I am a student in this course."

Luke, Lois, and Fast Eddy got into the airplane. Luke sat in the pilot's seat and flew the plane; Fast Eddy sat in the co-pilot's seat; and Lois sat in one of the two back seats. The flight went without incident for about 20 minutes, when the plane's engine suddenly quit. Luke attempted to make an emergency landing in a nearby field located on Fred Farmer's farm, but the plane overshot the field and struck Fred's house, causing extensive damages. Fast Eddy was not hurt, but Luke and Lois were seriously injured.

It was later determined that the plane's engine quit because the plane ran out of fuel. Lois will testify that Luke failed to visually check the fuel tanks prior to take-off, as he was required to do by FAA regulations. However, Luke denies this; he will testify that he told Fast Eddy to check the fuel, and he relied on Fast Eddy to make this check. Fast Eddy denies any such request. Luke maintains that he was further misled by the fact that the fuel gauges on the airplane were broken and were stuck in the "full" position, a fact which is undisputed.

Analyze and discuss the rights and liabilities of Luke, Lois, Fred Farmer, and Ace Flying School and Service. Be sure to discuss how damages will be apportioned. Do not discuss any product liability theories.

*

APPENDIX C

A Suggested Analysis Of The Practice Examination Questions

QUESTION ONE

I. BATTERY

A. Cause of Action. Dunham is guilty of a battery. Battery is an intentional and unprivileged harmful or offensive contact with the plaintiff's person, caused by defendant.

As used in the intentional torts, "intent" means to have a purpose to cause the harm or the knowledge that the harm is substantially certain to occur. Here, Dunham's purpose was to cause at least an offensive contact with unprivileged entrants on his premises. While he did not do so directly, he set in motion the force that was intended to accomplish this harm indirectly. That is sufficient. Although Dunham did not intend to harm *lawful* entrants—and Apple may have been a lawful entrant—he must have known that both lawful and unlawful entrants were substantially certain to be shocked. In the alternative, his intent to harm unlawful entrants will transfer to lawful entrants such as Apple. Therefore, the elements of a battery are present.

The question of Apple's status (trespasser, licensee, or invitee) is irrelevant for purposes of the basic cause of action, since a landowner is liable to even a trespasser for intentional or reckless torts.

B. Defenses

1. Defense of Property. The possessor of land or chattels has a privilege to use minimal force to prevent a trespass. Therefore, assuming for the sake of argument that Apple was a trespasser (a doubtful assumption), Dunham would have such a privilege.

    However, this privilege is subject to strict limitations. Ordinarily, the potential trespasser must first be asked to cease or leave. Only when he refuses is force allowed, and only then such minimal force as may be required to prevent the trespass. Moreover, the occupier assumes the risk of a mistake as to the status of the entrant. Thus, if Apple was not a trespasser (see part II.A., below), no privilege exists.

    Here, Dunham was not present; he used a mechanical device to prevent trespasses. The law is clear (as in the spring gun and other "trap" cases) that such a device can do no more than Dunham could do in person. Normally, such devices require a posted warning. It is doubtful that the warning here was adequate, as it did not apprise the visitor of the nature of the "electrical anti-theft system" he would encounter. Thus, the required warning was arguably missing. Moreover, although the force used was not calculated to cause serious bodily harm, it was probably excessive for this purpose. Thus, even if the privilege could be applicable, its scope was exceeded.

2. Consent. Dunham may argue that Apple consented to the harm (or assumed its risk) by proceeding in the face of his warning sign. However, consent is a subjective concept. Even assuming the text of the warning was adequate (which it probably wasn't), Apple did not in fact see the warning because of his condition. While voluntarily intoxicated persons are often deemed sober for purposes of certain *objective* criteria in tort law, that may not be the case if a *subjective* test such as consent is applicable. This defense is not available.

3. Contributory fault. Contributory fault is not a defense or a damage-reducing factor in intentional tort cases.

II. NEGLIGENCE

A. Cause of Action. In the event that, for some reason, the battery action fails, or if the plaintiff seeks to proceed on a non-intentional tort theory (e.g., to preserve defendant's liability insurance coverage), plaintiff could proceed in the alternative on a negligence theory.

The first issue in a negligence action is duty. Here, Apple's status on the premises would be important, since a general duty of ordinary care is owed to invitees (or, in some instances, to licensees). An invitee is one who enters the premises (a) held open to the public or (b) with the occupier's express or implied permission for a purpose involving business with the occupier. In the case of a store, the premises are usually held open to the public, and entrants come to do business with the occupier. Thus, both tests are applicable here.

The facts do not indicate whether Apple was standing on a public sidewalk or had crossed Dunham's property line when he touched the door. However, even assuming that he had entered the property, the evidence will support a jury finding that he was an invitee. While the scope of an invitation can be limited in time and space, custom suggests that past, present and future customers of a store have an implied invitation to enter the premises so far as they are able, to "window shop" or read the signs or look inside, at almost any time. Thus, in the absence of a clear warning to the contrary, Apple will probably be deemed an invitee.

Once having found a duty of ordinary care, a breach of that duty is easy to find. A jury could determine that there was no adequate warning (see I.B.1., above), and that the device itself was unreasonably unsafe. If there was negligence, that negligence was clearly the cause in fact of plaintiff's harm. The proximate cause issue is discussed below.

B. Defenses. Dunham will argue that Apple was contributorily negligent in grabbing the door without reading his warning sign. He will argue that Dunham's failure to read the sign was due to his voluntary intoxication, which is no defense. For this purpose, a drunk is treated as if he was sober. However, the jury could find that the warning was inadequate to convey the true nature of the harm. Whether, and to what extent, Apple was contributorily negligent would be for the jury. In Calinois, a pure comparative negligence jurisdiction, Apple's negligence (if any) will merely reduce his damages. It does not bar recovery.

For similar reasons, Apple will likely be found not to have assumed the risk. First of all, the warning is probably not sufficient to apprise Apple of the full nature and extent of the risk, an essential element of this defense. Moreover, unlike contributory negligence, assumption of risk is a subjective concept. Therefore, Apple's failure to read the sign does prevent this defense from operating. We do not reach the issue, whether it is a complete defense or only a damage-reducing factor.

C. Proximate Cause

From the foregoing, we see that Dunham may be liable in either battery or negligence for the injury caused by the electrical shock. But what about his injury from being run over by Garner's car? Dunham will undoubtedly argue that the foreseeable risk of injury that he created was, at most, the mild electrical shock and perhaps an injury from falling down as a result of that shock. He would agree that if plaintiff was unusually susceptible to side effects from the shock or fall, he would be liable for those side effects as well. But Apple was not such a person. Thus, under *Palsgraf* and *Wagon Mound* and their progeny, which represent the majority view, he is not liable for the unforeseeable event that occurred–Apple wandering all the way into the street, collapsing, and being run over. His duty, he says, is limited to the scope of the foreseeable risk, which did not include being run over by Garner.

Apple will counter that the risk that, as a result of the shock, he would stagger into the street was *not* unforeseeable. He will say that he was unusually susceptible by reason of his intoxication, and that under the "eggshell" plaintiff rule, which Dunham concedes, the aggravating effects of the intoxication cannot be disregarded. In any event, the foreseeable risk that Dunham created was the risk of some bodily harm to Apple, either from the shock itself or perhaps from a fall as a result of that shock. The rule is that if the same type of harm occurs as that which made defendant's conduct tortious, defendant cannot escape liability because the actual harm was greater than could have been foreseen, or because the exact manner in which the injury occurred was not foreseeable.

For similar reasons, Garner cannot be a superseding cause. Although the intervening cause itself may not have been foreseeable, the injury that occurred was of the same type as that which made defendant's conduct tortious. In such a case, the intervening cause is not a superseding cause.

The foregoing analysis applies primarily to Dunham's negligence liability. In the case of intentional torts, broader proximate cause rules are applied. Therefore, in the battery action, there is little chance of a successful proximate cause argument. Defendant is liable even for unforeseeable consequences.

QUESTION TWO

I. LOIS v. LUKE

The elements of a common law negligence action are (a) duty, (b) breach of duty (negligent conduct), (c) causation, and (d) damages.

As to Lois, a passenger in Luke's plane, the duty question turns on whether Calinois has an applicable guest statute. Some jurisdictions have had airplane guest statutes, similar to automobile guest statutes which limit the liability of the driver or owner for injuries to a "guest" (i.e., nonpaying) passenger to injuries caused by the driver's reckless ("willful and wanton") misconduct. The trend is to repeal such statutes, and some have been held unconstitutional. While Lois is clearly a guest here, it is unlikely that such a statute exists. Even if it does, Luke's conduct may qualify as reckless.

Assuming the guest statute hurdle is overcome, there are several possible specifications of negligence. Luke may have been negligent in (a) taking a passenger (Lois) in violation of FAA regulations, since Fast Eddy did not meet the required qualifications (Regulation 1); (b) failing to personally make a visual check of the fuel tanks, also in violation of FAA regs (Regulation 2); and (c) making an inadequate landing.

In most jurisdictions, violation of a safety statute, ordinance, or administrative regulation is deemed negligence per se, provided (1) the safety purpose of the statute coincides with the negligence charged, and (2) the injured person is a member of the class for whose protection the legislation was adopted. Negligence per se means that the statutory violation alone proves negligence; the burden is then upon the violator to establish some legally recognized excuse for his violation. (In some jurisdictions, a statutory violation is merely evidence of negligence, like safety codes and custom and practice.)

Luke clearly violated Regulation 1, and its purpose is clearly broad enough to include injuries to passengers such as Lois. Indeed, passengers are the named beneficiaries. However, it is still necessary to show that the violation of the reg was a cause in fact of plaintiff's harm. Here, it seems doubtful. Fast Eddy was on board; his license had expired. While it could be argued that he was not as sharp or current as if his license had been renewed, it may be difficult to show that the lapse of his license alone had any effect on his ability to handle ordinary flying or even emergencies such as loss of an engine. This situation is analogous to the cases where courts have refused to accept evidence that a driver is unlicensed as proof of his negligence.

Luke's violation of Regulation 2, however, is certainly negligence. The obvious purpose of requiring a visual fuel check is to prevent engine-out emergencies. The rule contemplates the possibility that fuel gauges may not be reliable. And the rule obviously is for the benefit of all on board.

Luke may seek to argue that his violation was excused because he delegated this task to Eddy, and reasonably assumed that it had been performed. However, this is not a recognized excuse, especially here where the duty will be deemed non-delegable because of the high risks involved. Moreover, Eddy had no duty to perform this task. At most, Eddy was guilty of nonfeasance of a gratuitous undertaking. Luke may also argue proximate cause, but to no avail. Such conduct can never be a superseding cause, where it was not intentional and was certainly foreseeable.

Luke may also have been negligent in performing his emergency landing. We first note that he will be held to the standard of the reasonably prudent pilot. No allowance will be made for his novice status, or for his youth even if he is a minor (the facts do not indicate). He may have failed to exercise the requisite skill in making the landing. Even though it was an emergency, he was required to exercise reasonable care under the circumstances (one of which was the emergency itself). His use of the emergency doctrine will be further curtailed because his own negligence created the emergency.

Another circumstance affecting the negligence issue is the dangerous nature of the activity. Although the aircraft is not a common carrier, Luke was required to exercise care commensurate with the danger involved in the activity.

Res ipsa loquitur cannot apply here, since res ipsa does not usually work against multiple tortfeasors (e.g., Luke and Ace).

Thus, it seems likely that Luke will be found liable to Lois in negligence. Does he have any defenses?

Lois could not have assumed the risk. Implied assumption of risk requires a full understanding and appreciation of a negligently created risk, followed by the plaintiff voluntarily encountering that risk. While Lois may have assumed the ordinary risks inherent in flying (primary sense), there is no indication that she was aware of any facts that would put her on notice of any pre-existing negligence or the likelihood of future negligence. In addition, in most jurisdictions, assumption of the risk no longer exists as a separate defense, having been merged into contributory fault.

It also appears doubtful that Lois could be found contributorily negligent. She did nothing that could be found to be unreasonably dangerous.

II. LOIS v. ACE

Ace owed Lois, a passenger in its plane, a duty of ordinary care. Even if there is a guest statute, Ace is not a party protected by such a statute.

Ace may have been negligent in failing to use reasonable care to (a) maintain the airplane (i.e., the fuel gauges), (b) ensure the fuel tanks were full when the plane was rented out, (c) warn Luke that the fuel gauges didn't work, and (d) make sure that Fast Eddy was a currently licensed flight instructor before renting the plane to Luke. Whether any of these was negligence is a question for the jury.

Lois may argue that the violation of the FAA regulation (Regulation 1) requiring a current flight instructor on board is negligence per se. (See discussion under I, above, as to the legal effect of a statutory violation.) There are two problems, however, with this argument. First, it is doubtful that this regulation was intended to apply to Ace; most likely, it creates a duty only on the part of Luke. Second, Ace can argue that its violation of the regulation was not the cause in fact or proximate cause of Lois's injury. See discussion in Part I, above.

Ace could also argue, as the allegations of negligence concerning the fuel, that Luke's failure to check the fuel visually was a superseding cause of Lois's injury, relieving Ace of liability. If an intervening cause is sufficiently significant, it can break the chain of causation between an actor's negligence and plaintiff's injury.

However, ordinary negligence is not deemed a superseding cause, especially when the intervening act was foreseeable and was part of what made the actor's conduct negligent in the first place. Such is the case here. Therefore, Luke's conduct is no defense to Ace.

III. LUKE v. ACE

Luke will argue that Ace was negligent in failing to use reasonable care to (a) maintain the airplane (i.e., the fuel gauges), (b) ensure the fuel tanks were full when the plane was rented out, and (c) warn Luke that the fuel gauges didn't work. Whether any of these was negligence is a question for the jury.

Here, Ace's major defense will be Luke's release. A release operates as an express assumption of risk, and is valid to relieve the actor of liability for his negligent conduct under certain conditions. In general, to be enforceable, the release must be clear on its face and the terms must be brought home to the plaintiff; its terms must clearly encompass defendant's negligence; and its enforcement must not be against public policy (e.g., where there is a great disparity in bargaining power between plaintiff and defendant and the activity is one in which there is a strong public interest or where plaintiff's choice of providers is restricted).

In this case, the terms of the release are clear and its enforcement does not appear to be against public policy. However, the terms of the release do not expressly refer to Ace's *negligence* liability. In such cases, the courts have usually declined to extend the effect of the release to defendant's negligence. Hence, it appears that the release would not bar an action by Luke based on Ace's negligence.

(Luke might also question whether the release should be construed as extending to activities outside the scope of the flying course. Here, Luke's relationship to Ace is the same as any other renter of aircraft. Since the release is ineffective for the reason stated above, however, we do not reach this issue.)

Ace's other defense will be contributory negligence. Calinois is a pure comparative negligence jurisdiction. This means that plaintiff's contributory negligence, if any, will be compared against the negligence of *all other persons* whose negligence contributed to plaintiff's injuries, and plaintiffs recovery will be reduced by the percentage of the total fault attributable to him. In this case, Luke was obviously negligent in failing to make a visual inspection of the fuel tanks before takeoff, and perhaps during the emergency landing. It will be up to the jury to decide if Luke was negligent, and if so the percentage of his fault. However, he can still recover part of his damages even if his fault is greater than 50%. Implied assumption of risk will not apply, because there is no evidence that Luke had actual knowledge of the risk and chose to encounter it.

IV. FARMER v. LUKE

The first issue is whether Luke is liable to Farmer for trespass to land. Trespass is an intentional entry upon the land of another without a privilege to do so. The question is, did Luke intend to enter Farmer's land? Although Luke apparently had no choice but to land the plane when it ran out of fuel, I will assume that Luke had a choice as to *where* he would land it. He could have chosen any of several fields. Therefore, it appears that his entry upon Farmer's land was intentional and therefore a trespass.

Luke's most likely defense is the privilege of private necessity. One is privileged to enter the land of another if it is (or reasonably appears to be) necessary to prevent serious harm to the actor. Luke probably chose to land in Farmer's field because it provided the safest choice available to him at the time. The privilege applies. But when the entry is for the benefit of the actor, the actor must pay damages for any harm done in the exercise of the privilege. Therefore, Luke will be liable for the damage to Farmer's land and buildings.

In the event that the trespass action should fail, or if the damages allowable to Farmer would be greater under a negligence theory (due to the necessity privilege), Farmer would undoubtedly have a cause of action in negligence based on Luke's negligent failure to check the fuel tanks, and possibly for making an inadequate landing.

V. FARMER v. ACE

As previously noted, Ace may have been negligent in failing to use reasonable care to (a) maintain the airplane (i.e., the fuel gauges), (b) ensure the fuel tanks were full when the plane was rented out, (c) warn Luke that the fuel gauges didn't work, and (d) make sure that Fast Eddy was a currently licensed flight instructor before renting the plane to Luke. Whether any of these omissions was negligence, and whether any of them was a cause in fact of the damage to Farmer's property, is a question for the jury.

VI. ACE v. LUKE

Ace may counterclaim against Luke for damage to the airplane, based on Luke's negligence in failing to make a visual check of the fuel tanks. In a pure comparative negligence jurisdiction, two parties who are both negligent and who each sustain damages in the same occurrence may both recover damages, reduced by the percentage of negligence attributable to each of them. Thus, Ace can maintain its counterclaim.

Ace would not have an action for conversion, because the use of the airplane was permissive and there was no intent to assert dominion or control inconsistent with Ace's ownership.

VII. ALLOCATION OF DAMAGES

Under the majority view, comparative negligence has no effect on the principle of joint and several liability. Therefore, all defendants who are found negligent are liable in accordance with Calinois' allocation of damages rules—each jointly and severally liable to each plaintiff whose injury was caused in part by that defendant's negligence for the full amount of that plaintiff's damages, reduced by that plaintiff's percentage of fault; severally liable; or liable under some hybrid joint liability scheme. Damages for trespass (an intentional tort) would probably not be reduced by comparative negligence, but Farmer could not possibly have been contributorily negligent.

In addition, to the extent defendants are jointly and severally liable, each such defendant can bring an action for contribution against the other. Under modern principles of comparative contribution, jointly and severally liable defendants who pay more than their proportionate share of plaintiff's damages may be entitled to recover from other such defendants who have paid less. In this phase of the case, the jury will assess each defendant's share of the total fault of all defendants. Thus, for example, assume the jury finds both Luke and Ace liable to Lois and Farmer, and Luke and Ace are jointly and severally liable. The jury might assess Luke's fault at 75% and Ace's fault at 25%. Plaintiffs Lois and Farmer could collect their judgments against either or both defendants, but Luke and Ace would then share the ultimate responsibility in a 75–25 ratio.

If Luke is found liable to Ace and Ace is found liable to Luke, each party to these claims can recover their damages from the other, reduced by the other's contributory negligence, without any offset.

APPENDIX D

Glossary

A

Abnormally Dangerous Activity The modern version of the doctrine of *Rylands v. Fletcher* imposes strict liability for harm caused by an abnormally dangerous activity. R.2d § 519; R.3d PH § 20.

Absolute Liability See **Strict Liability.**

Appropriation One of the subdivisions of the cause of action for invasion of privacy, in which D appropriates P's name or likeness for commercial gain. R.2d § 652C.

Assault An intentional tort in which D causes P to apprehend an imminent battery. R.2d § 21.

Assumption of Risk An affirmative defense to negligence and other tort actions which bars or reduces P's recovery based on his knowingly and voluntarily subjecting himself to a risk of harm. The two main forms are express and implied. R.2d §§ 496A–496G. Implied assumption of the risk is now usually no longer a separate defense, having been merged into a comprehensive contributory fault defense.

Attractive Nuisance A popular name for the "child trespasser" doctrine (R.2d § 339) which subjects a possessor of land to a duty of ordinary care to a child whose trespass is foreseeable.

Authority of Law A privilege (defense to an intentional tort) which excuses conduct which would otherwise be tortious because the conduct is authorized by law.

B

Battery An intentional tort in which D causes a harmful or offensive contact with P's person. R.2d §§ 13, 18.

Bodily Harm See **Harm**

Burden of Proof Rules of law determine which party has the burden of persuading the trier of fact that a fact is or is not true. In a civil (tort) case, the party having the burden of proof on a claim or defense must ordinarily prove it by a preponderance of the evidence. See R.2d § 328A.

Bystander One against whom tortious conduct was not directed, or who was not the user or consumer of a product. (1) In product liability cases, foreseeable bystanders are usually eligible to recover. (2) In actions for negligent infliction of emotional distress, a few jurisdictions allow recovery by closely related bystanders who witness an injury to a loved one; most do not permit recovery by bystanders unless they were themselves in the zone of danger.

C

Case, Action on the Under the common law writ system, the form of action in which the pleader could tailor his complaint to the facts of his particular case. The proper form of action for the tort of negligence.

Cause in Fact Any cause which one of the factual causes of P's injury. See **Proximate Cause (Scope of Liability).**

Collateral Source Rule The doctrine which prohibits D from receiving credit against the compensatory damages for which he is found liable to P for those items for which P was reimbursed from a source collateral to D. R.2d § 902A(2).

Colloquium In defamation, allegations of extrinsic facts connecting P to the defamatory statement, where that connection is not apparent. See also **Inducement, Innuendo.**

Common Law (1) English law promulgated by judges in the royal courts which was therefore "common" to the realm. (2) Any judge-made law, as distinguished from law created by statute or other legislation.

Comparative Fault The doctrine by which the negligence or other fault of P is compared to that of D and P's damages are reduced proportionately. It also includes comparing fault among tortfeasors for purposes such as contribution or several liability.

Compensatory Damages Damages awarded to compensate P. R.2d § 903.

Concert of Action Conduct by persons pursuant to a common plan such that the tort of one is imputed to all. R.2d § 876; R.3d AL § 15.

Concurrent or Consecutive Tortfeasors Concurrent tortfeasors are those whose tortious conduct operates at the same time. Consecutive tortfeasors are those whose tortious conduct occurs at different times. In either case, if their conduct results in a single, indivisible harm to P, they are deemed joint tortfeasors. R.2d § 879; R.3d PH § 26.

Conduct In tort law, "conduct" includes both acts and omissions to act, and liability can usually be based on either. However, in certain situations no duty arises from mere inaction. See **Misfeasance vs. Nonfeasance.**

Consent A privilege that negates an intentional tort. See also **Assumption of Risk.**

Consequential Damages Damages sustained as a result of an injury to another— e.g., a spouse's loss of consortium, a parent's loss of a child's services. See, e.g., R.2d §§ 693, 703.

Constitutional Tort Some constitutional violations can be redressed directly by an action for damages, e.g., under 42 U.S.C.A. § 1983. Such causes of action are sometimes called "constitutional torts." See R.2d § 874A.

Constructive Knowledge Constructive knowledge is knowledge that one had a legal duty to acquire, and therefore the law will treat the person as if he had that knowledge whether he did or not. See **Knowledge: Should Have Known.**

Contributory Negligence A plaintiff's failure to exercise ordinary care for his own safety. R.2d § 463.

Contribution A doctrine whereby one of two or more joint tortfeasors against whom plaintiff has obtained a common judgment, who has been required to satisfy that judgment in excess his pro rata or proportionate share, can recover that excess from any other joint tortfeasor(s) who paid less than his share. R.2d § 886A; R.3d AL § 23. Contribution is only available with respect to defendants who are jointly and severally liable.

Conversion An intentional tort in which D has so harmed or interfered with P's chattel that D can be required to pay P its full value. R.2d § 222A.

Covenant Not to Sue A contract to settle a claim in which P does not release his cause of action but merely promises not to file or pursue a suit against D. See R.2d § 885; R.3d AL § 24; **Release; Loan Receipt Agreement.**

D

Defamation A communication which tends to harm P's reputation by lowering him in the estimation of the community or deterring others from associating or dealing with him. R.2d § 559.

Discipline A privilege (defense to an intentional tort) based upon D's right as, e.g., P's parent or military superior, to impose discipline upon P. R.2d §§ 146, 147.

Dram Shop Liability (1) A statutory cause of action to recover limited damages from a commercial vendor of alcoholic beverages for injuries to P resulting from a customer's intoxication; (2) any common law cause of action recognized against such a commercial venture.

Duty A rule of tort law recognizing an obligation running from D to P, the violation of which gives rise to a tort cause of action.

E

Eggshell Plaintiff Rule A rule providing that D is liable for the full consequences of P's injury or damages, even though greater in degree than would normally be a foreseeable result of the occurrence in question, due to the fact that P was unusually susceptible to the injury (or, indeed, for any other reason), provided injury of the same general type could have been foreseen. Sometimes stated as the "thin-skulled plaintiff" rule, or "you take your plaintiff as you find him." R.2d §§ 435, 461; R.3d PH § 31.

F

False Imprisonment An intentional tort resulting when D forcefully confines P within boundaries set by D. R.2d § 35.

False Light in the Public Eye One of the subdivisions of the cause of action for invasion of privacy, in which D causes publicity which places P before the public in a highly offensive false light. R.2d § 652E.

Fault Most tort causes of action include an element of fault–intent, recklessness, negligence, and even strict products liability in which the fault is placing a defective product in the stream of commerce.

Foreseeability Foreseeability is not a separate element of any tort, but it can be a factor in determining issues such as duty, breach of duty, and proximate cause.

G

General Damages Damages which at common law were presumed to flow from a tort and therefore did not have to be pleaded specially, such as pain and suffering. R.2d § 904. See **Special Damages.** Today, this category is often called "non-economic loss."

H

Hand Formula A balancing test for determining whether conduct creates an unreasonable risk of harm, and is therefore negligent. Proposed by Judge Learned Hand in *United States v. Carroll Towing Co.* The actor compares (1) the **burden** (B) and utility of the conduct in question compared to alternative, safer conduct with (2) the **probability** (P) that harm will result form the proposed conduct multiplied by the **gravity** of the harm that will probably result (L, or loss) if the risk is realized. See **Negligence; Ordinary Care.**

Harm, Physical Harm, Bodily Harm As used in tort law, the term "harm" encompasses any loss or detriment. R.2d § 7(2). "Physical harm" means any physical impairment of the human body, land, or chattels. R.2d § 7(3); R.3d PH § 4. "Bodily harm" includes physical impairment in the condition of P's body, or physical pain or illness. R.2d § 15.

I

Immunity A doctrine that provides D a complete defense to conduct that otherwise would be an actionable tort, such as the family immunities, charitable immunity, and sovereign immunity. Unlike a privilege, an immunity does not negate the tort and must be raised as an affirmative defense or it is waived. R.2d §§ 895A–895J.

Impact Rule The traditional common law rule that negligently inflicted emotional distress is not actionable unless D's negligent conduct resulted in an "impact" with P's person, however slight, so that the damages for emotional distress would be parasitic to the action for negligently inflicted bodily harm. R.2d §§ 436A, 456. See **Harm.**

Imputed Negligence Doctrines by which the negligence of A is treated as if it were also the negligence of B. A typical example is the vicarious liability of a master for his servant's negligence.

Indemnity The right of D, against whom P has obtained a judgment, to shift the entire judgment to another tortfeasor. The right to indemnity may arise from an express agreement, operation of law, or a major disparity between D's faulty and that of the other tortfeasor. R.2d § 886B; R.3d AL § 22. The last form has generally been superseded by contribution.

Inducement In defamation, allegations of extrinsic facts which show the defamatory meaning of a statement that is not defamatory on its face. See also **Colloquium, Innuendo.**

Injury In tort law, the term "injury" includes the invasion of any interest which is protected by tort law. R.2d § 7(1). It is broader than terms such as "harm" and "physical harm," since it includes torts against relational and other intangible interests.

Innuendo In defamation, allegations explaining how a statement was claimed to be understood s having a defamatory meaning, when the statement is not defamatory on its face. See also Colloquium, Inducement.

Intent A term of art in tort law, meaning either (1) the purpose to cause a particular result, or (2) knowledge that the result is virtually certain to occur. R.2d § 8A; R.3d PH § 1. Intent is a necessary element of various torts.

Intervening Cause A cause of P's injury which comes into operation after the cause for which D is responsible and operates with or upon D's cause to produce the injury. R.2d § 441; R.3d PH § 34. See **Superseding Cause.**

Intrusion One of the subdivisions of the cause of action for invasion of privacy, in which D intrudes upon P's solitude, seclusion, or private life in a highly offensive manner. R.2d § 652B.

Invitee In premises liability, an entrant upon D's land who is either (1) a business visitor or (2) a public invitee. R.2d § 332. An invitee is owed a duty of ordinary care.

J

Joint Tortfeasor One whose tortious conduct contributed with one or more other tortfeasors to cause a single, indivisible injury to P. See R.2d § 875 (called "contributing tortfeasors").

K

Knowledge: Had Reason to Know "Had reason to know" means that D had information from which a person of reasonable intelligence would infer that the fact in question exists, or that such a person would govern his conduct on the assumption that the fact exists. R.2d § 12(1).

Knowledge: Should Have Known "Should have known" means that a person of reasonable intelligence and of reasonable prudence would have ascertained the fact, or would govern his conduct on the assumption that the fact exists. R.2d § 12(2).

L

Last Clear Chance A disappearing doctrine used to avoid the defense of contributory negligence. If P is negligently in a zone of danger from which he cannot escape in time, and D has the last opportunity to exercise care to prevent the harm but negligently fails to do so, D cannot use P's prior contributory negligence as a defense. R.2d §§ 479, 480.

Legal Cause (1) An obsolete term for proximate cause, which included "cause in fact." See R.2d § 431. (2) Some view legal cause as that part of proximate cause that is not "cause in fact," under an expanded view of proximate cause that includes both legal cause and cause in fact.

Libel The publication of defamatory matter by (1) written or printed words or (2) another comparably permanent or equally harmful form. See R.2d § 568.

Licensee In premises liability, an entrant upon D's land who is privileged to enter or remain but who is not an invitee. R.2d § 330.

Loan Receipt Agreement A form of settlement in which D loans money to P interest-free, and which need not be repaid except from the proceeds of any amounts recovered from other tortfeasors responsible for the same injury. P agrees to pursue his claim against the remaining tortfeasors. R.3d AL § 24.

M

Malice The term "malice" is used in various contexts in tort law, but has no fixed meaning. As applied to the intentional torts, it usually means an intent to cause harm; in that context, the rule is that malice is not required for liability, although it may be relevant as to punitive damages. In defamation law, "actual malice" means the same as constitutional malice—knowledge that the statement is false or a reckless disregard for its truth. R.2d § 580A.

Malpractice A term used to designate professional negligence—e.g., medical malpractice.

Misfeasance vs. Nonfeasance These terms are usually used when discussing the existence of a duty. If the only relationship between P and D is contractual, and D merely fails to perform their contract (i.e., nonfeasance), there is often no tort liability. But if D commences performance and is thereafter negligent (misfeasance), he may be liable because the commencement of performance is enough to activate a duty of ordinary care to P. See R.2d § 323.

Misrepresentation A misstatement of fact. At one time, only intentional misrepresentations were actionable; the name of the tort was "deceit." Today, the category is "misrepresentation" because some negligent (and even innocent) misrepresentations are actionable. R.2d §§ 525, 552, 552C.

Mistake An element in some privileges. Mistake itself is not a defense, but it is sometimes relevant in determining whether a privilege exists.

Misuse In product liability cases, using the product in some was that the manufacturer did not intend. If the misuse was foreseeable, it is ignored. If it was unforeseeable, then D is not liable.

Mitigation of Damages A doctrine that requires P, subsequent to an injury, to exercise ordinary care to try to alleviate its effects. If P fails to do so, he cannot recover damages for that part of the injury that could have been corrected. Sometimes referred to as the doctrine of "avoidable consequences." R.2d § 918.

Motive The reason for one's act. It is usually said that in tort law, motive is irrelevant; only intent counts. But motive may be relevant on the issue of exemplary damages.

N

Necessity A privilege (defense to an intentional tort) based upon D's right to trespass upon, covert, or appropriate P's property. Under the doctrine of private necessity, D must compensate P for the damage; but under public necessity, no compensation is due. R.2d §§ 196, 197, 262, 263.

Negligence The failure to exercise ordinary care for another's safety; the failure to act as a reasonably prudent person would act under the same or similar circumstances. R.2d § 283. The creation of an unreasonable risk of harm. R.2d § 282. The reasonably prudent person determines the reasonableness of the risk by use of a balancing test such as the Hand Formula.

Nominal Damages An insignificant sum (e.g., $1) awarded to P who has established liability but cannot prove the existence or amount of his actual damages. R.2d § 907. Not available as to some torts—e.g., negligence.

Nuisance, Private A thing or activity which substantially and unreasonably interferes with P's use and enjoyment of his land. R.2d § 821D.

Nuisance, Public An unreasonable interference with a right common to the general public. R.2d § 821B.

O

Offensive Contact In battery, an unprivileged contact is actionable, even if not harmful, if it is offensive—i.e., offends a reasonable sense of personal dignity. R.2d § 19.

Ordinary Care That care which would be exercised by the reasonable person in the same or similar circumstances. Also called "ordinary prudence," "reasonable care," and "reasonable prudence."

P

Per Quod In defamation law, the type of defamation which is not actionable without proof of special damages.

Per Se By itself; taken alone. The concept is a general one with various uses. For example, violation of a statute is sometimes deemed negligence per se. In defamation, statements that are defamatory per se are actionable without proof of special damages.

Physical Harm See **Harm.**

Premises Liability The special tort liability rules applicable to owners and occupiers of land, characterized by a group of duty limitations that provide restrictions on the negligence liability of possessors of land with respect to conditions or activities on the premises. See R.2d §§ 328E–387.

Prima Facie Case Evidence sufficient to make a submissible case (i.e., sufficient to support a jury's finding) on each element of a cause of action or defense. R.2d § 328B.

Privacy A tort of relatively recent origin based on (1) appropriation of P's name or likeness, (2) intrusion on P's seclusion, (3) public disclosure of private facts about P, and (4) placing P in a false light in the public eye. R.2d § 652A.

Privilege A type of defense to tort liability which negates the tort. R.2d § 10. See **Immunity.**

Products Liability A general term encompassing theories of tort liability of manufacturers or other suppliers of defective products, including (1) negligence, (2) breach of express or implied warranty, and (3) strict products liability. The special liability rules applicable to such actions.

Proximate Cause A concept that includes (1) rules of legal causation that cut off D's liability for certain unforeseeable, remote or indirect consequences and superseding causes; and, under some versions, (2) rules of cause in fact. R.2d §§ 430–61; R.3d PH § 26.

Public Disclosure of Private Facts One of the subdivisions of the cause of action for invasion of privacy, in which D publicizes P's private life in a highly offensive manner. R.2d § 652D.

Public Figure In defamation, one who has achieved a degree of fame or notoriety, either generally or as to a particular public issue or controversy. Different and more restrictive liability rules apply to defamation actions by public figures and public officials.

Publication In defamation, an intentional (or perhaps negligent), unprivileged communication of the defamatory statement to a third person. R.2d § 577.

Punitive Damages Damages awarded in addition to P's compensatory damages to punish D and to deter D and others from committing similar torts. Also called "exemplary" or "vindictive" damages. Available, if at all, only when D's tort was intentional or reckless, or when authorized by statute. R.2d § 908.

R

Reasonable Care See **Ordinary Care.**

Reasonable Person (Reasonably Prudent Person) The mythical person who serves as the standard of care in a negligence action. See **Ordinary Care; Negligence; Hand Formula.**

Reckless Conduct Tortious conduct involving a conscious disregard of risk of physical harm to P which is (a) known to D, (b) unreasonable, and (c) substantially greater than that which is necessary to make his conduct negligent. R.2d § 500; R.3d PH § 2. Also called "willful and wanton conduct."

Release A document by which P gives up his cause of action against D. See R.2d § 885; R.3d AL § 24; **Covenant Not To Sue; Loan Receipt Agreement.**

Res Ipsa Loquitur The thing speaks for itself. A codified rule of circumstantial evidence in which p can make out a prima facie case of D's negligence by proving that (1) the instrumentality causing P's injury was under D's control at the relevant time, and (2) the occurrence was such that it would not have happened in the absence of D's negligence. See R.2d § 328D.

Risk A set of circumstances giving rise to the possibility or probability of an injury. See **Negligence; Hand Formula.**

Rylands v. Fletcher An 1868 English case establishing strict liability for damage caused by the escape of water from D's premises in the course of D's unnatural use of the land. The forerunner of modern rules of strict liability for abnormally dangerous activities.

S

Scienter Actual knowledge. The term is often used to refer to D's knowledge of the falsity of his statement such as will support an action for deceit.

Self-defense A privilege (defense to an intentional tort) based upon D's right to use reasonable force to prevent an unprivileged tort against his person. Similar privileges may be used to defend one's property and other persons. R.2d §§ 63–87.

Slander The publication of defamatory matter by spoken words, transitory gestures, or other form of communication not amounting to a libel. R.2d § 568(2).

Special Damages Damages which at common law were NOT presumed to flow from a tort and therefore had to pleaded specially, such as medical bills and lost wages. R.2d § 904. See **General Damages.** Today, this category is often called "economic loss."

Statute of Limitations A statutory time period during which an action must be commenced. Ordinarily the statute begins to run when the cause of action accrues. The expiration of the statutory period gives D an affirmative defense to bar P's action. R.2d § 899.

Statute of Repose A statutory time period governing a particular activity (e.g., medical malpractice) which commences and expires at a fixed time, independent of the statute of limitations, so as to bar causes of action X years after D's tortious conduct occurred.

Strict Liability Liability which is imposed upon D for injury caused by D's activity (or for which D is similarly responsible) even though D has exercised reasonable care. Sometimes called "liability without fault" or "absolute liability" (although the latter term connotes a total absence of fault, whereas strict liability is sometimes said to contain a fault element).

Subject to Liability Refers to the situation where the actor has engaged in conduct which is (or may be found to be) tortious, without regard to whether the other conditions to a finding of liability are present. R.2d § 5,

Superseding Cause A superseding cause is an intervening cause that the law deems sufficient to override the cause for which D is responsible and exonerates D from liability for D's tortious conduct. R.2d § 440; R.3d PH § 34. See **Intervening Cause.**

Survival Statute A statute that overturns the common law rule that tort (and other) causes of action not reduced to judgment did not survive the death of either the victim or the tortfeasor. A "survival action" is a tort action brought on behalf of a decedent's estate for decedent's damages accruing between the moment of the occurrence and the moment of his death.

T

Tortious Conduct Conduct, whether by act or omission, which subjects the actor to tort liability. R.2d § 6. See **Subject to Liability.**

Transferred Intent An expanded rule of proximate cause applicable to and among the five original trespass actions (assault, battery, false imprisonment, trespass to land, trespass to chattels). D's intent to commit any one supplies the intent necessary for any other. D's intent also transfers from his intended victim to his actual (but unintended) victim. R.3d PH § 33.

Trespass (1) A tort cause of action for D's intentional (a) entry upon P's land (trespass to land) or (b) interference with P's chattel (trespass to chattel). (2) One of the forms of action under the common law writ system, traditionally limited to actions for injuries inflicted directly. Forms of this writ included (a) trespass vi et armis, for bodily harm, and (b) trespass quare clausum fregit, for trespass to land.

V

Vicarious Liability Tort liability imposed upon a for the tortious conduct of B, based upon the existence of some relationship between A and B. See **Imputed Negligence.**

W

Willful and Wanton Misconduct See **Reckless Conduct.**

Worker's Compensation A statutory system of compensation for an employee whose personal injury "arises out of" and occurs "in the course of" his employment. The employer is liable without fault. An employee whose employment is covered by such an act has no common law tort remedy against his employer for physical harm.

Wrongful Birth An action brought by the parents of an unwanted child born with a physical or mental defect (for which D was not responsible) based on D's negligence in sterilizing a parent or in failing to properly diagnose or treat a parent prior to or during the pregnancy.

Wrongful Death A tort action brought on behalf of a decedent's surviving next of kin for their damages resulting from a tortious injury to decedent causing his death. R.2d § 925.

Wrongful Life An action brought by a child born with a physical or mental defect (for which D was not responsible) based on D's negligence in sterilizing a parent or in failing to properly diagnose or treat a parent prior to or during the pregnancy.

Z

Zone of Danger Rule In actions for negligent infliction of emotional distress, most jurisdictions now allow recovery if P was in the zone of danger created by D's negligence and suffered fright as a result of the risk of harm to P. See R.2d § 436.

*

APPENDIX E

Text Correlation Chart

Torts: Black Letter Series	BEST & BARNES, BASIC TORT LAW: CASES, STATUTES, & PROBLEMS (Aspen 2003)	CHRISTIE, MEEKS, PRYOR, & SANDERS, THE LAW OF TORTS (4th ed. West 2004)	DIAMOND, CASES & MATERIALS ON TORTS (West 2001)	DOBBS & HAYDEN, TORTS & COMPENSATION (5th ed. West 2005)	EPSTEIN, CASES & MATERIALS ON TORTS (8th ed. Aspen 2004)	FARNSWORTH & GRADY, TORTS: CASES & QUESTIONS (Aspen 2004)	FRANKLIN & RABIN, TORT LAW & ALTERNATIVES (7th ed. Foundation 2001)	GOLDBERG, SEBOK, ZIPURSKY, TORT LAW: RESPONSIBILITIES & REDRESS (Aspen 2004)	HENDERSON, PEARSON, & SILICIANO, THE TORTS PROCESS (6th ed. Aspen 2003)	KEETON, SARGENTICH, & KEETING, TORTS & ACCIDENT LAW (4th ed. West 2004)
Part One: Introduction 1. General Considerations	1-14	1-31		2-34 *[CHP1-2]*			1-28	3-43		1-29
Part Two: Intentional Torts II. Liability Rules for Intentional Torts	15-49, 73-89	32-61, 1151-1185, 1382-1406	1-61	37-74 *[CHP3]*	3-19, 60-79	1-84	864-910	537-583	1-38	7-11, 30-56, 94-123
III. Defenses to Liability for Intentional Torts	49-73	62-106	61-71	82-109 *[CHP4]*	20-59	85-120	910-928	583-626	38-99, 653-694	56-93, 136-152
Part Three: Negligence IV. Liability Rules for Negligence	91-170	107-238	129-195, 265-313	111-207 *[CHP5&6]*	143-285	121-253	29-108, 130-189	47-208	147-217	11-14, 283-440
V. Defenses to Liability for Negligence	283-353	344-456, 540-587	402-454	271-343 *[CHP7-11]*	287-352	565-605	214-260, 435-497	377-448	353-377	503-562
Part Four: Causation VI. Cause in Fact	171-216	239-270	195-231	208-233 *[CHP7]*	393-435	307-350	341-398	209-262	101-145	563-591
VII. Proximate (Legal) Cause	217-281	271-343	231-265	234-270 *[CHP8]*	435-491	351-389	399-434	265-322	257-293	613-676
Part Five: Special Liability Rules VIII. Owners an Occupiers of Land	451-504	508-540	366-387	349-363 *[CHP12]*	513-534	253-270	190-213	739-814	217-230	461-483
IX. Products Liability	654-725	679-814	500-564	695-798 *[CHP14]*	651-771	447-513	540-651	815-955	437-534	925-1099
X. Vicarious Liability	387-403	407-413	612-636	624-660 *[CHP22]*	375-394	431-446	17-28	488-500	135-145	15-19, 771-809

XI. Employer's Liability to Employees	829-840	1021-1037	637-657	914-950 *(hw: chap 22)*	320-322, 390-392		793-816	659-680	628-634	1152-1176
XII. Automobiles	399-403, 840-851	412-413	657-674	347-349	149-150				634-651	
XIII. Medical and Professional Negligence	405-449	186-210, 210-212, 231-238	166-183	382-440 *(hw: chap 13)*	16-22, 164-169, 210-211, 317-322, 364-365, 579-580		109-129	166-182	201-203, 643-647	377-398, 564-577
XIV. Nuisance	727-770	1052-1083	565-583	670-683	608-650	741-783	658-678	778-798	379-412	123-136, 862-924
XV. Negligent Infliction of Emotional Distress	528-544	587-623	313-334	569-598 *(hw: ch 14)*	480-493	288-303	261-301	680-736	293-314	100-118
XVI. Prenatal Harm	553-560	952-962	343	599-610 *(hw: ch 20)*	409		325-340		322-338	
XVII. Alcoholic Beverages	183-184, 227-229		305, 356-365	133, 551-559	241-242			114-120		654-656, 235, 422-423
XVIII. Constitutional Torts		1407-1436		74-81	17, 78-79		928-947	622-624		
XIX. Economic Harm	544-553	1084-1102	396-401	1014-1039	1143-1198	277-288	301-325	82-93	338-353	
Part Six: Strict Liability	631-652	624	472-500	661-673 *(hw: chap 23)*	569-650	393	498-539		413-435	805-861
XX. Animals	631-640	624-630	495	669-670, 682	581-589	394-404		141-142, 146	413-417	807-813
XXI. Abnormally Dangerous Activities	640-652	631-678		683-687	589-608	414-431	510	798-813	417-435	816-837
Part Seven: **XXII.** Damages for Physical Harm	355-387, 573-630	414, 456, 815-952	454-471, 584-611	855-900	345-350, 515-547		368-391, 679-784	449-533	127-129, 535-608	591-721
Part Eight; **XXIII.** Survival and Wrongful Death	579-583	936-952	334-356	611-621 *(hw: chap 21)*	816-824		705-710	340-356	597-598	700-721
Part Nine: Non-Physical Harm **XXIV.** Misrepresentation		1102-1136	387-396	1040-1059	1101-1142		1216-1239		785-844	233-282, 993-1056
XXV. Defamation	771-828	1186-1313	675-723	983-999	931-1037	607-684	948-1097	538	695-740	154-222
XXVI. Privacy		1314-1381	724-750	1008-1011	1039-1099	685-740	1098-1215		741-784	222-232

Torts: Black Letter Series	LITTLE & LIDSKY, TORTS: THE CIVIL LAW OF REPARATION FOR HARM DONE BY WRONGFUL ACT (2d ed. Matthew Bender 1997)	PHILLIPS, TERRY, McCLELLAN, HADDON, GALLIGAN, TORT LAW (3d ed. Lexis 2002)	PROSSER, WADE & SCHWARTZ, CASES & MATERIALS ON TORTS (11th ed. Foundation 2005)	ROBERTSON, POWERS, ANDERSON & WELLBORN, TORTS (3d ed. West 2004)	SHAPO, TORT & INJURY LAW (2d ed. Matthew Bender 2000)	SHULMAN, JAMES, GRAY, & GIFFORD, LAW OF TORTS: CASES & MATERIALS (4th ed. Foundation 2003)	TWERSKI & HENDERSON, TORTS: CASES AND MATERIALS (Aspen 2003)	VANDALL, WERTHEIMER, & RAHDERT, TORTS: CASES & PROBLEMS (2d ed. Lexis 2003)	VETRI, LEVINE, FINLEY & VOGEL, TORTS LAW & PRACTICE (rev'd 2d ed. Matthew Bender 2003)
Part One: Introduction I. General Considerations	1-33	1-97	1-16	1-7	1-16	1-53	1-6	1-14	1-39
Part Two: Intentional Torts II. Liability Rules for Intentional Torts	487-539	99-175	17-90	8-48	17-100	948-1006	7-55	15-86	783-843
III. Defenses to Liability for Intentional Torts	539-563	177-220	91-130	49-72	101-154	954-970	57-107	87-132	844-877
Part Three: Negligence IV. Liability Rules for Negligence	35-78, 99-288	221-317	131-258	73-115	155-264	153-291	109-183	133-270	41-236
V. Defenses to Liability for Negligence	95-98, 349-400	727-816	586-659	375-435	265-368	413-507, 668-710	405-462	563-702	697-782
Part Four: Causation VI. Cause in Fact	78-82, 289-320	319-380	259-292	116-168	611-688	295-347, 390-392	185-230	271-298	413-506
VII. Proximate (Legal) Cause	82-86, 321-347	381-422	293-360	169-215	731-908	347-412	231-291	299-348	523-588

Part Five: Special Liability Rules VIII. Owners an Occupiers of Land	121-145	555-592	480-502	271-295	177-188	711-755	367-403	373-426	238-261
IX. Products Liability	597-669	999-1083	718-798	536-589	411-493	756-875	513-579	497-562	947-1090
X. Vicarious Liability	441-462	959-998	660-685	314-324	204	123-143	26-27	1041-1060	506-521
XI. Employer's Liability to Employees	719-753	848-858, 1328-1339	1191-1199	158, 363	720-726	884-890	675-684		
XII. Automobiles	755-779	199-200, 673-685				484-485	685-695		
XIII. Medical and Professional Negligence	781-794	853-958	168-197	512-526	214-251	211-228, 274-290, 324-331, 338-347	144-149	146-147, 206-223	189-211
XIV. Nuisance	700-718	1121-1156	799-828	590-599	925-978	88-111	581-607	931-986	903-930
XV. Negligent Infliction of Emotional Distress	106-120	504-518	450-464	235-253	805-857	547-573	336-352	155-173	334-383
XVI. Prenatal Harm	175-184, 194-205	528-553	464-479		883-890	583-591	352-365	174-184	396-406
XVII. Alcoholic Beverages					788-804, 1175-1177	392-396, 404-405	285-286		
XVIII. Constitutional Torts	887-915	1351-1398	984-1003		48-54, 570-573, 1358-1372				
XIX. Economic Harm	145-164	518-528	438-450, 1078-1133	253-271	891-908, 1089-1150	1207-1238	318-336	384-392	
Part Six: Strict Liability	565-596	1087	686, 710-717	525-535	391-508		487-511	475-496	930-931
XX. Animals	588-592	1087-1095	686-691	525-526		120-122	488-493		931
XXI. Abnormally Dangerous Activities	569-573	1095-1119	692-710	526-535	391-410	63-88	493-511		931-945

Part Seven: XXII. Damages for Physical Harm	87-95, 401-485	640-725, 817-839	361-402, 519-564	325-350	523-581, 689-730	490-507, 508-622	463-486, 609-672	349-372, 427-462	439-448, 589-648, 669-696
Part Eight; XXIII. Survival and Wrongful Death	184-193	687-702	565-586	350-374	582-609	537-538, 577-578	642-651	463-474	
Part Nine: Non-Physical Harm XXIV. Misrepresentation	145-155	1267-1288	1022-1077	253	82-89	1007-1087	71-74	897-930	392-396, 648-669
XXV. Defamation	795-862	1158-1223	829-938		979-1048	1088-1163	721-790	753-838	1091-1198
XXVI. Privacy	863-886	1223-1265	940-983	48	1048-1087	1164-1206	791-824	839-896	1199-1291

APPENDIX F

Table of Cases

APPENDIX G

Index

†